Life and Health Insurance

License Exam Manual

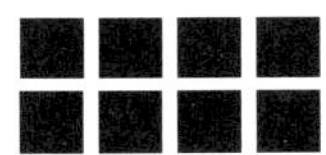

At press time, this edition contains the most complete and accurate information currently available. Owing to the nature of license examinations, however, information may have been added recently to the actual test that does not appear in this edition. Please contact the publisher to verify that you have the most current edition.

This publication is designed to provide accurate and authoritative information in regard to the subject matter covered. It is sold with the understanding that the publisher is not engaged in rendering legal, accounting, or other professional services. If legal advice or other expert assistance is required, the services of a competent professional should be sought.

LIFE AND HEALTH INSURANCE LICENSE EXAM MANUAL, 2ND EDITION

If you find imperfections or incorrect information in this product, please visit www.kfeducation.com and submit an errata report.

Published in June 2010 by Kaplan Financial Education.

Revised April 2016.

Printed in the United States of America.

ISBN: 978-1-4277-2505-9 / 1-4277-2505-5

PPN: 1000-0556

Contents

UNIT 5 Group Insurance 81

UNIT 6 Selling Life Insurance 93

UNIT 7 Policy Issuance and Delivery 111

UNIT 8 Types of Life Insurance Policies 127

UNIT 9 Policy Provisions 159

UNIT 10 Riders 179

UNIT 11 Policy Options 191

UNIT 12 Annuities 205

UNIT 13 Group Life Insurance 225

UNIT 14 Social Security and Tax Considerations 235

UNIT 15 Retirement Plans 253

UNIT 16 Health Insurance Basics 271

UNIT 17 Policy Underwriting, Issuance, and Delivery 305

UNIT 18 Policy Provisions 315

UNIT 19 Disability Income Insurance 347

Introduction

Important: Check for Updates

States sometimes revise their exam content outlines unexpectedly or on short notice. To see whether there is an update for this product because of an exam change, please go to **www.kfeducation.com** and check the Insurance Licensing Blog. If there is an update, it will be clearly noted in the blog entries.

We suggest that you check for updates when you first receive the course, again during your study period, upon completion of your studies, and one last time just before you take your insurance license exam.

Hints for Successful Exam Preparation

An examination must be taken and passed before an insurance producer's license is issued. This examination is designed to measure your basic knowledge of insurance coverages and practices to ensure that the public is served in a professionally responsible manner. The examination will also test your understanding of state laws and regulations pertaining to the insurance industry.

The Licensing Examination

All examination questions are four-part multiple-choice. The number of questions on the exam and the amount of time allowed to complete the exam varies depending on the state and the exam provider. Your exam may contain anywhere from 50–100 questions and have a time limit of 1–2.5 hours. Check with your state's license exam administrator for details.

Be sure to read each question carefully. While several of the possible answers may be partially correct, you must select the best answer to each question. Watch for words such as *all*, *never*, and *always*. They may help you eliminate some of the choices.

There is no penalty for guessing. If you can narrow the choice of four answers down to three or even two logical possibilities, you have a good chance of making an educated guess and picking the right answer.

Do not spend too much time on any one question. It is best to skip very difficult questions and return to them after you have completed all of the easier ones. Other questions on the exam may contain information that helps you answer more difficult questions.

Study Techniques

You may have a lot of experience taking training courses and their examinations or it may have been years since you've taken a course. Here are a couple tips we recommend to make your study most effective.

Read the Entire Course

Study the material in each unit until you understand it. A firm grasp of the material in the course is the best preparation for passing the exam.

Look for Question Areas as You Read Each Assignment

You can prepare for the exam by paying attention to the questions that appear throughout the course. They point to important areas that you should master. More importantly, study with the exam in mind. What questions would you put in the exam if you were creating it to test a student's knowledge of the material? This exercise will help you master the important material in the course and pass the exam.

UNIT

1

Introduction to Insurance

1. 1 INTRODUCTION

The future is notoriously unpredictable. Every day, each of us faces the possibility that something might happen that would result in a personal financial loss. Sickness, disability, premature death, and damage to property are all examples of things that might cause a financial loss. We know that these things will happen to some people and not to others, but we do not know which things will happen to any particular person. In the face of this uncertainty, insurance was developed as a means for spreading a financial loss among many persons so that the cost to any one person is relatively small.

1. 2 LEARNING OBJECTIVES

After completing this lesson, you will be able to:

- define insurance;
- explain how the insurance business is regulated;
- describe the underwriting process;
- define the following key terms: *insurance*, *insurer*, *premium*, *insured*, *policy*, *claim*, *loss*, *risk*, *hazard*, *peril*, *indemnity*, and *law of large numbers*;
- list and describe methods for managing risk;
- list and describe five characteristics of insurable risk;
- describe the following types of insurers: stock insurers, mutual insurers, nonprofit insurers, reciprocal insurers, fraternal insurers, Lloyd's of London, reinsurers, excess insurers, and surplus lines insurers;
- describe the role of the federal government in providing insurance; and
- list the two main insurance distribution systems and describe each one.

1. 3 WHAT IS INSURANCE?

Insurance is a contract that indemnifies another against loss, damage, or liability arising from an unknown event. **Indemnify** means to make a person whole by restoring that person to the same financial position that existed before the loss.

Insurance is a social device for spreading the chance of financial loss among a large number of people. Transfer of risk is the basic principle of all insurance. By purchasing insurance, a person shares risk with a group of others, reducing the individual potential for disastrous financial consequences.

A person protects themselves against risk by purchasing an insurance policy. The insured (**policyowner**), pays a set amount of money (the **premium**) to the insurance company (the **insurer**). In return, the insurer agrees to pay the other party (the insured beneficiary) a set sum (the benefit) upon the occurrence of some event. For example, in life insurance, the benefit is paid when the insured dies.

The agreement between the insurer and the **insured**, the person who is covered by the insurance, is established in a legal document referred to as a contract of insurance or a **policy**. The insurer promises to pay the insured according to the terms of the policy if a loss occurs. **Loss** is defined as reduction in the value of an asset. To be paid for a loss, the insured must notify the insurer by making a **claim**. The **claim** is a demand for payment of the insurance benefit to the person named in the policy.

Insurance plays an important role in society. As a result of the sharing, or pooling, of a large number of similar risks, insurance coverage is available to most individuals for a reasonably affordable premium.

1. 4 RISK

Every day, all of us face various risks, such as the risk of unemployment, disability, sickness, premature death, and damage or loss of property. These risks evolve from uncertainty that results in personal financial loss. Risk is the possibility that a loss might occur and is one of the reasons that people purchase insurance. The definition of risk used in the insurance industry is relatively simple and specific. It involves two things: a possibility of loss and an uncertainty about whether the loss will occur.

Risk simply means uncertainty of financial loss, or the chance of loss, when more than one outcome is possible. Anything through which we may experience a financial loss presents a risk. But there must be an element of doubt or uncertainty. Risk situations are those in which we may have financial loss. This does not necessarily mean we will have a loss.

1. 4. 1 Types of Risks

There are two different kinds of risk. Generally, insurance deals only with pure risks.

- **Pure risk** means that there is only a chance of loss—the loss may or may not happen—and there is no possibility for gain. The risk associated with the chance of an accident is an example of pure risk. Only pure risk is insurable.

- **Speculative risk** involves both an uncertainty of loss and of gain. Insurance does not protect individuals against losses arising out of speculative risk because these risks are undertaken voluntarily. For example, betting at the race track and investing in the stock market are examples of uninsurable risk.

1. 4. 2 Perils and Hazards

Perils and hazards are factors that cause or give rise to risk.

- A **peril** is the immediate specific event causing loss and giving rise to risk. It is the cause of a risk. For example, when a building burns, fire is the peril. When a person dies, death is the peril.
- A **hazard** is any factor that gives rise to a peril. For purposes of life insurance, there are three basic types of hazards: physical, moral, and morale.
- **Physical hazards** arise from material, structural, or operational features of a risk situation (slippery floors or unsanitary conditions would be physical hazards).
- **Moral hazards** arise from people's habits and values (filing a false claim is an example of moral hazard).
- **Morale hazards** arise out of human carelessness or irresponsibility (failing to take safety precautions is an example of morale hazard).

Exercise 1.A
Match the following examples with the type of hazard they represent.

_____ 1. Icy sidewalks	A. Morale hazard
_____ 2. Arson	B. Physical hazard
_____ 3. Leaving car keys in the ignition	C. Moral hazard

Answers to the exercises can be found at the end of the Unit 1 answers and rationales.

1. 4. 3 Managing Risk

Fortunately, there are a number of techniques for handling risks. The nature of a specific risk and the circumstances (extent of exposure, available resources, and so forth) often dictate which technique, or combination of techniques, is most appropriate. Basically, there are five methods for dealing with risk. It is easy to remember these by thinking of the acronym STARR.

Sharing—Sometimes, when a risk cannot be avoided and retention would involve too much exposure to loss, we may choose risk sharing as a means of handling the risk. By sharing risk with someone else, an individual also shares potential losses. That is, the individual's own loss may not be as great if it occurs, but the individual may have to pay a portion of the losses experienced by others.

Transfer—Risk transfer means transferring the risk of loss to another party, usually an insurance company, that is more willing or able to bear the risk. Some non-insurance transfers of risk occur, such as when one agrees to assume the risk of another under the terms of a written contract.

Avoidance—As the name implies, this technique deals with risk by avoiding the risk in the first place. This usually means not undertaking an activity that could involve the chance of loss. For example, by never flying, one could eliminate the risk of being in an airplane crash.

Reduction—Sometimes, when risks cannot be avoided, they can be reduced. Risk reduction can work in one of two ways: it can reduce the chance that a particular loss will occur, or it can reduce the amount of a potential loss if it occurs. For example, installing a smoke alarm in a home would not lesson the possibility of fire, but it would reduce the risk of the loss from the fire.

Retention—Retention simply means doing nothing about the risk. In other words, people assume or retain the risk and, in effect, become self-insurers. For example, the insured would pay a smaller portion of the loss than the insurer, such as paying a deductible.

Exercise 1.B

To help remember the ways of managing risk, we use the acronym STARR. Identify the ways of managing risk.

1. S____________
2. T____________
3. A____________
4. R____________
5. R____________

Answers to the exercises can be found at the end of the Unit 1 answers and rationales.

1. 4. 4 Law of Large Numbers

When an individual purchases insurance, the risk is transferred from the individual to the insurer. To make a successful business of accepting the transfer of individual risk, the insurer needs to have some idea of how many losses will actually occur.

Insurance companies cannot predict the losses expected for a given individual. However, using the law of large numbers, insurers are able to predict how many losses will occur in a group. The larger the group, the more predictable the future losses in the group will be for a given period. Large numbers make it possible to predict losses with some degree of accuracy. Insurance rates and premiums must be based on broad averages of expected losses.

Example

Consider two groups of 40-year-old males. The first group has 10,000 males, and the second group has 50,000 males. A more accurate prediction can be made of how many of those individuals will die in a year in the group of 50,000 than in the group of 10,000.

For the law of large numbers to operate, it is essential that a large number of similar risks or exposure units be combined. An exposure unit is the item of property or the person insured. The exposure unit in life and health insurance is the economic value of the individual person's life. In property and casualty insurance, it is the number of cars, homes, and so forth.

1. 4. 5 Insurable Interest

A basic rule governing insurance states that before an individual can benefit from insurance, that individual must have a legitimate interest in the preservation of the life or property insured. This requirement is called insurable interest.

A person is presumed to have an insurable interest in his own life. An individual is also considered to have an insurable interest in the life of a close blood relative or a spouse. In these cases, insurable interest is based on the love that individual would have for the family member and a real interest in protecting the life of that family member.

Insurable interest can also be based on a financial loss that will take place if an insured individual dies. An example would be two partners in a business, each of whom brings substantial expertise to that business. If one partner dies, the business could fail, resulting in a loss to the other partner.

For life insurance, insurable interest must exist at the time of the application for insurance, but it need not exist at the time of the insured's death. This prevents the insurer from needing to obtain proof of such emotional issues as existing love and affection in the emotional time following a death. In contrast, property and casualty insurance generally does require an insurable interest to exist at the time of loss. Loss of property is not generally as emotional as the loss of a life, and the existence of an insurable interest in property is more easily determined.

Insurable interest affects who may purchase a policy but not who may benefit from a policy. For example, an individual could purchase life insurance on her own life and name a charitable organization as the beneficiary.

1. 4. 6 Insurable Risks

Not all risks are equally insurable. Insurable risks have certain characteristics that make the rate of loss fairly predictable, allowing insurers to adequately prepare for the losses that do occur. The more closely a risk aligns with the following characteristics, the more insurable it is.

1. 4. 6. 1 Large Numbers of Homogeneous Units

A large number of similar exposure units is necessary in order for the pooling and sharing mechanisms of insurance to function.

1. 4. 6. 2 Loss Must Be Measurable

The insurer must be able to place a specific monetary value on exposures and losses in order to be able to calculate rates and premiums and reach settlements.

1. 4. 6. 3 Loss Must Be Uncertain

Insurance covers pure risks, which must involve an uncertainty of loss. If insurance policies covered certain losses (such as deliberate acts of destruction and inevitable loss events), insurance companies would lose money or coverage would be unaffordable.

1. 4. 6. 4 Economic Hardship

There must be a significant potential for economic loss. You cannot insure a $2 pen against loss (because there is no threat of hardship and it would cost more than $2 to issue the policy). You cannot insure your neighbor's house against loss by fire (you do not have an insurable interest and would suffer no loss if the house burned).

1. 4. 6. 5 Exclusion of Catastrophic Perils

The insurance system would collapse if it covered events that caused widespread losses to large numbers of insureds at the same time. There is no way to reasonably price catastrophic exposures. This is why many policies exclude losses resulting from war, nuclear hazards, flood, and earthquake. (Exclusion of catastrophic perils applies primarily to property and casualty insurance. Coverages for some of these exposures are available through government programs or specialty insurers.)

1. 5 COVERAGE CONCEPTS

1. 5. 1 Indemnity

The concept of **indemnity** states that insurance should restore the insured, in whole or in part, to the condition the insured enjoyed before the loss. Restoration may take the form of payment for the loss or repair or replacement of the damaged or destroyed property.

In life and health insurance, the concept of indemnity has a slightly different meaning in that a person's economic value or human life value is the individual's present and future earning power. For example, a family is indemnified for the financial loss of the breadwinner by being provided with life insurance proceeds with which to replace present and future income, thus enabling the family to maintain its lifestyle. An individual is indemnified for the financial loss of a broken arm by being provided with health insurance proceeds to pay the medical bills and perhaps to cover wages lost as a result of the injury.

1. 5. 1. 1 Subrogation

Subrogation entitles one who has paid for another's loss to take over the other's right to recourse from the party responsible for the loss. A subrogation clause in an insurance policy gives the insurer the right to sue (for itself or on behalf of the insured) the responsible party. It prevents the insured from collecting from both the insurer and the liable party. Subrogation is never used in life insurance and seldom in health insurance.

1. 5. 2 Limit of Liability

Although the term *limit of liability* is not used in the life and health insurance field as commonly as it is in the property and casualty field, it means the maximum amount the insurer will pay for a specified insured contingency.

Life insurance policies usually use the term *face amount* to refer to the maximum liability of the insurer for a death claim.

Health and disability policies are more likely to specify a maximum benefit amount or period instead of a limit of liability. Basic medical insurance often has a maximum benefit amount (such as $10,000), and major medical insurance usually has a lifetime maximum benefit (such as $1 million).

1. 5. 3 Deductibles

Deductibles are a common feature of medical insurance coverages (the term has no application in life insurance). A **deductible** is simply the initial amount of a covered loss (or losses) that the insured must absorb before the insurer begins to pay for additional loss amounts. For example, if a basic medical expense policy only pays losses above a $250 deductible and an insured incurs $1,000 of covered medical expenses, the insured would have to pay the first $250, and the insurer would then pay the additional $750 of expenses.

Although the term *deductible* is not used in disability income policies, disability insurance usually has a time deductible called the **elimination period** or a waiting period. The **elimination period** is simply the number of days an insured must be disabled before disability income benefits become payable. For example, if a policy specifies an elimination period of 7 days and an insured is disabled for 30 days, the policy would pay benefits for only the 23 days following the elimination period.

The purpose of a deductible is to minimize small nuisance claims and to keep premiums down. Insurers usually offer a standard deductible but give applicants the option of purchasing higher deductibles that result in even lower premiums.

1. 5. 4 Coinsurance

Coinsurance is another concept commonly found in medical insurance policies. It means that within a specified coverage range, the insured and insurer will share the allowable expenses. It is usually expressed in percentages (e.g., 20–80%). For example, if a policy has a $500 deductible and a 20%/80% coinsurance provision for the next $10,000 of expenses, a $5,500 medical bill would be settled in the following manner: the insured would pay the first $500 (the deductible amount) and $1,000 of the additional expenses (the insured's 20% share); the insurer would pay the remaining $4,000 (the insurer's 80% share).

A coinsurance provision also is designed to keep insurance premiums down, but it does so primarily by discouraging unnecessary or excessive treatments. An insured who is faced with paying 20% of the bill is more likely to question the doctor about whether proposed treatments are necessary and whether there might be less costly alternatives.

1. 6 TYPES OF INSURANCE

Insurers market a variety of insurance products. The most common products offered are property, casualty, life, and health insurance and annuities.

Property insurance protects the insured against the financial consequences of the direct or consequential loss or damage to property of every kind. Property insurance policies cover the risk of damage or loss to property, which is defined as building, equipment, stock, or contents.

Casualty insurance protects the insured against the financial consequences of legal liability, including that for death, injury, disability, or damage to real or personal property. Casualty insurance contracts include automobile policies, general liability policies, workers' compensation coverage, crime insurance, surety (bonding), boiler and machinery coverages, and many others.

Life insurance is insurance coverage on human lives, including endowments and annuities, and may include benefits in the event of accidental death or dismemberment and benefits for disability. It is designed to protect against the risk of premature death, which exposes a family or a business to certain financial risks, such as burial expenses, paying debts, loss of family income, and business profits.

An **annuity** provides guaranteed income for the life of an annuitant. Annuities are designed to protect against the risk of living too long—that is, outliving one's financial resources during retirement.

Accident and health or sickness insurance protects the insured against financial loss caused by sickness, bodily injury, or accidental death and may include benefits for disability income. It may reimburse the insured for actual medical expenses incurred as a result of an accident or illness (hospitalization insurance), or it may provide protection for loss of income experienced by the insured during periods of disability resulting from accident or sickness (i.e., disability income insurance). Health insurance can be written on either an individual or group basis and may include medical expense, hospital indemnity, major medical, hospital, surgical, disability, cancer, accident, dental expenses, eyeglasses, prescription medication, and other health-related expenses.

Variable life and variable annuity products include insurance coverage provided under variable life insurance contracts and variable annuities. Variable products carry investment risk—that is, the insured may lose money because of a decrease in the price of the securities underlying the policy. For this reason, individuals selling such products are required to carry a securities license as well as an insurance license.

Credit is a limited line of insurance protecting the insured, who is usually a creditor, against the financial consequences should a debtor be unable to pay debts as a result of illness or death.

Other types of insurance, such as title insurance or crop insurance, may be authorized in individual states. These limited lines of insurance are more narrowly focused than the types of insurance listed above, generally falling within the broad scope of one of the types of insurance listed earlier in this section.

1. 7 TYPES OF INSURERS

Insurance is provided to the public by three major sources: private commercial insurers (profit making), private noncommercial insurers (nonprofit service organizations), and the US government (special nonprofit). Other types of private insurers include reciprocals, fraternals, Lloyd's, reinsurers, and self-insurers.

Private life and health insurers are in the business to make a reasonable profit and are therefore called commercial insurers. Stock and mutual insurers are private insurers. Private noncommercial service organizations, such as Blue Cross and Blue Shield, operate on a nonprofit basis. A nonprofit status exists when profits are returned to subscribers in the form of reduced premiums or expanded benefits (similar to mutual insurers).

1. 7. 1 Stock Insurers

A **stock insurance company** consists of stockholders, also known as shareholders, who own shares in the company. Stockholders select the board of directors, and the board elects the officers who conduct the daily operations of the business. A stock company is referred to as a **non-participating company** because policyholders do not participate in dividends resulting from stock ownership.

1. 7. 2 Mutual Insurers

In a mutual company, there are no stockholders; ownership rests with the policyholders, also known as policyowners. They vote for a board of directors that in turn elects or appoints the officers to operate the company. Funds not paid out after paying claims and other operating costs are returned to the policyowners in the form of **policy dividends**. As such, mutual companies are sometimes referred to as **participating companies** because the policyowners participate in dividends.

1. 7. 3 Reciprocal Insurers

Reciprocal insurers are unincorporated groups of people that provide insurance for one another through individual indemnity agreements. Each individual who is a member of the reciprocal is known as a **subscriber**. Each subscriber is allocated a separate account through which his premiums are paid and earned interest is tracked. If any subscriber should suffer a loss provided for by the reciprocal insurance, each subscriber account would be assessed an equal amount to pay the claim. Administration, underwriting, sales promotion, and claims handling for the reciprocal insurance are handled by an *attorney-in-fact*. The attorney-in-fact is often controlled and overseen by an advisory committee of subscribers.

1.7.4 Fraternal Insurers

Fraternal benefit societies are primarily life insurance carriers that exist as social organizations and usually engage in charitable and benevolent activities. Fraternals are distinguished by the fact that their membership is usually drawn from those who are also members of a lodge or fraternal organization. They operate under a special section of the state insurance code and receive some income tax advantages. One distinctive characteristic of fraternal life insurance is the open contract, which allows fraternals to assess their certificateholders (charge additional, unscheduled premiums) in times of financial difficulty.

1.7.5 Lloyd's

Lloyd's of London is not an insurance company, but it provides a meeting place and clerical services to its members who actually transact the business of insurance. Members are individually liable and responsible for the contracts of insurance into which they enter.

1.7.6 Reinsurers

Reinsurers make up a specialized branch of the insurance industry that insures insurers. Reinsurance is an arrangement by which an insurance company transfers a portion of a risk it has assumed to another insurer. Usually, reinsurance takes place to limit the loss any one insurer would face should a very large claim become payable. The company transferring the risk is called the ceding company; the company assuming the risk is the reinsurer.

Facultative reinsurance is negotiated on an individual risk basis. The reinsurer retains the right to accept or reject each risk, so there must be an offer and acceptance on each reinsurance contract.

Treaty reinsurance involves an automatic sharing of risks by the ceding company.

1.7.7 Excess and Surplus Lines

Occasionally, it may be difficult to place a risk in the normal marketplace. If the risk is very large or unusual in nature, typical carriers may be unwilling to assume it. For some special risks, the only market may be with specialty carriers. Excess and surplus lines is the name given to insurance for which there is no market through the original producer or that is not available through authorized carriers in the state where the risk arises or is located. Such business must be placed through a licensed excess or surplus lines broker, who will attempt to place it with an unauthorized carrier.

1.7.8 Risk Retention Groups

Risk retention groups are composed of members who are engaged in similar businesses or activities. The group's primary activity consists of assuming and spreading all, or a portion, of the liability exposure of its members. These groups may only provide liability insurance, not workers' compensation or personal lines insurance. RRGs are regulated by the state where they are domiciled but can transact insurance in any other state without further regulation or the requirement to participate in the state guaranty fund.

1. 7. 9 Self-Insurers

Self-insurance is a means of retaining risk. Some businesses intentionally self-insure all or a portion of specified risks. Frequently, self-insurers set aside reserve funds to cover losses and purchase excess insurance to cover large losses or aggregate losses above a given level.

Individuals who neglect to purchase needed insurance coverage (such as health insurance or automobile insurance) are, in effect, self-insuring these exposures and risking their personal assets.

1. 7. 10 The United States Government as Insurer

The federal government provides a wide variety of insurance benefits through various programs. These include Social Security benefits, military life insurance benefits, federal employee compensation benefits, and various retirement benefit programs. It also provides, supports, or subsidizes a number of insurance programs designed to cover catastrophic risks, including insurance for war risks, nuclear energy liability, flood, and crop losses.

At the state level, governments are involved in providing unemployment insurance, workers' compensation insurance, disability insurance, and medical insurance for the needy. Local governments also participate in providing medical, disability, and retirement benefits.

1. 8 DOMICILE AND AUTHORIZATION

1. 8. 1 Insurer's Domicile (Domestic, Foreign, and Alien Insurers)

Insurance companies may be classified in terms of their place of origin where they are conducting business.

- **Domestic insurers** A company is a domestic insurer in the state in which it is incorporated.
- **Foreign insurers** A foreign insurer is licensed to conduct business in states (the District of Columbia or other US territories) other than the one in which it is incorporated.
- **Alien insurers** Alien insurers are companies incorporated in a country other than the United States, the District of Columbia, or any US territorial possession.

Exercise 1.C

Fill in the following blanks:

1. A company who receives a license to do business in a state is considered ________ into a state as a legal insurer and is ___________ to do business in that state.
2. A company that is doing business in a country where it is not domiciled is considered a ________ insurer.
3. A company that is doing business in a state where it is not domiciled is considered a ________ insurer.
4. Insurers not licensed to transact insurance within a state are considered ___________ or _______.
5. A company that is doing business in the state in which it is incorporated is considered a ________ insurer.

Answers to the exercises can be found at the end of the Unit 1 answers and rationales.

Insurers Classified By Origin

Alien insurers are companies incorporated in a country other than the United States, the District of Columbia, or any US territorial possession.

A **foreign insurer** is licensed to conduct business in states (the District of Columbia or other U.S. Territories) other than the one in which it is incorporated.

A company is a **domestic insurer** in the state in which it is incorporated.

1. 8. 2 Authorized Versus Unauthorized (Admitted Versus Nonadmitted)

Generally, an insurance company must receive authority from the state insurance department to transact business within a state. Some types of transactions (such as surplus lines or reinsurance) may be permitted by unauthorized companies, but these transactions are still regulated to some degree.

An *authorized (admitted) insurer* means an insurer that is entitled to transact insurance within the state, having complied with the law and satisfying all conditions to transacting insurance.

An *unauthorized (nonadmitted) insurer* means an insurer that is not entitled to transact insurance within the state.

1. 9 TYPES OF DISTRIBUTION SYSTEMS

Insurance companies market their products generally in one of two ways: by using producers to sell their products or by selling directly using mass marketing. The vast majority of policies are sold through producers.

1. 9. 1 Agency System

Insurance is made available to the public through a number of distribution systems, including the following.

Independent insurance agents sell the insurance products of several companies and work for themselves or other agents. The independent agent owns the expirations of the policies he sells, meaning the individual may place that business with another insurer upon renewal if in the best interest of the client.

Exclusive or captive agents represent only one company. These agents are sometimes referred to as career agents working from career agencies. Most often, these captive or career agents are compensated by commissions.

General agents or managing general agents (MGAs) hire, train, and supervise other career agents within a specific geographical area. The MGA is compensated by commissions earned on business sold by herself as well as an overriding commission (overrides) on the business produced by the other agents managed by the general agent. An MGA has field underwriting and binding authority only in property and casualty insurance.

Direct-writing companies usually pay salaries to employees whose job function is to sell the company's insurance products. Technically, these salaried employees do not function as agents. Commissions are usually not paid and the insurer owns all of the business produced.

1. 9. 2 Mass Marketing

Mass marketing has grown in general use over the past several years. The most common types of mass marketing systems are direct response, franchise, noninsurance sponsors, and vending machine sales.

1. 9. 2. 1 Direct Response

Direct-response marketing is conducted through the mail, by advertisements in newspapers and magazines, and on television and radio. Policies sold using this method have limited benefits and low premiums, such as disability only.

1. 9. 2. 2 Franchise Marketing

The franchise marketing system provides coverage to employees of small firms or to members of associations. Unlike group policies where benefits are standard for classes of individuals, persons insured under the franchise method receive individual policies that vary according to the individuals' needs.

Franchise plans are attractive to employers who do not, according to the laws of their state, meet the qualifications for a true group. These plans allow the employers to offer individual insurance to their employees at a lower premium than for insurance purchased on an individual basis. Premiums may be deducted from the individual's paycheck.

1. 10 PRODUCERS

The term *producer* is becoming increasingly common. Many states have replaced separate agent and broker licenses with a single **producer** license.

1. 10. 1 Categories of Producers

Producers may function as agents, representing the insurance company, or as brokers, representing the potential insured.

Producers acting as agents are not only categorized by their function in the industry but also by the line of insurance they sell.

1. 10. 1. 1 Life and Health Agents

Generally, life and health insurance agents represent the insurer to the buyer with respect to the sale of life and health insurance products. The agents are appointed by the insurer, and usually the agent's authority to represent the insurer is specified in the agency agreement between them, which is a working agreement between the agent and the insurer. Life and health insurance agents generally do not have the authority to issue or modify insurance contracts. Customarily, life and health insurance agents are authorized to solicit, receive, and forward applications for the contracts written by their companies. The agent may receive the first premium due with the application, but usually not subsequent premiums, except in industrial life insurance. The insurance company approves and issues the contract after receiving the application and premium from the applicant through the agent. The agent cannot bind coverage. This means that an agent cannot commit to providing insurance coverage on behalf of the insurance company.

1. 10. 1. 2 Property and Casualty Agents

Agents appointed by property and liability insurance companies generally are granted more authority. These agents may **bind** or commit their companies by oral or written agreement. They sometimes inspect risks for the insurance company and collect premiums due. They may be authorized to issue many types of insurance contracts from their own offices.

1. 10. 1. 3 Brokers

In contrast to the agent-client relationship in which the agent represents the insurer to the purchaser, a broker represents the buyer to the insurer. A broker may do business with several different insurers. Brokers are independent sales representatives who select insurance coverages from these various companies for their clients.

Brokers must be licensed just like agents, and generally their routine activities and functions are similar to those of agents. Brokers solicit applications for insurance, may collect the initial premium, and deliver policies. Brokers do not have the authority to bind coverages.

1. 10. 1. 4 Solicitors

A **solicitor** is a salesperson who works for an agent or a broker. This working relationship is most common in the property and casualty insurance field.

1. 10. 1. 5 Insurance Consultants

A very small group of insurance professionals call themselves insurance consultants. Consultants are not paid by commission for the sales of insurance policies. Instead, they work strictly for the benefit of insureds and are paid a fee by the insureds they represent.

UNIT TEST

1. The term used to describe the individual who is covered by the insurance is
   A. insurer
   B. insured
   C. policyowner
   D. risk

2. Which of the following is a risk?
   A. A car may need to have new brakes installed after several years of regular driving.
   B. An individual may need medical attention after slipping on the ice and falling.
   C. Both are examples of risk.
   D. Neither is an example of risk.

3. The application of the law of large numbers enables insurers to
   A. estimate the future losses of a class or group of people
   B. predict the future losses of specific individuals
   C. charge higher premiums for insurance
   D. calculate mortality charges

4. The estimation of future losses is more accurate when information is from
   A. a small select group
   B. a large group
   C. a medium-sized group
   D. any size group; group size does not matter

5. Which type of policy is designed to protect against the risk of living too long?
   A. Casualty
   B. Life
   C. Annuity
   D. Medical expense

6. Which of the following is a type of insurance company owned by its shareholders?
   A. Mutual
   B. Stock
   C. Lloyd's
   D. Reinsurer

7. The ZYX Insurance Company is incorporated in Alabama. While doing business in Texas, it is
   A. a domestic insurer
   B. a foreign insurer
   C. an alien insurer
   D. an export insurer

8. The ZYX Insurance Company is incorporated in Mexico. While doing business in Texas, it is
   A. a domestic insurer
   B. a foreign insurer
   C. an alien insurer
   D. an export insurer

9. Self-insurance is an example of which method of handling risk?
   A. Acceptance
   B. Transference
   C. Avoidance
   D. Reduction

10. Which of the following terms is used to denote insurance companies?
    A. Broker
    B. Exchange
    C. Corporation
    D. Insurer

11. A social device for spreading the chance of financial loss among a large number of people is the definition of
    A. hazard
    B. risk
    C. insurance
    D. peril

12. Which of the following risks is most likely to be insurable?
    A. George is concerned about the financial impact his premature death would have on his family.
    B. Talyn is concerned about the financial impact large betting losses at the horse track will have on his retirement savings.
    C. John is concerned about the financial impact on his savings when his car eventually becomes worn enough to need to be replaced.
    D. Jewel is concerned about the financial effect losing her hat would have on her weekly spending money.

13. Roger refuses to travel by airplane. Roger is managing the risk of being in a plane crash by
    A. reduction
    B. avoidance
    C. transference
    D. retention

14. Chianna becomes injured in a car accident caused when she took her eyes off the road to answer her cell phone. This is an example of
    A. a physical hazard
    B. a moral hazard
    C. a morale hazard
    D. a legal hazard

15. An arrangement in which an insurer transfers part of the insurance risk to another insurance company is known as
    A. avoidance
    B. fraud
    C. Lloyd's associations
    D. reinsurance

16. Which of the following is NOT an example of insurable interest?
    A. Jose wishes to take out a life insurance policy on his own life to provide for his family in the event of his death.
    B. Ana wishes to take out a life insurance policy on her mother to ensure that funeral costs will be covered when the time comes.
    C. Juan wishes to take out a life insurance policy on his neighbor because his neighbor is a careless driver and Juan thinks his neighbor is likely to die in a car accident.
    D. Carla wishes to take out a life insurance policy on her best salesperson to protect the business from lost sales in the event of the salesperson's death.

17. Kim is injured in a house fire. When the bills come, the insurance company pays 80% of the cost, and Kim pays the rest. This is an example of
    A. coinsurance
    B. a deductible
    C. extraneous insurance
    D. policy limits

18. Hoosier Insurance Company is owned by the policyholders. Hoosier Insurance is
    A. a stock insurer
    B. a mutual insurer
    C. a nonprofit insurer
    D. a fraternal insurer

19. Which of the following people represents several insurance companies but owns the policy expirations?
    A. Independent agent
    B. Exclusive agent
    C. Direct writing agent
    D. General agent

20. Which of the following can bind an insurance company by oral or written agreement?
    A. Property and casualty producer
    B. Life producer
    C. Broker
    D. Solicitor

ANSWERS AND RATIONALES TO UNIT TEST

1. **B.** The term used to describe the individual who is covered by the insurance is insured.

2. **B.** A possibility that an individual may need medical attention after slipping on the ice and falling is a risk.

3. **A.** The law of large numbers enables actuaries to estimate the future losses of a class or group of people.

4. **B.** The estimation of future losses is more accurate when information is from a large group.

5. **C.** An annuity is designed to protect against the risk of living too long.

6. **B.** A stock insurance company is owned by its shareholders.

7. **B.** A company doing business in another state in which it is incorporated is considered a foreign insurer.

8. **C.** This insurance company is an alien insurer.

9. **A.** Self-insurance is an example of accepting the risk.

10. **D.** Insurer denotes an insurance company.

11. **C.** Insurance is a social device for spreading risk.

12. **A.** George is most likely insurable.

13. **B.** Roger is avoiding the risk.

14. **C.** This is an example of a morale hazard.

15. **D.** Reinsurance is the process of transferring a portion of the risk to another insurer. Reinsurance may be negotiated on an individual risk or may involve the automatic sharing of risks by the ceding company.

16. **C.** Juan's interest is not insurable.

17. **A.** This is an example of coinsurance.

18. **B.** Hoosier Insurance is a mutual insurer.

19. **A.** Independent agents represent several insurance companies but own the policy expirations.

20. **A.** A property and casualty producer can bind an insurance company by oral or written agreement.

UNIT 1 EXERCISE ANSWERS

1. D. 1. 5. 1 Exercise 1.A

1. **B**
2. **C**
3. **A**

1. D. 1. 5. 2 Exercise 1.B

1. Sharing
2. Transfer
3. Avoidance
4. Reduction
5. Retain

1. D. 1. 5. 3 Exercise 1.C

1. Admitted, authorized
2. Alien
3. Foreign
4. Nonadmitted, unauthorized
5. Domestic

UNIT

2

Insurance Regulation

2. 1 INTRODUCTION

The general public has an interest in making sure that insurance activity actually is provided as a service and not a disservice. Insurance is highly regulated to protect the public interest and to make sure coverage is available on an equitable basis.

Another reason the insurance business is regulated is the large amount of money involved in the industry. Insurance companies control vast sums of money that, if misused, could impact consumers and even the economy.

2. 2 LEARNING OBJECTIVES

After completing this lesson, you will be able to:

- explain the role of the Insurance Commissioner in insurance regulation;
- describe the role of company ratings and how such information may be used with prospects;
- describe the role of state guaranty associations; and
- explain the requirements for maintaining a producer license.

2. 3 REGULATION OF THE INSURANCE BUSINESS

Regulation of the insurance industry is divided among a number of authorities. The three major channels of regulation of the insurance industry are:

- federal regulation;
- state regulation; and
- self-regulation.

2. 3. 1 Federal Regulation of the Insurance Industry

Most insurance regulation takes place at the state level, but there are some important regulations at the federal level. Federal jurisdiction applies to individuals or companies whose activities affect interstate commerce, which includes most insurance activity. Federal regulation of insurance is primarily used as a means to oversee areas not covered by state regulation of the industry. The most important sources of federal regulation are outlined below and include both legislative and judicial aspects.

2. 3. 1. 1 *Paul v. Virginia*

The case of *Paul v. Virginia* established that the transaction of insurance across state lines was not interstate commerce and therefore should be regulated by local law. This decision held for 75 years.

2. 3. 1. 2 *South-Eastern Underwriters Decision*

The South-Eastern Underwriters Association Supreme Court decision overturned *Paul v. Virginia* and stated that insurance transacted across state lines was, in fact, interstate commerce.

2. 3. 1. 3 *McCarran-Ferguson Act*

Congress enacted the McCarran-Ferguson Act in 1945. This act stated that the federal government had the right to regulate the business of insurance, but only to the extent that such business is not regulated by state law. The main intent of the law was to exempt the insurance industry from most of the provisions of the federal antitrust laws.

2. 3. 1. 4 *Privacy*

Because of the abundance of personal information and the numbers of agencies collecting and using personal information, it is vital that controls be established to protect the public from inaccurate or misused information.

2. 3. 1. 4. 1 Disclosure Authorization

It is the responsibility of a producer to explain to an applicant the various resources from which the insurer will obtain information regarding that applicant's insurability.

In almost every state, applicants for insurance must be given advance written notice of an insurer's practices regarding the collection and use of personal information related to insurance transactions.

Written disclosure authorization forms must be furnished stating who is authorized to disclose personal information, the kind of information that may be disclosed, the reason information is being collected, and how it will be used.

The applicant's signature on the disclosure form authorizes the insurer to collect and disseminate information in the manner described in the notice. The authorization is good only for a certain period. At the end of this period, another authorization must be obtained.

2. 3. 1. 4. 2 Penalties

A fine of $10,000 or up to one year in jail is the penalty for any person who obtains information about a client without having a legitimate reason to receive it.

2. 3. 1. 5 *Fair Credit Reporting Act*

All insurers and their producers must comply with the federal Fair Credit Reporting Act regarding information obtained from a third party concerning the applicant.

2. 3. 1. 5. 1 Consumer Rights

Consumers who feel that information in their files is inaccurate or incomplete may dispute the information, and reporting agencies may be required to reinvestigate and correct or delete information. Insurance companies may use consumer reports, or investigative consumer reports, to compile additional information regarding the applicant. If applicants feel that the information compiled by the consumer inspection service is inaccurate, they may send a brief statement to the reporting agency with the correct information.

2. 3. 1. 5. 2 Notice to Applicant

A **Notice to Applicant** must be issued to all applicants for life or health insurance coverage. This notice informs the applicant that a report will be ordered concerning their past credit history and any other life or health insurance for which they have previously applied. The agent must leave this notice with the applicant along with the receipt.

2. 3. 1. 5. 3 Penalties

Violators of the Fair Credit Reporting Act may be subject to fines and imprisonment and may be required to pay any actual damages suffered by a consumer, punitive damages awarded by a court, and reasonable attorney's fees. The maximum penalty for obtaining consumer information reports under **false pretenses** is $5,000, imprisonment for one year, or both.

2. 3. 1. 6 Consumer Reports

Consumer reports include written, oral, and other forms of communication that a consumer reporting agency has regarding a consumer's credit, character, reputation, or habits and are used or collected to determine whether a consumer is eligible for credit, insurance, employment, or other purposes. Consumer reports may be issued only to persons who have a legitimate business need for the information.

2. 3. 1. 7 Investigative Consumer Reports

An investigative consumer report includes information on a consumer's character, general reputation, personal habits, and mode of living that is obtained through investigation—that is, interviews with associates and friends and neighbors of the consumer. Such reports may not be made unless the consumer is clearly and accurately told about the report in writing. The consumer also must be notified that she is allowed to request an accurate disclosure of the report.

2. 3. 1. 8 Pretext Interviews

A **pretext interview** is an interview whereby a person, in an attempt to obtain information about another person, pretends to be someone else, misrepresents the true purpose of the interview, or refuses to properly identify himself.

Generally, pretext interviews are prohibited. However, such an interview may be conducted when there is evidence of criminal activity, fraud, or misrepresentation.

2. 3. 1. 9 *Consumer Reporting Agencies*

Consumer reporting agencies collect information on individuals, prepare reports, and make the reports available to persons or organizations with a legitimate reason to receive such information. These agencies may operate for profit (e.g., Experian or Equifax) or agencies may be nonprofit (e.g., the Medical Information Bureau or a credit union).

A consumer may choose to have her name and address excluded from any list provided by a consumer reporting agency in connection with a credit or insurance transaction that is not initiated by the consumer. The consumer simply needs to notify the agency that she does not consent to any use of a consumer report in connection with any credit or insurance transaction that is not initiated by the consumer.

Credit agencies are required to provide a notification system, including a toll-free telephone number, to allow consumers to request exclusion of their information. This notification is valid for two years. If notification is made in writing on a signed notice of election form issued by the agency, it is valid until the consumer revokes the request. The consumer may revoke the request at any time.

2. 3. 1. 10 *Fraud and False Statements*

Certain types of false or fraudulent statements have been specifically outlined in federal law as punishable by a fine, a prison sentence, or both. Persons engaging in the business of insurance whose activities affect interstate commerce are prohibited by federal law from knowingly (and with the intent to deceive):

- making any false material statement or report that willfully and materially overvalues any land, property, or security in connection with any financial reports or documents presented to an insurance regulatory official or agency, or an agent or examiner acting for an insurance regulatory official for the purpose of influencing the actions of such individual;
- making any false entry of material fact in any book, report, or statement of such person engaged in the business of insurance with intent to deceive any person, including any officer, employee, or agent of such person, engaged in the business of insurance regarding the financial condition or solvency of such business;
- willfully embezzling, abstracting, purloining, or misappropriating any of the monies, funds, premiums, credits, or other property of any person engaged in the business of insurance; or
- corruptly influencing, obstructing, or impeding the due and proper administration of the law under which any proceeding is pending before any insurance regulatory official or agency or any producer or examiner appointed by such official or agency to examine the affairs of a person engaged in the business of insurance.

The punishment for any of the offenses described here may include fines, imprisonment, or both.

2. 3. 1. 11 Financial Services Modernization

Also known as the Gramm-Leach-Bliley Act (GLBA), this legislation was passed in 1999 to remove Depression-era barriers between commercial banking, investment banking, and insurance. This law allows financial holding companies to engage in any activities that are financial in nature. Regulation of these holding companies is managed on a functional basis. This means that regulatory authority is based on what activity is occurring, rather than on what type of company is engaging in the activity. For example, the sale of insurance is regulated by state insurance regulators even if the company making the sale is a bank or securities brokerage.

Financial holding companies have the potential to capture unprecedented amounts of information about their customers. This law also establishes a minimum federal standard for financial privacy. The law requires that technical, administrative, and physical safeguards be established:

- to ensure the security and confidentiality of customer records and information;
- to protect against any anticipated threats or hazards to the security or integrity of such records; and
- to protect against unauthorized access to or use of such records or information that could result in substantial harm or inconvenience to any customer.

Anyone about whom a company collects information is a **consumer**. A customer is a consumer who has an ongoing relationship with the financial institution.

In some cases, consumers and customers are given the opportunity to keep the company from sharing the information it has about them. This is known as the right to **opt out**. Health information, such as that acquired during a medical exam, is subject to a stricter **opt-in** standard, meaning that companies may not share some health information without receiving specific permission to do so.

2. 3. 1. 11. 1 Disclosure Requirements

GLBA requires that a company make two primary disclosures to customers: one at the time of the establishment of the customer relationship and the second before the company discloses protected information. The first disclosure is to be made at the time a consumer becomes a customer, usually by purchasing a policy. At this point, the company is required to give a clear and conspicuous disclosure to the new customer regarding its policies and procedures for customer privacy. The customer must, at least on an annual basis, receive an updated notice containing the same information.

The second disclosure required by GLBA explains the customer's right to opt out of information sharing. Each customer must be given the right to opt out and must be told explicitly how that right may be exercised.

2. 3. 1. 12 *Other Regulating Agencies*

Some insurance products are regulated by both the federal and state governments. For example, the Securities and Exchange Commission (SEC) and the state Insurance Departments regulate variable contracts. Variable annuities and variable life insurance are insurance company products, but these products present a degree of investment risk to the buyer and, accordingly, have also been identified as securities in accordance with SEC regulations.

2. 3. 2 State Regulation of the Insurance Industry

Most insurance regulation takes place at the state level. The body of laws at the state level is called the **Insurance Code**. State regulation consists of statutes and rules and regulations. **Statutes** are the body of law developed by the legislative branch of government. They outline, in general terms, the duties of the Commissioner and the activities of the Department of Insurance. **Rules and regulations** are developed by the Department of Insurance to expand upon statutory requirements and legislative intent.

2. 3. 2. 1 *Commissioner's Scope and Duties*

The Insurance Code of each state authorizes the establishment of a department of insurance to administer and enforce the insurance laws. In each state, a public official will head the department, and the title of the official will be the **Commissioner**, **Superintendent**, or **Director of Insurance**. This person has broad powers to supervise and regulate the insurance affairs within the state.

Note that the Commissioner does not make the insurance laws. He is simply in charge of making certain all insurance operations within the state are in compliance with the laws made by the state legislature.

Exercise 2.A

1. All of the following are powers and duties of the Commissioner, Superintendent, or Director of Insurance EXCEPT
   A. issue a certificate of authority
   B. make insurance laws
   C. examine books, records, and documents of an insurer, agent, or broker
   D. approve insurance policy forms sold within a state

Answers to the exercises can be found at the end of the Unit 2 answers and rationales.

2. 3. 2. 2 *Regulating Insurance Companies*

The state Insurance Code prescribes the procedures that must be followed for an insurance company to be formed. It specifies the manner in which the company must be organized, the requirements for incorporation, and the amounts for minimum capital and surplus.

2. 3. 2. 3 Insurer Solvency

Insurance companies collect premiums before losses are paid. If the insurer later becomes insolvent, customers will have paid for protection the company is no longer in a position to provide. Protection against insurer insolvency is one of the principal concerns of the insurance industry. Insurance insolvency regulations govern such areas as the organization and ownership of a new company, capital and surplus requirements, reserves, accounting, investments, annual statements, and the rehabilitation and liquidation of impaired insurers.

The Department of Insurance has the right to compute the reserve liabilities of a company, to value its assets, and to approve or disapprove its investments, dividends, and expenses. and The Department of Insurance also has the power to require a company to deposit securities to cover its liabilities in the state.

Various state statutes impose capital and surplus requirements and require the preparation of annual financial statements and periodic examinations of insurers by the Department of Insurance. These laws establish initial financial requirements and help in the early detection of financial problems.

2. 3. 2. 3. 1 Annual Statement

Each insurance company must report its financial condition in an annual statement.

2. 3. 2. 3. 2 Investments

All states have regulations that are intended to ensure that insurers invest only in high-quality assets to prevent insolvencies. Life insurance companies may invest funds in concerns that are fairly stable in value. These safe investments include municipal bonds, corporate bonds, real estate mortgages, and even policy loans.

2. 3. 2. 3. 3 Company Financial Ratings

Producers have a responsibility to place coverage with financially sound carriers. Evaluating the financial health of an insurance company is a complex task. There are several organizations that rate the financial strength of insurance carriers on the basis of an analysis of a company's claims experience, investment performance, management, and other factors. These organizations include AM Best, Inc., Standard & Poor's Insurance Rating Services, Moody's Investors Service, Duff & Phelps Credit Rating Company, and Weiss Ratings. These ratings are one of the most widely used indicators of financial health (or the lack of it) in the insurance industry.

The firms do not all rate every company, and each firm has different criteria for which companies will be rated. Each firm also uses a different method for evaluating the financial strength of insurance companies. There are at least four different rating scales in use among the five firms.

Scaled in Use by Financial Rating Services	
Firm	**Scale, Highest to Lowest**
A.M. Best Company	A++, A+, A, A–, B++, B+, B, B–, C++, C+, C, C–, D, E, F
Weiss Research	A+, A, A–, B+, B, B–, C+, C, C–, D+, D, D–, E+, E, E–, F+, F, F–
Standard & Poor's/ Duff & Phelps	AAA, AA+, AA, AA–, A+, A, A–, BBB+, BBB, BBB–, BB+, BB, BB–, B+, B, B–, CCC, CC, D
Moody's Investors Service	Aaa, Aa1, Aa2, Aa3, A1, A2, A3, Baa1, Baa2, Baa3, Ba1, Ba2, Ba3, B1, B2, B3, Caa1, Caa2, Caa3, Ca1, Ca2, Ca3, C1, C2, C3

2. 3. 2. 3. 4 Examination of Insurers

The state Department of Insurance must examine the financial affairs, transactions, and general business records of domestic insurers in accordance with specific state insurance laws. Generally, these laws will state that the Commissioner of Insurance may examine the insurer's records as often as necessary but at least once every three to five years.

The nonfinancial regulatory activities of an insurance department fall under the broad heading of market conduct. **Proper market conduct** means conducting insurance business fairly and responsibly. In a market conduct examination, state Department of Insurance investigators examine the business practices and operations of an insurer and its agents to determine their authority to conduct insurance business in the state. During a market conduct examination, state examiners investigate the records and practices of an insurance company and determine whether the company is in compliance with state laws regulating the sales and marketing, underwriting, and issuance of insurance products.

2. 3. 2. 3. 5 Rehabilitation and Liquidation

Despite regulatory controls, some insurers become insolvent or find themselves in financial difficulty. In this event, the Department has the authority to assume control over company funds and management. If an insurer becomes impaired (in financial difficulty), the Department will attempt to put the insurer back in sound financial standing. If an insurer becomes insolvent (unable to meet financial obligations), the Department will attempt to make the insurer solvent again. Rehabilitation efforts are undertaken if the Department believes that an impaired insurer has a chance of restoring solvency. Liquidation proceedings are instituted when the insurer is insolvent and cannot be restored to solvency.

2. 3. 2. 4 Guaranty Associations

State **guaranty associations** are organized to protect claimants, policyholders, annuitants, and creditors of financially impaired or insolvent insurers by providing funds for the payment of claims and other related policy benefits. Associations are composed of insurers authorized to transact insurance business within the state. Association membership exceptions include fraternal organizations and nonprofit companies. Member insurers are assessed certain sums of money to cover the association's operating expenses. If insurer insolvency occurs, each member insurer will be assessed additional fees to cover the insolvency.

2. 3. 2. 5 *Marketing and Advertising Life and Health Insurance*

States often regulate the marketing and advertising of life and health insurance policies to ensure truthful and full disclosure of pertinent information when selling these policies. As a rule, the insurer is held responsible for the content of advertisements of its policies. Advertisements cannot be misleading or obscure or use deceptive illustrations and must clearly outline all policy coverages as well as exclusions or limitations on coverage (such as preexisting condition limitations).

Most states require insurers to keep a permanent advertising file of all advertisements used in the state until the next regular examination of the insurer by the Department of Insurance or for a specified minimum number of years, usually two or three.

Also, many states require the delivery of a buyer's guide and policy summary or outline of coverage at the time of policy delivery. The **buyer's guide** is a document providing basic information about insurance policies, and the **policy summary** (life insurance) or **outline of coverage** (health insurance) is a written statement describing the elements of the policy being sold. Generally, it must include the agent's name and address, the name and office address of the insurer, and the generic name of the policy and each rider.

2. 3. 2. 6 *Regulating Producers*

Producers may function as either agents or brokers. Agents represent their companies, and brokers represent their clients.

2. 3. 2. 6. 1 Licensing Regulation

Although much progress has been made in making producer licensing more uniform, it is important to refer to your *State Law Supplement* for more information on licensing regulations in your state.

2. 3. 2. 6. 2 License Required

Under the statutes of most states, no person is permitted to act as an insurance producer without being currently licensed as a producer for the class or classes of insurance involved. Acting as a producer includes selling, soliciting, or negotiating insurance.

2. 3. 2. 6. 3 Exceptions to License Requirements

Each state identifies exemptions from the licensing requirements. Generally speaking, people who are not paid commissions for selling insurance do not need a license.

2. 3. 2. 6. 4 Nonresident Producer Licensing

The majority of states allow for reciprocity in nonresident licensing. Reciprocity means a mutual exchange of privileges. In the case of producer licensing, it means the recognition of two states of the validity of licenses or privileges granted by the other.

Check your *State Law Supplement* to see what the rules are in your state.

A nonresident producer who moves from one state to another state or a resident producer who moves to another state must file a change of address and provide certification from the new resident state within 30 days of the change of legal residence. No fee or license application is required.

2. 3. 2. 7 *Obtaining a License*

2. 3. 2. 7. 1 Application for Examination

A resident individual applying for an insurance producer license has to pass a written examination unless exempt. The exam is developed to test the knowledge of the individual concerning the lines of authority for which the application is made, the duties and responsibilities of an insurance producer, and the insurance laws and regulations of the state.

2. 3. 2. 7. 2 Exemptions from Examination

A person licensed as an insurance producer in one state who moves to another state has 90 days after establishing legal residence to become a resident licensee. Prelicensing education is generally not required to obtain a line of authority previously held in another state.

2. 3. 2. 7. 3 Issuance of License

Licenses contain the licensee's name, address, personal identification number, date of issuance, lines of authority, expiration date, and any other information the Commissioner deems necessary.

2. 3. 2. 7. 4 Temporary Agent Licenses

In most states, temporary agent licenses may be issued for up to 180 days to:

- the surviving spouse or court-appointed personal representative of a licensed producer who dies or becomes disabled in order to maintain the producer's business;
- a member of a business entity licensed as an insurance producer, upon the death or disability of an individual designated in the business entity application or the license; or
- the designee of a licensed insurance producer entering active service in the armed forces of the United States.

A temporary license may not continue after the licensee disposes of the business.

2. 3. 2. 8 *Maintaining a License*

2. 3. 2. 8. 1 Change of Address

Every licensee must promptly give to the head of the Department of Insurance written notice of any change of business address. Most states require this notice be made within 30 days.

2. 3. 2. 8. 2 Assumed Names

An insurance producer doing business under any other than the producer's legal name is required to notify the Commissioner before using the assumed name.

2. 3. 2. 8. 3 Office and Records

Every resident producer must have and maintain in the state issuing the license a place of business accessible to the public. The designated place of business must be where the licensee principally conducts transactions under the license. Licenses must be conspicuously displayed in a part of the place of business that is customarily open to the public. The producer must keep at the place of business the usual and customary records pertaining to insurance transactions.

2. 3. 2. 8. 4 Continuation, Expiration, and Renewal of License

Producer licenses generally remain in effect unless they are revoked or suspended, as long as the appropriate fee is paid and the continuing education requirements are met by the due date.

An insurance producer who is not able to comply with the license renewal procedures because of military service or some other extenuating circumstance (for example, medical disability) may request a waiver.

2. 3. 2. 8. 5 Appointment

If a producer is going to function as an agent of an insurer, the producer generally needs to be appointed by that insurer. To appoint a producer as its agent, the appointing insurer needs to file a notice of appointment within 15 days from the date the agency contract is executed or the first insurance application is submitted.

Note that producers are licensed by the state and appointed by an insurer. Loss of an appointment does not necessarily mean that the producer has lost his license. It simply means that the producer may no longer represent that particular company, although he is still licensed within the state.

2. 3. 2. 8. 6 Termination of Appointment

Subject to a producer's contract rights, if any, an insurer may terminate any of its appointed producers at any time. The insurer must give prompt written notice of the termination and the date to the Department of Insurance (and to the producer when reasonably possible) and must file a statement of facts related to the termination and reasons for it.

If the appointment was terminated because the producer was found to have done something that would be grounds for revocation, denial, or suspension of his license, the insurer is obligated to notify the Commissioner, generally within 30 days.

2. 3. 2. 8. 7 License Denial, Nonrenewal, or Revocation

The Commissioner may place on probation, **suspend**, **revoke**, or **refuse to issue or renew** an insurance producer's license or may levy a civil penalty for:

- providing incorrect, misleading, incomplete, or materially untrue information in the license application;
- violating insurance laws or violating any regulation, subpoena, or order of the Commissioner or of another state's Commissioner;
- obtaining or attempting to obtain a license through misrepresentation or fraud;
- improperly withholding, misappropriating, or converting money or property received in the course of doing insurance business;
- intentionally misrepresenting the terms of an actual or proposed insurance contract or application for insurance;
- having been convicted of a felony;
- having admitted or been found to have committed insurance unfair trade practices or fraud;
- using fraudulent, coercive, or dishonest practices or demonstrating incompetence, untrustworthiness, or financial irresponsibility in the conduct of business in this state or elsewhere;
- having an insurance producer license or its equivalent denied, suspended, or revoked in any other state, province, district, or territory;
- forging another's name to an application for insurance or to any document related to an insurance transaction;
- improperly using notes or any other reference material to complete an examination for an insurance license;
- knowingly accepting insurance business from an individual who is not licensed;
- failing to comply with an administrative or court order imposing child support obligations; and
- failing to pay state income tax or comply with an administrative or court order directing payment of state income tax.

If the Commissioner **nonrenews** or **denies** an application for a license, the applicant or licensee must be notified and advised, in writing, of the reason for the denial or nonrenewal of the license.

A civil fine may be imposed in addition to or instead of license denial, suspension, or revocation.

2. 3. 2. 9 *Regulated Practices*

2. 3. 2. 9. 1 License for Controlled Business Prohibited

Coverage written on a producer's own life or health and on the lives or health of such persons as the producer's relatives or business associates is called **controlled business**. Because of the effect that controlled business could have on the insurance industry if people became licensed solely to sell insurance to family and friends, such activities are limited.

2. 3. 2. 9. 2 Unfair Trade Practices

The Unfair Trade Practices Act is divided into two parts: unfair marketing practices and unfair claims practices. In each state, statutes define and prohibit certain trade and claims practices that are unfair, misleading, and deceptive.

2. 3. 2. 9. 3 Misrepresentations

A **misrepresentation** is simply a lie. It is a violation of unfair marketing practices for any person to make, issue, or circulate any illustration, sales material, or statement that is false, misleading, or deceptive. Misrepresentations include (but are not limited to):

- misrepresenting the benefits, advantages, or terms of a policy;
- misrepresenting policy dividends by implying or stating that they are guaranteed;
- misrepresenting the financial condition of an insurer by means of an inaccurate or incomplete financial comparison; and
- misrepresenting an insurance policy by using a name or title that is untrue or misleading or by indicating that an insurance policy represents shares of stock.

In some cases, misrepresentation can occur unintentionally. To prevent this, the producer must know the products being sold and accurately explain these products to a population largely ignorant about insurance. To assist in explaining the products being sold, many states require that life insurance buyer's guides be distributed by an insurance company to its prospects to explain basic insurance plans and identify the types of insurance available.

2. 3. 2. 9. 4 False or Deceptive Advertising

It is an unfair trade practice for any person to formulate or use an advertisement or make a statement that is untrue, deceptive, or misleading regarding any insurer or person associated with an insurer.

2. 3. 2. 9. 5 Twisting

Twisting occurs when a producer convinces a policyowner to lapse or surrender a present policy in order to sell him another one, usually from a different company. Any attempt by the producer to misrepresent another insurer by falsely making statements about the financial condition of the company or by giving an incomplete comparison of policies is an unfair trade practice.

2. 3. 2. 9. 6 Churning

Closely allied with twisting is **churning**, which is the practice of using misrepresentation to induce replacement of a policy issued by the insurer the producer is representing, rather than the policy of a competitor. The impetus behind churning is to allow the producer to collect a large first-year commission on a new policy. Churning is the result of a producer putting his interests above those of the client.

2. 3. 2. 9. 7 False Financial Statements

It is a violation of unfair marketing practices for any person to deliberately make a false financial statement regarding the solvency of an insurer with the intent to deceive others.

2. 3. 2. 9. 8 Defamation

It is an unfair trade practice for any person or company to make oral or written statements or to circulate literature that is false, maliciously critical, or derogatory to the financial condition of any insurer or that is calculated to injure anyone engaged in the insurance business.

2. 3. 2. 9. 9 Discrimination

It is illegal to permit discrimination between individuals of the same class or insurance risk in terms of rates, premiums, fees, and policy benefits because of their place of residence, race, creed, or national origin.

2. 3. 2. 9. 10 Rebating

Splitting a commission with a prospect is prohibited in almost every state. **Rebating** is any inducement in the sale of insurance that is not specified in the insurance contract. An offer to share commissions with the insurance applicant is an inducement in the sale of insurance that is not part of the insurance policy, and thus, constitutes rebating. Rebates include not only cash but also personal services and items of value.

2. 3. 2. 9. 11 Illegal Premiums and Charges

It is unlawful for a person or insurer to collect premiums or make charges that are not specified in the insurance contract.

2. 3. 2. 9. 12 Boycott, Coercion, and Intimidation

It is a violation of the act for a person or organization to commit or be involved in an act of boycott, coercion, or intimidation that is intended to create a monopoly or restrict fair trade in the transaction of insurance.

Exercise 2.B

Match the following definitions of unfair trade practices with the proper terms.

____ 1. Making a false or misleading statement regarding the benefits, advantages, or terms of a policy

____ 2. Making an oral or written statement that is false, malicious, or derogatory to the financial condition of any insurer and is done with the intent to harm

____ 3. Using threat or force to create a monopoly or restrict fair trade in the transaction of insurance

____ 4. Inducing an insured to lapse, forfeit, or surrender a policy based on misrepresentations or making an incomplete comparison of another policy from a different company

____ 5. Making false statements regarding the solvency of an insurer with the intent to deceive

____ 6. Offering any inducement in the sale of insurance that is not specified in the contract such as commission splitting

____ 7. Formulating an advertisement that is untrue, deceptive, or misleading

____ 8. Charging a different rate for individuals of the same class and life expectancy

____ 9. Replacing a policy repeatedly with the same company allowing the producer to collect continuous first year commissions

____ 10. Collecting additional charges from the insured that are not specified in the contract

A. Illegal premiums and charges

B. Boycott, coercion, and intimidation

C. Discrimination

D. Rebating

E. Misrepresentation

F. Churning

G. Defamation

H. False advertising

I. Twisting

J. False financial statements

Answers to the exercises can be found at the end of the Unit 2 answers and rationales.

2. 3. 2. 10 Unfair Claims Practices

Claims settlement practices are regulated in the public interest for two main reasons.

It is for the purpose of settling claims that insurance companies have collected policyowners' money.

When insureds are denied claims or claim payments are delayed or altered, the consequences go beyond the policy benefits and can drastically affect other areas of the insured's financial situation. The unfair claims practices provisions are designed to protect insureds and claimants from any claims settlement practices that are unfair, deceptive, or misleading. The following are considered unfair claims practices:

- Misrepresenting pertinent facts or insurance policy provisions relating to coverage at issue
- Failing to acknowledge and act reasonably promptly upon communications with respect to claims arising under insurance policies
- Failing to adopt and implement reasonable standards for the prompt investigation of claims arising under insurance policies
- Refusing to pay claims without conducting a reasonable investigation based on all available information
- Failing to affirm or deny coverage of claims within a reasonable time after proof of loss statements have been completed
- Not attempting in good faith to effectuate prompt, fair, and equitable settlements of claims in which liability has become reasonably clear
- Compelling insureds to institute litigation to recover amounts due under an insurance policy by offering substantially less than the amounts ultimately recovered in actions brought by such insureds
- Attempting to settle a claim for less than the amount to which a reasonable person would have believed he was entitled by reference to written or principal advertising material accompanying or made part of an application
- Attempting to settle claims on the basis of an application that was altered without notice, knowledge, or consent of the insured
- Making claims payments to insureds or beneficiaries not accompanied by statements setting forth the coverage under which the payments are being made
- Making known to insureds or claimants a policy of appealing arbitration awards in favor of insureds or claimants for the purpose of compelling them to accept settlements or compromises less than the amount awarded in arbitration
- Delaying the investigation or payment of a claim by requiring an insured, claimant, or the physician of either to submit a preliminary claim report and then requiring the subsequent submission of formal proof of loss forms, both of which submissions contain substantially the same information

- Failing to promptly settle claims where liability has become reasonably clear under one portion of the insurance policy coverage to influence settlement under other portions of the insurance policy coverage
- Failing to promptly provide a reasonable explanation of the basis relied on in the insurance policy in relation to the facts or applicable law for denial of a claim or for the offer of a compromise settlement

Some states have added another provision that makes it an unfair claim practice to offer a settlement or payment in any manner prohibited by law.

2. 3. 2. 10. 1 Penalties

Following an investigation and a hearing, if the Department of Insurance finds that any person or insurer is engaged in any unfair trade or unfair claims practice, the Commissioner may issue a **cease and desist order** prohibiting the individual or company from continuing the practice. Failure to comply with the cease and desist order can result in a substantial fine. In addition, fines and loss of license also may be imposed for a company or person guilty of violating the Unfair Trade Practices Act.

The Department of Insurance also may issue a **consent order**, which is a disciplinary action in which the party at fault (the insurance company or agent) agrees to discontinue a particular practice (usually an unfair trade or claims practice) through a written agreement with the Department of Insurance.

2. 3. 3 Self-Regulation

The last channel of regulation of the business is self-regulation. There are several intercompany organizations and industry associations that impose codes of ethical behavior on their members, including national, state, and local agent associations and associations made up of insurance companies.

2. 3. 3. 1 NAIC

Although without legal authority as a group, the **National Association of Insurance Commissioners (NAIC)**, an association of state Commissioners, also imposes a strong influence in the area of the industry's self-regulation. The NAIC is the organization that has done the most to standardize law between the states. The model laws passed by the NAIC include the Individual Accident and Sickness Policy Provisions Law, Standard Nonforfeiture and Valuation Laws, Fair Trade Practices Act, Unauthorized Insurers Service of Process Act, Insurance Holding Company System Regulatory Act, Variable Contract Law, Group Life Definition and Standard Provisions Bill, and Credit Life and Credit Health Insurance Regulation Bill.

UNIT TEST

1. Pretext interviews are
   A. always illegal
   B. not permitted without a warrant sworn by a sitting judge
   C. generally accepted practice in the industry
   D. not permitted unless some evidence of criminal activity exists

2. A customer is anyone
   A. about whom a company collects information
   B. with whom a company has an ongoing relationship
   C. who prohibits the sharing of nonpublic personal information
   D. who permits the sharing of nonpublic personal information

3. The federal government
   A. is the primary authority for regulating the business of insurance
   B. does not get involved in regulating the business of insurance
   C. has the right to regulate the business of insurance to the extent that such business is not regulated by state law
   D. is prohibited by executive order from regulating any aspect of the insurance business

4. Insurance laws generally are written by
   A. the federal government
   B. the state legislature
   C. the state Department of Insurance
   D. the Commissioner

5. The head of the state Department of Insurance (usually called the Commissioner) is responsible for all of the following EXCEPT
   A. examining individual insurance policies before issuance
   B. administering and enforcing state insurance laws
   C. imposing penalties for violations of the Insurance Code
   D. issuing insurance licenses and certificates of authority

6. The nonfinancial regulatory activities of an insurance department fall under the broad heading of
   A. company conduct
   B. regulatory conduct
   C. market conduct
   D. producer conduct

7. Which of the following individuals would NOT be exempt from a producer licensing requirement?
   A. Alicia works in an insurance office conferring directly with or offering advice to prospective purchasers about the benefits, terms, and conditions of insurance policies and urges a person to apply for policies Alicia thinks would be a good match.
   B. Brenda works for an insurer acting in the capacity of a special agent or agency supervisor assisting insurance producers by providing technical advice and assistance to licensed insurance producers on nonsales-related areas.
   C. Connie gathers information for the purpose of enrolling individuals under a group life insurance plan at her company. Connie also issues certificates and assists in administering the plan.
   D. Del inspects, rates, and classifies risks. At times, Del also supervises the training of insurance producers.

8. Producers may act as
   A. agents representing the insurance company
   B. brokers representing the individual seeking insurance
   C. either agents representing the insurance company or brokers representing the individual seeking insurance
   D. neither agents representing the insurance company nor brokers representing the individual seeking insurance

9. Most insurance regulation takes place at
   A. the international level
   B. the national level
   C. the state level
   D. the local level

10. Applicants for insurance must be given advance notice including all of the following types of information EXCEPT
    A. the persons who are collecting information
    B. the kind of information to be collected
    C. the sources of information
    D. the persons with access to personal information

11. Under the financial privacy safeguards of the Gramm Leach Bliley Act, an individual about whom a financial institution collects information is
    A. a customer
    B. a consumer
    C. a client
    D. a patron

12. Under the financial privacy safeguards of the Gramm Leach Bliley Act, an individual with whom a financial institution has an ongoing relationship is
    A. a customer
    B. a consumer
    C. a client
    D. a patron

13. The Commissioner of Insurance has all of the following powers EXCEPT
    A. conducting investigations and examinations
    B. making reasonable rules and regulations
    C. promulgating insurance law
    D. approving insurance policy forms sold within the state

14. Nonfinancial regulatory activities of an insurance department fall under the broad heading of
    A. market regulation
    B. conduct regulation
    C. market conduct
    D. insurance conduct

15. Associations organized to protect claimants, policyholders, annuitants, and creditors of financially impaired insurers are known as
    A. insurance associations
    B. department associations
    C. liability associations
    D. guaranty associations

16. Which of the following people would be required in most states to obtain an insurance license?
    A. Rachel, a salaried employee of a large department store chain, who counsels her employer on insurance-related matters
    B. Adam, who works in an advertising agency, supervising the advertising business of a major insurer
    C. Henry, who works as an underwriter for a small insurer
    D. Sarah, who sells insurance to businesses only

17. A person licensed as an insurance producer in another state who moves to this state has how many days after establishing legal residence to become a resident licensee without taking prelicensing education or an examination?
    A. 30
    B. 60
    C. 90
    D. 120

18. Which of the following individuals is least likely to be granted a temporary license?
    A. Georgia, whose insurance producer-husband passed away unexpectedly, leaving her with a business to either learn or sell
    B. Kim, who wants to try selling insurance on a temporary basis before investing the time and money into being licensed
    C. Dave, an employee of a business entity, when the individual designated as the licensee in the business entity is disabled in an auto accident and unable to return to work for several months
    D. Lee, whose insurance producer-fiancée was recalled to active duty by the Navy and appointed Lee her designee

19. Business written on the producer's own life or interests is known as
    A. controlled business
    B. personal business
    C. conflicted business
    D. producer business

20. Which of the following is considered an unfair claims practice?
    A. Splitting a commission with a prospect
    B. Failing to affirm or deny coverage within a reasonable time after proof of loss
    C. Convincing a policyowner to lapse or surrender an existing policy to sell another policy
    D. Making any oral or written statement that is false, maliciously critical, or calculated to injure a competing producer

21. An organization that establishes model laws that are often adopted by states with only slight differences is
    A. the National Association of Insurance Companies
    B. the National Association of Independent Commissioners
    C. the National Association of Insurance Consultants
    D. the National Association of Insurance Commissioners

ANSWERS AND RATIONALES TO UNIT TEST

1. **D.** Pretext interviews are not permitted unless some evidence of criminal activity exists.

2. **B.** A customer is anyone with whom a company has an ongoing relationship.

3. **C.** The federal government has the right to regulate the business of insurance to the extent that such business is not regulated by state law.

4. **B.** Insurance laws generally are written by the state legislature.

5. **A.** The Commissioner is not responsible for examining individual policies prior to issue.

6. **C.** The nonfinancial regulatory activities of an insurance department fall under the broad heading of market conduct.

7. **A.** Alicia would not be exempt from a producer licensing requirement.

8. **C.** Producers may act either as agents representing the insurance company or as brokers representing the individual seeking insurance.

9. **C.** Insurance is state regulated as defined by the McCarron-Ferguson Act.

10. **A.** Applicants for insurance do not have to be given advance notice of the persons who will be collecting information.

11. **B.** Under the financial privacy safeguards of the Gramm Leach Bliley Act, an individual about whom a financial institution collects information is a consumer.

12. **A.** Under the financial privacy safeguards of the Gramm Leach Bliley Act, an individual with whom a financial institution has an ongoing relationship is a customer.

13. **C.** The Commissioner of Insurance does not have the power to promulgate insurance laws.

14. **C.** Nonfinancial regulatory activities of an insurance department fall under the broad heading of market conduct.

15. **D.** Associations organized to protect claimants, policyholders, annuitants, and creditors of financially impaired insurers are known as guaranty associations.

16. **D.** Sarah would be required to obtain an insurance license in most states.

17. **C.** A person licensed as an insurance producer in another state who moves to this state has 90 days after establishing legal residence to become a resident licensee without taking prelicensing education or an examination.

18. **B.** Kim is least likely to be granted a temporary license.

19. **A.** Business written on the producer's own life or interests is known as controlled business.

20. **B.** Failing to affirm or deny coverage within a reasonable time after proof of loss is considered an unfair claims practice.

21. **D.** The National Association of Insurance Commissioners establishes model laws that are often adopted by states with only slight differences.

UNIT 2 EXERCISE ANSWERS

Exercise 2.A

1. **B**

Exercise 2.B

1. **E**
2. **G**
3. **B**
4. **I**
5. **J**
6. **D**
7. **H**
8. **C**
9. **F**
10. **A**

UNIT

3

Insurance Law

3. 1 INTRODUCTION

Life and health insurance policies are legal contracts. As such, they are governed by many of the same legal principles that are applicable to the formation of any **contract**, plus specific principles that are pertinent to insurance only. A **contract** is an agreement enforceable by law. It is the means by which one or more parties bind themselves to certain promises. With a life insurance contract, the insurer binds itself to pay a certain sum upon the death of the insured. In exchange, the policyowner pays premiums. Because contracts of insurance are binding and enforceable, certain legal concepts extend to the contract parties: the applicant and the insurer, as well as the agent who brings them together.

3. 2 LEARNING OBJECTIVES

After completing this lesson, you will be able to:

- explain the law of agency;
- list and define three types of authority granted in an agency relationship;
- define fiduciary and explain the role of an insurance producer as a fiduciary;
- explain the legal doctrines of waiver and estoppel;
- describe the responsibilities of an agent;
- describe the responsibilities an insurer has to its agents;
- explain what errors and omissions policies cover and their importance;
- define *contract* and list and describe the elements that form a valid contract;
- describe the four basic parts of life and health insurance contracts;
- list and explain the characteristics unique to insurance contracts;
- explain the difference between warranties and representations; and
- explain the difference between misrepresentation, concealment, and fraud.

3. 3 AGENCY LAW

3. 3. 1 Agency Law Principles

An understanding of the law of agency is important because an insurance company, like other companies, must act through agents.

Agency is a relationship in which one person is authorized to represent and act for another person or for a corporation. An **agent** is a person authorized to act on behalf of another person, who is called the **principal**. In the field of insurance, the principal is the insurance company and the sales representative or producer is the agent. Contracts made by the agent are the contracts of the principal. Payment to the agent, within the scope of the agent's authority, is payment to the principal. The knowledge of the agent is assumed to be the knowledge of the principal.

3. 3. 2 Presumption of Agency

If a company supplies an individual with forms and other materials (signs and evidences of authority) that make it appear that he is an agent of the company, a court will likely hold that a presumption of agency exists. The company is then bound by the acts of this individual whether or not he has been given this authority.

3. 3. 3 Authority

The authority of an agent is of three types: express, implied, or apparent.

Express authority is the explicit, definite authority which the insurer has given the producers under the terms of the agent's written contract.

Implied authority is not expressly granted under an agency contract, but it is actual authority granted to an agent in accordance with general business practices. Implied authority addresses the relationship between the producer and the company. For example, these authorities are not written into the contract but are necessary to conduct insurance business; for example, when the producer collects the initial premium from an applicant on behalf of the insurer.

Apparent authority is authority the agent seems to have because of certain actions undertaken by the agent, thereby giving members of the public reason to believe that the agent does indeed have such authority to conduct business. For example, business cards and rate books give the impression to the applicant that the producer works for and represents the company; the agent's words could appear to be the company's words.

3. 3. 4 Collection of Premium

All premiums received by an agent are funds received and held in trust. The agent must account for and pay the correct amount to the insured, insurer, or other agent entitled to the money.

Any agent who takes funds held in trust for personal use is guilty of theft and will be punished as provided by law.

An agent may establish an account separate from a personal account to deposit the trust funds. All trust funds may be deposited into the single separate account. However, the agent's records must clearly distinguish the funds held for each individual.

3. 3. 5 Agent's Responsibility to Insured/Applicant

An agent has a fiduciary responsibility to the insured, the applicant for insurance, and the insurer. A **fiduciary** is a person in a position of financial trust. As a fiduciary, the agent has an obligation to act in the best interest of the insured. The following are examples of an agent's fiduciary responsibility.

All premiums received by an agent are funds received and held in trust. The agent must account for and pay the correct amount to the insured, insurer, or other agent entitled to the money. The insured's premiums must be kept separate from the agent's personal funds.

Failure to do this can result in **commingling**—mixing personal funds with the insured's or insurer's funds.

Any agent who takes funds held in trust for personal use is guilty of theft and will be punished as provided by law.

The agent must be knowledgeable about the features and provisions of various insurance policies and be able to explain important features to the insured.

Suitability considerations Before an agent takes an application for insurance or an annuity product, the agent and the insurer should obtain information from the prospective applicant that will help determine if either an insurance or annuity product is an appropriate means of addressing the prospect's needs and, if so, what kind of product will best address those needs.

An agent or insurer can obtain this information by asking questions like the following.

- Will the proposed insurance or annuity replace an existing insurance product or annuity?
- What other insurance policies or annuity contracts does the prospect have in effect?

Specific questions that agents must ask are often mandated by a state's insurance regulations.

3. 3. 6 Waiver and Estoppel

Waiver is defined as the intentional and voluntary giving up of a known right.

Estoppel means that one party who has given up a right may be blocked (or stopped) from changing conduct and reasserting the right, after another party has begun to rely upon it, if doing so would be to the detriment of the second party.

Waiver and estoppel often occur together, but they are separate and distinct doctrines. For example, by repeatedly accepting late premium payments, an insurance company may have waived its right to cancel a policy for nonpayment of premium. In the future, the insurer may be legally estopped from making any prompt cancellation for nonpayment because the policyholder has begun to rely on the prior acceptance of late payments.

3. 3. 7 Agent's Responsibilities to the Company

The agent's contract or agency agreement with the insurer will specify the agent's duties and responsibilities to the principal. In all insurance transactions, the agent's responsibility is to act in accordance with the agency contract and for the benefit of the insurer. If the agent is in violation of the agency agreement, the agent may be held personally liable to the insurer for breach of contract.

In accordance with the agent's fiduciary obligation to the insurer and his agency agreement, the agent has a responsibility of accounting for all property, including money that comes into his possession. The agent must not embezzle or commingle these funds.

It is important that pertinent information be disclosed to the insurer, particularly with regard to underwriting and risk selection. If the agent knows of anything adverse concerning the risk to be insured, it is his responsibility to provide this information to the insurer. In accordance with agency law, information given to the agent is the same as providing the information to the insurer.

It is the agent's responsibility to obtain necessary information from the insurance applicant and to accurately complete the application for insurance. A signed and witnessed copy of the application becomes part of the legal contract.

Finally, the agent has a responsibility to deliver the insurance policy to the insured and collect any premium that may be due at the time of delivery. The agent must be prepared to provide the insured with an explanation of some of the policy's principal benefits and provisions. If the policy is issued with changes or amendments, the agent also will be required to explain these changes and obtain the insured's signature acknowledging receipt of these amendments.

3. 3. 8 Company's Responsibility to the Agent

The company likewise has a responsibility to the agent. It is required to permit the agent to act in accordance with the terms of the agent's employment contract, and the company must recognize all of the provisions of that contract.

In addition, the company must pay the agent the compensation agreed upon in the contract, must reimburse the agent for proper expenditures made on behalf of the principal, and must indemnify the agent for losses or damages suffered without fault on the part of the agent but occurring on account of the agency relationship.

3. 3. 9 Potential Liabilities of Agent (Errors and Omissions Exposure)

Errors and omissions (E&O) insurance is needed by professionals who give advice to their clients. It covers negligence, error, or omission by the insurer or by the producer who is the insurer's representative. E&O policies protect producers who face an insured's claim that the producer provided incorrect advice (error) or failed to inform them of an important issue (omission).

Producers must take special care to follow strict procedures (and train all employees to do the same) in taking applications, explaining coverages, collecting premiums, submitting changes to policies upon an insured's request, and submitting claims. All E&O policies have certain basic characteristics in common.

- The policy covers only losses resulting from negligence, error, or omission. For example, a producer who fails to tell a client that purchasing a new policy means that waiting periods have to be met again can be sued for this omission if a loss that was previously covered occurs and the insured finds that he is not currently covered.
- The policy usually has a high deductible, such as $500 or $1,000. The high deductible provides an added incentive for a producer to reduce errors.
- The coverage may be written with both a limit per claim and a limit for all claims during the policy period.
- Except for obvious exclusions, such as a producer committing unfair trade practices or intentional fraud, the policy has few other exclusions.

3. 4 FORMATION OF A LIFE OR HEALTH INSURANCE CONTRACT

The formation of a life or health insurance contract differs from the formation of other insurance contracts in that the life or health producer usually does not have the authority to bind the insurer (put a policy into effect). The producer can solicit applications and collect initial premium payments from prospective insureds, but the application and premium must be sent to the insurance company underwriter, who determines whether the company will accept the risk.

Life insurance policies are generally noncancelable, long-term contracts. A life insurance policy is contestable for a one- or two-year period. Life and health insurance underwriting decisions frequently rest on medical questions. The insurance company is in a much better position than the producer to evaluate the applicant's insurability.

3. 4. 1 Contract Elements

Insurance policies are legal contracts and are subject to the general law of contracts. This is a distinct body of law that is separate from criminal law (crimes against society) and tort law (legal liability issues usually involving damages for negligence). Contract law dictates the formation and enforcement of legal contract rights.

A contract is a legal agreement between two or more parties promising a certain performance in exchange for a valuable consideration. Under the law, the following elements are necessary for the formation of a valid contract:

- Agreement (offer and acceptance)
- Consideration
- Competent parties
- Legal purpose

3. 4. 1. 1 Agreement (Offer and Acceptance)

There can be no contract without the agreement or mutual assent of the parties.

The parties to an insurance contract are the insurance company and the applicant, who may become the insured or may name another person to be insured.

3. 4. 1. 2 Offer

An **offer** is a proposal that creates a contract if accepted by another party.

The offer may come from the insurer (company) or the applicant. If an applicant gives the insurer a completed application and pays the first premium, the application is an offer. If the policy is issued as applied for, the insurer accepts the offer.

There is no offer if the applicant sends the application to the insurance company without payment of the premium. Such an application is merely an invitation to the company to make an offer. The insurance company makes an offer by issuing the policy. The applicant accepts it by paying the first premium.

3. 4. 1. 3 Acceptance

An acceptance must be unconditional and unqualified. (A qualified or conditional acceptance rejects the offer and may constitute a counter offer.)

3. 4. 1. 4 Consideration

Consideration refers to an exchange of value. Each party to the contract must give valuable consideration such as statements, promises, and/or monetary payments. The applicant is giving the premium (as well as representation statements) and the insurer is giving its promise to fulfill its part of the contract; in other words, the insurer agrees to pay for any valid claim.

Part of the applicant's consideration consists of the statements in the application. A great deal of importance is placed on the representations in the application because the insurance company bases its entire decision on whether to issue the policy on statements made in the application.

3. 4. 1. 5 *Competent Parties*

For a contract to be binding, both parties must have the legal capacity to make a contract.

The insured or applicant must be of legal age and be mentally competent to make an insurance contract. Applications of minors usually must be signed by an adult parent or guardian.

3. 4. 1. 6 *Legal Purpose*

To be valid, a contract must be for a legal purpose and not contrary to public policy.

Exercise 3.A

1. All of the following are parts of a legal contract EXCEPT
   A. conditions
   B. legal purpose
   C. offer and acceptance
   D. competent parties

2. All of the following parties must be competent to enter into a contract EXCEPT
   A. the insurance company
   B. the company's representative (producer)
   C. the applicant
   D. the beneficiary

Answers to the exercises can be found at the end of the Unit 3 answers and rationales.

3. 4. 2 Parts of the Insurance Contract

Although it is not a legal requirement that all contracts be in writing, insurance contracts always are in writing because of their complex nature. All life and health insurance contracts contain the following four basic parts:

- Policy face (title page)
- Insuring clause
- Conditions
- Exclusions

3. 4. 2. 1 *Policy Face (Title Page)*

The **policy face** is usually the first page of the insurance policy. It includes the policy number, name of the insured, policy issue date, the amount of premium and dates the premium is due, and the limits of the policy. The policy face also includes the signatures of the secretary and president of the issuing insurance company. In addition, generally there are clauses required by law to give the insured information on the right to cancel and a warning to the insured to read the policy carefully.

3. 4. 2. 2 *Insuring Clause*

The **insuring clause** generally also appears on the policy face. It is a statement by the insurance company that sets out the essential element of insurance—the promise to pay for losses covered by the policy in exchange for the insured's premium and compliance with policy terms.

3. 4. 2. 3 *Conditions*

This section spells out in detail the rights and duties of both parties. **Conditions** are provisions that apply to the insured and insurer.

3. 4. 2. 4 *Exclusions*

In this section, the company states what it will not do/pay for. The **exclusions** are a basic part of the contract, and a complete knowledge of them is essential to a thorough understanding of the agreement. Certain risks must be excluded from insurance contracts because they are not insurable. Such risks include war and acts of war, self-inflicted injuries, and certain hazardous occupations or avocations, such as sky diving, scuba diving, and auto racing.

3. 5 LEGAL REQUIREMENTS

3. 5. 1 Contract Construction

When the courts have a case involving contracts, they look at the **rules of construction** to interpret the contract. The **rules of construction** help to identify and establish the intent of the parties to the contract.

3. 5. 1. 1 *Plain Language and Word Definitions*

If the language of the contract is clear, the courts do not have to interpret the meaning of the contract. The courts give the words in the contract their ordinary meaning. In cases where ordinary words have been used in a technical capacity, the technical meaning of the word is accepted.

3. 5. 1. 2 *Entire Contract*

The courts look at the entire contract to determine the intent of the parties. They do not consider material added to the basic contract, nor do they take only parts of the contract to make a determination.

3. 5. 1. 3 *Interpretation in Favor of Valid Contract*

Because the courts assume that when people make a contract they intend for it to be valid, the courts will, if possible, render an interpretation of the contract that makes it valid rather than invalid.

3. 5. 1. 4 *Unclear Contract of Adhesion Interpreted Against the Insurer*

If a contract contains wording that is unclear, the courts will interpret the language used against the writer of the contract unless the wording used is required by law to be stated in a specific manner. Insurance contracts are contracts of adhesion, which means the insured had no part in determining the wording of the contract. Therefore, the courts will interpret the contract in favor of the policyholder, insured, or beneficiary.

3. 5. 1. 5 *Written Contracts*

If a contract contains unclear or inconsistent material between printed, typed, or handwritten material in the contract, the typed or handwritten material will determine intent. Where there is a discrepancy between typed material and handwritten material, the handwritten material will determine the intent. This procedure is used because printed material is standard and for general use, but typed or handwritten material is added to the existing printed material and is a better indication of the parties' intent.

3. 5. 2 Contract Characteristics

Insurance policies have certain characteristics that are not always found in other types of contracts. A number of legal terms are used to describe these features.

3. 5. 2. 1 *Utmost Good Faith*

The insurance contract requires **utmost good faith** between the parties. This means that each party is entitled to rely on the representations of the other, and each party should have a reasonable expectation that the other is acting in good faith without attempts to conceal or deceive.

3. 5. 2. 2 *Aleatory*

An insurance contract is said to be an **aleatory** contract because performance depends upon an uncertain event. Each party may not give and receive the same value. An insured who has a loss may receive a greater payment than was paid in premiums, while an insured who never has a loss will pay premiums and not receive a monetary return.

3. 5. 2. 3 *Adhesion*

Insurance policies are said to be contracts of **adhesion** because the insurance company drafts the wording of the contract and the insured simply adheres to it. As a result, any ambiguity in the contract is usually resolved in favor of the insured. Courts will usually grant any reasonable expectation on the part of the policyowner or the beneficiaries from a contract that was drawn up by the insurance company.

3. 5. 2. 4 *Unilateral*

Insurance policies are unilateral contracts because after the insured has completed the act of paying the premium, only one party of the contract is legally required to do something. For example, the insurer promises to pay the death benefit in the event of a loss.

3. 5. 2. 5 *Conditional*

Insurance policies are conditional contracts because when a loss occurs certain conditions must be met to make the contract legally enforceable. For example, a policyholder might have to satisfy the test of having an insurable interest and satisfy the condition of submitting proof of loss.

3. 5. 2. 6 *Personal Contract*

Generally, insurance policies are personal contracts between the insured and insurer. With few exceptions, once a policy is formed it cannot be transferred to another person (insured) without the consent of the insurer. However, life and health insurance policies are not personal contracts, as it is possible to assign ownership of a life or health policy to another person.

3. 5. 2. 7 *Warranties and Representations*

A **warranty** is something that becomes part of the contract itself and is a statement that is considered to be guaranteed to be true. Under a strict interpretation, any breach of warranty provides grounds for voiding the contract.

A **representation** is a statement believed to be true to the best of one's knowledge. An insurer seeking to void coverage on the basis of a misrepresentation usually has to prove that the misrepresentation is material to the risk.

Under most state laws, an applicant's statements or responses to questions on an application for insurance (in the absence of fraud) are considered to be representations and not warranties.

3. 5. 2. 8 *Impersonation*

Impersonation means assuming the name and identity of another person for the purpose of committing a fraud. The offense is also known as **false pretenses**. In the case of life insurance, an uninsurable individual applying for insurance may ask another person to substitute for him to take the physical examination.

3. 5. 2. 9 *Misrepresentation and Concealment*

A **misrepresentation** is a written or oral statement that is false. Generally, for a misrepresentation to be grounds for voiding an insurance policy, it has to be material to the risk.

Concealment is the failure to disclose known facts. Generally, an insurer may be able to void the insurance if it can prove that the insured intentionally concealed a material fact.

Material information or a **material fact** is something that is crucial to acceptance of the risk. For example, if the correct information about something would have caused the insurance company to deny a risk or issue a policy on a different basis, the information is material. If a person misrepresents her age or gender, this may be considered material misrepresentation, and the policy could be voided as a result. However, the policy would only be voided if the company would not have issued the policy at all had the company possessed the correct information.

3. 5. 2. 10 *Fraud*

Fraud is an intentional act designed to deceive and induce another party to part with something of value.

Fraud may involve misrepresentation, concealment, or both, but not all acts of misrepresentation or concealment are acts of fraud. If someone intentionally lies to obtain coverage or to collect on a false claim, it would be a matter of fraud. If someone misrepresents something on an application (perhaps a medical treatment the person is embarrassed to talk about) without intent to obtain something of value, no fraud has occurred.

3. 5. 2. 11 *Parol (Oral) Evidence Rule*

The parol evidence rule limits the impact of waiver and estoppel on contract terms by disallowing oral evidence based on statements made before the contract was created. It is assumed that oral agreements made before contract formation were incorporated into the written contract. An oral statement may waive contract provisions only when the statement occurs after the contract exists.

3. 5. 2. 12 *Void and Voidable Contracts*

The terms *void* and *voidable* are often incorrectly used interchangeably. A *void contract* is simply an agreement without legal effect. In essence, it is not a contract at all, for it lacks one of the elements specified by law for a valid contract. A void contract cannot be enforced by either party. For example, a contract having an illegal purpose is void, and neither party to the contract can enforce it. A *voidable contract*, however, is an agreement which, for a reason satisfactory to the court, may be set aside by one of the parties to the contract. It is binding unless the party with the right to reject it wishes to do so. Say that a situation develops under which the policyholder has failed to comply with a condition of the contract: he ceased paying the premium. The contract is then voidable and the insurance company has the right to cancel the contract and revoke the coverage.

This raises another possibility under a voidable contract. In the situation previously described, the insurance company may choose not to exercise its right to cancel the contract after the policyholder fails to pay the premium. The same possibility does not exist under a void contract.

Exercise 3.B

Fill in the following blanks regarding contract characteristics.

1. Insurance contracts are ____________ contracts because certain conditions must be met to make the contract legally enforceable.
2. In a Contract of ________ __________ __________, the parties have a duty to each other to disclose all material facts relating to the contract.
3. Since policyowners can give their contracts away by the use of an assignment, life insurance contracts are NOT considered to be ____________ contracts.
4. Since the insurance company draws up the insurance contract and it is not negotiable, if it is found to be ambiguous the courts will interpret the contract against the party who prepared it. This is an example of a Contract of __________.
5. One party may receive much more in value that he gives in value. Because insurance is dependent on chance or an uncertain outcome, it is considered an _________ contract.
6. A ___________ contract is one in which there is an exchange of an act for a promise. Once the insured pays the premiums, the contract is no longer binding to the insured and cannot be held for breach of contract.

Answers to the exercises can be found at the end of the Unit 3 answers and rationales.

UNIT TEST

1. Insurance agents are appointed by
   A. the federal government
   B. the state Department of Insurance
   C. the Insurance Commissioner
   D. insurance companies

2. Life and health insurance producers have the authority to bind an insurance company to a contract agreement.
   A. True
   B. False

3. Ralph is a producer for Hoosier Insurance Company. His contract states that he is allowed to put the company's logo on his business cards and the door to his office. This is an example of
   A. express authority
   B. implied authority
   C. lingering implied authority
   D. apparent authority

4. Tom has always made a practice of having his policyholders mail their premium checks directly to his home address and forwarding them on to the insurer so that he is aware of anyone missing a payment and can contact policyowners directly if that should happen. His contract does not allow this practice, but the insurer is aware of the actions and has not asked him to stop. This practice is an example of
   A. express authority
   B. implied authority
   C. lingering implied authority
   D. apparent authority

5. Gina accepts the initial premium when she sells an insurance policy and sends it to the company with the application. Nothing in her contract mentions handling of initial premiums. This is an example of
   A. express authority
   B. implied authority
   C. lingering implied authority
   D. apparent authority

6. Albert's life insurance premium is due on the 10th of the month. Because he gets paid at the end of the month, he has always sent the premium in late. The insurer has been accepting his premium this way for 3 years when a new CEO comes in and decides to crack down on late premiums, canceling Albert's policy for nonpayment of premium. Albert contests this decision legally and gets the policy reinstated. The decision to reinstate the policy is an example of
   A. estoppel
   B. waiver
   C. contract of adhesion
   D. express authority

7. Which element is NOT necessary for the formation of a valid contract?
   A. Consideration
   B. Competent parties
   C. Written document
   D. Legal purpose

8. The initial premium payment sent with an application constitutes which part of the insurance contract?
   A. Consideration
   B. Acceptance
   C. Agreement
   D. Legal purpose

9. Life insurance contracts contain all of the following EXCEPT
   A. a policy folder
   B. an insuring clause
   C. conditions
   D. exclusions

10. Ken has paid only 4 premiums on his health insurance policy when he is hit by a car. The insurance company pays out nearly half a million dollars to cover his treatment and a lengthy stay in intensive care. This is an example of
    A. contract of adhesion
    B. aleatory contract
    C. unilateral contract
    D. utmost good faith

11. Carol applies for a life insurance policy and pays the initial premium. Carol has
    A. accepted an offer from the insurer
    B. made an offer to the insurer
    C. accepted a counteroffer from the insurer
    D. made a counteroffer to the insurer

12. The insurer looks at Carol's application and decides to offer Carol a modified policy, including an exclusion Carol did not request. The insurer has
    A. accepted an offer from Carol
    B. made an offer to Carol
    C. accepted a counteroffer from Carol
    D. made a counteroffer to Carol

13. The failure to disclose known facts is
    A. misrepresentation
    B. concealment
    C. fraud
    D. impersonation

14. When one party may receive much more from the contract than she gives in exchange, this is known as
    A. utmost good faith
    B. concealment
    C. aleatory
    D. entire contract

15. Both parties to the contract have an affirmative duty to disclose all information relevant to the contract, whether or not it is requested. This is known as
    A. utmost good faith
    B. consideration
    C. aleatory
    D. waiver/estoppel

ANSWERS AND RATIONALES TO UNIT TEST

1. **D.** Insurance agents are appointed by insurance companies.

2. **B.** Life and health insurance producers do not have the authority to bind an insurance company to a contract agreement.

3. **A.** Express authority is authority the company gives to the producer in writing.

4. **D.** This is an example of apparent authority.

5. **B.** This is an example of implied authority.

6. **A.** The decision to reinstate the policy is an example of estoppel.

7. **C.** A written document is not necessary for the formation of a valid contract.

8. **A.** The initial premium sent with the application is a consideration or exchange in value.

9. **A.** Life insurance contracts do not contain a policy folder.

10. **B.** This is an example of aleatory contract.

11. **B.** Carol has made an offer to the insurer.

12. **D.** The insurer has made a counteroffer to Carol.

13. **B.** The failure to disclose known facts is concealment.

14. **C.** An insurance contract is said to be aleatory, or dependent on chance or an uncertain outcome, because one party may receive much more in value than she gives in value under the contract.

15. **A.** Utmost good faith means both parties to the contract have an affirmative duty to disclose all information relevant to the contract, whether or not it is requested.

UNIT 3 EXERCISE ANSWERS

Exercise 3.A

1. **A**
2. **D**

Exercise 3.B

1. Conditional
2. Utmost good faith
3. Personal
4. Adhesion
5. Aleatory
6. Unilateral

UNIT

4

Underwriting Basics

4. 1 INTRODUCTION

Underwriting is the process of selection, classification, and rating of risks. The risk selection process consists of evaluating information and resources to determine whether a risk is acceptable. If a risk is acceptable, it will then be classified accordingly.

4. 2 LEARNING OBJECTIVES

After completing this lesson, you will be able to:

- explain the importance of the underwriting process in regard to policy issuance;
- define adverse selection and explain why it is relevant to policy issuance;
- list five sources of underwriting information and briefly describe the type of information available from each;
- list the four parts of the typical life or health insurance application and describe the type of information requested on each;
- list and define the three types of insurance risk;
- list and describe the factors used in determining life or health insurance rates; and
- list the types of premium payment modes and explain the effect that varying premium modes have on the total cost of the policy.

4. 3 AFTER THE PROSPECT AGREES TO BUY

Once the prospect has agreed to purchase the insurance contract, three important functions take place.

- The underwriting process begins.
- The application will be submitted, and the policy will be issued (or declined).
- The producer will deliver the policy to the policyowner.

It is important to clearly understand all of the individuals who might be involved and the parts they play in the insurance process. They might include the **applicant**, the **insured**, the **policyowner**, and the **beneficiary**.

An **applicant** is the individual who fills out the application and applies for the insurance.

A **policyowner** is the individual who pays the premium, accepts the policy when it is delivered by the agent, and has the special owner's rights, such as designating beneficiaries. The policyowner is usually, but not necessarily, also the applicant.

An **insured** is the individual whose life is covered by the policy.

A **beneficiary** is the individual or individuals who the policyowner has named to receive the benefits of the policy.

Most of the time, the applicant, policyowner, and the insured are the same person. For example, a person who applies for insurance on his own life will be the insured and most often will also be the policyowner.

The term **third-party ownership** refers to a situation where the policy is owned by someone other than the insured. For example, in a business situation, a corporation may apply for insurance on the life of a key employee. In this case, the corporation is the applicant and the policyowner, and the key employee is the insured. The corporation would also be the beneficiary.

4. 4 THE UNDERWRITING PROCESS

4. 4. 1 The Underwriter's Job

Careful underwriting is a critical function of any insurance company. An underwriter's job is to select risks that can be assumed by the insurance company at a reasonable price and to reject other risks. Part of an underwriter's job is to protect the insurance company against something known as adverse selection. The goal is to achieve a profitable distribution of exposures—a broad base of risks where average losses fall within a normal range.

The process of **underwriting** life and health insurance policies includes reviewing the background information and medical history of the applicant. This information permits an insurance company to determine whether to accept or reject an applicant for coverage. In addition, this information also determines whether the insurer will charge standard or modified premium rates.

Adverse selection exists when the group of risks insured is more likely than the average group to experience loss. The potential for adverse selection exists because people who perceive that they have a higher risk of loss have a greater tendency to apply for insurance, and to apply for higher limits of coverage, than those who perceive that they have very little chance of loss. For example, if there were no underwriting controls, a disproportionate number of people with serious health problems or diseases would apply for life, health, and disability insurance, and the insurance companies would lose money.

It is the underwriter's job to identify the risks that have a higher probability of loss, and to either obtain a higher premium for the risk (if it is within an acceptable range) or to reject the risk (if it cannot be assumed at any price).

4. 4. 2 Sources of Underwriting Information

The underwriter has various sources of information to provide the necessary information for the risk selection process. These sources include:

- the insurance application;
- medical exams and history;
- the attending physician's statement;
- consumer reports (general or investigative);
- Medical Information Bureau (MIB);
- a federal credit report; and
- an agent report.

4. 4. 3 The Application

The application is a vital document because it usually is attached to and made a part of the contract. The producer must take special care with the accuracy of the application in the interest of both the company and the insured.

The application is divided into sections or parts. Each section is designed to obtain specific types of information. The form of the application may differ from one company to another. However, most applications consist of the following:

- Part I—General Information
- Part II—Medical Information
- The agent's statement or report
- Proper signatures of all parties to the contract

4. 4. 3. 1 Part I

Part I of the application asks for general or personal data regarding the insured. This would include such information as name and address, date of birth, business address and occupation, Social Security number, marital status, and other insurance owned. In addition, if the applicant and the insured are not the same person, the applicant's name and address will be included in Part I.

4. 4. 3. 2 Part II

Part II of the application is generally designed to provide information regarding the insured's medical history, current physical condition, and personal morals. If the insurance applied for qualifies as nonmedical (no physical exam required), the producer and the insured will complete Part II of the information. In some cases, the proposed insured is required to take a medical examination and Part II of the application is completed as part of the physical exam.

In addition, Part II requires information regarding the current health of the insured by asking for current medical treatment for any sickness or condition and types of medication taken. The name and address of the insured's physician are also required.

Usually Part II of the application also will include questions regarding alcohol and drug use by the insured. Avocations and high-risk hobbies are also usually reported in Part II. Generally, plans for a prolonged trip or stay in a foreign country also are reported in Part II.

4. 4. 3. 3 Attending Physician's Statement

In addition to requiring a medical examination, an underwriter may request an **Attending Physician's Statement (APS)** from the proposed insured's doctor. Usually, the APS is designed to obtain more specific information about a particular medical problem revealed in the application or during the medical examination.

4. 4. 3. 4 Medical Examinations and Testing

When modest amounts of insurance are involved, the applicant and agent are usually permitted to complete the medical portion of the application. This is referred to as underwriting on a non-medical basis, or simplified issue. If the amount of insurance applied for is relatively high, the proposed insured is usually required to take a medical examination, in which case the medical portion of the examination will be completed by the doctor as part of the medical exam. Medical examinations, when required by the insurance company, are conducted at the company's expense.

4. 4. 3. 5 AIDS Considerations

In general, insurance applications for life or health insurance cannot ask applicants questions that are designed to elicit information for the purpose of determining sexual preferences or lifestyles. Sexual orientation cannot be used in the underwriting process or to determine insurability. However, applicants may be asked questions relating to their having or having been diagnosed as having AIDS or ARC (AIDS-related complex) if the questions are factual and intended to determine the existence of the condition.

Insurers may require that applicants take the test, at the insurer's expense.

When an applicant is asked to take an AIDS-related test for an insurance application, the insurer must tell the applicant how the test will be used and obtain the applicant's written consent.

If an applicant undergoes an AIDS-related test, the results are kept confidential. Applicants can designate individuals who they want the results to be shared with. For example, an applicant can request that positive results be reported to a particular physician or medical provider.

Results are reported to the insurer, who may not release this information. Positive results will be reported to the MIB that the individual has abnormal blood test results but not the presence of AIDS antibodies.

4. 4. 3. 6 Agent's Statement

Many companies require an agent's statement to be completed and submitted as part of the application. Generally, this includes information regarding the agent's relationship to the proposed insured and general knowledge about the proposed insured's financial status, habits, general character, and any other information that may be pertinent to the risk being assumed by the insurer.

Signatures of both the applicant and agent are usually required at the time of completion of the application. If the applicant is not to be the insured, the signature of the proposed insured may be required as well.

4. 4. 3. 7 Inspection Reports

To supplement the information on the application, the underwriter orders an inspection report on the applicant from an independent investigating firm or credit agency, which covers financial and moral information. If the amount of insurance applied for is average, the inspector will write a general report in regard to the applicant's finances, health, character, work, hobbies, and other habits. The inspector will make a more detailed report when larger amounts of insurance are requested. This information is based on interviews with the applicant's associates at home (neighbors and friends), at work, and elsewhere.

4. 4. 3. 8 Investigative Consumer Reports

An **investigative consumer report** includes information on a consumer's character, general reputation, personal habits, and mode of living that is obtained through investigation (i.e., interviews with associates and friends and neighbors of the consumer). Such reports may not be made unless the consumer is clearly and accurately told about the report in writing.

4. 4. 3. 9 Medical Information Bureau (MIB)

Reports issued by the **Medical Information Bureau** are another source of information which may aid the underwriter in determining whether or not to accept a risk. This is a non-profit trade association that maintains medical information on applicants for life and health insurance. Applicants who are denied coverage due to information in an MIB report must be given explanations and an opportunity to challenge information about their medical history that may be inaccurate.

4. 4. 3. 10 National Do Not Call Registry

The National Do Not Call Registry is a list of phone numbers from consumers who have indicated their preference to limit the telemarketing calls they receive. The registry is managed and enforced by the Federal Trade Commission (FTC), the Federal Communications Commission (FCC), and state officials.

The registry applies to any plan, program, or campaign to sell goods or services through interstate phone calls, including insurance. This includes telemarketers who solicit consumers on behalf of third parties. It also includes sellers who provide, offer to provide, or arrange to provide goods or services to consumers in exchange for payment.

Calls from or on behalf of political organizations, charities, and telephone surveyors are still permitted, as well as calls from companies that have the express written permission of the consumer. Calls are also permitted to consumers with whom the company has established a business relationship, as follows.

- A consumer can establish a business relationship with an insurer by requesting information from it or submitting an application to it. In this case, the business can call for three months from the date of inquiry or application.
- A company with which a consumer has an established business relationship may call for up to 18 months after the consumer's last purchase or last delivery, or last payment, unless the consumer asks the company not to call again.

Telemarketers and sellers are required to search the registry at least once every 31 days and drop from their call lists the phone numbers of consumers who have registered.

A consumer who receives a telemarketing call despite being on the registry will be able to file a complaint with the FTC either online or by calling a toll-free number. Violators could be fined up to $11,000 per incident.

4. 4. 3. 11 *HIPAA Disclosures*

The Health Insurance Portability and Accountability Act (HIPAA) imposes specific requirements on health care providers with respect to the disclosure of insureds' health and medical information or protected health information. Health care providers must preserve patient confidentiality and protect this information. If this information is inadvertently disclosed, providers must mitigate the harm to patients. Insurers and producers are under similar requirements when dealing with the protected health information of applicants and insureds.

When examining an applicant for underwriting purposes, all medical information is to remain confidential and the insurer must protect the applicant's privacy. If the insurer wishes to share this information (such as in communications with medical professionals), including information related to HIV infection, the applicant must be given full notice of the insurer's practices with respect to the treatment of this information, the applicant's rights to maintain privacy, and an opportunity to refuse the dissemination of the information.

Exercise 4.A

Match the following definitions with correct terms relating to sources of underwriting and the application.

_____ 1. A general report in regard to the applicant's finances, health, character, work, hobbies, and other habits

_____ 2. A part of the application that requires the agent to provide information regarding the proposed insured, such as the relationship between the agent and the insured

_____ 3. A nonprofit trade association that maintains medical information on applicants for life and health insurance

_____ 4. A list of phone numbers from consumers who have indicated their preference to limit the telemarketing calls they receive

_____ 5. Medical exam conducted by physicians or paramedics at the company's expense

_____ 6. A vital document that is divided into sections or parts and is attached to and made part of the contract

_____ 7. A document that is requested from the proposed insured's doctor to obtain more specific information about a particular medical problem that is included in the application

_____ 8. The section of the application that includes information regarding the proposed insured's current physical condition, medical history, and alcohol and drug use

_____ 9. The section of the application that includes information regarding the proposed insured's name, address, date of birth, occupation, and marital status

_____ 10. A requirement that the insurer must keep all medical information confidential and protect the applicant's privacy

A. Application

B. Part I

C. Part II

D. Attending physician's statement

E. Medical examination and testing

F. Agent's statement

G. Inspection or investigative report

H. Medical Information Bureau

I. National Do Not Call Registry

J. HIPAA disclosures

Answers to the exercises can be found at the end of the Unit 4 answers and rationales.

4. 4. 4 Field Underwriting

An agent plays an important role in underwriting. As a field underwriter, the agent initiates the process and is responsible for many important tasks, including:

- making proper solicitation;
- ensuring the suitability of the product being underwritten;
- completing the application with the applicant;
- obtaining all proper signatures;
- explaining the sources of insurability;
- disclosures at point of sale;
- collecting the initial premium and issuing a receipt;
- completing the agent's report; and
- delivering and explaining the policy.

4. 4. 5 Required Signatures

Several signatures are required to complete a life insurance application. Required signatures include the applicant, the proposed insured (if different from the applicant), and the agent soliciting the insurance.

In situations where a corporation is the policyowner, one or more of the partners or officers must sign the application.

A minor may not sign for a juvenile policy; the guardian is required to sign for that policy.

The agent's report must be completed and signed by the agent only. The Fair Credit Reporting Act Notice of Disclosure ("Notice to the Applicant") is also to be completed with the appropriate signatures.

4. 4. 6 Changes in the Application

Any changes made to an insurance application after it is completed must be initialed by the applicant.

Some insurers require that the agent also initial application changes.

The reason an insurer would require initialing is to protect itself in the event a dispute arises and the applicant and the agent do not recall the changes that were made.

4. 4. 7 Incomplete Applications

Because the application is the critical tool used by the company in the underwriting process, the agent has the responsibility to see that an applicant's answers to the questions are recorded accurately and completely.

Any incomplete applications sent to the underwriting department will be returned to the agent for completion.

This means that a delay in the underwriting process will ensue, requiring that the applicant wait to have the proper protection issued.

If an insurance company accepts an application that is incomplete, then it waives its right to that information. In the event of a claim, the insurance company cannot deny that claim based on missing information in the application.

4. 4. 8 Selection Criteria and Unfair Discrimination

While insurers must use actuarially sound principles to determine whether to insure a risk and at what premium, they cannot impose underwriting criteria that unfairly discriminate among members of the same or similar actuarial class.

4. 5 CLASSIFICATION OF RISKS

Risks that are acceptable to an underwriter are classified for rating purposes. Generally, acceptable risks fall into one of three classifications.

4. 5. 1 Standard Risks

Standard risks reflect average exposures and fall into a normal range. These risks can be insured for standard rates and premiums.

4. 5. 2 Substandard Risk

Substandard risks reflect an above average risk of loss (due to health, occupation, habits, or some other factor), but are still within an acceptable range. The underwriter must use some rating technique in order to obtain a relatively higher premium for these risks (flat additional charge, rating at a higher age, or other adjustment of premium or benefits).

4. 5. 3 Preferred Risks

Preferred risks reflect a below average risk of loss. These risks may be insured at preferred or discounted premium rates due to favorable risk factors (such as healthy lifestyle, favorable medical history, or low-risk occupation).

4. 5. 4 Declined Risks

A declined risk is one that an insurer has decided not to insure. The insurer declines the application for insurance. Insurers rarely do this; rather, they seek to insure for a higher premium, and/or by limiting or excluding certain losses.

Classes of Risks	
Standard	Average Risk
Substandard	Higher Risk of Loss Rated Up Age Flat Additional Premium Tabular Ratings Graded Death Benefit
Preferred	Lower Risk of Loss

Exercise 4.B
Use the four classifications of risk to fill in the blanks in the following statements.

1. A risk that does not measure up to underwriting standards is a ___________ risk.
2. A___________ risk is one that the insurer decides not to insure.
3. A below average risk of loss is considered a ___________ risk.
4. A ___________ risk bears the same health, habits, and occupational characteristic as the persons on whose lives the mortality table was based upon.

Answers to the exercises can be found at the end of the Unit 4 answers and rationales.

4. 6 DETERMINING PREMIUMS OR RATING CONSIDERATIONS

The final step in the underwriting process is the rating of the risk or the determination of the premium. There are three factors used in determining insurance rates:

- Mortality (life insurance rates) or morbidity (health insurance rates)
- Interest
- Expenses

4. 6. 1 Mortality or Morbidity

Insurance companies have kept the kind of records required to produce precise predictions, and the result is called a **mortality table**. The table is based on statistics kept by insurance companies over the years on mortality by age, sex, and other characteristics.

The **mortality rate**, which is defined as the number of deaths per 1,000 people, is taken from the mortality table and is converted into a dollar and cents rate.

The mortality portion of a rate is simply the charge for the expected number of deaths per 1,000 insureds based on the insured's attained age.

Premium Components				
Mortality	–	Interest	+	Expense Acquisition costs General overhead Contingency fund Immediate payment of death claims

Health insurance policies use related but much more complex statistics to determine morbidity rates. **Morbidity** is the likelihood that a person will suffer an accident, contract a disease, or otherwise require medical care. For many years, insurance companies have kept records that document the outcome of insuring various types of risks. For instance, they know that older people are more likely to become ill than younger people, so health insurance premiums tend to be higher for older people. Similarly, insurers know that people employed in certain occupations are more likely to be injured than those in other occupations.

To set rates for health insurance, insurers need to consider not only how often people will become ill or injured, but also how much it will cost when they do. Insurers look at how frequently claims happen among a particular population, or the **claim frequency rate**, as well as the average dollar amount per claim. These two figures are multiplied to create the **aggregate claim** amount, which is a primary element in calculating health insurance rates.

4. 6. 2 Interest

Because premiums are paid in advance of claims, insurance companies have money to invest to earn interest. This interest helps to lower the premium rate.

It is assumed that all premiums are paid at the beginning of the year and all claims are paid at the end. Therefore, it becomes necessary to determine how much should be charged at the beginning of the year, assuming a given rate of interest, to have enough money at the end of the year to pay all claims.

4. 6. 3 Expenses

If the cost of mortality is calculated (discounting for interest), there is enough money to pay claims, but the insurance company has no money with which to pay operating expenses. The premium without expense loading is a **net premium**.

An expense loading is added to the net premium to:

- cover all expenses and contingencies;
- have funds for expenses when needed; and
- spread cost equitably among insureds.

Loading consists of four main items:

- **Acquisition costs**—All costs in connection with putting the policy on the books are charged as incurred in the insurance accounting. In most cases, these costs will be so proportionately high compared with those for ensuing years that they must be amortized over a period of years. One of the highest acquisition costs is the producer's first-year commission. This is the reason a policy that lapses during the first two or three years creates a loss for the insurer. It has not yet recovered acquisition costs.

- **General overhead loading**—Clerical salaries, furniture, fixtures, rent, management salaries, and so forth must be considered when determining expenses.
- **Loading for contingency funds**—Once a level premium policy has been issued, the premium can never be increased. However, unforeseen contingencies could make the rate inadequate.
- **Immediate payment of claims**—In rate making, it is assumed that all claims are paid at the end of the year. This is not literally true, of course. Relying on the law of large numbers, it is safe to assume that claims will be spread throughout the year. Allowance must be made for this loss in the expense loading.

The **gross annual premium**, or the amount the policyowner actually pays for the policy, equals the mortality risk discounted for interest, plus expenses. By definition, the **net premium** is the mortality risk discounted for interest, without any expense adjustment.

By formula:
gross premium = mortality − interest + expenses;
net premium = mortality − interest.

The **level premium** concept was devised to solve the problem of increasing premiums. Mathematically, the level premiums paid by the policyowner are equal to the increasing sum of the premiums caused by the increased risk of mortality. Accordingly, in the early years of the policy, the level premiums paid are actually more than the amount necessary to cover the cost of mortality. Conversely, in the later years of the policy, the premiums paid are less than the amount necessary to cover the increased cost of mortality. This shortage in the later years of the policy is accounted for by the overcharges (plus interest earned) in the early policy years.

Premium mode—The premium mode is simply the frequency with which a policy premium will be paid. The most common premium modes for life insurance are annual, semi-annual, quarterly, and monthly.

The more payments the insured wishes to break the premium into, the higher the total premium will be. For example, the cost of 12 monthly premiums (gross annual premium) will be slightly higher than a single annual premium (net single premium) for the same policy. Because the insurance company will not receive as much money in advance and must bill more frequently, it must charge something extra to offset the interest it would have earned on the full premium as well as its increased administrative expenses.

4. 6. 3. 11. 1 Loss Ratios

Loss and expense ratios are basic guidelines as to the quality of company underwriting. A **loss ratio** is determined by dividing losses by total premiums received. Loss ratios are often calculated by account, by line of insurance, by book of business (all accounts placed by each producer or agency), and for all business written by an insurer. Loss ratio information may be used to make decisions about whether to renew accounts, whether to continue agency contracts, and whether to tighten underwriting standards on a given line of insurance.

$$\text{Loss ratio} = \frac{\text{losses}}{\text{premiums}}$$

$$\text{Loss ratio} = \frac{\$3 \text{ million}}{\$10 \text{ million}} = 30\%$$

An **expense ratio** is determined by dividing an insurer's operating expenses (including commissions paid) by total premiums. When the combined loss and expense ratio is 100%, the insurer breaks even. If the combined ratio exceeds 100%, an underwriting loss has occurred. If the combined ratio is less than 100%, an underwriting profit, or gain, has been realized.

$$\text{Expense ratio} = \frac{\text{operating expenses}}{\text{premiums}}$$

$$\text{Expense ratio} = \frac{\$2 \text{ million}}{\$10 \text{ million}} = 20\%$$

4. 7 RESERVES

By law, a portion of every premium must be set aside as a reserve against the future claim under the policy as well as other contractual obligations, such as cash surrender and nonforfeiture values. Reserves are accounting measurements of an insurer's liabilities to its policyholders. Theoretically, the reserve is the amount, together with the interest to be earned and future premiums to be paid, that will exactly equal all of the company's contractual obligations. The extent to which an insurer's assets exceed its liabilities is known as *surplus*. Policy dividends are paid out of an insurer's surplus.

UNIT TEST

1. The tendency for poor risks to seek and be covered by insurance more often than average risks is
   A. inappropriate selection
   B. adverse selection
   C. inappropriate risk
   D. adverse risk

2. John fills out an application for a life insurance policy to insure his own life, for which he plans to pay the premiums. John is playing all of the following roles EXCEPT
   A. applicant
   B. policyowner
   C. insured
   D. beneficiary

3. Life insurance that requires no medical exam and asks only basic medical questions is known as
   A. simplified policy
   B. simplified issue
   C. simplified risk
   D. preferred risk

4. If an applicant is rated or declined an insurance policy, the reasons for this decision will be explained to the applicant by
   A. the producer
   B. the underwriter
   C. the insurer
   D. the Insurance Commissioner

5. Robin is a 25-year-old man who drinks occasionally, does not smoke, and has no known health problems. He probably would be classified by an insurer as
   A. a standard risk
   B. a substandard risk
   C. a superstandard risk
   D. a preferred risk

6. Which of the following factors does NOT have an effect on insurance premium rates?
   A. Mortality or morbidity
   B. Interest rates
   C. Producer certification
   D. Expenses

7. To be certain that insurers have the money available to pay claims as they arise, they are required to maintain
   A. a risk-based capital ratio
   B. reserves
   C. expense ratios
   D. reinsurance

ANSWERS AND RATIONALES TO UNIT TEST

1. **B.** The tendency for poor risks to seek and be covered by insurance more often than average risks is adverse selection.

2. **D.** The insured cannot ever be the beneficiary in a life insurance contract.

3. **B.** Life insurance that requires no medical exam and asks only basic medical questions is known as simplified issue.

4. **A.** If an applicant is rated or declined an insurance policy, the reasons for this decision will be explained to the applicant by the producer.

5. **A.** Robin probably would be classified as a standard risk.

6. **C.** Producer certification does not have an effect on insurance premium rates.

7. **B.** Insurers maintain reserves to be certain they will have the money available to pay claims as they arise.

UNIT 4 EXERCISE ANSWERS

Exercise 4.A

1. **G**
2. **F**
3. **H**
4. **I**
5. **E**
6. **A**
7. **D**
8. **C**
9. **B**
10. **J**

Exercise 4.B

1. Substandard risk
2. Declined risk
3. Preferred risk
4. Standard

UNIT

5

Group Insurance

5. 1 INTRODUCTION

Group life insurance is frequently issued to employers, labor unions, trusts, or associations to cover employees or members. States generally define a true "group" as having at least 10 people covered under one master contract. The **plan sponsor** (employer, union, association, and so forth) is the policyholder responsible for administering the plan and making premium payments to the insurance company. Premiums are based on the experience of the group as a whole. A person who is covered by group insurance does not receive a policy as proof of insurance. As the master policyowner, the group receives and holds the insurance policy. The insured group members receive a certificate of insurance that certifies the coverage, the benefits under the policy, the name of the covered individual or individuals, and the name of the beneficiary, if applicable.

5. 2 LEARNING OBJECTIVES

After completing this lesson, you will be able to:

- explain certificates of insurance;
- list and describe common types of groups that are eligible for insurance;
- explain the difference between contributory and noncontributory policies and list the minimum participation percentage for each;
- explain the difference between underwriting for group insurance policies and individual insurance policies respectively; and
- explain the probationary and eligibility periods.

5. 3 THIRD-PARTY OWNERSHIP

Third-party ownership exists when a party other than the insured is the owner of the policy. For example, third-party owners could include a wife who is the owner of a husband's policy, a parent who is the owner of a child's policy, or a corporation that is the owner of a director's or officer's policy.

5. 4 TYPES OF GROUPS

Employee or individual employer group—The first type of group would be the employees of an eligible employer. This is called an employee group or an individual employer group. The employer is the policyowner and establishes the eligible class of employees to be covered under the group policy (full-time, salaried, retired, and so forth).

Multiple employer group—A second type of group could be composed of several employers forming a trust to combine their workers for life insurance eligibility. This is known as a multiple employer group. The trusts are called **multiple employer trusts (METs)**.

A policy may be issued to the trustees of a trust group if the fund has been established by:

- two or more employers in the same or related field; or
- one or more labor unions or associations (this is known as a Taft-Hartley trust).

The trustees are the policyholders of the plan that covers eligible employees. This type of plan must not be for the benefit of the employer, union, or association.

Association or labor group—A third type of organization eligible for group insurance includes members of labor organizations, such as the United Auto Workers. An association or labor group must have the following characteristics to be considered an authorized group:

- Have a constitution and bylaws
- Be organized and maintained in good faith for purposes other than obtaining insurance
- Have insurance for the purpose of covering members and their employees for the benefit of persons other than the association or its officers or trustees

Credit insurance is written to provide payment of the insured's debt when he dies prematurely or is disabled as a result of accident or sickness. The **creditor** is the policyowner and the **debtor** is the insured. Benefits under credit insurance are not permitted to exceed the amount of indebtedness.

5. 5 PREMIUMS

Group insurance policies are often able to provide coverage at a lower premium than individual policies can.

Group insurance premiums are based on the experience of the group as a whole. The premium may be paid entirely by the policyowner, or it may be paid jointly by the policyowner and the insured. If the insured contributes money toward the premium, the plan is considered **contributory**. In most states, at least 75% of eligible employees must participate under a contributory plan. If the premium is paid entirely by the policyowner, the plan is considered **noncontributory**. All of the eligible members must participate in noncontributory plans.

5. 6 GROUP UNDERWRITING CONSIDERATIONS

Group life insurance is usually written on a group basis as opposed to an individual basis. Each group participant completes a very short application that usually consists of the individual's name, address, Social Security number, dependent information, and beneficiary designation. No medical underwriting takes place. (Under contributory plans, the period of time during which the employee may enroll and receive coverage without evidence of insurability is known as the **eligibility period (or enrollment period)**. Evidence of insurability must be furnished by an employee who wants to join a contributory group after the eligibility period has ended.)

5. 7 ADVERSE SELECTION

Adverse selection is the tendency for poor risks to seek and be covered for insurance more often than average risks. Thus, in a group situation, the underwriter must consider such things as the type of work done, the ages of the participants, and the probability of this particular group being an adverse risk to the company. For example, a group of coal miners presents a much higher risk of disability/premature death than a group of bank employees.

The larger the group to be insured, the more predictable will be the expected losses from the group. Thus, it is more difficult for the underwriter to anticipate expected losses from relatively small groups (10, 20, or 25 participants).

5. 7. 1 Adverse Underwriting Decisions

A risk will be rejected when the insurer believes the policy cannot be profitable at a reasonable premium or with reasonable coverage modifications. If a risk is rejected on the basis of information in an investigative report, the applicant must be notified and given the name and address of the reporting company. In health insurance, when renewal is denied, the insured must be given a written explanation for nonrenewal or be notified that the explanation is available upon written request.

5. 8 PROBATIONARY PERIOD

A probationary period may be required for new employees, which means they must wait a certain period of time (usually one to six months) before they can enroll in the plan.

5. 9 ELIGIBILITY (ENROLLMENT) PERIOD

If the group plan is noncontributory, all individuals become covered immediately after the probationary period. If an employee does not enroll in the plan during the eligibility (enrollment period), she may be required to provide evidence of insurability and take a medical exam if she wants to enroll later. This is to protect the insurer against adverse selection.

5. 10 STATUTORY REQUIREMENTS IN GROUP UNDERWRITING

5. 10. 1 Statutory Requirements

5. 10. 1. 1 Nondiscriminatory Classifications

An eligible group must not discriminate in favor of individuals in a manner that increases the opportunity for adverse selection against the insurance company. For instance, if an employer has five data entry clerks in the same job classification (job title and salary range), the employer cannot single out one to receive benefits greater than the other four. Therefore, employees will be grouped under such classifications, as eligible full-time employees, clerical workers, hourly employees, salaried employees, executives, and so forth.

5. 10. 2 Optional Requirements

5. 10. 2. 1 Employer Control

The employer should be in charge of enrollment, premium payment, benefit selection, and all other areas of administration that are not an insurance company function. It is the employer's duty to see that plan administration is conducted in a confidential, legal, and objective manner.

5. 10. 2. 2 Group Size

Most insurers require a minimum number of employees or plan participants before a group health insurance plan may be written. This requirement may vary depending on state laws. Typically, the minimum group size for health insurance is 10, but it could be as few as 5 or some other number.

5. 10. 2. 3 Predetermined Coverage Amount

Coverage must be uniform for plan participants. Individual members of the group cannot select the level of benefits for their own coverage. Coverage can be based on such things as the number of years with the company, occupation, or salary.

5. 10. 2. 4 *Enrollment Percentage*

The underwriter should determine that individual participation meets company guidelines to prevent adverse selection. A majority of eligible individuals should be members of the group of insureds.

5. 10. 2. 5 *Insurance Incidental to Group*

The underwriter should determine that the group has not been formed only for the purpose of purchasing insurance.

5. 10. 2. 6 *Eligibility*

The underwriter first should determine that the business is one that the insurer will cover. There was a time when certain occupations were of such a high risk that employees could not get insurance. Today, virtually all occupations can get insurance coverage. However, the higher the risk, the higher the premium.

5. 10. 2. 7 *Composition of Group*

The underwriter should determine that there is a reasonably steady flow of new members into the group. If a group were to keep the same individuals in the group, the chance of accident, illness, or death would increase as the group became older, and rates also would increase.

The group underwriter also must be concerned about currently disabled employees or their dependents. A new insurer may decide to decline the entire group because of a large number of current claims.

A new insurer may establish a preexisting condition provision in the group contract that excludes coverage for any condition that exists before the effective date of coverage. This provision normally will exclude these conditions for a period of 6 or 12 months after the effective date of coverage.

Although there have been changes to underwriting standards because of the passing of unisex (anti-discrimination) laws, there remain instances when a group composed largely of women in general, young women, or older employees pays higher premiums.

5. 10. 2. 8 *Group Contract and Certificate of Coverage*

The basic principle of *group insurance* is that it provides insurance coverage for a number of people under a single *master contract* or *master policy*. The employer (or group) is the applicant and contract policyholder; the employees, as group members, are not parties to the contract. In fact, they are not even named in the contract. The employee does not receive a policy and instead receives a **certificate of insurance** which summarizes the coverage terms and explains the employee's rights under the group contract.

Exercise 5.A

1. To protect against adverse selection, minimum mandatory participation requirements are established in group insurance. A plan in which the employer pays the entire premium and requires 100% participation is referred to as a(n) ________________________ group.

2. A group plan in which the employer and employee both contribute to the premium and requires a minimum of 75% participation is referred to as ________________________ group.

3. All of the following are correct regarding the underwriting procedures of group insurance EXCEPT
   A. individual members cannot select the level of benefits for their own coverage
   B. a group cannot be formed only for the purposes of purchasing insurance
   C. an individual policy will be provided to all members of the group
   D. the employer cannot discriminate when determining eligibility of its members

Answers to the exercises can be found at the end of the Unit 5 answers and rationales.

5. 11 FUNDING OF GROUP INSURANCE

There are several mechanisms for funding group insurance.

A **shared funding arrangement** allows the employer to self-fund health care expenses up to a certain limit. The employer can select a deductible and pay covered expenses for any individual incurring claims up to that maximum, at which point the insurer assumes the risk.

Under a **retrospective premium** arrangement, the insurer agrees to collect a provisional premium but may collect additional premium or make a premium refund at the end of the year based on actual losses.

A **minimum premium** plan occurs when the employer agrees to fund expected claims and the insurer funds excess claims. The employer and insurer agree to a trigger beyond which the insurer is liable. The employer is responsible for a minimum premium consisting of administrative expenses, reserves, and a premium for stop-loss to fund claims over the trigger.

A large employer may elect to fully self-fund or may self-fund the group benefits but contract for administrative services via an administrative services only (ASO) contract.

UNIT TEST

1. To be eligible to purchase insurance, an association group must
   A. have a constitution and bylaws
   B. be organized and maintained strictly for the purpose of obtaining insurance
   C. have insurance for the purpose of covering the association or its officers or trustees only
   D. have at least 200 members

2, For group insurance policies, the covered individual receives proof of coverage in the form of
   A. an insurance policy
   B. an insurance contract
   C. a certificate of insurance
   D. a certificate of policy

3. If a group insurance policy is contributory, what percentage of employees must participate?
   A. No set percentage
   B. 50%
   C. 75%
   D. 100%

4. Albert works as a window washer at the top of skyscrapers. Bernie works as a window washer on the ground floor. The fact that Albert is more likely to seek insurance coverage than Bernie is an example of
   A. risk selection
   B. adverse underwriting
   C. adverse selection
   D. risk underwriting

5. Gianna starts work at a new job on March 1. She is not eligible for insurance coverage until July 1. The period between start date and her eligibility date is
   A. the probationary period
   B. the eligibility period
   C. the selection period
   D. the waiting period

6. Gianna is eligible for coverage on July 1. She enrolls on July 15. She does not need to take a medical exam because she enrolled within
   A. the probationary period
   B. the eligibility period
   C. the selection period
   D. the waiting period

7. Tom started work the same day Gianna did, at the same company. Tom does not try to enroll in the company insurance plan until August 15. What will Tom probably need to do?
   A. Pay an extra premium
   B. Fulfill the probationary period again before coverage is available
   C. Look for insurance somewhere else
   D. Submit to a medical exam and full individual underwriting

8. The baker's union and the butcher's union worked together to form a trust to provide insurance to their employees. This type of group is called
   A. an employee group
   B. a multiple employer trust
   C. a Taft-Hartley trust
   D. a labor group

9. Jimmy's Print Shop and Bryan's Boutique join together to form a trust to provide insurance to their employees. This type of group is called
   A. an employee group
   B. a multiple employer trust
   C. a Taft-Hartley trust
   D. a labor group

10. A candlestick maker offers insurance to its employees. This type of group is called
    A. an employee group
    B. a multiple employer trust
    C. a Taft-Hartley trust
    D. a labor group

11. The United Auto Workers union provides insurance to its employees. This type of group is called
    A. an employee group
    B. a multiple employer trust
    C. a Taft-Hartley trust
    D. a labor group

12. General Electricians offers insurance to its employees. About 80% of its eligible employees are currently covered under the plan. This plan is
    A. contributory
    B. noncontributory
    C. inclusive
    D. noninclusive

13. Group insurance generally does NOT require
    A. stringent medical underwriting
    B. a short application form
    C. a minimum level of participation among eligible insureds
    D. a master policyowner to hold the policy

14. Sara is hired to work at a restaurant. She is not eligible to join the group insurance plan for 30 days. This is an example of
    A. an introductory period
    B. a weeding-out period
    C. a probationary period
    D. an eligibility period

15. Which of the following group underwriting characteristics generally is required by law?
    A. Employer control
    B. Predetermined coverage amount
    C. Nondiscriminatory classifications
    D. Insurance incidental to group

16. Kelsey's Printing funds all the claims in a year, regardless of the amount of the claim. Kelsey's insurer just manages the paperwork for the claims. Which of the following option's is Kelsey's Printing using?
    A. Retrospective premium
    B. Minimum premium
    C. Variable premium
    D. Administrative services only

17. Al's Print Shop pays a provisional premium at the beginning of the year. At the end of the year, Al's insurer has the right to change that premium by charging more or issuing a refund. Al's policy is funded using which premium option?
    A. Retrospective premium
    B. Minimum premium
    C. Variable premium
    D. Administrative services only

18. PDQ Printing pays for all routine claims. PDQ's insurer pays for excess or unexpected claims beyond a specified trigger point. PDQ's policy is funded using which premium option?
    A. Retrospective premium
    B. Minimum premium
    C. Variable premium
    D. Administrative services only

ANSWERS AND RATIONALES TO UNIT TEST

1. **A.** An association must have a constitution and bylaws; it cannot discriminate among the officers and trustees or be organized strictly for the purpose of obtaining insurance.

2. **C.** An individual covered by a group insurance policy receives proof of coverage in the form of a certificate of insurance.

3. **C.** To be a contributory group insurance policy, 75% of employees must participate.

4. **C.** The fact that Albert is more likely to seek insurance coverage than Bernie is an example of adverse selection.

5. **A.** The probationary period is the time period from the hire date to when the employee is eligible to enroll in the group plan. There is no coverage during the probationary period.

6. **B.** Gianna does not need to take a medical exam because she enrolled within the eligibility period.

7. **D.** Tom will need to submit to a medical exam and full individual underwriting.

8. **C.** The Taft-Hartley Trust is a group that is made up of one or more unions to form a group.

9. **B.** This type of group is called a multiple employer trust.

10. **A.** This type of group is called an employee group.

11. **D.** This type of group is called a labor group.

12. **A.** It is most likely that this plan requires employees to contribute toward the premiums.

13. **A.** Group insurance generally does not require stringent medical underwriting.

14. **C.** This is an example of a probationary period.

15. **C.** Nondiscriminatory classifications generally are required by law.

16. **D.** Kelsey's Printing is using administrative services only.

17. **A.** Al's policy is funded using the retrospective premium.

18. **B.** PDQ's policy is funded using the minimum premium.

UNIT 5 EXERCISE ANSWERS

Exercise 5.A

1. noncontributory
2. contributory
3. **C**

UNIT

6

Selling Life Insurance

6. 1 LEARNING OBJECTIVES

After completing this lesson, you will be able to:

- list costs commonly associated with death;
- list two different approaches to needs analysis;
- list the three income periods a surviving spouse may encounter;
- list four living benefits of life insurance;
- explain the advantages of life insurance as property;
- describe the traditional net cost method and the interest-adjusted cost method of comparing insurance policy costs;
- explain the difference between accelerated benefits and viatical/life settlements and explain when each might be used; and
- list the types of organizations that might use life insurance for business reasons.

6. 2 MEETING CONSUMER NEEDS

6. 2. 1 The Importance of Life Insurance

The loss of human life is tragic in many ways. The financial results alone of such a loss can be devastating. If the principal breadwinner dies, the spouse might not be able to maintain the family on Social Security benefits. If there were two breadwinners in the family, the surviving spouse might not be able to maintain the family's lifestyle on a single income. The death of a single parent might leave dependent children without an adequate source of support.

Life insurance products provide a number of unique and powerful features, especially financial security.

Studies show that less than half of American adults own individual life insurance and the average policy amount is just $45,000 of life insurance. Relying on the group life insurance provided at work can build a false sense of security because coverage is usually insufficient for family needs and ceases when employment terminates. Experts agree that few people protect their own full value with life insurance, leaving their families at risk.

6. 2. 2 Costs Associated with Death

In order to help applicants plan ahead, agents should be familiar with the wide range of costs and financial needs that may arise after the death of an insured. For example, a consumer who has purchased life insurance to cover funeral costs and pay off the balance of a mortgage may not realize that if there is a prolonged final illness, health care costs could eat into the proceeds and not leave enough to cover the mortgage.

Potential costs and ongoing financial needs create opportunities during sales presentations for agents to expand the applicant's understanding of the uses of life insurance. Agents should be aware of the following primary areas of potential financial need:

- Doctor and hospital bills from a final illness
- Funeral expenses
- Estate taxes
- Paying off debts (mortgage, loans, credit cards)
- Continuing income needs for family
- Future need to pay for children's education
- Future need of retirement income for spouse

The insurance producer is the person most qualified to help potential insureds select the contract of insurance that will best meet their needs.

A thorough needs analysis can be accomplished by identifying the specific financial objectives of the individual by means of a fact-finding interview. This interview covers the following financial needs:

- Cash needs to cover the expenses of dying (e.g., funeral, taxes, and last illness)
- Cash needs for payment of debts (e.g., credit cards, loans, and bank notes)
- Home mortgage payments
- Family income needs during the dependency period and in later years
- Funds for children's college education
- Retirement income needs
- Health insurance needs such as hospitalization insurance and disability income coverage

After the needs analysis is complete, the producer should make recommendations as to the amount and type of insurance needed by the individual. These recommendations should consider the following.

- Should the coverage be permanent insurance, term insurance, or a combination of the two?
- How much premium can the individual afford to pay?
- Should the premium be level, increasing, or decreasing?
- Is the individual insurable?

6. 2. 3 Human Life Value Approach

Once the costs associated with death are determined, various techniques are available to guide agents in assessing the consumer's need for life insurance. The following are two of the major approaches.

Human life value—This approach focuses on an individual's future stream of income. It considers such things as annual salary and expenses, years remaining until retirement, and the future value of current dollars, and translates this into an amount of insurance needed to replace the income stream in the event of an early death. In other words, this approach addresses the following question:

HOW MUCH WILL THE INSURED MAKE?

6. 2. 4 Needs Approach

Needs approach—This technique focuses more on the needs of survivors. It considers such things as funeral expenses, final illness, continuing family income needs, children's education, and spousal retirement income, and translates this into an amount of insurance designed to provide for the survivors. In other words, this approach asks a different question:

HOW MUCH WILL THE SURVIVOR NEED?

Exercise 6.A

True or False

_____1. The Human Life Value Approach uses the individual's net annual salary, annual expenses, number of years to retirement, and the depreciation of the dollar to determine the amount of insurance that is needed.

_____2. The Needs Approach considers the cost of final expenses, maintenance income for the family, the cost of education for dependent children, and continuing income for the spouse when calculating the amount of insurance that is needed.

Answers to the exercises can be found at the end of the Unit 6 answers and rationales.

6. 2. 5 Income Periods

A typical married couple with children will have fluctuating income needs based on the changes in their family. To properly determine how much life insurance protection they will need if an income earner dies, it is useful to understand three different income periods:

Family dependency period—The first period is called the *family dependency period* because the surviving spouse will have children to support during this time. The family's income needs will be greatest during this period.

Preretirement period—When the children are no longer dependent on the surviving spouse, he enters the *preretirement period*. Because the surviving spouse only qualifies for Social Security survivor benefits when he has dependent children in his care or after reaching age 60, this period is also referred to as the **blackout period**. Usually, the surviving spouse's income needs lessen during this period.

Blackout Period
A 40-year-old widow with a 12-year-old daughter will receive monthly Social Security survivors' benefits until the daughter turns 16. (Benefits to the child continue until she is age 18 but are payable directly to the child.) At age 60, the widow becomes eligible for Social Security retirement benefits. Between the ages of 44 and 60, there is a 16-year blackout period.

Retirement period—The final period is called the *retirement period*. During this period, the surviving spouse's working income ceases and his Social Security and outside retirement benefits begin.

6. 2. 6 Capital Conservation and Capital Liquidation

There are two methods used to calculate the amount of life insurance needed to supply an individual or family with the desired amount of capital to generate income if an income earner should die prematurely. **Capital conservation** (sometimes called capital retention) and **capital liquidation** (sometimes called capital utilization) differ in how capital is used to generate income for the surviving family.

Under the capital conservation method, income is derived only from interest gained on the principal. Under the capital liquidation method, both interest and principal are used to generate income. Generally, this means that a smaller fund is needed when using the capital liquidation method because there is no concern for leaving the principal intact.

6. 2. 7 Estate Planning

Life insurance creates an **immediate estate** for the insured and provides funds that will help preserve the greatest amount of value in the estate. The field of estate planning is very complicated. It requires expertise in the areas of wills, taxes, law, and life insurance. Some of the items to be considered when planning an estate are:

- the needs of the beneficiaries;
- the type and amount of property in the estate;
- how best to administer the estate to fulfill the wishes of the insured;
- the amount of insurance needed to cover expenses and costs;
- how to dispose of any business interest; and
- who will settle and administer the estate.

6. 2. 8 Other Sources of Funds

Regardless of the approach taken when determining insurance needs, other sources of funds should be considered when calculating the need for additional life insurance. Sources to consider include the following:

- Social Security
- Medicare
- Medicaid
- Group retirement plans
- Savings
- Investments
- Other income (rental property income, and so forth)
- Annuities
- Other insurance

6. 2. 9 Living Benefits

The primary reason to own life insurance is the death benefit—the money the beneficiaries will receive when the insured dies. However, life insurance policies that grow cash value can be used during the lifetime of the insured. The cash accumulation in these policies gives liquidity to the policyowner. For example, the insured can use the cash value to provide funding to pay off debts, cash for emergencies, or funding for children's education.

Another type of policy provides for withdrawals from the policy's cash value, which can be used to meet emergencies or pay off debts, further meeting the policyowner's needs. Many policies also offer dividends, which may be defined as payments to policyowners when the insurance company makes a profit.

So, although not all types of life insurance policies accumulate cash values or make payments to policyowners, you should recognize these living benefits of life insurance:

- Loan values
- Retirement income
- Cash withdrawals
- Dividends

6. 2. 10 Advantages as Property

Life insurance actually qualifies as a type of property. Many of the characteristics and advantages of property apply to life insurance.

A life insurance policy's cash value can be used as collateral for borrowing money.

Another advantage of life insurance as property is that it creates an immediate estate. The instant a life insurance policy goes into effect, the policyowner has established a fund that will be paid to his beneficiary—even if only one premium payment has been made.

- Yet another advantage is the convenience of paying for life insurance in installments. In the case of a $100,000 life insurance policy, the entire premium required to purchase the policy does not have to be paid up front.
- Safety of principal is of considerable concern to anyone purchasing property. A $100,000 life insurance policy will pay that amount to the beneficiary at the death of the insured as long as premiums are met and there are no outstanding loans against the policy.
- As for return on investment, life insurance offers plans that can be very advantageous, especially with regard to taxation of cash values.
- Many kinds of property require physical maintenance or upkeep. Apart from paying premiums, a policyowner has no other obligations with regard to life insurance.

6. 3 COMPARING INSURANCE POLICIES

Life insurance cost comparison methods are used to compare the cost of one life insurance policy with another. The comparative interest rate method and the interest-adjusted net cost method are just two of many cost comparison methods used in insurance.

6. 3. 1 Comparative Interest Rate Method

This analysis examines the rate of return that must be earned on a hypothetical side fund in a buy-term-invest-the-difference plan so that the value of the side fund will be exactly equal to the surrender value of the higher-premium policy at a designated point in time. The higher the comparative interest rate (CIR), the less expensive the higher-premium policy relative to the alternative plan.

6. 3. 2 Interest-Adjusted Net Cost Method

This analysis is conducted over a set period and considers a policy's premiums, death benefits, cash values, and dividends, recognizing the accumulated interest over the set period. The NAIC Model Life Insurance Solicitation Regulation requires two interest-adjusted cost indexes for a policy: a surrender cost index and a net payment cost index.

To compare two different policies, it is not enough just to compare premiums. A lower premium does not automatically mean a low-cost policy. Cost indexes have been developed to help in the process of measuring the cost of a policy. These indexes use compound interest factors to produce interest-adjusted cost and payment figures.

Policy illustrations normally include a surrender cost index and a net payment cost index. These indexes show average annual costs and payments per $1,000 of insurance on a basis that recognizes that $1 payable today is worth more than $1 payable in the future. Both assume that the insured will live and pay premiums for a period of years. Most companies provide these index numbers on both a guaranteed and an illustrated basis.

6. 3. 2. 1 *Traditional Net Cost Method*

Under the traditional net cost method, premium payments for a specified number of years are added together, the projected cash value accumulation and any dividend payments for the period are then subtracted, and the result is divided by the number of years under consideration to produce an average annual net cost. The traditional method makes a comparison without regard to the *time value of money*, which takes into account both the ability to earn interest and the tendency for cash value accumulations to lose relative value during inflationary periods.

6. 3. 2. 2 *Interest-Adjusted Cost Method*

Under the interest-adjusted cost method, the calculation is similar except that an adjustment is made for an interest rate. For example, dividends will be assumed to earn a specified interest rate and the future aggregate of cash value, and dividends will be discounted by an interest rate when determining the interest-adjusted average annual net cost. This method factors in the time value of money.

6. 4 USES OF LIFE INSURANCE

6. 4. 1 Personal Uses of Life Insurance

Life insurance may be used to fulfill a number of personal and family needs. With life insurance, the death of the insured creates an immediate estate for the benefit of the insured's family. Life insurance is primarily used for the following:

- Providing funds for last illness and funeral
- Immediate creation of an estate upon death of the insured
- Providing income for survivors

Survivor protection The beneficiaries use the proceeds of a life insurance policy to help maintain a standard of living for survivors by replacing the lost flow of income. This may also be referred to as estate creation because there is a liquid asset in the insured's estate.

Security When death takes the life of a family provider prematurely, surviving family members suffer when they are left without adequate income or the means to provide basic necessities. On the other hand, some people face the unpleasant prospect of outliving their incomes; retirement may be forced on them before they have prepared adequately for a non-income-earning existence. Life insurance, based on actuarial or mathematical principles, guarantees a specified sum of money on the death of the insured person. Annuities provide a stream of income by making a series of payments to the annuitant for a specific period of time or for a lifetime. The true significance of insurance is its promise to substitute uncertainty with future economic certainty and to replace the unknown with a sense of security.

Living benefits/cash accumulation Life insurance policies that grow cash value can be used during the lifetime of the insured. The cash accumulation in these policies gives liquidity to the policyowner with availability for loans. For example, the insured can use the cash value to provide:

- funding to pay off debts;
- cash for emergencies; or
- funding for children's education.

Estate conservation The death benefit can be used to pay estate taxes so a hard asset such as a business or a farm does not need to be sold (liquidated) for cash, thus preserving an estate by avoiding forced liquidation of assets.

Accelerated benefits are living benefits paid by the insurance company that reduce the remaining death benefit available for the beneficiary.

Under a **viatical settlement**, the policyholder actually sells all rights to the policy to a viatical settlement company, which advances a percentage (usually 60% to 80%) of the eventual death benefit. The viatical settlement company then receives the entire death benefit when the insured ultimately dies.

6. 4. 2 Business Uses of Life Insurance

There are several reasons a business might buy life insurance on the lives of employees. These reasons will be discussed in further detail:

- Buy-sell funding
- Key person
- Executive bonuses
- Corporate-owned policies

6. 4. 2. 1 Key Person Life Insurance

Life insurance is often used to protect businesses from the financial consequences of the loss of a key person. When an owner, director, executive, or manager dies, a business may suffer losses due to the gap in expertise and the expense of finding, hiring, and training a replacement.

The **business** is the applicant, policyowner, and beneficiary and is responsible for paying the premiums. Because this is a third-party owned contract, the consent of the insured is required.

Key-employee life insurance also receives favorable tax treatment. The death proceeds of key-employee life insurance are not taxable. However, premiums are not deductible for business income tax purposes.

6. 4. 2. 2 Buy-Sell Agreements

Buy-sell agreements help with the orderly continuation of a business where survivors receive a fair cash settlement for a deceased owner's interest. A buy-sell agreement is a **legal document** outlining the business continuation plan. The most common way in which to fund a buy-sell agreement is through the use of life insurance. Funding the agreement with life insurance proceeds guarantees that the cash necessary to pay for the deceased owner's interest in the business will be available. It allows an individual to purchase the deceased owner's interest so the business will continue without further disruption.

Legal contracts (the buy-sell agreement) are drawn which set a predetermined value on each person's portion of ownership in the business. Premiums are not tax deductible, and benefits are not taxed.

The two most common types of buy-sell funding agreements are the entity or "stock redemption" type of plan (this is where the business purchases the life insurance coverage) and the cross-purchase plan (with this plan, the individuals purchase coverage on each other). For example, in a cross-purchase plan, if there are three partners, each partner will own a policy covering the life of each of the other partners. Therefore, six policies are purchased all together.

6. 4. 2. 3 Executive Bonus Plans

Some companies set up benefit plans for executives that allow highly paid officers to defer current income or bonuses and to receive the funds at a later date (such as after retirement) when they might be in a lower tax bracket. Life insurance products are often used to fund such programs. Executives purchase an individual life insurance policy and the company pays the executive the cost of the premium.

Because the company pays the executive the cost of the premium, the premium is considered part of the executive's compensation, and this is reported as taxable income to the executive.

Because the premium is considered part of the executive's compensation, it is tax deductible for the employer as part of payroll.

The death benefit is not taxable to the executive's beneficiary.

6. 4. 2. 4 Deferred Compensation

Deferred compensation is an arrangement whereby an employee or owner agrees to forgo some portion of current income (for example, employee raises or bonuses) until a specified future date—typically, at retirement. Life insurance is one method of funding a deferred compensation plan.

Deferred compensation is an example of a nonqualified plan because the plan favors highly paid executives. The plan is not in the employee's name during the contribution phase: it exists as a "promise" to pay a future benefit. (The benefit generally will be forfeited if the employee leaves the company.) Contributions are not deductible to the employer until the employee retires and takes distributions. In addition, the employee does not pay tax on the employer's contributions until the employee takes distributions.

6. 4. 2. 5 *Business Continuation Plan*

A **sole proprietorship** is an unincorporated form of business whereby an individual, using his own special talents and abilities, owns and manages a business. Even though a sole proprietorship may have several employees, it is the sole proprietor who is directly responsible for the success of the business.

The sole proprietor has **unlimited liability** with regard to the business operation. Creditors can claim both the sole proprietor's business assets as well as personal assets. When the sole proprietor dies, the business also dies. This business asset becomes part of the deceased's estate and is subject to taxation, the payment of debts, and claims of creditors.

Generally, the business is the principal asset in the sole proprietor's estate. It is also normally the only source of income for the family. Upon the death of the sole proprietor, family income ceases and the business may have to be liquidated for a fraction of its value to pay estate settlement costs.

Life insurance can be used to solve the problems created by the death of the sole proprietor. Life insurance may fund a **business continuation agreement** (also known as a **buy-sell agreement**) by providing necessary cash with which to keep the business doors open until the business can be sold at its fair market value for the benefit of the family. Life insurance also can be used to provide funds for a competent employee or other qualified person to purchase the business from the surviving family members.

If the business is to survive the death of the sole proprietor and the family is to be able to maintain its standard of living, adequate planning and the implementation of agreements, such as a business continuation agreement, are necessary. Finally, these plans and agreements must be funded with adequate amounts of life insurance to guarantee that the sole proprietor's financial plans will be realized.

6. 4. 2. 6 *Corporate Owned Life Insurance*

Corporations may also face financial losses when the owner dies or even if one of the key employees dies. To protect against those financial losses, the corporation may purchase life insurance on the owner or key person. The corporation is the owner, premium payor, and beneficiary on the policy. The face amount generally relates to the amount of lost corporate income plus the costs of hiring and training a replacement for the deceased owner or key person.

The death of a stockholder in a closely held corporation means the loss of services of this key person and quite possibly loss of business income. However, the most immediate effect will be the loss of income to the deceased's family. The choices available to the family are to sell the deceased's stock, attempt to live off of any dividends the corporation may pay, or assume a working position within the corporation.

Probably the most desirable alternative is to sell the deceased's stock.

Business planning to resolve the problems created by the death of a stockholder involves the implementation of a stock purchase or stock redemption plan. A **stock purchase plan** is similar to a cross-purchase partnership plan in which a price is determined and each stockholder agrees to purchase a proportionate share of the deceased shareholder's stock. The purchase price is naturally funded with life insurance, and each shareholder is the owner, premium payor, and beneficiary of a life policy on the lives of the other stockholders. This arrangement is feasible when there are only a few shareholders.

In situations with several shareholders, the **stock redemption plan** is better. Under a **stock redemption plan**, the corporation is the owner, beneficiary, and premium payor of the life insurance policies and the corporation agrees to purchase the deceased's stock.

The advantages of the life insurance-funded corporate buy-sell plan include:

- the establishment of a fair price for the stock;
- a binding agreement that identifies the buyers;
- security of corporate assets and jobs; and
- guaranteed delivery of the purchase price.

Example

Section 303 stock redemption is a special type of stock redemption that permits a corporation to partially redeem a shareholder's stock for purposes of providing cash to cover estate settlement costs. Tax laws generally require that stock redemptions be total to avoid taxing the proceeds payable to the family as a dividend. The Internal Revenue Service will permit a partial redemption by the corporation to pay funeral expenses, taxes, and related estate settlement costs.

6. 4. 2. 7 Split Dollar Plans

These plans allow employees and employers to share premium payments and benefits. This arrangement often allows a key employee to have additional life insurance at a reasonable cost, and the employer to eventually recapture its investment in premiums. For example, assume a key or valued employee has a definite need for life insurance protection but lacks the funds necessary to the coverage. With a split-dollar plan, the employer contributes to the premium each year in an amount equal to the increase in the policy's cash value, and the employee pays only the balance of the premium. If the policy is surrendered at any time, the cash savings value amount is returned to the employer. If the insured dies, the employer gets back the money paid out for the premiums (the employer is generally listed as beneficiary for an amount of the death proceeds equal to the premiums paid) and the balance is paid to the deceased's beneficiary.

Split dollar is considered a nonqualified plan because it is offered only to highly valued employees.

If the employee retires, he can borrow cash value to repay the employer equal to the premium paid by the employer, and the employee can take the policy with him.

The employer's contributions are considered taxable compensation to the employee in the year paid.

6. 4. 3 Charitable Uses of Life Insurance

Another use of life insurance is for charitable purposes. In accordance with tax laws, a policyowner may purchase a life insurance contract on his life, pay the premiums, and designate a charitable organization as the beneficiary, such as a church, school, hospital, or similar organization. Generally, the premium paid by the insured donor is tax deductible.

Exercise 6.B

1. Life insurance can be purchased to meet all of the following needs EXCEPT
   A. charitable giving
   B. guaranteed lifetime retirement income
   C. business uses
   D. personal uses

Answers to the exercises can be found at the end of the Unit 6 answers and rationales.

UNIT TEST

1. Which of the following costs are associated with death?
   A. Doctor or hospital bills from a final illness or accident
   B. Paying off debts such as credit cards and other loans
   C. Taxes
   D. All of the above

2. An insurance producer analyzed Bonita's life insurance needs, taking into account Bonita's net annual salary, her expenses, her current age, and depreciation of the dollar over time. This producer was using
   A. the analytical approach to needs analysis
   B. the human life value approach to needs analysis
   C. the needs approach to needs analysis
   D. the planning approach to needs analysis

3. An insurance producer analyzed Dwight's life insurance needs, taking into account the amount of money Dwight anticipated needing for his funeral and the amount of income that would be required to maintain his family's standard of living in the event of his death, including projected college costs and the costs of supporting his spouse. This producer was using
   A. the analytical approach to needs analysis
   B. the human life value approach to needs analysis
   C. the needs approach to needs analysis
   D. the planning approach to needs analysis

4. Wilma's husband died 3 years ago, leaving her with 2 grade school-aged children. Which income period is Wilma in?
   A. Family dependency period
   B. Preretirement period
   C. Retirement period
   D. Grieving period

5. Which of the following is an advantage of life insurance as property?
   A. Life insurance is generally paid for in one lump sum.
   B. Life insurance requires no physical upkeep.
   C. Life insurance requires careful managerial care on the part of the policyholder.
   D. Life insurance has little potential for a positive return on investment.

6. Life insurance proceeds are generally the only source of income for surviving dependents of a breadwinner.
   A. True
   B. False

7. Which of the following factors should NOT be taken into account when a producer makes recommendations as to the amount and type of insurance needed by an individual?
   A. How much premium can the individual afford to pay?
   B. Should the premium be level, increasing, or decreasing?
   C. How much commission does the product offer?
   D. Is the individual insurable?

8. Ana wishes to purchase enough insurance to support her husband for the rest of his life if she should die prematurely and then leave a sizeable inheritance for her children upon his death. Which method should be used to calculate the amount of insurance necessary?
   A. Capital conservation
   B. Capital liquidation
   C. Human life value
   D. Needs analysis

9. Ken has terminal cancer and wants to access the death benefit of his life insurance policy to pay medical expenses. How might he be able to do this?
   A. He won't be able to access the policy funds until after his death.
   B. He may access the funds through accelerated benefits.
   C. He may access the funds through a viatical settlement.
   D. He may access the funds either through a viatical settlement or by use of the accelerated benefits provision.

10. Shane is a master carpenter in business for himself. His business is probably operated as
    A. a corporation
    B. a sole proprietorship
    C. a partnership
    D. a limited liability company

11. Which of the following is NOT financed using life insurance?
    A. Buy-sell agreement
    B. Section 303 stock redemption
    C. Cross-purchase agreement
    D. Split-dollar plan

ANSWERS AND RATIONALES TO UNIT TEST

1. **D.** All of these costs are associated with death.

2. **B.** The human life value approach looks at net annual salary, expenses, current age, and depreciation of the dollar over time.

3. **C.** This is an example of the needs approach because it focuses on the financial needs that will arise as a result of Dwight's death.

4. **A.** Wilma is in the family dependency period because she still has children to support.

5. **B.** Life insurance does not require any physical maintenance or upkeep aside from paying the premiums.

6. **B.** Surviving dependents are often entitled to benefits from retirement plans and government programs such as Social Security.

7. **C.** A producer should not recommend a product based on the amount of commission he will receive.

8. **A.** The capital conservation method should be used to calculate the amount of insurance needed because of the concern to leave the principal intact for her children.

9. **D.** Ken may access the funds either through a viatical settlement or by use of the accelerated benefits provision.

10. **B.** Shane probably operates his business as a sole proprietorship.

11. **D.** A split-dollar plan is not financed using life insurance.

UNIT 6 EXERCISE ANSWERS

Exercise 6.A

1. True

2. True

Exercise 6.B

1. **B**

U N I T

7

Policy Issuance and Delivery

7. 1 LEARNING OBJECTIVES

After completing this lesson, you will be able to:

- list two important reasons for the potential insured to pay the premium at the time of initial application;
- list three types of receipt and explain the differences among them;
- explain what happens when a potential insured dies between the application and issuance of the policy and how that changes depending on the type of receipt issued;
- explain the importance of personally delivering life insurance policies;
- define replacement and explain when it is and is not appropriate; and
- list duties commonly required of producers and insurers when replacing insurance.

7. 2 COLLECTION OF PREMIUM

The producer is encouraged to collect the initial premium with the application. If the applicant does not pay the initial premium at the time of application, chances increase that the applicant will not accept the issued policy. Also if the applicant waits to pay the premium, he may become uninsurable or may die before the policy takes effect.

When the initial premium is not paid with the application, no contract is in force. When the producer delivers the policy and collects the initial premium, there may be additional underwriting requirements to be satisfied. Most commonly, the insurance company may require that the insured sign a health statement verifying that no change in health has occurred since application.

7. 3 RECEIPTS

Once the underwriting process is complete and the applicant has been approved, the life insurance policy will be issued by the insurance company. The coverage is not effective until the policy is delivered and the initial premium has been paid. Usually the applicant will pay the initial premium with the application. When this occurs, the producer will provide the applicant with a receipt for the initial premium and the effective date of coverage will depend on the type of receipt issued.

7. 3. 1 Conditional Receipt

This receipt usually makes the coverage effective as of the date of application, if the applicant is found to be insurable under the company's general underwriting rules. Some conditional receipts make coverage effective on the date of application, or the date of a required medical examination, whichever is later.

According to the conditional receipt, if the proposed insured should die before the policy is issued, one of the following will occur.

- The proceeds will be paid to the beneficiary named in the policy if the company would have issued the policy to the proposed insured if he had been living.
- The proceeds will not be paid to the policy's beneficiary if the company would not have issued the policy. Instead, the premium will be returned.

Example

An applicant has paid the initial premium and completed and signed the application. The producer provides the applicant with a conditional receipt, which basically states that the applicant is covered as of the date of the application (or receipt) provided she is insurable as a standard risk. Thus, if the applicant were to die before the policy was issued, the beneficiary would receive the face amount of the policy.

However, if the applicant is found to be a substandard risk, then the conditional receipt is null and void and no coverage would be effective until the substandard policy was delivered and the additional premium paid.

7. 3. 1. 1 Statement of Good Health

When the initial premium is not paid until the policy is delivered, the agent must also obtain a statement signed by the insured attesting to the insured's continued good health before leaving the policy with the insured.

7. 3. 2 Binding Receipt

A few companies use an **unconditional** or **binding receipt** that makes the company liable for the risk from the date of application, regardless of the applicant's insurability. This coverage lasts for a specified time (usually 30 to 60 days) or until the insurer issues the policy, if earlier. If the application is rejected, coverage terminates at the end of the specified period.

This type of receipt is rarely used for life insurance policies, though it is commonly used for auto or homeowners insurance.

7. 3. 3 Inspection Receipt

Occasionally, the proposed insured wants to examine the policy carefully before actually purchasing it. In this situation, the policyowner does not pay the first full premium at the time the application is completed. The policyowner signs an inspection receipt for the policy, examines the policy, and then pays the first full premium.

7. 3. 4 Temporary Insurance Agreement

This type of receipt or agreement provides the applicant with immediate life insurance coverage whether or not the individual is found to be insurable, while the underwriting process is taking place.

The insurer has the right to cancel this coverage if the applicant fails to meet the company's normal underwriting requirements. However, claims incurred during the underwriting period will be paid whether or not the application ultimately would have been approved.

Example

An applicant submits the initial premium and application and is provided with a temporary insurance agreement that states that coverage is effective immediately and will continue during the underwriting process. If the applicant should die during this period, the coverage is in force regardless of the individual's insurability or risk classification as a result of the underwriting process.

7. 3. 5 Amendments

The insurer may amend the policy's terms depending on the results of the underwriting process. The insurer may, for instance, amend the policy to exclude certain losses or conditions, or it may classify the applicant as a substandard risk for which it will charge a higher premium. The applicant is not obligated to accept the amended policy and may withdraw the application.

7. 4 SUBMITTING THE APPLICATION AND INITIAL PREMIUM

It is important for the producer to submit the application, initial premium, and any questionnaires or other forms promptly after reviewing all forms for completeness and making sure that they are properly signed.

Because producers are handling money belonging to their clients, it is extremely important that an accurate record of transactions be kept.

7. 4. 1 Issuing the Policy

A life insurance policy may be issued as applied for, modified, or even amended, provided the applicant meets the underwriting standards of the insurance company. In some cases, the insurer may issue a policy with a waiver attached, stating that death by a particular event (perhaps reflecting an occupation or recreational exposure) will not be covered. In other cases, an insurer might issue a more limited form of coverage or a policy with lower limits than those applied for by the applicant.

7. 5 DELIVERING AND SERVICING THE POLICY

7. 5. 1 Personal Delivery

Delivery is necessary to complete the sale of a life insurance policy, so the best way to ensure delivery is to do it in person. If a conditional receipt has not been issued, the insurer may require the producer to obtain a statement of good health at the time of policy delivery. Regardless of whether personal delivery is required, it is usually recommended because it also gives the agent an opportunity to enhance the agent-client relationship by:

- conducting a policy review of both new and existing coverages;
- explaining coverages and policy provisions and answer any questions the client has;
- identifying the effective date of coverage;
- explaining the possible need for any additional coverages or amounts of insurance; and
- asking the client for referrals.

7. 5. 2 Mailing the Policy

Legally, the policy is considered delivered when it is mailed to or turned over to the policyowner or someone acting on the policyowner's behalf. In some cases, a **constructive delivery** is deemed to occur when the insurer mails a policy to its producer for actual delivery to the policyowner because the insurer has issued the policy and released it for delivery. However, a legal delivery has not yet occurred if the insurer requires personal delivery for verification of good health at the time of delivery or if the policy is being provided to the applicant merely to review and inspect at that time and not necessarily to buy.

7. 5. 3 Policy Review

Once the policy is delivered to the policyowner, the producer should thoroughly explain all coverage provisions, particularly the exclusions, and any riders.

7. 5. 4 Effective Date of Coverage

The effective date is important for two reasons: not only does it identify when the coverage is effective, it also establishes the date by which future annual premiums must be paid.

If a receipt (either conditional or binding) was issued in exchange for the payment of an initial premium deposit, the date of the receipt will generally be the policy effective date.

If a premium deposit is not given with the application, the policy effective date is usually the date the policy is issued by the insurance company. However, the policy will not be truly effective until it is delivered to the applicant, the first premium is paid, and a Statement of Good Health is obtained.

7. 5. 5 Policy Summary

The policy summary addresses the specific product being presented for sale. It identifies the agent, the insurer, the policy, and each rider. It includes information about premiums, dividends, benefit amounts, cash surrender values, policy loan interest rates, and life insurance cost indexes.

7. 5. 6 Buyer's Guide

An agent is required to deliver to the applicant a *Life Insurance Buyer's Guide* and a *Policy Summary*. These documents are usually delivered before the agent accepts the applicant's initial premium. Typically, the buyer's guide is a generic publication that explains life insurance in a way that average consumers can understand. It does not address the specific product or policy being considered.

7. 6 HANDLING A CLAIM

A claim and its payment are the end result of the insurance process. With respect to life insurance, it means the insured has died and the beneficiary stands ready to collect from the insurer what is due. Unlike property or casualty insurance, claims made on a life insurance policy are rarely negotiated. They are either paid or denied. When proof of the death of the insured arrives at the insurer's claims department, the records are checked to make sure the policy was in force at the time of death and that the person to whom the policy proceeds are to be paid is indeed the rightful beneficiary.

7. 6. 1 Payment of Claims

When an insured dies, the life insurance company should be notified as soon as possible. In many cases, it is the producer's responsibility to make sure that the company is notified of the claim at the earliest possible opportunity.

Once a company has been given the proper forms, there is usually little or no delay in payment of the claim, especially when the claim is valid—the policy is in force, the beneficiary is available, there is no evidence of suicide within the limitations of the suicide clause, and so on. Insurers usually pay valid life claims within a few days.

In most states, life insurance companies are required to pay death claims within a specified period after proper notification is received (usually 60 days).

If there is a delay in a death claim payment, the usual reason is that the company has not been properly notified of the insured's death. A formal proof of death of some type is usually required by the company, in addition to a death certificate completed by the attending physician or the coroner. When an insured dies, the agent should complete any proof of death form the company requires, have it signed by the necessary parties, and forward it to the company as soon as possible along with a death certificate.

7. 6. 2 Payment Less than Face Amount

In property or casualty insurance, the amount of claims paid is often less than the face amount of the policy. In contrast, life insurance is generally paid for the full face amount of the policy. There are three exceptions.

The first exception is when there is an outstanding loan against the cash value of a policy. The amount of the loan, plus any interest outstanding, is deducted from the face amount of the policy before payment is made to the beneficiary.

The second exception is when a premium payment is due. With insurance premiums, as with many other types of bills, there is a grace period of somewhere between a week and a month after the due date. If the insured dies within this grace period, the amount of premium due is deducted from the face amount of the policy before payment is made to the beneficiary.

The third exception happens when there is an error made in determining the age or gender of the insured when the policy was issued. If such an error is discovered at the time of death, the insurance company will compute the face amount that the premium would have purchased if the accurate information was used and pay that amount to the beneficiary.

7. 6. 3 Producer Responsibilities Upon Insured's Death

When the producer is made aware of an insured's death, the first task is to notify the company immediately. Sometimes a beneficiary, the beneficiary's legal representative, or an heir of the deceased will notify the company directly of the insured's death. In these instances, the company will then contact the producer or will advise the beneficiary to do so.

The producer should contact the beneficiary (or the beneficiary's legal representative). The producer should help the beneficiary complete a proof of death form and send it to the company along with a death certificate.

The important thing at this point is to render the best possible service to the beneficiary.

Life insurance policy proceeds can be taken in forms other than cash. The insured can select a settlement option when the policy is purchased, or it may be left up to the beneficiary as to which option to select. Even if the insured had chosen an option, the right to change it to another one may have been given to the beneficiary.

Exercise 7.A

1. If the initial premium is paid at the time of the application on May 1, the company issues the policy as a standard issue on May 30, and the producer delivers the policy to the owner on June 5, when is coverage effective, assuming a conditional receipt was given and there was no medical exam required?
   A. May 1
   B. May 30
   C. June 5
   D. After the statement of good health is signed
2. An application is completed and submitted without an initial premium on July 1. A medical exam is required and completed on July 12. The company issues the policy as a standard issue on August 1, and the producer hand delivers the policy on August 4. When is coverage effective?
   A. July 12
   B. August 1
   C. August 4, after the premium is paid
   D. August 4, after the premium is paid and the statement of good health is signed

Answers to the exercises can be found at the end of the Unit 7 answers and rationales.

7. 7 REPLACEMENT

Replacement is the purchase of one life insurance policy to replace another. Because of the cash values that can build up in a policy and the favorable loan interest rates in older policies, replacement can be disadvantageous to consumers. However, there are also good reasons to replace a policy, particularly if it does not meet the current needs of the consumer.

Commissions paid to producers for selling a new policy are particularly lucrative. For this reason, unscrupulous producers have persuaded consumers to give up old policies for new ones, even if it was not in the consumers' best interests.

When replacing existing life insurance, the producer must comply with all pertinent state regulations. Each state has rules and regulations regarding replacement of life insurance products that are designed to protect the interests of the insuring public. There are several reasons that a new policy might not be in the insured's best interests.

- New insurance requires the applicant to prove insurability.
- Premiums may be higher for a new policy.
- New policy provisions will have to be complied with, such as a new incontestable period.

- The existing policy's provisions may be more liberal than a new policy's provisions.
- Generally, a new policy will not have current cash values.

7. 7. 1 Duties of Producers

Replacement means any transaction in which new life insurance or a new annuity is to be purchased, and it is known, or should reasonably be known, that as part of the transaction, existing life insurance or annuities will be:

- lapsed, forfeited, surrendered, or terminated;
- converted to reduced paid-up insurance, continued as extended term insurance, or reduced in value by the use of nonforfeiture benefits or other policy values;
- amended to produce a reduction in the benefits or in the term for which coverage would otherwise remain in force or for which benefits would be paid; or
- reissued with a reduction in cash value.

Generally, the duties of the producer include obtaining, along with the application, a signed statement from the applicant as to whether insurance is to be replaced and submitting the statement to the insurer.

If replacement is involved, the producer is required to:

- list all existing life insurance policies to be replaced;
- give the applicant a Notice to Applicants Regarding Replacement of Life Insurance (a copy of the forms should be left with the applicant); and
- give the insurer a copy of any proposals made and the name of the insurer of the policy that is to be replaced.

The producer must take special care when replacing an existing policy to make sure that the insured is not misled into purchasing a policy that is to the insured's disadvantage.

7. 7. 2 Duties of the Insurer

The duties of the replacing insurer include the following:

- Making sure that all replacements are in compliance with state regulations
- Notifying each insurer whose insurance is being replaced and, upon request, furnishing a copy of any proposal
- Maintaining copies of proposals and receipts

7. 8 POLICY RETENTION

Although much of the business of the producer is involved in attracting potential clients, retaining the account and servicing it through the years is very important as well.

The client's needs change at such times as marriage, the birth of a child, and death. The producer acts as the representative of the company in changing beneficiaries, adding amounts of insurance, and facilitating payment of claims. The effectiveness of the producer at these times will lead to retention of the account for the lifetime of the client and often over generations.

7. 9 PROFESSIONALISM AND ETHICS

All business transactions are based to a certain extent on trust. When it comes to life insurance, the trust factor is especially significant. When asked what factors matter most in a financial advisor, consumers choose ethical performance more than twice as often as financial performance. Ethics and professionalism are critical components of a successful career as an insurance producer.

Ethics means setting a standard of conduct or behavior based on established values. Insurance producers have long sought to distinguish themselves as professionals. A **professional** is defined as a person in an occupation requiring an advanced level of training, knowledge, or skill. Professionals relate to their clients in a way that reflects well on the entire industry.

7. 9. 1 Fiduciary Responsibility

Insurance producers have a **fiduciary** duty to just about any person or organization that they come into contact with as a part of the day-to-day business of transacting insurance. By definition, a **fiduciary** is a person in a position of financial trust. Attorneys, accountants, trust officers, and insurance producers are all considered fiduciaries.

As a fiduciary, the producer has an obligation to act in the best interest of the insured. The producer must be knowledgeable about the features and provisions of various insurance policies as well as know the use of these insurance contracts. The producer must be able to explain the important features of these policies of the insured.

As a fiduciary, the producer must know and comply with the state's insurance laws.

7. 9. 2 Summary of the Producer's Responsibilities

The insurance producer is a key player in the marketing, underwriting, and delivery of insurance policies. As a marketing representative of the insurer, it is the producer's responsibility to represent and market the insurer's products in an ethical and professional manner. This requires knowledge of insurance products, awareness of a prospect's insurance needs and problems, and the ability to address these needs with the proper insurance products.

The producer also has a responsibility to be aware of insurance laws that pertain to the marketing of insurance products, such as state-required standards for advertising and sales literature.

As part of the underwriting process, the producer is the primary source of underwriting information. It is the producer's duty to accurately and thoroughly complete all applications for insurance, collect initial premiums, and promptly submit them to the company. In addition, the producer is responsible for providing the insurance applicant with privacy notices and information, such as the Notice of Insurance Information Practices, as well as necessary receipts for the initial premium collected.

Another objective of the producer as a field underwriter is to help protect the insurer from adverse risks. If an applicant is determined to be a substandard risk, the producer is responsible for delivering the substandard policy and explaining its limitations and/or extra premium to the applicant.

UNIT TEST

1. Alice decides to buy a policy. She pays the first premium; the producer issues a receipt and tells her that she is covered immediately, until she is notified that the policy is either issued or declined. What kind of receipt has Alice received?
   A. Conditional receipt
   B. Binding receipt
   C. Inspection receipt
   D. Premium receipt

2. Brenda decides that she wants to buy a policy. She fills out the application but does not pay the initial premium. What kind of receipt will Brenda receive?
   A. Conditional receipt
   B. Binding receipt
   C. Inspection receipt
   D. Premium receipt

3. Camille decides to buy a policy. She pays the first premium, and the producer issues a receipt and tells her that she is covered immediately, unless the company decides she would have been a substandard risk. What kind of receipt did Camille receive?
   A. Conditional receipt
   B. Binding receipt
   C. Inspection receipt
   D. Premium receipt

4. Which kind of receipt is most commonly used in life insurance?
   A. Conditional receipt
   B. Binding receipt
   C. Inspection receipt
   D. Premium receipt

5. Insurers sometimes require personal delivery so that
   A. the producer has another opportunity to sell policies
   B. the producer can verify the insured's good health at the time of delivery
   C. the insurer can save mailing costs of delivering the policies
   D. the first premium may be collected

6. If payment of a valid death claim is delayed, what is the usual reason?
   A. A dispute over the validity of the claim
   B. A dispute over the amount of the claim
   C. The insurer has not received proper notification of the death
   D. The insurer has not received proper notification of the policy

7. Lee applies for a policy, pays the initial premium, and receives a conditional receipt on March 14. On March 15, he passes the medical exam with flying colors. On March 16, an undiagnosed brain aneurysm bursts, killing Lee instantly. On March 17, the insurer receives the results of the medical exam, which includes no information about the aneurysm. On March 19, the insurer receives the notice of claim. The insurer will
   A. pay the claim
   B. return the premium
   C. pay the claim plus the amount of the first premium
   D. pay the claim minus a processing fee

8. Rich applies for a policy, pays the initial premium, and receives a binding receipt on Friday, September 1. On Monday, September 4, the underwriting department decides not to issue the policy and places the file in a pile for notification letters to be sent out at the end of the week. On Wednesday, September 6, Rich is killed in an auto accident. On Thursday, September 7, the insurer receives the notice of claim. The insurer will
   A. return the premium and not pay the claim because the underwriting decision had been made
   B. return the premium and not pay the claim because death occurred before the policy was issued
   C. pay the claim because a binding receipt ensures coverage until the potential insured is notified of a rejection
   D. pay the claim because any receipt assures coverage until the potential insured is notified of a rejection

9. Brit purchases a policy and tells the producer he wants immediate coverage, regardless of what the underwriting outcome is. To meet Brit's demand, the producer most likely will accept the premium and
   A. set up a temporary insurance agreement
   B. issue an inspection receipt
   C. issue a binding receipt
   D. issue a conditional receipt

10. A policy may be issued in all of the following ways EXCEPT
    A. as applied for
    B. as a modified or amended policy
    C. as an exchange policy, covering someone other than the original applicant
    D. with a waiver excluding death by a certain cause

11. Which of the following statements describes the best use of a producer's time when personally delivering the policy?
    A. Mr. Jones delivers a policy and makes a special point of finding out how the insured's son performed in the gymnastics competition.
    B. Ms. King delivers a policy and reiterates the same sales pitch she used to make the initial sale.
    C. Mrs. Ritley delivers a policy and restates the advantages of the policy and how it can be amended to meet future insurance needs.
    D. Mr. Bourne delivers a policy early in the morning, before the client is home, so that he can simply leave the policy in the mailbox.

12. Which of the following statements is NOT true?
    A. Replacement is illegal.
    B. Replacement is the purchase of one life insurance policy to replace another.
    C. Replacement laws are designed to protect the interests of life insurance purchasers.
    D. Replacement laws concern themselves with the use of false and misleading statements used in the sale of insurance.

ANSWERS AND RATIONALES TO UNIT TEST

1. **B.** A binding receipt is effective on the day of application.

2. **C.** An inspection receipt is used when the applicant wants to inspect the policy before actually purchasing it.

3. **A.** This is a conditional receipt because Camille is covered conditionally. The receipt makes coverage effective on the date of the application if the insurer finds that Camille is insurable under the insurer's general underwriting rules.

4. **A.** Conditional receipts are the type most commonly used in life insurance transactions.

5. **B.** The insurer may require personal delivery so the producer can verify the insured's good health at the time of delivery, especially if a conditional receipt was issued.

6. **C.** Most insurance companies pay death claims as soon as possible after they receive proper notification and proof of death. If there is a delay, the usual reason is that the company has not received proper notification.

7. **A.** The insurer will pay the claim because the applicant met underwriting standards and would have been issued the policy.

8. **C.** The insurer will pay the claim because a binding receipt ensures coverage until the potential insured is notified of a rejection.

9. **A.** To meet Brit's demand, the producer most likely will accept the premium and set up a temporary insurance agreement.

10. **C.** A policy cannot be issued as an exchange policy, covering someone other than the original applicant.

11. **C.** When a producer delivers a policy personally, the producer should restate the advantages of the policy and tell the policyowner how the policy can be amended to meet future insurance needs.

12. **A.** Replacement is legal.

UNIT 7 EXERCISE ANSWERS

Exercise 7.A

1. **A**

2. **D**

UNIT

8

Types of Life Insurance Policies

8. 1 LEARNING OBJECTIVES

After completing this lesson, you will be able to:

- describe the types of life insurance policies, including term, whole life, and flexible policies;
- explain the death benefits for various types of life insurance policies;
- describe industrial life insurance, home service life insurance, credit life insurance, and specialized policies; and
- describe viatical/life settlements and how they work.

8. 2 INTRODUCTION

All life insurance provides a death benefit. However, living benefits, such as loan values, retirement income, and cash withdrawals, set certain life insurance policies apart from others. Life insurance can be structured to provide:

- a guaranteed death benefit only, using term insurance;
- a guaranteed death benefit plus cash accumulation, using some type of permanent insurance;
- a guaranteed death benefit plus premium flexibility, using universal life;
- a guaranteed death benefit plus premium and investment flexibility, using variable or variable universal life; and
- liquidity for estates.

8. 3 TERM INSURANCE

Term life insurance policies:

- provide temporary insurance protection for a specified period of time, also called the policy term (for example, the term may be 1 year, 5 years, 10 years, 30 years, or to a specified age, such as age 65);
- pay a death benefit (or mature) only if the insured dies during the term of coverage; and
- do not accumulate cash value.

Term insurance provides pure protection and is the least expensive form of life insurance.

8. 3. 1 Characteristics of Term Policies

Term policies are defined by the way the **face amount** of the policy changes throughout the life of the policy. The **face amount**, or **face value**, of the policy is the amount of money listed on the face page (first page) of the policy. This is the amount that will be paid in the event of the insured's death. Term insurance policies may be characterized according to their renewability and convertibility provisions.

8. 3. 2 Types of Term Policies

8. 3. 2. 1 Renewable Term

A **renewable term policy** is issued for a specified term and may be renewed at the end of that term without evidence of insurability. Renewable term policies may be limited in the number of renewals or to a specified age beyond which renewals will not be available. The renewal policy premium will be based on the insured's attained age at the time of renewal. A popular (and initially less expensive) form of renewable term insurance is annual renewable term (ART) insurance.

Step-Rate Premiums in Renewable Term

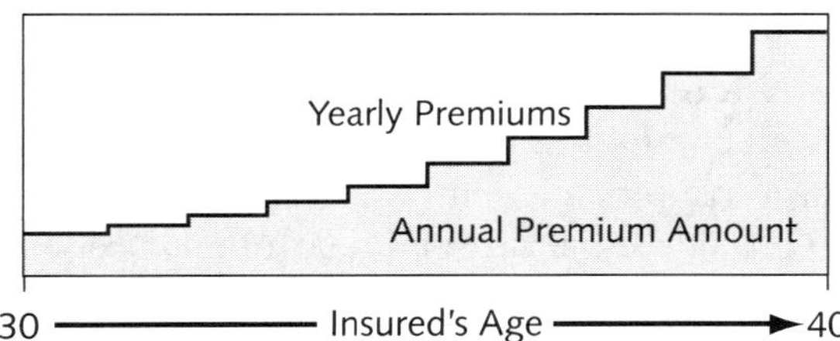

A **nonrenewable term policy** is issued for a specified term and may not be renewed. (An insured may always apply for a new policy at the end of the term, but there are no guarantees and the risk may be accepted or rejected based on current underwriting standards.)

8. 3. 2. 2 Convertible Term

A **convertible term policy** allows a policyowner to convert or exchange the temporary protection for some form of permanent protection without evidence of insurability. The conversion must be made prior to expiration of the term. When a policy is converted, the premium will be based on attained age.

8. 3. 2. 3 Reentry Term

A **reentry term policy** gives the insured the opportunity to provide evidence of insurability at the end of the term and qualify for reduced premium rates (lower than the guaranteed rate that is available for a renewable term policy).

8. 3. 2. 4 *Level Term*

Level term policies are issued for a fixed face amount, which remains the same during the term of coverage. A level term policy may be issued for an annual period, for a specified number of years, or until a specified age. Premiums may increase annually or be level for the term of coverage (level premium, level term).

Example

An insured has purchased $50,000 of one-year renewable and convertible term insurance. Each year the policy is renewed at the same face amount by the payment of the new, higher premium. A new application is not required nor is a new policy issued. The only thing that changes is the age of the insured and subsequently the policy's premium.

8. 3. 2. 5 *Decreasing Term*

Decreasing term policies are issued for an initial face amount that declines during the term period and reaches zero at policy expiration. For example, a 20-year decreasing term policy issued for $100,000 may only provide a death benefit of $50,000 after 10 years. This type of policy is ideal for many types of insurance needs that decrease over time (such as protecting the unpaid balance of a mortgage).

8. 3. 2. 6 *Increasing Term*

Increasing term policies begin with little or no insurance protection, and the face amount grows over time. Although not very common, increasing term insurance is sometimes sold as a rider to another type of policy in order to provide an additional death benefit equal to total premiums paid or some other value.

8. 3. 2. 7 *Interim Term*

When a person wants immediate protection and is thinking of starting a permanent insurance policy in the near future, interim term may be used to cover the period before permanent protection is to begin. Many companies write interim term on an automatically convertible basis—that is, they provide the insured with temporary term protection that will covert automatically at some future date, usually no later than 11 months. The premium for the interim term is based on the age at application. The premium for the permanent coverage is also based on attained age when permanent protection begins.

8. 3. 3 Advantages and Uses of Term Insurance

Term insurance has a variety of useful applications. One of the most common uses for term is to provide a substantial amount of coverage at a minimum cost. Since term insurance provides pure protection, it allows a person with a limited income to purchase more coverage than might otherwise be affordable. This is particularly important when there is a clear need for additional protection.

Example

A husband has a relatively small whole life policy and becomes a father of twins. His responsibilities have suddenly changed, and there is a need for large amounts of additional life insurance. Term insurance could provide the solution to this problem. Often, the additional insurance is added to the existing policy by means of a rider.

8. 3. 4 Disadvantages of Term Insurance

Some of the disadvantages of term insurance are include the following.

- Over time, renewable term insurance becomes more and more expensive. Although initially the level term premium is low, it increases with each renewal on the basis of the increased age of the insured and the increased risk of mortality for the insurance company. Thus, a relatively low premium at age 35 becomes an expensive premium at age 55 or 60.
- Because term insurance provides temporary protection for a limited time, the insured can be left without insurance at a time (older age) when protection is needed the most.
- Term insurance is pure death protection only. It offers no living benefits such as guaranteed cash values.
- Even if the term policy is renewable, it generally is not renewable beyond a certain age, such as age 65 or 70.

Exercise 8.A

Match each definition with the proper term relating to term insurance.

____ 1. This option gives the insured the opportunity to show evidence of insurability at the end of the term to qualify for a lower premium at renewal.

____ 2. The death benefit increases and the premium remains level throughout the term.

____ 3. This feature allows the policy to be renewed at the end of a specified period without evidence of insurability.

____ 4. The annual premium remains level throughout the policy and the death benefit decreases throughout the term.

____ 5. This feature allows the policyowner to exchange the term coverage for whole life coverage without evidence of insurability.

____ 6. The annual premium remains level while the death benefit also remains level.

A. Renewable term

B. Convertible term

C. Re-entry term

D. Level term

E. Decreasing term

F. Increasing term

Answers to the exercise can be found at the end of the Unit 8 answers and rationales.

8. 4 WHOLE LIFE INSURANCE

Whole life insurance gets its name from the fact that the policy is designed to provide coverage for the whole of life (usually up to age 100, although some mortality tables have been adjusted to age 120).

Whole life is also called **permanent insurance** because the maturity date is beyond the life expectancy of most individuals. However, a whole life policy actually consists of a combination of a savings element (the advancing cash value) and a decreasing amount of net insurance. When a whole life policy reaches its maturity date (age 100), the cash value would equal the face amount.

Because whole life policies include cash values in addition to net insurance protection, the premiums have to cover mortality costs, expenses, and the savings account. For this reason, whole life policies are more expensive than term life policies.

Cash values accumulate within the policy as illustrated below.

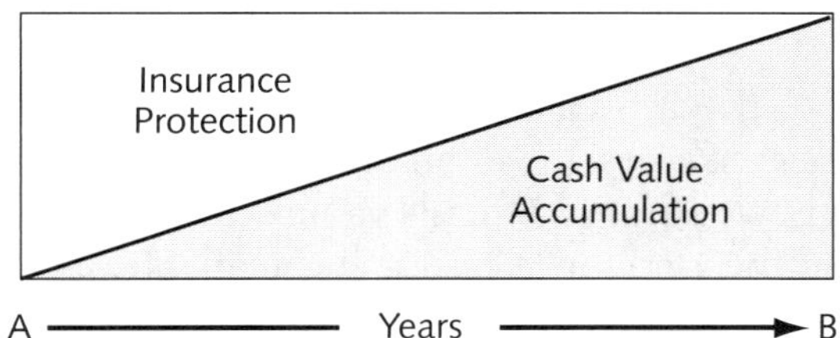

Assume the face value of the above policy is $100,000. The first day the policy is in force, the insured has $100,000 of protection. If the insured should die one week, one month, one year, 10 years, or 50 years later, the insured's beneficiaries would be paid $100,000 at the time of death. The face amount of the policy remains the same throughout the life of the policy (and the insured).

8. 4. 1 Characteristics of All Whole Life Policies

8. 4. 1. 1 Level Premiums

Premiums for permanent insurance policies are designed to remain level during the entire period the policy is in force. In the early years of the contract, the insured actually pays in more premium than is needed to provide the current year's insurance protection, whereas in later years less than is needed is paid in. The net result is that the premium remains the same for the entire life of the contract. In addition, the company has the opportunity to invest the money at a favorable return, which helps reduce the cost of insurance.

8. 4. 1. 2 Level Face Amount

The face amount of the policy (the amount payable upon death at any age) is fixed and will not change while the policy remains in effect.

8. 4. 1. 3 Guaranteed Cash Value

Whole life policies include a savings element that is guaranteed to accumulate and earn a specified rate of interest. Usually, the policy has little or no cash value during the first couple of policy years (due to the way front end expenses are allocated). In the third year, cash values begin to accumulate.

Once an insured has accumulated cash value, it cannot be forfeited. An insured may **cash in** a policy at any time by surrendering it in exchange for its cash value. An insured may also borrowed a portion of the cash value in the form of a **policy loan**, but this must be paid back (with interest) in order to restore policy values. When a policyowner takes a cash value loan, the amount borrowed and any accumulated interest due on the loan become an **indebtedness** against the policy. If the insured dies before the loan has been repaid, any indebtedness will reduce the face amount of the policy accordingly: it will be subtracted from any death benefit.

8. 4. 1. 4 Nonforfeiture Value

The cash value in the policy belongs to the policyowner. If the policyowner wishes, some or all of the cash value may be withdrawn from the policy. Any withdrawal of cash value will reduce both the face value of the policy and the amount of cash value available.

8. 4. 2 Types of Whole Life Policies

8. 4. 2. 1 Continuous Premium Whole Life

Continuous premium whole life is the most common type of whole life insurance sold. These policies stretch the premium payments over the whole life of the insured (to age 100). This type of policy is often referred to as straight life insurance.

8. 4. 2. 2 Limited-Payment Whole Life

Limited-payment whole life policies allow the policyowner to pay for the entire policy in a shorter period of time or to a specific age. Common forms of limited payment whole life are 20-payment life (meaning payments spread out over 20 years), 30-payment life, and life paid-up at age 65. Although the policy is fully paid-up at the end of this period, it has not yet matured. It will continue to provide protection and cash value accumulation until the scheduled maturity date at age 100, or death.

Premiums for limited payment policies will be higher than those for continuous payment policies because the total premiums have to be paid over a shorter period of time (the cash value will also be slightly higher because more money is paid into the contract during the early years). For example, the policyowner will pay a higher premium in a 20-pay whole life policy than the policyowner would have in a 30-pay whole life. The shorter the payment period, the higher the premium.

Comparison of Whole Life and Limited Pay Life

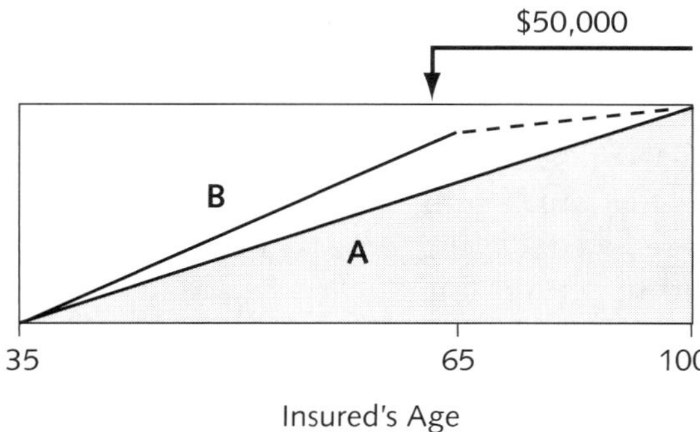

Example

20-pay life means premium payments for 20 years but lifetime (to age 100) protection. Life paid up at 65 means premium payments to age 65 but lifetime protection. A 20-pay life policy matures at age 100 or upon the death of the insured, whichever occurs first. The principal difference with limited-pay policies is simply the length of the premium paying period.

8. 4. 2. 3 Single Premium Whole Life

A single premium whole life policy is simply a whole life policy with one premium payment (a lump sum amount which, together with the interest it will earn, will be sufficient to cover all future premium payments). The entire cost of this policy is paid up at the time of purchase. Single premium whole life policies accumulate immediate cash value.

The premium for such a policy might be many thousands of dollars. The advantage offered by a single premium policy is that the policyowner will pay less for the policy than if the premiums were stretched over several years.

Exercise 8.B

Use the following premium methods to answer the questions below.
Continuous premium (CP)
Limited payment (LP)
Single premium (SP)

_____ 1. Which method will cost the least over the life of the insured?

_____ 2. Which method may be called 20-pay life?

_____ 3. Which method allows for immediate cash value?

_____ 4. Which method will have cash value that grows the slowest?

_____ 5. Which method has the lowest annual premium?

_____ 6. Which method requires lifetime premium payments?

Answers to the exercise can be found at the end of the Unit 8 answers and rationales.

8. 4. 2. 4 Current Assumption Whole Life

Current assumption whole life policies (also known as **interest-sensitive whole life**) offer flexible premium payments that are tied into current interest rate fluctuations. The insurance company reserves the right to increase or decrease the premium within a certain range depending on interest rate fluctuations. During a period of relatively high interest rates, premiums could be reduced. During periods of low interest rates, premiums could be increased within certain limits. Usually, premium adjustments are made on an annual basis. There are two rates of return received on the cash value, either a guaranteed rate or a current rate, whichever is higher. Interest-sensitive policies can receive a rate of return other than just a fixed (guaranteed) rate.

8. 4. 2. 5 Economatic

An **economatic** policy is a whole life-type policy with a term rider that uses dividends to purchase additional paid-up insurance.

As policy dividends are declared, they are used to purchase additional paid-up insurance. As the paid-up insurance is added, an equal amount of term insurance is removed from the policy, thus maintaining the full face amount at no additional cost.

8. 4. 3 Advantages and Uses of Whole Life

- The principal advantage of whole life is that it is permanent insurance and can be used to satisfy permanent needs such as the cost of death, dying, and final burial expenses.
- The level premium allows the policyowner to know exactly what the cost of insurance will be and offers a form of forced savings.
- Whole life builds a living benefit through its guaranteed cash value, which enables the policyowner to use some of this cash for emergencies, as a supplemental source of retirement income, and for other living needs.

8. 4. 4 Disadvantages of Whole Life Insurance

Two of the disadvantages of whole life insurance are the following.

- The premium-paying period may last longer than the insured's income-producing years.
- It does not provide as much protection per premium dollar as term insurance does.

8. 5 FLEXIBLE POLICIES

Although traditional policies have served the needs of the public for many decades, other types of life insurance products have been developed to meet different financial goals. These new products include adjustable life, universal life, and variable life insurance. These newer life insurance products generally offer the policyowner flexibility in terms of premiums, face amounts, and investment objectives.

8. 5. 1 Characteristics of Flexible Policies

Ordinary whole life policies offer premiums, cash values, and face amounts that are determined at the time the policy is purchased and, unless the policyowner takes out a loan or partial withdrawal, generally do not change over the life of the policy.

Flexible policies, in contrast, offer the policyowner the opportunity to change one or more of these components in response to changing needs and circumstances.

8. 5. 2 Types of Flexible Policies

8. 5. 2. 1 Adjustable Life Insurance

Adjustable life insurance is a policy that offers the policyowner the option to adjust the policy's face amount, premium, type of protection, and/or length of protection, without having to complete a new application or actually exchange policies. The flexibility of adjustable life is accomplished by allowing conversion from one form of insurance to another, and by making appropriate premium adjustments, if necessary. For example, a given amount of term insurance could be converted to a lesser amount of whole life insurance, or a lesser amount of whole life insurance could be converted to a greater amount term insurance, without a premium change. Converting a given amount of term insurance into an equal amount of whole life insurance would require a higher premium charge. The insurance company may require evidence of insurability if any change is made that increases the death benefit. The policyowner chooses two features to adjust, which will dictate the third feature of the insurer.

Example

The insured is now 50 years old and planning for retirement. The same $500 premium now could be used for some form of permanent insurance protection with guaranteed cash values. The temporary protection would be changed to permanent coverage, and the death benefit (face amount) would be reduced because of the insured's age and premium commitment.

8. 5. 2. 2 Universal Life

Universal life insurance was developed in response to the relatively low interest rates (generally 3.5–5%) earned by traditional whole life insurance cash values, which made the whole life product less attractive during periods of high inflation. In order to be more competitive, insurers introduced universal life policies that might pay higher interest rates (such as 8%, 10%, or 12%) during inflationary times. These policies also provide greater flexibility because they allow policyowners to adjust the death benefits and/or premium payments.

A universal life policy is similar to a whole life policy in the sense that it has the same two components: death protection and cash value. However, instead of being fixed and guaranteed amounts, the death protection resembles one-year renewable term insurance and the cash account grows according to current interest rates. Generally, universal life policies have these characteristics.

Premium payments are separated and paid toward the insurance protection; the loading cost and the remaining balance is used to build the cash value (with interest).

The policyowner may increase or decrease the death benefit during the policy term, subject to any insurability requirements.

Premium amounts may be changed as long as enough premium is paid to maintain the policy.

The interest earned by the cash account will vary, subject to a guaranteed minimum.

Universal life contracts are actually subject to two different interest rates—the current annual rate and the contract rate. The **current annual rate** varies with current market conditions and may change every year. The **contract rate** is the minimum guaranteed interest rate, and the policy will never pay less than that amount. For example, if the guaranteed contract rate is 5% and the current rate is 8%, the cash account would grow by the higher 8% during that year. But if the current rate falls below 5%, the cash account would still grow by the minimum rate of 5% during that year.

Generally, there are two options available regarding the death benefit payable under a universal life policy.

Option 1 (also known as option A) provides a level death benefit equal to the policy's face amount. As the policy's cash value increases, net death protection actually decreases over the life of the policy, which making the policy structure similar to a whole life contract.

Option 2 (also known as option B) provides for an increasing death benefit equal to the policy's face amount plus the cash account. In terms of policy structure, this contract is more like a combination of level term insurance and increasing cash value than whole life insurance.

Universal life provides for cash value loans in the same manner that whole life or any permanent plan of insurance does. If a loan is taken, it is subject to interest and, if unpaid, both the interest and the loan amount will reduce the face amount of the policy. Many UL policies continue to credit the outstanding loan amount at the guaranteed interest rate and the remaining cash value amount at the current interest rate. For this reason, there is an advantage to the policyowner to take a loan out (if the policyowner is going to take a loan out on one of her life policies) on a UL policy versus a whole life policy.

Many universal life policies will also permit a **cash withdrawal**, also called a partial surrender, from the cash account. This is not treated as a loan.

A partial surrender is not subject to any interest and will reduce the total cash value in the account (rather than the face amount). If this withdrawal is later repaid, it will be treated as a premium payment.

Option A—Universal Life Level Death Benefit

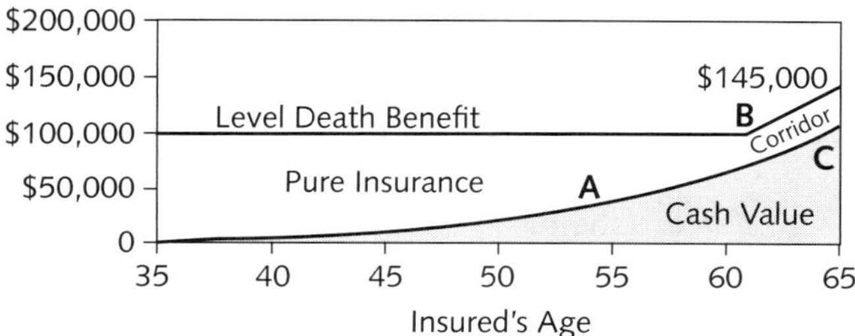

Option B—Universal Life Increasing Death Benefit

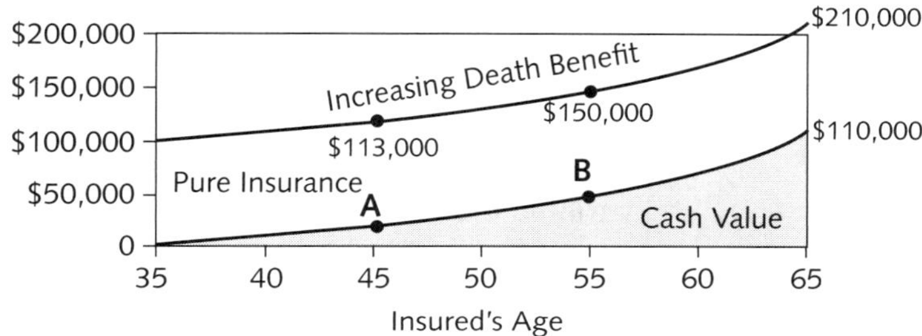

8. 5. 2. 3 *Variable Life*

Variable life insurance, also called variable whole life, is another product that was developed in response to the low returns earned by traditional cash value policies. Once again we find that the policy has two elements: death protection and a savings/investment element. However, instead of the cash values being linked to interest rates, they are backed by equity investments and securities and are not guaranteed. Variable life insurance has the following characteristics.

- They have a **guaranteed minimum death benefit** (the actual death benefit may be higher and will vary with the success of the investments).
- They have **cash values that are not guaranteed** (these vary with investment success and may change daily).
- These contracts are **regulated as securities**.

For fully guaranteed contracts (such as whole life insurance), an insurer maintains a **general account**, also called a general asset, that consists primarily of safe and conservative investments (such as high grade bonds, real estate, and certificates of deposit). The safety of these investments makes it possible for the insurer to guarantee its policies. In contrast, an insurer must establish a **separate account**, also called a separate asset, for its variable products. Premiums paid for variable life insurance must be placed in the insurer's separate account, which consists primarily of a portfolio of common stocks and other securities-based investments. Because this portfolio is subject to considerable investment risk, there can be no guarantees as to future value.

Because variable contracts are equity products, they are subject to regulation by the Securities and Exchange Commission (SEC), the Financial Industry Regulatory Authority (FINRA), and other federal bodies, as well as by state insurance departments. In order to sell variable life insurance, an agent must be licensed to sell life insurance and must pass the appropriate securities exam.

In order to prevent agents from misleading members of the public about the possible returns that can be expected with variable life insurance, during sales solicitations they must follow the 12% Rule. This means that variable life illustrations may not be based on projected interest rates greater than 12%. For example, if a policy actually earned 15% during one exceptional year, the agent would be prohibited from projecting that return annually for a 20-year period. This prevents both the agent and the policyholder from assuming excessive and unrealistic rates of return. A variety of policy performance illustrations at different rates (such as 8%, 10%, and 12%) would be the preferred method for clearly explaining variable life products. Agents should also stress that rates are not guaranteed and that historical performance may not be duplicated in the future.

Variable life policies have a level premium.

Variable Life Insurance Death Benefit

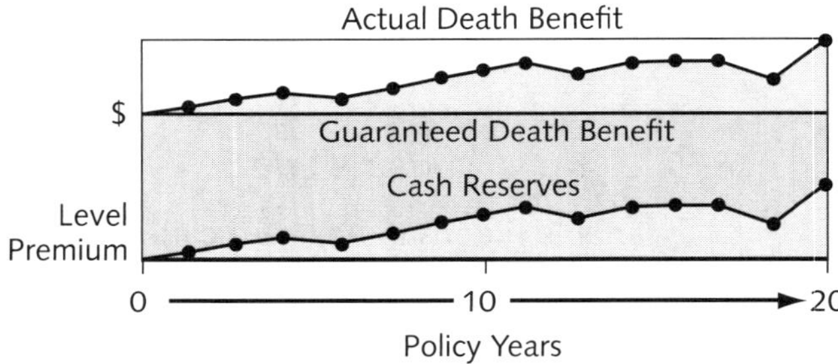

8. 5. 2. 4 Variable Universal Life

This product blends a combination of the variable and universal life insurance concepts. The policy has elements of variable life insurance because it is backed by equity investments. The policy has elements of universal life insurance because it allows the policyowner to adjust the amount of the death benefit and/or the premium.

Separate Account Investment Options

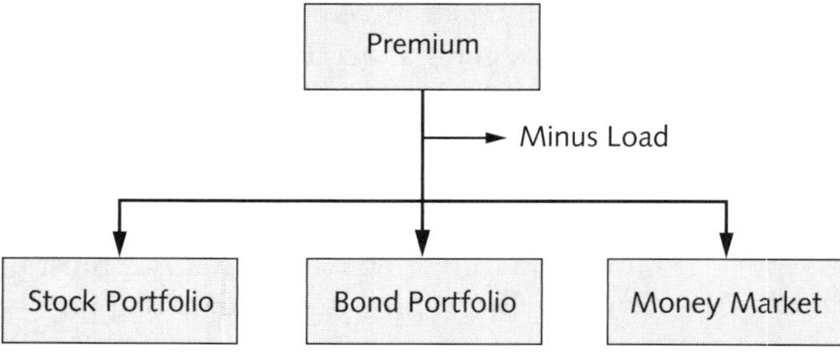

8. 5. 2. 5 Equity Indexed Life Insurance

Some companies offer policies with face amounts that are linked to an equity index, for example the S&P 500. Naturally, an additional premium must be charged for the increased amount of protection, and it may be obtained in one of two ways: the insurance company may simply increase the premium when it increases the coverage, or it might make advance assumptions about the rate of inflation and charge a slightly higher premium from the original inception date.

Exercise 8.C

Match the following features with the respective types of policies. Remember more than one feature may apply to each policy.

	Policy		Feature
___ 1.	Ordinary whole life	A.	Fixed, level premiums
___ 2.	Adjustable life	B.	Flexible premiums
___ 3.	Universal life	C.	Adjustable premiums
___ 4.	Variable life	D.	Two death benefit options
___ 5.	Variable-universal life	E.	Part or all of the cash value is deposited into a separate account
___ 6.	Current assumption whole life	F.	No guaranteed minimum return
___ 7.	Equity indexed life	G.	Guaranteed minimum death benefit
		H.	Guaranteed minimum rate of return
		I.	Requires a life insurance license to sell to the public
		J.	Requires a securities license to sell to the public
		K.	Face amount is adjustable with evidence of insurability
		L.	Part or all of the premium is deposited into the general account

Answers to the exercise can be found at the end of the Unit 8 answers and rationales.

8. 5. 3 Advantages and Uses of Flexible Policies

There are some of advantages of flexible policies.

- Flexible policies provide the opportunity to customize the policy to the needs and wants of the insured.
- Flexible policies may include a securities component, which is considered an effective hedge against inflation.
- Premium flexibility allows policyowners to pay what they can, when they can. This provides the opportunity to increase cash values more rapidly when the policyowner has the resources to do so. It also provides the opportunity for policyowners to skip payments when their financial circumstances dictate without losing insurance protection.

8. 5. 4 Disadvantages of Flexible Policies

There are also some disadvantages associated with flexible policies.

- Flexible policies that include a securities component may not have guaranteed returns. Returns may be low, or even negative, in policies based on separate securities accounts.
- Some policyowners need the forced discipline of a mandated premium schedule to ensure that they regularly contribute enough to ensure adequate cash value growth. Many flexible premium policies lack a required premium schedule.

Comparison of Life Products					
Features	**Term**	**Permanent Whole Life**	**Universal Life**	**Variable Life**	**Current Assumption Whole Life**
Death Benefit	Fixed and level	Fixed and level	Adjustable level or increasing options	Varies with investment performance, guaranteed minimum	Fixed and level
Premiums	Fixed schedule, increasing amount	Fixed schedule, level amount	Flexible schedule, flexible amount	Fixed schedule, level amount	Fixed schedule, amount may rise to guaranteed maximum
Cash Values	None	Fixed and guaranteed	Current interest with guaranteed minimum rate	Varies with investment performance	Current interest with guaranteed minimum rate and cash value level
Mortality Rates	Fixed and guaranteed	Fixed and guaranteed	Current, guaranteed maximum	Fixed and guaranteed	Current, guaranteed maximum
Partial Surrenders	N/A	No	Yes	Some policies	Some policies
Regulated As	Insurance	Insurance	Insurance	Insurance and security	Insurance

8. 6 INDUSTRIAL LIFE INSURANCE

The industrial policy is written for a small face amount, usually $2,000 or less, and the premiums are payable as frequently as weekly and, occasionally, monthly.

8. 6. 1 Characteristics of Industrial Life Insurance

The basic characteristics of industrial life insurance are as follows.

- Premium payments are made frequently.
- Benefits are usually less than $2,000.
- Premiums are collected by the agent at the insured's home or workplace.
- Sales are made in premium units rather than in insurance units. The rate book lists the amount of insurance that can be bought with a specified weekly or monthly premium. (This has been changing for larger amounts of insurance.)
- All family members are covered from birth to age 65 or 70.
- Usually a medical examination is not required.

8. 6. 2 Industrial Life Policy Provisions

Most of the provisions found in individual life insurance policies also are found in industrial life insurance.

- A 31-day grace period (28 days for weekly premium policies) is provided.
- The application is not required to be part of the policy.
- Medical examinations are not required.
- Cash values do not accumulate sufficiently to provide loans.
- Settlement options do not apply because of limited cash value.
- Suicide provisions are not included in the policy because of the small benefit amount.
- Nonforfeiture provisions do not allow the cash option until premiums have been paid for five years (compared with three years for ordinary policies).
- Dividends are used to reduce the premium payment or to purchase paid-up additions.

8. 6. 2. 1 Home Service Life Insurance

Another variation in the industrial life concept is known as **home service life insurance**. Policies are usually modest in size, ranging from $10,000 to

$15,000 in face value, and are typically sold on a monthly debit plan (automatic bank draft) or payments by mail, which eliminates the need for an agent to collect the premiums.

8. 7 CREDIT LIFE INSURANCE

Credit life insurance is designed to insure the lives of debtors for the benefit of a creditor (who is the policyowner). In the event that the insured debtor dies, it pays the outstanding balance of the loan.

Credit life insurance may be written on an individual or group basis. It is usually written as decreasing term insurance in connection with a purchase being financed. Usually, the individual debtor pays the total premium, which is often added to the installment loan payments so that, in effect, the insurance premium is being financed along with the item being purchased.

Credit life insurance may not be written for an amount greater than the total debt.

In the event of death, if the coverage exceeds the loan amount, the remainder of the death benefit will be paid to the estate.

Credit life insurance is a collateral (temporary) assignment. The creditor is the owner and beneficiary, and the debtor pays the premiums. Credit insurance is often written as decreasing term insurance. Insureds are given a certificate of coverage. In addition, the debtor's coverage terminates if debt is paid off, transferred, refinanced, or becomes significantly overdue.

8. 7. 1 Credit Life Policy Provisions

Some of the major provisions found in credit life insurance policies are those that provide the following.

- The number of insureds under the policy must be maintained at a specified level (usually 100); if participation drops below that number, the insurer may not insure new debtors.
- Unlike standard group insurance policies, the policy does not have a conversion privilege.

8. 8 SPECIALIZED POLICY FORMS

A variety of specialized life insurance policies are available to meet different types of insurance needs. Many of these exist in the form of a base policy with one or more other types of coverage attached as riders.

8. 8. 1 Endowments

An endowment policy provides for the payment (to the beneficiary) of the face amount upon the death of an insured during a specified period or the payment of the face amount at the end of the specified period if the insured is still alive, whichever comes first. Endowments are not as popular today as they once were. These contracts were originally designed to combine life insurance and savings elements.

Endowment policies may be issued for specified periods such as 5, 10, 20, 25, or 30 years, or up to a specified age such as age 65.

Once the specified period has passed and the insured is living, the face amount would be paid to that insured in a lump sum or in installments.

The premium payments for an endowment policy are higher than for traditional whole life contracts because their savings features and premium levels depend upon the endowment period selected.

8. 8. 1. 1 Types of Endowments

Endowments generally are not sold today because the tax consequences have changed, eliminating many of the benefits that once made them attractive.

A **retirement endowment** was one of the most commonly sold endowment contracts. This type of policy was issued to mature at age 65 when the insured planned to retire. Like whole life insurance, the face value was payable as a death benefit if the insured died before the maturity date. However, at maturity, the full face amount became payable, usually in the form of monthly installment income.

The **pure endowment** provided for the payment of the policy's face amount only if the insured lived to the maturity date. If the insured died before the endowment date, all benefits were forfeited. Because this was essentially a high-risk savings plan (all savings were lost upon early death), it was rarely sold.

Endowment life insurance was a combination of a pure endowment plus term insurance for a specified period. The pure endowment provided a living benefit at the end of the endowment period. The term insurance paid a death benefit if the insured died before the end of the endowment period.

Juvenile endowment policies were designed to mature at a specific age, such as age 18, to help fund a college education.

8. 8. 1. 2 Family Income Policies

Family plans are not commonly sold but sometimes appear on state license exams. Combining whole life insurance with decreasing term coverage, the **family income policy** provides an income to be paid upon the death of the breadwinner. This policy combines decreasing term insurance with a permanent policy. Income payments begin when the insured dies and continue for a period specified from the date of policy issue (not from the date of the insured's death).

8. 8. 1. 3 Family Maintenance Policies

This type of policy combines ordinary life insurance and level term insurance. It affords the payment of a monthly income during a stated period of 10, 15, or 20 years or to age 65 as preselected by the insured. The monthly income is payable from the date of death to the end of the preselected period. The payment of the face amount of the policy is payable at the end of such preselected period.

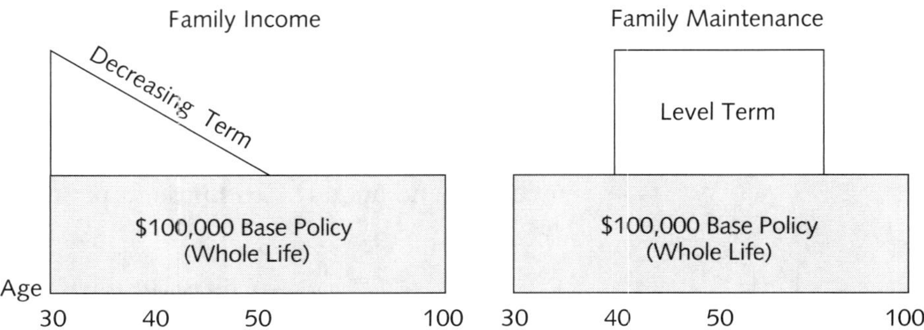

Family income and family maintenance plans are both designed to provide a period of monthly income following the death of the insured, if death occurs during the specified period.

8. 8. 1. 4 *The Family Policy (Family Protection Policy)*

This type of policy consists of whole life on the breadwinner and convertible term on the spouse and children. Once the policy is issued, additional children are automatically included at no extra cost.

Example
Bob's policy might provide $100,000 on himself, $25,000 on his wife, and $20,000 on each child. In this example, the wife's and children's coverages would ordinarily be term insurance, and Bob's would be a permanent policy. These additions to Bob's permanent coverage are sometimes referred to as riders. Spouse term rider and family rider are common names for these coverages.

Under a family policy, term insurance coverage is provided without additional premium for children born or adopted after the policy is issued. The term insurance expires on each child as that child reaches a specified age—18, or perhaps 21, and sometimes as late as 25. Coverage on the children is usually convertible to any permanent insurance without evidence of insurability.

8. 8. 1. 5 *Retirement Income*

A **retirement income policy** accumulates a sum of money for retirement while providing a death benefit. Upon retirement, the policy pays an income such as $10 per $1,000 of life insurance for the insured's lifetime or a specified period.

8. 8. 1. 6 *Joint Life Policies*

A joint life policy is a whole life contract written with two or more persons as named insureds. Most commonly, the policy is issued on two lives with the insured amount payable on the death of the first insured. A variation of the joint life policy is the **survivorship life policy**. It pays the insured amount, not upon the death of the first insured to die but upon the death of the last surviving insured. Joint life policies can also be sold as term life.

8. 8. 1. 7 Juvenile Policies

Juvenile life insurance is any form of coverage written on the lives of minors. One type of policy is commonly called the **jumping juvenile** policy because it automatically increases in face amount at a given age, usually 21, but the premium remains level.

8. 8. 1. 8 Minimum Deposit

Minimum deposit or **financed insurance** is technically a method of paying for insurance and not a type of policy. It is a high cash and loan value whole life policy. The cash value of a permanent policy is used to pay the premiums on that policy through the use of policy loans. To achieve sufficient cash value, the first two of these premium payments must be paid by the policyowner and then loans may be used, but only if during the first seven years of the policy at least four of the seven annual premiums are paid from funds other than policy loans. (This is a rule imposed by the IRS.)

One of the advantages of minimum deposit insurance is that, under certain circumstances, interest paid on policy loans used to finance premium payments still may be deductible. Disadvantages include the fact that its administration is complex.

8. 8. 1. 9 Modified Premium Plan

Modified whole life policies are distinguished by premiums that are lower than typical whole life premiums during the first few years (usually three to five years) and then higher than typical thereafter. During the initial period, the coverage and premium are based as if it was a term life policy. Afterward, the premium is higher than that of a typical whole life policy.

8. 8. 1. 10 Graded Premium Plan

Graded premium whole life policies are slightly different than modified life policies. A graded premium whole life policy is a gradual increase in premiums compared with a modified life, which has just one increase. With a graded premium whole life policy, the premium increases each year during the early years of the contract (usually five years) and remains the same after that time.

8. 8. 1. 11 Mortgage Redemption

The **mortgage redemption policy** or **rider** is simply decreasing term insurance. The benefit amount of the term element is intended to be sufficient to pay off the unpaid remainder of the mortgage loan if the insured dies before paying it off.

8. 8. 1. 12 Multiple Protection

Multiple protection policies are combinations of whole life and term in which the amount of protection is higher in the early years of the policy and less in the later years.

Example

The current death benefit may be described as equal to two times the benefit at age 65 (double protection). If the age 65 (and thereafter) benefit is $5,000, the insured has $10,000 of protection up to age 65. In essence, the additional death benefit before age 65 is term insurance.

8. 8. 1. 13 Index-Linked Policies

As a hedge against high inflationary periods, many companies offer policies with face amounts that increase by the amount of inflation. The policy amounts are generally linked to the Consumer Price Index. There are two ways of providing this additional coverage. Either the premium is increased every year to cover the increased insurance amount or the life insurance company makes assumptions about what it expects the increases to be at policy inception, and the insured pays the same (but higher than average) premium over the life of the policy.

8. 8. 1. 14 Deposit Term Insurance

Deposit term insurance is a level term insurance policy that has a much higher premium for the first year than for subsequent years. The initial premium is significantly higher than the average premium needed to cover the cost of mortality during the term period. The excess front-end premium (the deposit) is then set aside to earn interest, and these dollars (deposit plus interest) will be applied to reduce the premium payments required in the following years. The premium levels are set so that the entire deposit will be exhausted when the final annual premium is paid. In effect, this arrangement provides a method of paying a portion of the premium in advance.

8. 8. 1. 15 Preneed Funeral Insurance

Funeral insurance or preneed burial insurance is a type of life insurance used to pay for an insured's funeral (usually at a particular funeral home). Funeral insurance pays the face amount upon an insured's death. Really, it is just a contract to provide a preplanned funeral and cemetery services funded by a life insurance contract or annuity. Typically, the funeral home has the insured buy a life insurance policy, naming the funeral home as the beneficiary. The funeral home usually is paid a commission on the policy sale as well. The policy will have an increasing face amount so that the funeral will be fully funded, even if burial costs increase.

8. 8. 2 Advantages and Uses of Specialized Policies

Some of the advantages and uses of specialized policies are as follows.

- Specific combinations of term and permanent insurance can be used to match the need exactly.
- The cost of the policy may be lower than ordinary whole life insurance.

8. 8. 3 Disadvantages of Specialized Policies

The following are two of the disadvantages of specialized policies.

- Policies set up to meet a specific need may become obsolete if the need changes over time.
- Certain policies, if not set up carefully, may incur negative tax consequences.

8. 9 VIATICAL/LIFE SETTLEMENTS

Through *viatical settlements*, individuals with a terminal illness or severe chronic illness sell their life insurance policies to viatical companies.

During the underwriting process, the viatical settlement provider will contact the insured's physician or clinic to verify records and determine the insured's life expectancy. Throughout this process, the insured's information may be shared only with the appropriate people involved in the settlement to protect the insured's privacy.

Life settlements are similar to viatical settlements, except the policyowner is not necessarily terminally or chronically ill. Many states are reclassifying viatical settlements as a type of life settlement.

A life settlement transaction is a transfer of an ownership interest in a life insurance policy to a third party for compensation less than the expected death benefit under the policy or the sale of a life insurance policy for a dollar amount that is less than the policy's face.

It is important that the life settlement broker ensure that the transaction is suitable and appropriate for the seller, and the broker should perform due diligence to obtain and evaluate offers from multiple providers.

When a policyowner applies for a life settlement transaction, it is important that the following disclosures be made.

- There are possible alternatives to the life settlement (i.e., accelerated benefits).
- The transaction may have tax implications and advice should be sought from a qualified tax advisor.
- The transaction may affect creditors' rights.
- There may an effect on conversion rights and waiver of premium benefits.
- A life settlement transaction may limit ability to purchase future life insurance.

- Rescission rights exist.
- The date by which funds will be available must be disclosed.
- The owner will be required to disclose medical, financial, and personal information.
- The insured will be contacted periodically to determine health status.

When the life settlement contract is executed, the following disclosures should be made:

- Affiliations between broker and provider and affiliations between provider and issuer
- Provider disclosures
  - Gross purchase price paid for policy
  - Amount to be paid to policy owner
  - Full disclosure of compensation to broker or any party involved in the life settlement transaction
  - Contact information for broker
- Broker disclosures
  - Complete description of all offers, counteroffers, acceptances, and rejections
  - Affiliation between broker and person making an offer on a proposed life settlement contract
  - All estimates of life expectancy of the insured

8. 9. 1 Privacy Concerns

For life settlement transactions, the insured's identity and personal financial and medical information should not be disclosed unless it is:

- necessary to put the life settlement contract in place and the owner and insured have provided prior written consent;
- necessary in order to sell the life settlement contracts as investments, provided the applicable securities laws are followed and the owner and insured have provided prior written consent;
- provided in response to an investigation/examination by the Commissioner;
- a condition to the transfer of a settled life insurance policy by one provider to another provider, and the receiving provider agrees to comply with the Insurance Code's confidentiality provisions; or
- necessary to allow the provider, life settlement broker, or their authorized representative to make contact for purposes of determining health status of the insured.

UNIT TEST

1. Term insurance provides
   A. cash values
   B. the ability to take a loan against the policy
   C. pure insurance protection
   D. lifelong protection

2. Carl's insurance policy is designed to cover the mortgage on his house if he should die before paying it off. The policy is
   A. convertible term
   B. renewable term
   C. increasing term
   D. decreasing term

3. The least common of the following types of insurance is
   A. convertible term
   B. renewable term
   C. increasing term
   D. decreasing term

4. Pam owns a 1-year term policy. At the end of the year, she may purchase another identical policy without showing proof of insurability. Pam's policy is
   A. convertible term
   B. renewable term
   C. increasing term
   D. decreasing term

5. Whole life insurance policies provide all of the following EXCEPT
   A. cash values
   B. the ability to take a loan against the policy
   C. pure insurance protection
   D. an opportunity for significant investment gains

6. Zelda agrees to pay premiums on her policy every year for 20 years. After that, she will no longer have to pay premiums, but her insurance protection will continue until she dies. Zelda has
   A. a whole life policy
   B. a limited-pay policy
   C. a single premium policy
   D. an economatic policy

7. Jerry has a policy that pays dividends, which are used to purchase additional paid-up insurance to increase the face value of the policy. Jerry has
   A. a whole life policy
   B. a limited-pay policy
   C. a single premium policy
   D. an economatic policy

8. Ashley has a policy that she must pay premiums on until she is 100 years old or until she dies. Ashley has
   A. a continuous premium whole life policy
   B. a limited-pay policy
   C. a single premium policy
   D. an economatic policy

9. Which of the following is NOT flexible in a universal life policy?
   A. Premium amounts
   B. Premium schedule
   C. Guaranteed interest rate
   D. Death benefits

10. Adam purchases a universal life policy. In his second year, he decides to pay a $1,000 premium. What happens to the cash value of his policy at this point?
    A. Adam's cash value is increased by $1,000.
    B. The front-end load is deducted from the premium and the premium is added to the cash value.
    C. The front-end load is deducted from the premium, the premium is added to the cash value, and the cost of insurance is deducted from the cash value.
    D. The front-end load is deducted from the premium, the premium is added to the cash value, the cost of insurance is deducted from the cash value, and the current interest rate is credited to the cash value.

11. Martha has a universal life policy she purchased several years earlier. At that time, the death benefit in the policy was $100,000. Her cash value is now $20,000, and she has selected death benefit option A. How much is her current death benefit?
    A. $20,000
    B. $80,000
    C. $100,000
    D. $120,000

12. Karen has a universal life policy she purchased several years earlier. At that time, the death benefit in the policy was $100,000. Her cash value is now $20,000, and she has selected death benefit option B. How much is her current death benefit?
    A. $20,000
    B. $80,000
    C. $100,000
    D. $120,000

13. Assume that Martha and Karen are identical twins. Martha selects death benefit option A, and Karen selects death benefit option B. Who is probably paying more for her universal life policy?
    A. Martha
    B. Karen
    C. They are probably paying the exact same amount for their policies because they are twins
    D. None of the above

14. Which of the following is NOT required to be able to sell variable policies?
    A. A state insurance producer license
    B. Registration with FINRA
    C. Registration with the NAIC
    D. A passing score on the appropriate securities exam

15. Which of the following must be the case once a year for a variable policy to meet the federal definition of life insurance?
    A. The face amount must be higher than the cash value by a certain percentage.
    B. The cash value must be higher than the face amount by a certain percentage.
    C. The cash value and the face amount must be exactly equal.
    D. The cash value must equal zero.

16. Julia's variable policy deducts a certain percentage from the premiums as they are paid. What type of load does Julia's policy have?
    A. Back-end load
    B. Front-end load
    C. Premium load
    D. Face-value load

17. Laura collects insurance premiums every Friday at the home of several policyholders. Which type of policy do these policyholders probably have?
    A. Home service life insurance
    B. Credit life insurance
    C. Term life insurance
    D. Industrial life insurance

18. George has several policyowners at the factory set up on a plan that deducts the premium automatically from their bank accounts every month. Which type of policy do these policyowners probably have?
    A. Home service life insurance
    B. Credit life insurance
    C. Term life insurance
    D. Industrial life insurance

19. Which type of insurance policy is most common today?
    A. Home service life insurance
    B. Credit life insurance
    C. Industrial life insurance
    D. Endowment insurance

20. Sarah has a policy that will pay her family a monthly income until 2020 if she passes away before that time. Which type of policy does Sarah have?
    A. Family security policy
    B. Family maintenance policy
    C. Family income policy
    D. Family plan policy

21. Tracy has a policy that provides permanent life insurance on him, along with term insurance on his wife and children. Which type of policy does Tracy have?
    A. Family security policy
    B. Family maintenance policy
    C. Family income policy
    D. Family protection policy

22. Which type of policy would not provide a tax-free death benefit under current law?
    A. Joint life policy written on a survivorship basis
    B. Minimum deposit policy
    C. Endowment policy
    D. Mortgage redemption policy

23. Which of the following types of insurance is designed to provide life insurance protection for only a limited time?
    A. Whole life insurance
    B. Variable life insurance
    C. Term life insurance
    D. Universal life insurance

24. Which of the following types of insurance requires a level premium and provides lifelong protection?
    A. Whole life insurance
    B. Variable life insurance
    C. Term life insurance
    D. Universal life insurance

25. A flexible premium, adjustable benefit life insurance contract that accumulates cash values is called
    A. whole life insurance
    B. variable life insurance
    C. term life insurance
    D. universal life insurance

26. Securities-based whole life insurance is called
    A. whole life insurance
    B. variable life insurance
    C. term life insurance
    D. universal life insurance

27. Christy has a term policy that will allow her to switch over to a whole life policy at any time during the first half of the term without providing evidence of insurability. What type of policy is this?
    A. Level term insurance
    B. Renewable term insurance
    C. Convertible term insurance
    D. Reentry term insurance

28. Which of the following is an advantage of term insurance?
    A. The initial cost of the policy tends to be low.
    B. The policy becomes more expensive over time.
    C. It provides temporary protection for a limited time.
    D. Even if the policy is renewable, it is probably not renewable beyond a certain age such as 65.

29. Which of the following is NOT an advantage of whole life policies?
    A. Low initial cost
    B. Level face amount
    C. Guaranteed cash value
    D. Nonforfeiture values

30. Janice and Julie are identical twins who both work as teachers and live next door to each other. They each purchase a $75,000 whole life policy at the same time. Janice chooses continuous premium whole life, and Julie chooses a 20-pay whole life policy. Which sister is probably paying a higher premium?
    A. Janice is probably paying more.
    B. Julie is probably paying more.
    C. They are probably paying the same amount.
    D. It is not possible to determine from the information provided.

31. Sally purchases $100,000 of participating whole life and $50,000 of term insurance. Over time, she intends to use the dividends from the whole life policy to purchase paid-up additions to replace the term insurance. Sally owns
    A. an adjustable life insurance policy
    B. an economatic life insurance policy
    C. an universal life insurance policy
    D. a variable universal life insurance policy

32. Gerald has a state insurance license but no other training or licenses. Gerald can sell any of the following EXCEPT
    A. an adjustable life insurance policy
    B. an economatic life insurance policy
    C. a whole life insurance policy
    D. a variable universal life insurance policy

33. LaKita buys a policy that allows her to adjust the face amount, premium, and length of protection without having to complete a new application or have a new policy issued. LaKita has
    A. an adjustable life insurance policy
    B. an economatic life insurance policy
    C. a whole life insurance policy
    D. a variable universal life insurance policy

34. Which type of policy is least likely to be sold today?
    A. Term
    B. Whole life
    C. Endowment
    D. Variable universal life

35. Which type of policy combines whole life insurance with decreasing term coverage?
    A. Family stability policy
    B. Family maintenance policy
    C. Family income policy
    D. Family protection policy

36. Which type of policy combines whole life insurance with level term coverage?
    A. Family stability policy
    B. Family maintenance policy
    C. Family income policy
    D. Family protection policy

37. Which type of policy combines whole life insurance on one family member with term coverage on other family members?
    A. Family stability policy
    B. Family maintenance policy
    C. Family income policy
    D. Family protection policy

38. Dan and Dawn want to purchase a single policy that will provide a death benefit upon the death of either of them. The type of policy that might best fits this need is
    A. a juvenile policy
    B. a minimum deposit policy
    C. a joint life policy
    D. a multiple protection policy

39. Devon wants to purchase a policy that will cover his nephew until the nephew turns 21 in order to help his nephew start out on the right foot in terms of insurance. The type of policy that best fits this need is
    A. a juvenile policy
    B. a minimum deposit policy
    C. a joint life policy
    D. a multiple protection policy

40. Tim has a life insurance policy that will pay $100,000 if he dies before age 65 and $50,000 if he dies after age 65. Tim probably has
    A. a juvenile policy
    B. a minimum deposit policy
    C. a joint life policy
    D. a multiple protection policy

41. Minimum deposit policies have become less popular as a result of tax regulations, but they still can be used as long as a certain number of the initial payments are made from sources other than cash value. How many payments must be made from other sources?
    A. 2 of 7
    B. 3 of 7
    C. 4 of 7
    D. 5 of 7

ANSWERS AND RATIONALES TO UNIT TEST

1. **C.** Term insurance provides pure insurance protection.

2. **D.** This policy is decreasing term because it provides a decreasing death benefit as the balance on the mortgage declines.

3. **C.** Increasing term is not used as often as level term or decreasing term.

4. **B.** Renewable term may be renewed at the end of a specified period without proof of insurability.

5. **D.** Whole life insurance policies do not generally provide significant opportunities for investment gain.

6. **B.** This is a limited-pay policy because Zelda is required to pay premiums for only a limited period.

7. **D.** An economatic policy is a whole life policy that uses dividends to purchase additional paid-up insurance.

8. **A.** Ashley's policy is a continuous premium whole life policy because she is required to pay premiums for her whole life or until she is 100.

9. **C.** The guaranteed interest rate is not flexible in a universal life policy.

10. **D.** With a universal life policy, the front-end load is deducted from the premium, the premium is added to the cash value, the cost of insurance is deducted from the cash value, and the current interest rate is credited to the cash value.

11. **C.** Option A in a universal life policy provides a level death benefit equal to the policy's face amount.

12. **D.** Option B provides for an increasing death benefit equal to policy's face amount plus the cash value.

13. **B.** Option B is generally more expensive than option A for the same coverage because, unlike the case with option A, the mortality risk under option B does not decrease over the life of the policy.

14. **C.** Registration with the NAIC is not a requirement.

15. **A.** For a policy to meet the federal definition of life insurance, the face amount must be higher than the cash value by a certain percentage at least once a year.

16. **B.** The percentage is deducted from the premiums, so this is a front-end load.

17. **D.** Industrial life policies are characterized by weekly collection of premium at the policyholder's home or workplace.

18. **A.** These policyowners probably have home service life insurance because premiums are deducted automatically from the policyowners' bank accounts.

19. **B.** Credit life insurance is common because almost everybody uses credit.

20. **C.** This is a family income policy because it provides an income for a stated number of years from the insured's death.

21. **D.** This is a family protection policy because it insures each member of the family at the time the policy is issued.

22. **C.** Under current tax law, endowments do not provide a tax-free death benefit.

23. **C.** Term life insurance provides insurance protection for a limited time.

24. **A.** Whole life insurance requires a level premium and provides lifelong protection.

25. **D.** A flexible premium, adjustable benefit life insurance contract that accumulates cash values is called universal life insurance.

26. **B.** Securities-based whole life insurance is called variable life insurance.

27. **C.** A term policy that will allow the insured to switch over to a whole life policy at any time during the first half of the term without providing evidence of insurability is a convertible term insurance policy.

28. **A.** The initial cost of a term insurance policy tends to be low.

29. **A.** Low initial cost is not an advantage of whole life policies.

30. **B.** Julie is probably paying more than her sister is.

31. **B.** Sally owns an economatic life insurance policy.

32. **D.** Gerald cannot sell variable universal life insurance policies.

33. **A.** LaKita has an adjustable life insurance policy.

34. **C.** Endowments generally are not sold today because the tax consequences have changed, eliminating many of the benefits that once made endowments attractive investment vehicles.

35. **C.** A family income policy combines whole life insurance with decreasing term coverage.

36. **B.** A family maintenance policy combines whole life insurance with level term coverage.

37. **D.** A family protection policy combines whole life insurance on one family member with term coverage on other family members.

38. **C.** A joint life policy will provide a death benefit upon the death of either of them.

39. **A.** A juvenile policy will cover Devon's nephew until the nephew turns 21.

40. **D.** Tim probably has a multiple protection policy.

41. **C.** Four of seven payments must be made from sources other than cash value.

UNIT 8 EXERCISE ANSWERS

Exercise 8.A

1. C
2. F
3. A
4. E
5. B
6. D

Exercise 8.B

1. SP
2. LP
3. SP
4. CP
5. CP
6. CP

Exercise 8.C

1. A, G, H, I, L
2. C, G, H, I, L, K
3. B, D, H, I, K, L
4. A, E, G, F, I, J
5. B, D, E, F, I, J, K
6. B, G, H, I, L
7. A, G, H, I, L

UNIT

9

Policy Provisions

9. 1 LEARNING OBJECTIVES

After completing this lesson, you will be able to:

- explain life insurance policy provisions, clauses, and exclusions; and
- describe the different types of beneficiaries.

9. 2 INTRODUCTION

An insurance policy is a legal contract and contains provisions setting forth the rights and duties of parties to the contract. **Policy provisions** identify the rights and obligations of both the policyowner and the insurer under the insurance contract. Many states require certain provisions to be included in all life policies, so the following provisions have become more or less standard.

9. 3 STANDARD PROVISIONS

9. 3. 1 Insuring Clause

The insuring agreement or insuring clause states that the insurer agrees to provide life insurance protection for the named insured which will be paid to a designated beneficiary when proof of death is received by the insurer.

The insuring clause states the party to be covered by the life contract and names the beneficiary who will receive the policy proceeds in the event of the insured's death. If no beneficiary is named in the contract, the policy proceeds will be paid to the insured's estate.

The policy face expresses the promise of the insurer and lists the name of the company, insured, amount of insurance carried, the mode and amount of premium, and when coverage is effective.

9. 3. 2 Entire Contract Clause

The entire contract provision is also referred to as the **entire contract clause**. This provision states that the policy and a copy of the application constitutes the entire contract between the insurer and the insured. A copy of the life insurance application is attached to the policy.

The life insurance contract provides that all statements made by the insured in the application will be considered as representations and not warranties.

The basic purpose of the clause is to provide assurance to the policyowner that he has in his possession all necessary documents with regard to his life insurance coverage.

The clause also prevents the policyowner and the producer from unilaterally amending the policy. (Only an executive officer of the insurance company can amend the policy.)

9.3.3 The Consideration Clause

This provision or clause in a life insurance policy provides that the insurance coverage is granted in consideration of the application and the payment of the initial premium. The payment of the initial premium is required to place the insurance coverage in effect.

The insured's consideration is the premium paid and the representations made in the application.

The insurer's consideration is the promise to pay the face amount of the contract to the named beneficiary upon the death of the insured.

9.3.4 Payment of Premium

This provision specifies when, where, and how premiums are to be paid. Usually premiums are to be paid in advance either at the company's home office or to the agent. The various modes of paying the premium also are identified, such as monthly, quarterly, semiannually, and annually.

The least expensive way to pay the premium is annually. The other premium modes require the payment of a service charge added to the basic premium. For example, an annual policy premium may be $300. The monthly premium may be $25.50, which would total $306 of premium in a year.

9.3.5 Ownership Rights

The owner of a life insurance contract is usually the applicant, the insured, or the premium payer. The owner of a policy has several stipulated rights in the contract. Some of these rights include:

- changing the beneficiary;
- receiving dividends if any are paid;
- borrowing funds from the cash value if they exist; and
- assigning of some or all the rights of the contract to another party.

9.3.6 Applicant Control or Ownership Clause

When the proposed insured is a minor, the applicant can be the minor's parent or other relative or legal guardian. In such a situation, the applicant—let's say a parent who is applying for insurance on her son's life—will probably want to maintain control of the policy until the insured is of age. This can be accomplished by including a clause that designates the parent (the applicant) as the controller (or owner) of the policy. Because this clause designates the applicant as the person in control of the policy, it is called the **applicant control clause** or the **ownership clause**.

9.3.7 Grace Period

Every life insurance contract contains a **grace period**. This is the period of time following the date that each premium is due during which the insurance policy remains in force and coverage is provided, even though the premium has not yet been paid.

The grace period protects the policyowner from an unintentional lapse of the policy. Since the policy remains in force during the grace period, the face amount of the contract will be paid to a named beneficiary should the insured die during the grace period. If proceeds are paid out during the grace period, any outstanding premium owed to the insurer will be deducted from the face amount of the contract. Generally, the grace period in life insurance contracts is 31 days.

9. 3. 7. 1 Automatic Premium Loan Provision

The **automatic premium loan** (APL) provision may be added to a cash value life insurance contract and protects the policyowner against the inadvertent lapsing of the contract. If the cash value is sufficient, a loan in the amount equal to the premium due is subtracted from the cash value to pay the premium.

In most instances, this provision must be requested by the policyowner at the time of application. Many companies do not allow it to be added once the policy is issued.

If the policyowner allows the automatic premium loan to always pay the premium, the policy will lapse when the cash value is reduced to zero. If this happens, the policyowner will not be able to reinstate the policy.

All outstanding loan amounts will be deducted from the death benefit upon the death of the insured.

9. 3. 8 Reinstatement

If a life insurance contract was not surrendered for the cash savings value, many contracts permit reinstatement of the policy if it is effected within three years of the policy lapse.

Proof of insurability may be requested by the insurer. In addition, all owed premiums (back premiums) as well as any outstanding loans must be paid.

Many insurers request that a reinstatement application be completed. This means that statements made by the policyowner/applicant are again contestable for two years.

The advantage of reinstating a lapsed policy instead of purchasing a new one is the insured original issue age is used when reinstated; therefore, the premium is lower.

9. 3. 9 Policy Loan Provisions

A policyowner has the right to borrow from the cash value, and there is no legal obligation to repay the loan. Interest is assessed by the insurer for these borrowed funds, and the interest rates are determined by each state. Currently, most life insurance contracts charge approximately 8% on some contracts and a variable interest rate on others.

Partial surrenders are allowed with a Universal Life or a Variable Universal Life Policy.

Any outstanding policy loans that are in existence at the time of the insured's death would reduce the policy proceeds. The outstanding loan would be subtracted from the face amount of the contract and the remainder paid to the named beneficiary.

Interest on policy loans is payable annually at the rate specified. However, interest that is not paid when due will be added to the loan and bear interest at the same rate.

If the total indebtedness equals or exceeds the cash value of the contract, the policy will terminate (subject to 30 days' notice to the insured or other policyowner).

In a whole life policy, the policyowner can usually borrow up to 90% of the policy's cash value. In a variable policy, the policyowner can borrow 75% to 90%.

Policy Loans Example	
$50,000	Face Amount
–20,000	Outstanding Loan
–1,600	Interest on Loan
$28,400	Death Benefit

9. 3. 9. 1 *Withdrawals and Partial Surrenders*

Partial cash value distributions may be classified as loans or withdrawals.

A *loan* is just that—a loan against one's own money. It is withdrawn with either the presumption that it will be repaid (with accrued interest) or the understanding that by not repaying it the amount of future benefits—including the death benefit—will be reduced by the loaned amount (plus accrued interest).

A *withdrawal* has generally the same impact on policy benefits, but there is no presumption that it will be repaid.

Generally, only universal life and variable universal life policies, with their inherent policy flexibility, permit withdrawals. Because cash value withdrawals (versus loans) are taxable income to the extent they exceed the policyowner's cost basis in the contract, most sizeable withdrawals are technically regarded as "withdrawals" up to the owner's basis. Withdrawn amounts above basis are regarded as "loans," which are not taxable.

9. 3. 10 Incontestability

The incontestable clause of a life insurance policy states that after a specified period of time (two years), the insurer may not dispute or contest the validity of the contract or the statements. After the contract has been in effect for a specific length of time, the insurance company agrees not to challenge any statements made by the applicant on the application.

The existence of this clause is unique to insurance contracts because it is contrary to general fraud laws. It simply indicates that an insurer, following the contestable period, may not claim that any misstatements in the application were made with the intent of the policyowner/insured to defraud.

The incontestable clause also assures that a named beneficiary will not have to substantiate any statements that were made on the application several years after the policy has been issued. In this situation, it would be extremely difficult for the named beneficiary and others to supply or substantiate information if the insurer contested the contract at the time of the insured's death.

9. 3. 11 Suicide Clause

When this clause is inserted in a life insurance contract, death by suicide is not covered during the policy's first two years.

If suicide occurs during this initial two-year period, premiums are refunded but no face amount (death benefit) is paid.

Following the two-year period, coverage is provided for suicide.

9. 3. 12 Assignment

An assignment of a life insurance contract involves the transfer of some or all of the policyowner's legal rights under the contract to another party. The policy provisions concerning assignment do not usually grant the owner/insured any rights to assign, but do set out the procedures by which assignments may be made. When assignments are effected, the insurer must be notified. The party receiving the assigned rights is known as the **assignee**. The person transferring these rights is known as the **assignor**. There are several types of assignments utilized, including the following.

9. 3. 12. 1 Collateral, Partial, Conditional Assignment

This involves the assignment of some but not all policy rights to an assignee. A lender may wish that a life contract be collaterally assigned so that it may draw upon the cash savings value if loan payments are not paid promptly.

Collateral assignment transfers a portion of the ownership right temporarily. Rights are returned to the policyowner when the debt is repaid. In addition, the amount of the assignment cannot exceed the amount of the debt.

9. 3. 12. 2 Absolute, Voluntary, Complete Assignment

Sometimes the policyowner decides to sell or make a gift of a life insurance policy by assigning all rights in the policy to the assignee. This type of assignment is made voluntarily, so it's sometimes called a **voluntary assignment**.

A voluntary assignment usually involves turning all rights—including the right to use the cash value—over to the assignee. For this reason, it can be called an **absolute** or **complete assignment**.

When an absolute assignment is made, the original policyowner usually has no means of recovering surrendered rights. This type of assignment is usually permanent.

9. 3. 12. 3 Beneficiaries' Assignment Rights

In some cases, the policy's beneficiary can assign a portion of the proceeds. However, unless the beneficiary has been named irrevocably, there is actually little to assign.

A revocable beneficiary expects to receive the proceeds, unless the policyowner changes the designation to another person. A lending institution is unlikely to advance money based on such an expectancy.

An irrevocable beneficiary is more likely to receive the death benefit. An irrevocable beneficiary, then, is more likely to find a lending institution willing to lend money.

9. 3. 13 Misstatement of Age or Sex

Under this provision, the policy provides for an adjustment of benefits payable if it is discovered that, after an insured's death, or at the time of claim, the insured's age was misstated on an insurance policy application. Specifically, the benefit payable will be adjusted to an amount that the premium would have purchased at the correct age. If the misstatement is discovered during the policy period, there may be an adjustment of the face amount or a refund of excess premiums paid. An adjustment is involved whether the age was misstated higher or lower than it actually was.

Any inaccuracy regarding the applicant's sex would be treated in the same manner, since premiums for females may be less expensive than those for males.

9. 3. 14 Medical Examinations and Autopsy

Some states require life insurance policies to include a provision that gives the insurer the right, at its own expense, to examine an insured while a claim is pending, and in the event of death to perform an autopsy, at its own expense, and where not prohibited by law.

9. 3. 15 Modifications

Modifications or changes in the policy, or any agreement in connection with the policy, such as changes in the beneficiary, face amount, or additional coverage, must be endorsed on or attached to the policy in writing over the signature of a specified officer or officers of the company. Only an executive officer of the insurer can change the contract, not the agent.

9. 3. 16 Policy Change Provision (Conversion Option)

The policy may contain a provision that permits the insured to exchange a policy for another type of policy form permitted by the company.

If the exchange is to a policy with a higher premium, the insured merely has to pay the higher premium and no proof of insurability would be required.

If the exchange is to a policy form with a lower premium, proof of insurability may be required as this could result in adverse selection against the insurer.

Example

If Charlie discovers that he has only six months to live, he might decide to exchange his higher-premium 20-pay life for one-year term insurance with the same face amount. The insurer's risk has increased while its premium income has decreased. Thus, Charlie will have to prove insurability.

9. 3. 17 Free Look

This policy provision permits the policyowner to take a specified number of days to examine the life insurance contract. If the new policyowner decides that the purchase was unnecessary or unwise, the contract may be cancelled with the entire premium refunded by the insurer.

The free look laws vary in each state and range from 10- to 20-day periods (longer for senior insurance products). The free look period begins when the policyowner receives the policy. For the applicant to receive a premium refund, the policy must be returned within 10 or 20 days from the date the policy is delivered.

Exercise 9.A

Fill in the blanks with the correct provisions.

1. The ________ __________ provision allows the insured to borrow against the cash value in a whole life policy.
2. The ________________ clause states that after a specified period the insurer can no longer void an insurance contract except for nonpayment.
3. The time period immediately after the premium is due in which the policy will not lapse is called the ________ __________.
4. The ___________ clause includes the company's promise to pay.
5. The __________ __________ clause spells out the obligations of both the insured and the insurer, as well as all parts to the contract.
6. The rights of the policyowner are spelled out in the provision known as the __________ __________.
7. The ___________ clause identifies that the policyowner must pay something of value for the contract.
8. After a policy lapses, the ___________ clause sets forth the requirements to bring the policy back up to date within a certain period of time.
9. ___________ refers to the right to transfer rights in the policy.
10. The right to examine the policy and return it for a full refund is referred to as the ________ ________ provision.

Answers to the exercises can be found at the end of the Unit 9 answers and rationales.

9. 3. 18 Beneficiaries

Life insurance companies place few restrictions on who may be named the beneficiary of a life insurance policy. The decision rests solely with the owner of the policy. Only when the applicant for a policy is not the insured (third party) does the question of insurable interest come into play. When a third-party applicant names himself as beneficiary, insurable interest must exist between the applicant and insured at the time of application.

All of the following can be beneficiaries of a life insurance policy:

- Individuals
- Businesses
- Trusts
- Estates
- Charities
- Minors

Classes as beneficiaries Rather than specifying one or more beneficiaries by name, the policyowner can designate a class or group of beneficiaries. For example, "children of the insured" and "my children" are class designations.

9. 3. 18. 1 Revocable Versus Irrevocable

Revocable beneficiary A **revocable beneficiary** is one that may be changed by the policyowner. The policyowner may change revocable beneficiaries without their knowledge or consent.

Irrevocable beneficiary The policyowner may also designate an individual to be an **irrevocable beneficiary**. In this case, the beneficiary designation cannot be changed without the consent and signature of that named beneficiary. The policyowner is responsible for paying the premium but needs consent and a signature from the irrevocable beneficiary in order to exercise ownership rights such as borrowing from the cash value, assigning, or cancelling the policy. An irrevocable designation might be used when a court orders a husband in a divorce settlement or annulment to continue payment on an insurance policy on his own life, with an irrevocable beneficiary designation on behalf of his wife (the primary beneficiary) and his children (the contingent beneficiaries).

9. 3. 18. 2 Naming Beneficiaries

There are two methods for naming and changing beneficiaries: the filing method and the endorsement method.

9. 3. 18. 2. 1 Filing Method

This method of effecting a beneficiary change is also known as the **recording method**. The request must be filed in writing to the insurer and is made effective by the insurance company recording the change in its records.

9. 3. 18. 2. 2 Endorsement Method

This method requires that the beneficiary change be typed or affixed directly to the policy. The insured must make a written request and mail the request along with the policy to the insurance company.

9. 3. 18. 3 Succession of Beneficiaries

Primary beneficiary The **primary beneficiary** is the person designated by the applicant to receive the face amount of the proceeds upon the insured's death. In most cases, a husband stipulates that his wife will be the primary beneficiary, and a wife usually designates her husband as her primary beneficiary.

Contingent beneficiary The **contingent beneficiary** is the individual who will be paid the policy proceeds if the primary beneficiary predeceases the insured. In other words, the **secondary beneficiary** will receive the face amount of the contract if the primary beneficiary is not living at the time the insured dies. If a tertiary beneficiary is named, the tertiary beneficiary will receive the face amount if the secondary beneficiary is not living at the time the insured dies.

If no contingent beneficiary is present, proceeds are left to the insured's estate.

9. 3. 18. 4 Changing Beneficiaries

Careless wording of beneficiary designations can result in confusion, conflict, and litigation. For this reason, the life insurance producer should insist that the applicant word the beneficiary designation carefully.

Example

If the insured designates his wife (not specifically named) as the beneficiary, a problem may arise. If the insured has married several times, it may be difficult to identify the true beneficiary. In such case, does *wife* mean the insured's present wife, or does it mean his wife at the time the beneficiary was designated? Does it apply to a wife who is now caring for the insured's minor children? Who was the intended beneficiary in such a case? It is important that the beneficiary be designated by full name to avoid misunderstanding.

9. 3. 18. 5 Designation Options

9. 3. 18. 5. 1 A Minor as Beneficiary

Naming a minor as the beneficiary of a life insurance policy presents problems. The most immediate of these problems is that a minor would not be competent legally to receive payment of and provide receipt for the policy proceeds if the insured dies before the minor comes of age.

An insurance company may hold on to the proceeds, paying interest on them until the beneficiary reaches legal age, or the company may insist that a trustee or guardian be appointed for the minor, someone who is legally entitled to receive and manage the policy proceeds.

Some parents anticipate this problem by establishing a trust to administer the life insurance proceeds and all other property in the estate of the parents in the event that both parents die leaving minor children.

9. 3. 18. 5. 2 A Trust as Beneficiary

A trust is formed when the owner of property (the grantor) gives legal title of that property to another (the trustee) to be used for the benefit of a third individual (the trust beneficiary).

When a trust is designated as the beneficiary of a life insurance policy, the policy proceeds provide funds for the trust. Upon the death of the insured, the trustee administers the funds in accordance with the instructions set forth in the trust provisions.

Life insurance trusts often are used to provide management of insurance proceeds on behalf of a beneficiary. An **inter vivos trust** is one that takes effect during the lifetime of the grantor. A **testamentary trust** is a trust created after the grantor's death, according to the provisions of the grantor's will.

9. 3. 18. 5. 3 The Insured's Estate as Beneficiary

The insured's estate can be named as beneficiary. The insured may direct that the policy proceeds be payable to his executors, administrators, or assignees to pay estate taxes, expenses of past illness, funeral expenses, and any other outstanding debts before the settlement of the estate. However, in general it is not desirable to name the estate as beneficiary. When money enters an estate and there is no will, the court handling the disposition of that estate is required to distribute the assets according to state law, which may or may not be the way the deceased would have wished.

In addition, estate costs usually are determined by the size of the probate estate. This means that adding life insurance policy proceeds to the probate estate increases the costs of settling the estate.

Finally, when a policyowner leaves policy proceeds to a named beneficiary, there are ways to protect these funds from the beneficiary's creditors. When the proceeds go into the estate, the heirs receive the proceeds in cash, which is more vulnerable to creditors.

9. 3. 18. 6 Class Designations

Another way of designating beneficiaries of life insurance policies is by group or by class, rather than by individual name. An example of such a designation would be "all my children" or "my brothers and sisters still living."

This designation saves the policyowner the trouble of making changes if the membership of the group is altered because of births or deaths.

Exercise 9.B

1. All of the following can be named beneficiaries in a life insurance contract EXCEPT
   A. the insured's estate
   B. a trust
   C. the insured
   D. a minor

2. All of the following are designations of beneficiaries EXCEPT
   A. secondary beneficiary
   B. primary beneficiary
   C. tertiary beneficiary
   D. final beneficiary

Answers to the exercises can be found at the end of the Unit 9 answers and rationales.

9. 3. 18. 7 Per Capita and Per Stirpes

When life insurance proceeds are to be distributed to a person's descendants, a *per stirpes* or a *per capita* approach generally is used.

Per stirpes means by the root or by way of branches. A per stirpes distribution means that a beneficiary's share of a policy's proceeds will be passed down to the beneficiary's living child or children in equal shares should they (the named beneficiaries) predecease the insured.

Therefore, per stirpes means the proceeds go to the descendents of the named beneficiary. The per stirpes beneficiary does not have to be named because it goes through the bloodline.

Per capita means per person or by the head. A per capita distribution means a policy's proceeds are paid only to the named beneficiaries who are living.

Therefore, per capita means the proceeds go to the named beneficiary.

In short, the per capita beneficiary claims the policy's proceeds in his own right, while the per stirpes beneficiary receives the proceeds through the rights of another.

9. 3. 18. 8 Uniform Simultaneous Death Act

This law stipulates that if the insured and the primary beneficiary are killed in the same accident and there is insufficient evidence to show who died first, the policy proceeds are to be distributed as if the insured died last. This law allows the insurance company to pay the proceeds to a secondary or other contingent beneficiary. If no contingent beneficiary has been named, the insured's estate will receive the proceeds.

9. 3. 18. 8. 1 Common Disaster Provision

Common disaster clause This clause states that in case of death in a common accident (disaster), the insured will be presumed to have survived the beneficiary. This prevents the payment of the insurance proceeds to the estate of the beneficiary and thus permits the proceeds to be distributed to any contingent beneficiaries or wherever else provided for by the policy.

The common disaster clause only goes into effect if the insured and primary beneficiary are involved in the same accident.

Most policies specify that the death of the primary beneficiary must occur within 30 to 90 days of the accident.

If the primary beneficiary lives past the minimum time period, then the death benefit would be paid to the estate of the primary beneficiary.

9. 3. 18. 9 Spendthrift Clause

A person who spends money extravagantly is known as a **spendthrift**. The insured can protect the proceeds of an insurance policy from the actions of a spendthrift beneficiary through the use of a **spendthrift clause**. This clause in a life insurance policy provides the following features.

- The proceeds will be paid in some way other than a lump sum.
- The proceeds or payments to be made to the beneficiary are protected from the beneficiary's creditors while they are still held by the insurance company.

The spendthrift clause also prevents the beneficiary from:

- transferring the proceeds—assigning payments to a creditor;
- commuting the proceeds—taking the present value of future payments in a lump sum; and
- encumbering the proceeds—borrowing money on the strength of the proceeds of the policy.

The insured normally elects the spendthrift clause at the time of the application for insurance.

9. 3. 18. 10 Facility of Payment Provision

This provision allows the insurer to select a beneficiary if the named beneficiary is a minor, is deceased, or cannot be found. This provision is found most commonly in group life insurance contracts and industrial life policies. Normally, the insurer would select an immediate family member.

Exercise 9.C
True or False

____ 1. The spendthrift clause is designed to protect the beneficiary against the insured's creditors.

____ 2. The Uniform Simultaneous Death Benefit assumes that if the insured and primary die in the same accident that the insured died last.

____ 3. The common disaster clause is only used when there is no proof of the order of death.

Answers to the exercises can be found at the end of the Unit 9 answers and rationales.

9. 3. 19 Exclusions and Limitations

Most life insurance contracts contain exclusions, or defined circumstances, that would not be covered if death occurs. Some of the more common exclusions are as follows.

9. 3. 19. 1 Aviation Exclusion

This exclusion restricts coverage in the event of death from aviation activities, except when the insured is a fare-paying passenger. This exclusion is generally found in double indemnity (accidental death) provisions as well.

This exclusion generally restricts coverage for military pilots and crew members. Aviation-related deaths of test pilots, stunt pilots, student pilots, or crop dusting pilots are not covered (but may be covered for an additional premium). Commercial airline pilots and crew members are usually covered at standard rates.

For example, a person who applies for life insurance coverage and is a private pilot, for example, may be issued a policy, but an aviation rider or exclusion (excluding coverage for aviation activities) will be added to it.

9. 3. 19. 2 War or Military Service Exclusion

This exclusion normally provides for the return of premium with interest in the event that death occurs under conditions excluded in the policy. This clause is generally included in a life insurance contract that is issued during wartime or in time of impending military action. The purpose of this clause is to control adverse selection against the company by those individuals entering military service. Especially during wartime, an individual entering the military may purchase more insurance than he normally would. There are two basic types of war clauses.

Status-type clause If this clause is included in a life insurance contract, the policy will not pay in the event of death while the insured is in the military, regardless of the cause of death. This would hold true even if the insured were home on leave and the death had nothing to do with military action.

Results-type clause This type of clause is much less restrictive than the status type clause. A contract that includes this clause would not provide coverage for a member of the military if the member was killed as a result of military exercises or service in general. However, if the individual was home on leave and fatally injured in an accident or died as a result of a nonservice related illness, the insurer would pay the face amount of the contract.

9. 3. 19. 3 Hazardous Occupation or Hobby Exclusion

Few applicants are declined life insurance because of their occupations. Firefighters and police personnel generally can purchase life insurance at standard rates.

Instead, underwriters focus on the applicant's avocations or hobbies. If an applicant participates in a hazardous hobby such as auto racing, sky diving, or scuba diving, the amount of insurance that may be purchased may be limited or an extra premium may be charged because of the additional risk. Also, the death benefit may be excluded if death occurred as a result of the hazardous avocation.

9. 3. 20 Prohibited Provisions

By law in most states, life insurance policies are not permitted to contain the following provisions:

- A provision that limits the time for bringing any lawsuit against the insurance company to less than one year after the reason for the lawsuit occurs
- A provision that allows a settlement at maturity of less than the face amount plus any dividend additions, less any indebtedness to the company and any premium deductible under the policy
- A provision that allows forfeiture of the policy because of the failure to repay any policy loan or interest on the loan if the total owed is less than the loan value of the policy
- A provision making the soliciting agent the agent of the person insured under the policy or making the acts or representations of the agent binding on the insured (agent must only be an agent of the company, not the insured)
- **Backdating** An insurer may not backdate a policy for more than six months before the original application was made to preserve age and reduce premium. Premium must be collected for each month the policy is backdated.

UNIT TEST

1. Which clause contains the basic promise of the life insurance company to pay a specified sum of money to a beneficiary upon the death of the insured?
   A. Consideration clause
   B. Insuring clause
   C. Policy loan clause
   D. Payment clause

2. Which clause identifies the fact that the policyowner must pay something of value for the insurer's promise to pay benefits?
   A. Consideration clause
   B. Insuring clause
   C. Entire contract clause
   D. Payment clause

3. Which clause identifies the components of the contract?
   A. Consideration clause
   B. Insuring clause
   C. Entire contract clause
   D. Payment clause

4. Which of the following is NOT generally an ownership right in an insurance policy?
   A. Naming the beneficiary
   B. Deciding how the proceeds are to be paid out
   C. Assigning the policy when an irrevocable beneficiary has been named
   D. Using the cash value

5. How long is the typical grace period?
   A. 10 days
   B. 31 days
   C. 60 days
   D. 90 days

6. Which of the following is NOT usually a condition of policy reinstatement?
   A. The policyowner must pay all back dividends due plus interest on the amount.
   B. The policyowner must pay all back premiums due plus interest on the amount.
   C. The insured must show proof of insurability.
   D. Less than 3 years must have elapsed.

7. Which of the following statements about an automatic premium loan provision is TRUE?
   A. It applies only to term policies.
   B. It is included automatically in all policies.
   C. It keeps the policy in force when it would otherwise lapse because of nonpayment of premiums.
   D. Money used to pay premiums is treated as a partial withdrawal and is not subject to interest charges.

8. The incontestable clause is usually in effect after
   A. 2 years
   B. 4 years
   C. 5 years
   D. 6 years

9. Harry decides to borrow some money from a bank. What type of assignment will Harry probably use to secure the loan?
   A. Voluntary assignment
   B. Partial assignment
   C. Complete assignment
   D. Absolute assignment

10. Carol has a policy on her ex-husband that she wants to give to their daughter. Carol no longer wants any control over this policy. What type of assignment will Carol probably use to accomplish this?
    A. Collateral assignment
    B. Voluntary assignment
    C. Partial assignment
    D. Conditional assignment

11. Ginny is a revocable primary beneficiary on her mother's life insurance policy. Which of the following statements is TRUE?
    A. Ginny can probably assign her rights in the policy as collateral on a loan.
    B. Ginny will receive benefits only if another beneficiary has died before her mother dies.
    C. Ginny's mother may not change the beneficiary without Ginny's permission.
    D. Ginny will receive benefits before any other beneficiary upon her mother's death.

12. Carl purchased a life insurance policy when he was 44. The insurer accidentally recorded his age as 42. When the accident is discovered in a review of the files 5 years later
    A. the policy will be canceled because of misrepresentation
    B. the policy will not change because the incontestable period will have passed
    C. Carl will be charged the difference in premium between his actual age and his stated age, along with the interest on the back payments
    D. Carl will be credited the difference in premium between his actual age and his stated age, along with the interest on the back payments

13. Steve is the beneficiary on his wife's life insurance policy. When they divorce, his wife cannot remove him as beneficiary on the policy without his written permission because
    A. most states require the beneficiary's written consent
    B. Steve is a revocable beneficiary
    C. Steve is an assigned beneficiary
    D. Steve is an irrevocable beneficiary

14. When Tom dies, Rosemary receives the death benefit. If Rosemary had died before Tom, George would have received the benefit. Which of the following statements is TRUE?
    A. Rosemary is the primary beneficiary, and George is the contingent beneficiary.
    B. Tom is the primary beneficiary, and Rosemary is the contingent beneficiary.
    C. Rosemary is the contingent beneficiary, and George is the primary beneficiary.
    D. George is the contingent beneficiary, and Rosemary is the tertiary beneficiary.

15. John leaves his $300,000 estate to his 3 children to split equally according to a per capita distribution. One of his children dies before John does. Upon John's death, which of the following statements is TRUE?
    A. The proceeds are split 3 ways between the remaining children and John's estate.
    B. The proceeds are split 2 ways between the remaining children only.
    C. The proceeds are split 3 ways between the remaining children and the beneficiary of the deceased child's estate.
    D. The proceeds are split 4 ways between the remaining children, John's estate, and the deceased child's estate.

16. John leaves his $300,000 estate to his 3 children to split equally according to a per stirpes distribution. One of his children dies before John does. Upon John's death, which of the following is TRUE?
    A. The proceeds are split 3 ways between the remaining children and John's estate.
    B. The proceeds are split 2 ways between the remaining children only.
    C. The proceeds are split 3 ways between the remaining children and the beneficiary of the deceased child's estate.
    D. The proceeds are split 4 ways between the remaining children, John's estate, and the deceased child's estate.

17. Alice and Ken are in a fatal car crash that kills them both. Alice is the primary beneficiary of a policy on Ken's life. What happens to the policy proceeds?
    A. The proceeds are retained by the insurance company.
    B. The proceeds are paid to Alice's estate.
    C. The proceeds are paid to any contingent beneficiaries or to Ken's estate.
    D. The proceeds are paid directly to Ken's estate.

18. Which of the following is allowed when policy proceeds are being paid through a spendthrift clause?
    A. The proceeds are paid directly to the beneficiary in monthly installments.
    B. The proceeds may be transferred directly to a creditor by the beneficiary.
    C. The proceeds may be commuted by the beneficiary to receive the present value of future payments in a lump sum.
    D. The beneficiary may borrow against the strength of the proceeds.

19. Under the facility of payment provision
    A. the insurer may select a beneficiary if the named beneficiaries cannot be found
    B. the insurer may retain the proceeds if the named beneficiaries cannot be found
    C. the state may select a beneficiary if the named beneficiaries cannot be found
    D. the state may retain the proceeds if the named beneficiaries cannot be found

ANSWERS AND RATIONALES TO UNIT TEST

1. **B.** The insuring clause contains the promise of the life insurance company to pay a specified sum of money to a beneficiary upon the death of the insured.

2. **A.** The consideration clause identifies the fact that the policyowner must pay something of value for the insurer's promise to pay benefits.

3. **C.** The entire contract clause stipulates that the documents, attachments, forms, etc. are to be considered parts of the insurance contract.

4. **C.** Assigning the policy when an irrevocable beneficiary has been named is not generally an ownership right in an insurance policy.

5. **B.** The typical grace period is 30 days.

6. **A.** Requiring the policyowner to pay all back dividends due plus interest on the amount is not usually a condition of policy reinstatement.

7. **C.** An automatic premium loan provision keeps the policy in force when it would otherwise lapse because of nonpayment of premiums.

8. **A.** The incontestable clause is usually in effect after 2 years.

9. **B.** Harry will probably use a partial assignment to secure the loan from a bank.

10. **B.** Carol will probably use a voluntary assignment to give the policy to her daughter.

11. **D.** Upon her mother's death, Ginny will receive benefits before any other beneficiary.

12. **C.** Carl will be charged the difference in premium between his actual age and his stated age, along with the interest on the back payments.

13. **D.** When they divorce, his wife cannot remove him as beneficiary on the policy without his written permission because Steve is an irrevocable beneficiary.

14. **A.** Rosemary is the primary beneficiary, and George is the contingent beneficiary.

15. **B.** The proceeds are split 2 ways between the remaining children only.

16. **C.** The proceeds are split 3 ways between the remaining children and the beneficiary of the deceased child's estate.

17. **C.** The proceeds are paid to any contingent beneficiaries or to Ken's estate.

18. **A.** The proceeds are paid directly to the beneficiary in monthly installments.

19. **A.** Under the facility of payment provision, the insurer may select a beneficiary if the named beneficiaries cannot be found.

UNIT 9 EXERCISE ANSWERS

Exercise 9.A

1. Policy loan
2. Incontestability
3. Grace period
4. Insuring clause
5. Entire contract clause
6. Policyowner rights
7. Consideration clause
8. Reinstatement
9. Assignment
10. Free look

Exercise 9.B

1. **C**
2. **D**

Exercise 9.C

1. False
2. True
3. False

UNIT

10

Riders

10. 1 INTRODUCTION

Riders are special policy provisions that attach to the policy, or "ride" it. A rider also can refer to a term policy that is attached to a permanent policy to provide additional coverage. Riders can be used to enhance or add benefits to the policy, or they can be used to take benefits away from the policy.

A **waiver** is a type of rider that is used to exclude benefits and for which no premium is charged. For example, a waiver may be attached to a policy that excludes benefits for death by a specified cause such as a particularly hazardous hobby.

Riders that add benefits generally require the payment of additional premium.

10. 2 LEARNING OBJECTIVES

After completing this lesson, you will be able to:

- define a policy rider;
- explain why riders are used in policies; and
- describe how different riders enhance, expand, or reduce policy benefits.

10. 3 TYPES OF RIDERS

10. 3. 1 Accidental Death (Double Indemnity)

An accidental death benefit (ADB) rider may be added to a life insurance policy. This benefit is sometimes referred to as **double indemnity** because it provides double the face amount of the policy if the insured dies due to an accident.

An additional premium will be charged for this benefit.

To be covered, death must occur within 90 days of an accident. The basic purpose of this restriction is to make sure that the **accident is the only cause of death**.

Payment will not be made by an insurer if death results from certain causes, including:

- illegal activities;
- war;
- aviation activities (except passenger travel on scheduled or commercial airlines); or
- where an accident was involved in conjunction with illness, disease, or mental infirmity.

Accidental death or double indemnity coverage is usually limited to age 60, 65, or, in few cases, age 70.

Accidental death and dismemberment insurance (AD&D) This also provides benefits for death due to an accident, or for the loss of one or more hands, feet, arms, legs, or loss of sight. The principal sum would be paid for death or loss of two or more of the primary parts; the capital sum is paid for loss of one of the primary parts.

10. 3. 2 Waiver of Premium

The waiver of premium rider found in a life insurance contract states that if an insured becomes **permanently and totally** disabled during the term of the policy, premium payments will be waived during the period of disability. The contract will remain in force just as if the premiums were paid. An additional premium is charged for this benefit, and it is subject to a waiting period (typically, three to six months). If the insured is still totally disabled after this period, premiums are waived retroactively from the date of disability. (Usually the insured and the policyowner are the same.)

Some life insurance contracts stipulate that disability must occur prior to a specified age, such as age 60 or 65.

The additional premium paid for this benefit does not increase the face amount of the policy nor the policy's cash value.

10. 3. 2. 1 Waiver of Cost of Insurance (Universal Life Policies)

This rider, also found in universal life insurance policies, will pay the minimum amount of premium to keep the policy in force if the insured becomes permanently and totally disabled. When the average premium payment is calculated, there would be enough premiums to not only cover the cost of insurance, but also to contribute, in part, towards cash value accumulation.

10. 3. 3 Disability Income Rider

This rider waives premium payments while the policyowner is totally disabled and pays a specified amount each month (income) to the policyowner while the disability continues. Under the disability income rider, the company guarantees the insured policyowner a regular monthly income for as long as the insured remains totally and permanently disabled. The amount of the income is usually based on the face amount of the policy—for instance, $X per month per $1,000 of coverage.

Example

If a policyowner has the disability income rider on a $100,000 policy and the company guarantees $10 per month on each $1,000 of coverage, the policyowner will receive $1,000 per month.

An income under the disability income rider continues for the length of the disability. However, a waiting period is required by most companies to ensure that the disability is, in fact, permanent (by the company's definition) and total (as determined by a company-approved physician).

10. 3. 4 Payor Rider

This rider or provision may be added to a life insurance contract which provides for the continuance of insurance coverage on the life of a juvenile in the event of the death or total disability of the individual responsible for the payment of the premiums (a parent or guardian). The premium payor must prove insurability. This benefit may be added for an additional premium and is also referred to as the **payor clause**. The premium payor must prove insurability.

This benefit provides that premiums will be waived until the insured attains a specified age or the maturity date of the contract, whichever is earlier, in the event that the payor dies or becomes totally disabled.

10. 3. 5 Guaranteed Insurability

Many insurance companies now offer a **guaranteed-insurability option (GIO)**, also known as a **guaranteed-insurability benefit (GIB)**, which allows a policyholder to purchase specified amounts of additional insurance without evidence of insurability.

The new insurance is issued at standard rates on the basis of the insured's attained age when the option is exercised.

In most cases, this benefit allows an insured to purchase additional insurance coverage at three-year intervals beginning with the policy anniversary nearest the insured's 25th birthday and terminating with the anniversary nearest the insured's 40th birthday.

The amount of additional insurance that may be purchased on each of the specified dates is equal to the face of the original policy or $10,000, whichever is less.

Some insurers provide additional option dates at other important periods in the insured's life, such as marriage or the birth of a child.

10. 3. 6 Return of Premium

This rider was developed primarily as a sales tool to enable the agent to say, for example, "In addition to the face amount payable at your death, we will return all premiums paid if you die within the first 20 years." The rider is simply an increasing amount of term insurance that always equals the total of premiums paid at any point during the effective years. In reality, the rider does not return premium but pays an additional amount at death that equals the premiums paid up to that time, as long as death falls within the time specified in the rider. By purchasing this rider, the policyowner is buying term insurance and is charged for it accordingly.

10. 3. 7 Return of Cash Value

The return of cash value rider is similar to the return of premium rider in that it is merely an additional amount of term insurance that is equal to the cash value at any point while effective. Buying it, the policyowner is simply getting additional term insurance. In reality, this rider does not return the cash value; it pays an additional amount of insurance equal to the cash value.

10. 3. 8 Cost of Living

Some companies offer their applicants the ability to guard against the eroding effects of inflation. A cost of living (COL) or cost of living adjustment (COLA) rider can provide increases in the amount of insurance protection without requiring the insured to provide evidence of insurability. The amount of increase is tied to an increase in an inflation index, most commonly the Consumer Price Index (CPI). Depending on the type of base policy, these riders can take several forms.

The purpose of a cost of living rider is to increase the death benefit to keep pace with inflation, tied to the CPI.

No proof of insurability is required. Premium is based on attained age.

10. 3. 9 Additional Insureds

Coverage for a spouse may be obtained to cover the extra expenses of child care and home-related costs by purchasing some sort of family term insurance. This insurance may also be used to protect dependent parents. A term policy can be added to policy to provide this coverage.

Spouse/other-insured term riders are used to purchase insurance on a spouse or someone other than the original person. These riders are often level premium term riders. Examples include:

- a child term rider—used to purchase term insurance on a life of a child; and
- a family term rider—combines the spouse and the children's rider for temporary coverage on the family.

10. 3. 10 Substitute Insured Rider

Although it seems unusual to allow for the substitution of insureds in life insurance, the **substitute insured rider** actually does permit a change of insureds. This rider is also known as an **exchange privilege rider**.

The ability to substitute or exchange insureds is desirable, for instance, in business-owned life insurance, when a key employee or business executive is insured for the benefit of the corporation. If this employee terminates employment or retires, the insurance can be switched over to apply to the employee's replacement, subject to evidence of insurability. This way, the policy can continue (rather than be terminated and a new policy issued) with the same face amount, and premiums can be calculated on the basis of the new insured's age, sex, and other factors.

Exercise 10.A

Match the rider being used to the example.

____ 1.	Nelson increases the face amount of his life insurance policy without having to submit proof of insurability.	A. Return of premium rider
____ 2.	Cody's policy will pay an additional amount at death that equals the premiums paid on the policy up to that time.	B. Future increase option rider
____ 3.	Sharon's policy automatically increases the amount of insurance protection according to an inflation index.	C. Cost of living rider

Answers to the exercise can be found at the end of the Unit 10 answers and rationales.

10. 3. 11 Accelerated Benefits

Accelerated benefit riders or provisions are standard in most individual and group life insurance policies. Through these provisions, people who are terminally or chronically ill have tax-free access to policy death benefits. People suffering from AIDS, cancer, heart disease, Alzheimer's disease, or other terminal or severe chronic illnesses often experience devastating financial hardship. These funds are usually used for such necessities as rent, food, and medical services.

Qualifying conditions for payment of benefits All of the following are qualifying conditions that would trigger payment of benefits under an accelerated benefits provision:

- A medical condition that would drastically limit a life span as specified in the policy, for instance, to 24 months or less
- A medical condition that requires extraordinary medical intervention, without which the insured would die
- A condition that usually requires continuous confinement in an eligible institution as specified in the policy if the insured is expected to live there for the rest of the insured's life
- A medical condition that would, in the absence of extensive or extraordinary medical treatment, drastically limit a life span, including
  - — coronary artery disease resulting in an acute infarction or requiring surgery,
  - — permanent neurological deficit resulting from cerebral vascular accident,
  - — end stage renal failure, and
  - — AIDS

Disclosures When a policy or certificate containing an accelerated benefit provision is applied for or delivered, the producer is responsible for providing the applicant a summary of coverage that includes:

- a brief summary of the accelerated benefit and definitions of the conditions or occurrences triggering payment of the benefit; and
- an explanation of any effect of the payment of an accelerated benefit on the cash value, accumulation account, death benefit, premium payments, and any loans or liens.

When an accelerated benefit option is exercised, the insurer must provide to the policyholder or certificate holder and any irrevocable beneficiary an illustration that:

- numerically demonstrates any effect the payment of the benefit will have on the cash value, accumulation account, death benefit, premium payments, and any loans or liens; and
- includes a statement that receipt of accelerated benefit payments may adversely affect the recipient's eligibility for Medicaid or other government benefits or entitlements, that benefits may be taxable, and that assistance should be sought from a personal tax advisor.

10. 3. 11. 1 Effect on Death Benefit

Whatever amount is withdrawn will be deducted from the face amount when death occurs.

Accelerated death benefits are received income tax-free as long as the insured is terminally ill. This provision is given without an increase in premium.

10. 3. 12 Living Benefits Provision

Long-term care (LTC) insurance, which reimburses health and social service expenses incurred in a convalescent or nursing home facility, can be marketed as a rider to life insurance policies.

LTC rider benefits are similar to those found in a LTC policy. The benefit structure includes the following.

- There are elimination periods of 10–100 days.
- Benefit periods are three to five years or longer.
- Prior hospitalization for at least three days may be required.
- Benefits may be triggered by impaired activities of daily living.
- Levels of care include skilled, intermediate, custodial, and home health care.

In addition, certain optional benefits also may be provided such as adult day care, cost-of-living protection, hospice care, and others.

There are two approaches to the LTC rider concept. The generalized or independent approach recognizes the LTC rider as independent from the life policy because the benefits paid to the insured will not affect the life policy's face amount or cash value. The integrated approach links the LTC benefits paid to the life policy's face amount and/or cash value.

The living benefit or living needs rider combines life insurance and LTC benefits, drawing on the life insurance benefits to generate LTC benefits. In a sense, it's like borrowing from the life insurance to pay LTC benefits. Under the LTC option, up to 70–80% of the policy's death benefit may be used to offset nursing home expenses. Under the terminal illness option, 90–95% of the death benefit may be used to offset medical expenses. Of course, payment of LTC benefits reduces the face amount of the life policy.

UNIT TEST

1. Garth has a $100,000 whole life insurance policy that has been in effect for 10 years. The policy includes a double indemnity rider. Garth jumps off a bridge and dies. How much will the policy pay?
   A. Nothing because all policies exclude death resulting from suicide
   B. $100,000 because the base policy excludes death resulting from suicide, but the multiple indemnity rider does not
   C. $100,000 because the multiple indemnity rider excludes death resulting from suicide, but the base policy's suicide exclusion has expired
   D. $200,000 dollars because death was accidental

2. Tammy has a total of $10,000 loan and interest outstanding against her $100,000 policy. The policy has a double indemnity rider. Tammy is killed in an automobile accident. How much will the policy pay?
   A. Nothing until the outstanding loan is repaid
   B. $180,000
   C. $190,000
   D. $200,000

3. Kumar has a life insurance policy with a rider that will pay him $1,000 per month if he is totally and permanently disabled. Which type of rider does he have?
   A. Waiver of premium rider
   B. Accidental death and disability rider
   C. Disability income rider
   D. Payor rider

4. Paul has a life insurance policy on his son for which he pays all the premiums. A rider to this policy states that if Paul becomes permanently and totally disabled, the premiums will be paid until his son reaches age 21, at which point his son will take over the premium payments. Which type of rider does he have?
   A. Waiver of premium rider
   B. Accidental death and disability rider
   C. Disability income rider
   D. Payor rider

5. Alberta is concerned that if she became totally and permanently disabled, she would not be able to pay her life insurance premiums and the policy will lapse. Which type of rider should she consider to protect against this possibility?
   A. Waiver of premium rider
   B. Accidental death and disability rider
   C. Disability income rider
   D. Payor rider

6. Which of the following riders is increasing term insurance that always equals the total premiums paid during the time the policy is in effect?
   A. Guaranteed insurability
   B. Return of premium
   C. Accidental death
   D. Waiver of premium

7. Double payment may be made because of which occurrence?
   A. Guaranteed insurability
   B. Return of premium
   C. Accidental death
   D. Waiver of premium

8. Which of the following is waiver of all future premiums in the event of total and permanent disability?
   A. Guaranteed insurability
   B. Return of premium
   C. Accidental death
   D. Waiver of premium

9. Which of the following is a guarantee that at specified ages, dates, or events, the insured may buy additional insurance without a medical exam?
   A. Guaranteed insurability
   B. Return of premium
   C. Accidental death
   D. Waiver of premium

10. The amount of money paid by an accidental death benefit rider if the insured dies in an accident is referred to as
    A. the principal sum
    B. the principle sum
    C. the capital sum
    D. the capitol sum

11. The amount of money paid by an AD&D rider if the insured is disabled in an accident is referred to as
    A. the principal sum
    B. the principle sum
    C. the capital sum
    D. the capitol sum

12. For the waiver of premium to apply under a waiver of premium rider, the disability must be
    A. total
    B. permanent
    C. total and permanent
    D. total, permanent, and disfiguring

13. All of the following statements about accelerated living benefits are correct EXCEPT
    A. the proceeds must be spent on the insured's medical expenses
    B. they are standard in life insurance policies
    C. they allow access to the policy's face value
    D. they are provided at no additional cost to the policyowner

ANSWERS AND RATIONALES TO UNIT TEST

1. **C.** $100,000 because the multiple indemnity rider excludes death resulting from suicide, but the base policy's suicide exclusion has expired.

2. **C.** The policy will pay a death benefit of $200,000 minus the outstanding policy loan of $10,000.

3. **C.** Kumar has a disability income rider.

4. **D.** This is a payor rider because it provides for a waiver of premiums on the son's coverage if the payor (Paul) becomes disabled.

5. **A.** A waiver of premium rider will waive the premiums on Alberta's policy if she becomes disabled.

6. **B.** A return of premium rider is increasing term insurance that always equals the total premiums paid during the time the policy is in effect.

7. **C.** Double payment may be made in the case of accidental death.

8. **D.** Waiver of premium is waiver of all future premiums in the event of total and permanent disability.

9. **A.** Guaranteed insurability is a guarantee that at specified ages, dates, or events, the insured may buy additional insurance without a medical exam.

10. **A.** The amount of money paid by an ADB rider if the insured dies in an accident is referred to as the principal sum.

11. **C.** The amount of money paid by an AD&D rider if the insured is disabled in an accident is referred to as the capital sum.

12. **C.** For the waiver of premium to apply under a waiver of premium rider, the disability must be total and permanent.

13. **A.** Accelerated benefits provisions are standard in life insurance policies and are included at no additional cost to the policyowner. They allow access to the policy's face value if the insured suffers from a terminal illness or injury. (The death benefit, less any accelerated payment, is still payable.) The insured can spend the proceeds in any manner."

UNIT 10 EXERCISE ANSWERS

Exercise 10.A

1. **B**
2. **A**
3. **C**

UNIT

11

Policy Options

11.1 LEARNING OBJECTIVES

After completing this lesson, you will be able to:

- explain settlement options, nonforfeiture options, and dividend options; and
- know how permanent policies accumulate cash values.

11.2 INTRODUCTION

The life insurance policy provides important policy options that give the life insurance contract flexibility to meet the needs of the insuring public. Of particular importance are the settlement, nonforfeiture, and dividend options available under a life insurance contract.

11.3 SETTLEMENT OPTIONS

At the time a life insurance contract is purchased, a policyowner should consider the manner in which the proceeds of the policy will be paid when it matures or when the insured dies. Any failure to adequately prepare for these contingencies may defeat the purpose for which the insurance was purchased. The policyowner may select from several settlement options to have the policy accomplish for the insured what the insured would like it to do. Death benefit settlement options are usually designated in the insurance contract and are used to define how the policy proceeds will be paid to the named beneficiary or the insured's estate.

The most common form of distribution is the **lump sum payment.** A lump-sum settlement is not really considered an option since life insurance contracts automatically provide for a lump-sum settlement in the event of an insured's death.

11.3.1 Interest Only

Under this settlement option, the policyowner may leave policy proceeds with the insurer to earn interest. The proceeds are left with the insurer, and the interest is paid to the beneficiary on an installment basis.

This type of settlement option is generally selected when the policyowner wants to provide for contingent beneficiaries (such as children) after the death of the primary beneficiary (such as a parent).

This option may also provide additional flexibility for the beneficiary since the proceeds are retained by the insurer until needed.

11. 3. 2 Fixed Period Option

This settlement option involves liquidating the proceeds and interest over a period of years, without reference to a life contingency (paid even if the beneficiary dies). It provides for the payment of policy proceeds in equal installments over a definite period of months or years.

The amount of proceeds, the period of time, the guaranteed rate of interest, and the frequency of payments all determine the amount of each installment.

The fixed-period option is the best option when the most important consideration is to provide income for a definite period of time.

Example

If the policy proceeds total $100,000, earn 6% annual interest, and are to be paid out over a 10-year period, the beneficiary can expect to receive approximately $1,100 each month for a total of $132,000. However, if the proceeds are paid out over a 15-year period, the beneficiary would receive approximately $845 per month for a total of $152,100. Note that in both examples the total amount paid exceeds the policy proceeds because of the interest earned.

11. 3. 3 Fixed Amount Option

Under this settlement option, the amount of income is the primary concern rather than a period of time (e.g., fixed-period) during which policy proceeds and interest earned are to be liquidated. Under this option, a fixed amount of income is designated to be paid at specific intervals (e.g., $2,000 per month). This amount is continued until the proceeds and any interest earned are exhausted.

In most cases, this settlement option is more advantageous than the fixed-period option, since it is much more flexible. Insurers allow the insured to specify varying amounts of income at various times.

The amount of each installment is the controlling factor under this option as the dollar amount to be paid is established and not the length of time for which installments are to be paid.

11. 3. 4 Life Income Option

This option distributes policy proceeds and interest with reference to life contingencies. Life income options are a form of life annuity and serve the same functions.

The amount of each installment paid depends upon the type of life income selected, the amount of the proceeds, the rate of interest assumed, the age of the beneficiary when the income begins, and the sex of the beneficiary.

Several life income options are available.

- The **pure life income option** provides installment payments for as long as the primary beneficiary lives, with no return (refund) of principal guaranteed.
- **Refund life income options** may take the form of a cash refund annuity or an installment refund annuity.

- **Life income with period certain** (e.g., a specified number of years), occurs where installments are payable as long as the primary beneficiary lives, but should this beneficiary die before a predetermined number of years, the insurer will continue the installment to a second beneficiary until the end of the certain period.
- The **joint and survivorship life income option** occurs when, if at the death of the first party the second party is still living, installments are continued during the latter's lifetime.

11. 3. 5 Withdrawal Provisions

The withdrawal provision is used in connection with settlement options. Under this provision, the proceeds of a policy are held by the insurance company and earn interest. The insured has the right to withdraw the funds left on deposit with the insurer at any time. The beneficiary may withdraw only a limited amount each year.

11. 3. 6 Other Settlement Arrangements

Many insurance companies will permit other types of settlement arrangements.

Administration of the special arrangement must strictly follow the terms of the contract. Insurance companies will handle settlement option elections by individually drafting the agreements.

11. 3. 7 Third-Party and Creditor's Rights

Although the life insurance contract is between the policyowner and the insurer, once the insured has died, a contractual arrangement exists between the insurer and the beneficiary.

Similarly, once the insured dies, the proceeds of a life insurance policy belong to the beneficiary and the insured's creditors have no right to them. The beneficiary's creditors, however, may have a right to the life insurance proceeds.

11. 3. 8 Advantages of Settlement Options

One of the principal advantages of the various settlement options is freedom from investment concerns. If a beneficiary elects a lump-sum settlement of the death benefit, the beneficiary must decide how to use or invest the money. By electing a settlement option other than a lump sum, the beneficiary is trusting the expertise and knowledge of the insurance company to administer the proceeds and provide some form of guaranteed income.

Another advantage of settlement options is that any of the options will guarantee a greater return than by simply taking the face amount of the policy. A $100,000 policy will generate a greater death benefit than $100,000 if the proceeds are paid to a beneficiary over time.

Exercise 11.A

1. Which settlement option pays only the earnings on the death benefit to a beneficiary?
   A. Life income
   B. Fixed amount
   C. Fixed period
   D. Interest only

Answers to the exercise can be found at the end of the Unit 11 answers and rationales.

11. 4 NONFORFEITURE OPTIONS—GUARANTEED VALUES

Nonforfeiture options protect a policyowner from losing her entire investment when a life insurance policy is cancelled, surrendered, or when premium payments stop. (Nonforfeiture options are available only for life policies that accumulate cash value.) There are three nonforfeiture options:

- Cash surrender value
- Extended term insurance
- Reduced paid-up insurance

11. 4. 1 Cash Surrender Value

The first option available to the policyowner is to surrender the policy for its cash value. All types of permanent life insurance contracts may be surrendered to the company for the amount of cash which has accumulated. The cash surrender value increases each year that the policy remains in force. Therefore, the cash surrender value forms the basis of all the other surrender or nonforfeiture values.

When an insured exercises the cash surrender value option, the policy is returned to the insurer and the company has up to six months to pay the cash surrender value to the insured.

In the majority of instances, the insurer will send the cash surrender value payment to the insured within 30 days.

A policy that is surrendered for its cash value cannot be reinstated.

$100,000 Whole Life Policy, Male, Age 35, Nonsmoker

End of Policy Year	Cash Surrender or Loan Value	Reduced Paid-Up Insurance	Extended Term Insurance	
			Years	Days
1	$ .00	$ 0	0	0
2	.00	0	0	0
3	641.00	3,658	2	169
4	1,632.00	8,927	5	312
5	2,659.00	13,944	8	246
6	3,727.00	18,741	11	4
7	4,832.00	23,304	12	316
8	5,978.00	27,656	14	116
9	7,165.00	31,803	15	174
10	8,395.00	35,759	16	146
11	9,657.00	39,483	17	40
12	10,965.00	43,042	17	236
13	12,320.00	46,442	18	18
14	13,727.00	49,705	18	123
15	15,183.00	52,822	18	197
16	16,691.00	55,807	18	244
17	18,251.00	58,666	18	268
18	19,860.00	61,397	18	271
19	21,519.00	64,010	18	256
20	23,225.00	66,506	18	222
25	31,461.00	75,080	17	29
27	34,993.00	77,940	16	124
30	40,464.00	81,688	15	59
35	49,800.00	86,687	13	42

11. 4. 2 Reduced Paid-Up Insurance Option

With this option, the insurance company uses the cash value of the contract to purchase a single premium insurance contract of the same form (e.g., 20-pay life, ordinary life, and modified life) as the original policy. The amount of coverage will be much less than the original policy, but no more premium payments will be required. Thus, the policyowner/insured will receive a policy that is paid in full for life.

11. 4. 3 Extended Term Option

This nonforfeiture option provides extended term insurance in place of the cash value policy. Under this option, the policyowner may request that the insurance company use the existing cash value to purchase term insurance equal to the face amount of the original policy with a single net premium. This term insurance will remain in effect for as long a period of time that can be purchased with the cash value available. Extended term is not available for rated policies.

Cash value is used as a single premium to purchase the same amount of coverage as the original policy, but it is now a term policy.

"Default Option": If a policyowner fails to select one of the nonforfeiture options when premium payments cease, this option generally goes into effect automatically.

Exercise 11.B

1. Amanda has stopped paying the premium on her $50,000 whole life policy. She has accumulated $5,000 in cash value, but she has not contacted the insurance company or selected a nonforfeiture option. What will happen next?
   A. The insurance company will mail her a check for $5,000.
   B. The insurance company will use the cash value to purchase $50,000 worth of term insurance.
   C. The insurance company will use the cash value to purchase a reduced amount of whole life insurance.
   D. The insurance company will pay back the cash value in monthly installments.

Answers to the exercise can be found at the end of the Unit 11 answers and rationales.

11. 5 DIVIDENDS

Life insurance policies that pay dividends are referred to as **participating policies**. Life contracts that do not pay dividends are referred to as **nonparticipating policies**. A participating policy refunds a portion of the premium to the insured in the form of an annual dividend. Dividends cannot be guaranteed by the insurer but, when paid, are based on the difference between the gross premium charged and the actual experience of the insurer.

The experience of an insurer is determined by its ability to meet current obligations, such as paying policy proceeds to a named beneficiary, maintaining sound insurance company operations on a solvent financial basis, and other management and administrative expenses. There are several types of dividend options available to policyowners/insureds, including the following.

11. 5. 1 Not Guaranteed, Not Taxable

When dividends are possible in participating policies, it is common for clients to believe that the dividends are earnings similar to those associated with stocks. Producers must explain that dividends are a return of premium, which is why they are not taxed. Most of all, producers must make sure they never give clients the impression that dividends are guaranteed. Also, a company's past dividend performance must be presented as just that—a history of past performance, which in no way can be interpreted as a projection of future dividends.

11.5.2 Participating Versus Nonparticipating Company

Life insurance policies may be either participating or nonparticipating, and it is important to distinguish between the two to understand the source of policy dividends. At any given age, people who buy participating (par) policies normally pay premiums that are slightly higher than premiums paid by those who purchase nonparticipating (nonpar) policies.

At the end of each year, the insurance company analyzes its operations. If fewer insureds have died than was estimated, a "divisible surplus" results and the company can return to the policyowners a part of the premiums paid for participating policies. These payments are called dividends but should not be confused with the dividends paid on stocks. Because policy dividends are really a return of part of the premiums paid, they are generally not taxable income, unlike corporate dividends, which are reportable for income tax purposes.

11.6 POLICY DIVIDEND SOURCES

The source of funds from which life insurance policy dividends are paid is the same as the three factors used in premium computations, which are Mortality, Interest, and Expense:

- Mortality—The mortality tables tell us that a certain number of insureds in each age group will probably die during the next year. If fewer people die than predicted, the life insurance company experiences a mortality savings.
- Assumed interest—A life insurance company estimates that invested money will earn a given rate over the long run, usually around 4%. If a company assumes its investments will earn 4% but the invested premiums actually earn 8%, the company has earned excess interest.
- Operating expenses or loading—Past experience tells a company that it will cost so many dollars per $1,000 coverage to keep the company going. Such costs as accounting, rent, office equipment, and so forth are relatively predictable. Any savings realized will help reduce operating expenses or loading.

11.7 DIVIDEND OPTIONS

11.7.1 Cash Dividend Option

Dividends credited to a policyowner may be paid in cash to that individual and the insurer simply sends a check to the policyowner. Dividends paid in cash are not considered taxable income because it is a return of unused premium.

11. 7. 2 Accumulation at Interest Option

The policyowner may leave dividends with the insurer to accumulate at interest in much the same fashion as a savings account. The interest earned will be at a rate no less than the minimum rate specified in the contract. Dividends left with an insurer may be withdrawn at any time.

If the insured dies, the insurer will add the dividends that have accumulated at interest to the face amount of the contract (which is paid to the named beneficiary).

The interest earnings on dividends is considered taxable income when paid, even though the dividends themselves are not.

11. 7. 3 Paid-Up Additions Option

Dividends may be used to purchase additional amounts of insurance which are added to the face amount of the contract. Paid-up additions are actually single premium purchases of as much life insurance as the amount of the dividend will purchase at the insured's attained age.

The insurance additions will be paid-up or paid in full for life and actually increase the insured's death benefit.

11. 7. 4 Reduce Premium Dividend Option

A policyowner may apply dividends to reduce future premium payments. In this manner, the policyowner will pay the difference between the premium due and the dividend amount.

Example

An insured has a policy with an annual premium of $480. The dividend due for one year is $150. If the insured chose the reduce premium dividend option, the net annual premium due would be $330 ($480 less $150).

11. 7. 5 Accelerated Endowment

Occasionally, a policyowner with an endowment policy will use dividends to accelerate the endowment.

- Dividends may remain as accumulations until they, together with the cash value, equal the face amount of the policy, at which time the face amount may be paid as an endowment.
- The dividends may also be used each year to shorten the endowment period. Under this option, a policy will mature more quickly because its cash value will reach the desired face amount of the insurance in a shorter time.

11. 7. 6 Paid-Up Option

This option actually allows the policyowner to pay up the policy early. For example, the insured has a 20-pay life policy. By using the dividends over the life of the policy, it may be paid up after 16 or 17 years instead of the full 20 years.

11. 7. 7 One-Year Term Dividend Option

With this option, the policyowner may use dividends to purchase additional one-year term insurance up to the amount of the cash value of the policy. The cost is based on the attained age of the insured. This particular option may be advantageous to a policyowner/insured whose life insurance needs fluctuate from year to year.

Exercise 11.C

Match the dividend option to the example.

____ 1. Virgil uses his dividend every year toward paying for the policy early.

____ 2. Bonita applies her annual dividend toward the net annual premium.

____ 3. Charlotte allows her policy dividends to remain with the insurer, where they are subject to annual earnings.

A. Accumulated at interest option

B. Paid-up option

C. Reduce premium dividend option

Answers to the exercise can be found at the end of the Unit 11 answers and rationales.

UNIT TEST

1. Emily has chosen to receive the payout from her husband's life insurance policy so that she will receive an income for the next 15 years. At the end of that time, the entire proceeds from the policy will have been paid out. Emily has selected
   A. the interest-only option
   B. the fixed-period option
   C. the fixed-amount option
   D. the life-income option

2. Heath has chosen to receive the payout from his wife's life insurance policy in such a way that he will have an income for the remainder of his life, regardless of how long he lives. Heath has selected
   A. the interest-only option
   B. the fixed-period option
   C. the fixed-amount option
   D. the life-income option

3. Jim has selected to receive only the interest from his mother's life insurance policy. When Jim dies, his children will receive the lump-sum benefit in addition to the benefit from his life insurance policy. Jim has selected
   A. the interest-only option
   B. the fixed-period option
   C. the fixed-amount option
   D. the life-income option

4. Carmen has selected to receive $10,000 per month until the principal and interest on her husband's life insurance policy have been paid out. Carmen has selected
   A. the interest-only option
   B. the fixed-period option
   C. the fixed-amount option
   D. the life-income option

5. Tina has a whole life insurance policy on her life that has been in effect for 15 years. Tina and her husband review their insurance coverage and decide that this policy, which was purchased before their marriage, is no longer necessary for their financial future. If Tina decides to stop paying the premiums, what will happen?
   A. The policy will lapse when the grace period expires, and Tina will lose the cash values built up in the policy.
   B. The policy has not built up cash values because it is a whole life policy.
   C. The policy has not been in force long enough to have built up cash values, so when it lapses, Tina will receive nothing.
   D. The policy will lapse, and Tina will be able to select a nonforfeiture option to receive value for the cash value built up in the policy.

6. Ann quits paying premiums on her whole life policy that has been in effect for 17 years. She does not select a nonforfeiture option. What happens to the cash value in her policy?
   A. The insurer will issue a paid-up term insurance policy with the same face value as the policy with a term as long as the cash value will purchase.
   B. The insurer will issue Ann's beneficiary check for the eligible amount of cash value in the policy.
   C. The insurer will issue a check for the eligible amount of cash value in the policy.
   D. The insurer may keep the cash value if a nonforfeiture option is not selected.

7. Which of the following statements about reduced paid-up insurance option is NOT true?
   A. The new policy will build cash values for the policyowner.
   B. No further premiums need to be paid on the reduced policy—it is paid up.
   C. The new protection is for the same amount as the original policy.
   D. A full share of expense loading is usually not included in the premium on the reduced coverage because the costs of setting up the coverage are greatly reduced.

8. Which of the following statements regarding settlement options is NOT true?
   A. Most insurers will agree to distribute the proceeds under any reasonable and actuarially sound settlement model.
   B. Interest earnings on the retained proceeds are guaranteed.
   C. The money is safe with the insurance company.
   D. The beneficiary invests the money at the suggestion of the insurer.

9. Ken is receiving interest-only payments on the settlement of his father's life insurance policy. If Ken dies before the lump sum is paid to him, what happens to the balance of the money?
   A. It is retained by the insurer.
   B. It is paid to any contingent beneficiary named in the original policy, or if there is no contingent beneficiary, it is paid to Ken's estate.
   C. It is paid to any primary beneficiary named in the original policy or into Ken's father's estate.
   D. It is paid directly into Ken's estate.

10. Which of the following is NOT a factor in determining the amount the beneficiary will receive each time a payment is made under the fixed period option?
    A. The age of the beneficiary
    B. The principal amount
    C. The interest earned on the principal
    D. The length of time payments are to be made

11. Which of the following is not a factor in determining the amount the beneficiary will receive each time a payment is made under the fixed amount option?
    A. The specified amount of each payment
    B. The principal amount
    C. The interest earned on the principal
    D. The capital amount

12. Thomas has chosen to receive the settlement from his wife's $100,000 life insurance policy according to the life income option. Under the option he chooses, he will receive an income for his life and his daughter will receive payments if he dies before receiving $100,000 in income. Thomas has selected
    A. a straight life income option
    B. a refund annuity option
    C. a life income certain option
    D. a joint and survivorship life income option

13. Walter is the beneficiary of his mother's life insurance policy. He wants to make sure the proceeds will last not only as long as he lives but also as long as his wife is alive. Walter should select
    A. the straight life income option
    B. the refund annuity option
    C. the life income certain option
    D. the joint and survivorship life income option

14. Which of the following factors does NOT affect the payment of dividends?
    A. Mortality
    B. Assumed Interest
    C. Morbidity
    D. Operating expenses or loading

15. Carl has not selected a dividend option for his nonparticipating policy. What happens to his dividends?
    A. No dividends are paid.
    B. They are used to purchase paid-up additions to the policy.
    C. They are used to purchase one-year term insurance.
    D. They are paid to Carl in cash.

16. Which of the following statements about paid-up additions is TRUE?
    A. The dividends are used to purchase additional insurance protection.
    B. The additional protection is almost always restricted to term insurance.
    C. The single premium for the added coverage will be based on the insured's original age.
    D. The operating expenses of putting this coverage in force are higher than original policy expenses.

ANSWERS AND RATIONALES TO UNIT TEST

1. **B.** Emily has selected the fixed period option.

2. **D.** This is an example of the life-income option because the proceeds will be paid over the beneficiary's life, regardless of how long that might be.

3. **A.** Because Jim has elected to receive only the interest, this example represents the interest-only option.

4. **C.** Carmen has elected to receive a fixed amount per month until all the proceeds have all been paid, so this is an example of the fixed-amount option.

5. **D.** If Tina stops paying the premiums, the policy will lapse, and Tina will be able to select a nonforfeiture option for the cash value built up in the policy.

6. **A.** Usually, the extended term nonforfeiture option goes into effect automatically if the policyowner fails to make an election.

7. **C.** The reduced paid-up amount is simply the amount of paid-up insurance that can be purchased using the existing cash value.

8. **D.** It is not true that the beneficiary invests the money at the suggestion of the insurer.

9. **B.** The balance of the money is paid to any contingent beneficiary named in the original policy. If there is no contingent beneficiary, it is paid to Ken's estate.

10. **A.** The age of the beneficiary is not a factor in determining the amount the beneficiary will receive each time a payment is made under the fixed period option.

11. **D.** The capital amount is not a factor in determining the amount the beneficiary will receive each time a payment is made under the fixed amount option.

12. **B.** Thomas has selected a refund annuity option.

13. **D.** Walter should select the joint and survivorship life income option.

14. **C.** Morbidity does not affect the payment of dividends.

15. **A.** No dividends are paid.

16. **A.** With paid-up additions, the dividends are used to purchase additional insurance protection.

UNIT 11 EXERCISE ANSWERS

Exercise 11.A

1. **D.** The interest only settlement option pays earnings on principal only to the beneficiary.

Exercise 11.B

1. **B.** The "extended term" option is used when the policyowner has not otherwise selected a nonforfeiture option.

Exercise 11.C

1. **B**
2. **C**
3. **A**

UNIT

12

Annuities

12. 1 LEARNING OBJECTIVES

After completing this lesson, you will be able to:

- describe and explain the different types of annuities;
- list the three types of annuity premium contract payments;
- list the five factors used to determine annuity contract payments;
- explain how variable annuities are regulated; and
- explain how accumulation units and annuity units are calculated.

12. 2 PURPOSES OF ANNUITIES

Annuities are not life insurance. Annuities are the exact opposite. The principal function of a life insurance contract is to create an *estate* (sum of money) by the periodic payment of money into the contract. An annuity's principal function is the liquidation of an estate. However, in contrast to life insurance, which is designed to protect against the risk of premature death, annuities are designed to protect against the risk of living too long.

Annuities may be purchased on an individual or a group basis. *Individual annuities* are usually purchased to provide retirement income or to fund other specific needs. *Group annuities* are most often used to fund employer-sponsored retirement plans for employees.

12. 2. 1 Distribution of a Lifetime Income

The basic function of an annuity is to systematically liquidate a principal sum over a specified period of time. An annuity is usually purchased as a means to save for retirement. The benefit of purchasing an annuity is that the cash accumulated in the account grows tax deferred.

12. 2. 2 Lump Sum Settlements

If an annuitant dies before the annuity fund (the principal) is depleted, a lump-sum cash payment of the remainder is made to the beneficiary. Thus, the beneficiary receives an amount equal to the beginning annuity fund less the amount of income already paid to the deceased annuitant.

12. 2. 3 Accumulation of a Retirement Fund

An annuity contract provides for a series of periodic payments that begin on a specific date (such as when the annuitant reaches a stated age) or a contingent date (such as the death of another person), and continue for the duration of a person's life or for a fixed period. Usually, but not always, an annuity guarantees a lifetime income for the recipient.

12. 2. 4 Accumulation of Education Funds

While annuities are designed to create and accumulate income for retirement, they can be used for other purposes such as to accumulate funds for a college education. Annuities serve a variety of purposes for which a stream of income is needed for a few years or a lifetime.

12. 2. 5 Tax-Deferred Growth

Annuity benefit payments are a combination of principal and interest. Accordingly, they are taxed in a manner consistent with other types of income: the portion of the benefit payments that represents a return of principal (i.e., the contributions made by the annuitant) is not taxed; the portion representing interest earned on the declining principal is taxed. The result, over the benefit payment period, is a tax-free return of the annuitant's investment and the taxing of the balance.

An *exclusion ratio* is applied to each benefit payment the annuitant receives:

$$\frac{\text{Investment in the contract}}{\text{Expected return}} = \text{Exclusion ratio}$$

The ratio is applied to the benefit payments, allowing the annuitant to exclude from income a like percentage.

Deferred annuities accumulate interest earnings on a tax-deferred basis. While no taxes are imposed on the annuity during the accumulation phase, taxes are imposed when the contract begins to pay its benefits. To discourage the use of deferred annuities as short-term investments, the Internal Revenue Code imposes a penalty as well as taxes on early withdrawals and loans from annuities. Partial withdrawals are treated first as earnings income (and are thus taxable as ordinary income); only after all earnings have been taxed are withdrawals considered a return of principal. Furthermore, a 10% penalty tax is imposed on withdrawals from a deferred annuity before age 59½.

12. 3 HOW ANNUITIES WORK

Like an insurance policy, an annuity is a contract between a purchaser and an insurance company. The purchaser pays the premium and generally is the contract owner. The **contract owner** has certain rights under the contract.

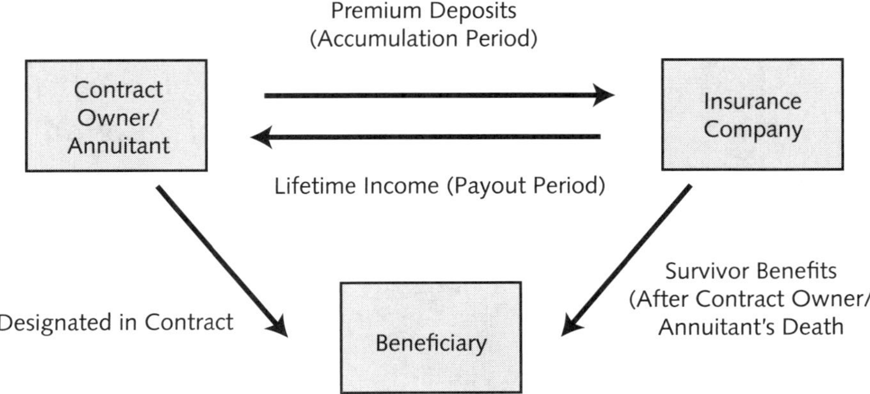

Annuities may be considered a true insurance product because there is an amount at risk. With an insurance policy, the insurer is counting on the insured living long enough so that the premiums paid and interest earned will equal or exceed the policy's death benefit. With an annuity, the insurer is counting on the annuitant not outliving the principal and interest.

12. 3. 1 The Accumulation Period

The accumulation period is the "putting in" time and the growth time. For a single premium deferred annuity, it is the time between the purchase date and the date benefits begin. For a periodic premium deferred annuity, it includes all the time between the first and last premium payments as well as any additional time before benefits begin. The owner has the ability to make changes during the accumulation period.

In all types of annuities, the principal earns interest. The first year's interest is added to the original principal, and the combined sum then earns more interest in the second year. In other words, we earn interest on interest, or compound interest, in the second and every subsequent year, as demonstrated by the following.

Accumulation Period—Single, Lump-Sum Deposit

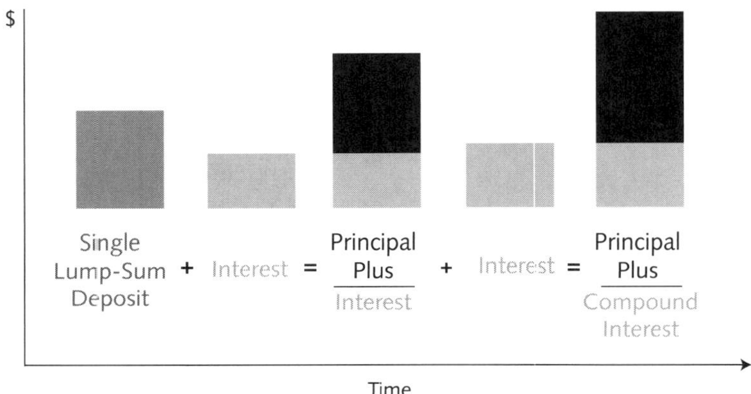

The interest earned by the annuity contract is not currently taxed as it is with other savings investment vehicles. Instead, if an individual owns the annuity, the interest generally is not taxed until it is paid out of the contract. Meanwhile, during the accumulation period, this untaxed interest goes right on earning even more interest, which is also added to principal and not currently taxed. This tax advantage is an important reason why people buy annuities.

12. 3. 2 The Annuity Period

The annuity period is the "taking out" time. This is the period following the accumulation of the annuitant's payments (principal and interest) during which annuity benefits are received.

During the annuitization period, the insurance company controls the funds in the annuity and disburses them according to the contract terms.

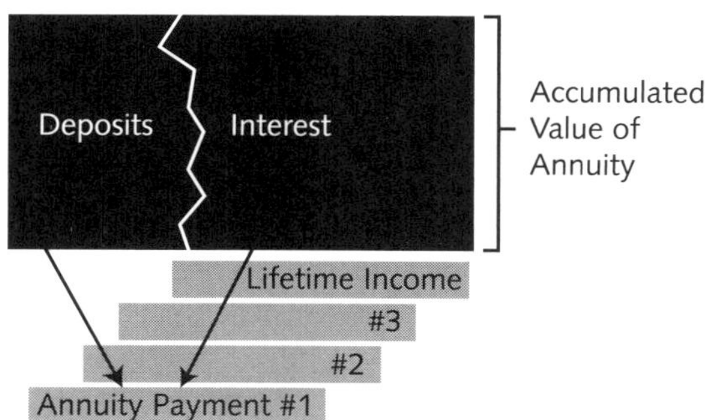

12. 3. 2. 1 *Fixed Payout*

For a fixed annuity, the cash value accumulation at the beginning of the annuity period is simply annuitized—that is, the accumulation is converted into a stream of periodic payments. The result is a fixed dollar amount payout that remains the same for the rest of the contract.

12. 3. 2. 2 *Variable Payout*

A different payout measure is used for variable annuities, and we'll look at it in detail later. Suffice it to say, the payout can fluctuate, reflecting the investment experience of the principal.

12. 3. 3 Nonforfeiture Provisions

An annuity contract owner who stops making premium payments during the accumulation period does not lose the value accumulated in the annuity up to that point. Instead, the contract holder will have **nonforfeiture options** or rights to the cash value accumulation in the annuity.

Surrender The contract may be surrendered for its cash value in a lump sum payment. However, most companies will level some kind of surrender charge, which is higher in the early years of the contract and then scales downward as time goes on, called a "back-end load." The surrender charge discourages surrender of the annuity and it compensates the company for loss of investment value. In some cases, surrender charges can be waived for an annuitant entering a long-term facility.

An annuity can only be surrendered during the accumulation period.

If the policy is surrendered for a lump sum prior to the age 59½, a 10% tax penalty will apply, in addition to the surrender charge.

If a nonqualified annuity is surrendered or withdrawn during the accumulation period, the cash withdrawals are made on a last in, first out basis (LIFO). In other words, the first monies withdrawn from the nonqualified annuity are considered to be from the interest earned on the principal, and they are taxed accordingly.

A **bail out provision** allows the annuity owner to surrender the annuity without surrender charges if interest rates drop a specific amount within a specific time period.

12. 3. 4 Owner Versus Annuitant Versus Beneficiary

The annuity **company** or insurer is most often a private insurance company because annuities are generally sold by life insurance companies.

The **annuitant** is the insured (the person on whose life the annuity contract has been issued) and is usually also the owner of the contract. The annuitant is the intended recipient of the annuity payments and the person upon whose life expectancy the payments will be based.

In an annuity, only the **owner** can:

- change the beneficiary, make withdrawals, or surrender the annuity;
- pay the premium; and
- make changes to the contract during the accumulation period.

Depending on the type of annuity and the method of benefit payment selected, a **beneficiary** may also be named in an annuity contract. In such cases, the annuity payments begin or continue after the death of the annuitant, for the lifetime of the beneficiary, or for a specified number of years.

Exercise 12.A

Match the sentences below with the terms that describe the annuity principle at work.

____ 1. The period during which annuity benefits are received

____ 2. The period between the annuity purchase date and when benefits begin

____ 3. A stream of equal, periodic annuity payments

____ 4. A stream of payments that fluctuate based on the investment performance of the principal funds

A. Fixed payout

B. Annuity period

C. Accumulation period

D. Variable payout

Answers to the exercise can be found at the end of the Unit 12 answers and rationales.

12. 4 IMMEDIATE AND DEFERRED ANNUITIES

There are two categories of annuities based on when annuity payments are to begin: immediate and deferred annuities.

Under an **immediate annuity**, the benefit payments begin within 12 months of purchase. Frequently, an immediate annuity is purchased with life insurance proceeds, an inheritance, or a settlement received for injuries.

Under a **deferred annuity**, the benefit payments are postponed until a later date, such as a planned retirement age.

The combination of premium method and commencement of benefits is often used to describe an annuity. Single premium annuities may be **single premium immediate annuities**. However, we also find **single premium deferred annuities**, under which a single premium is paid but benefits are deferred. All periodic premium annuities are **periodic payment deferred annuities**, but different deferral periods may be involved—benefits may begin immediately after the last premium payment, or be postponed until a later date.

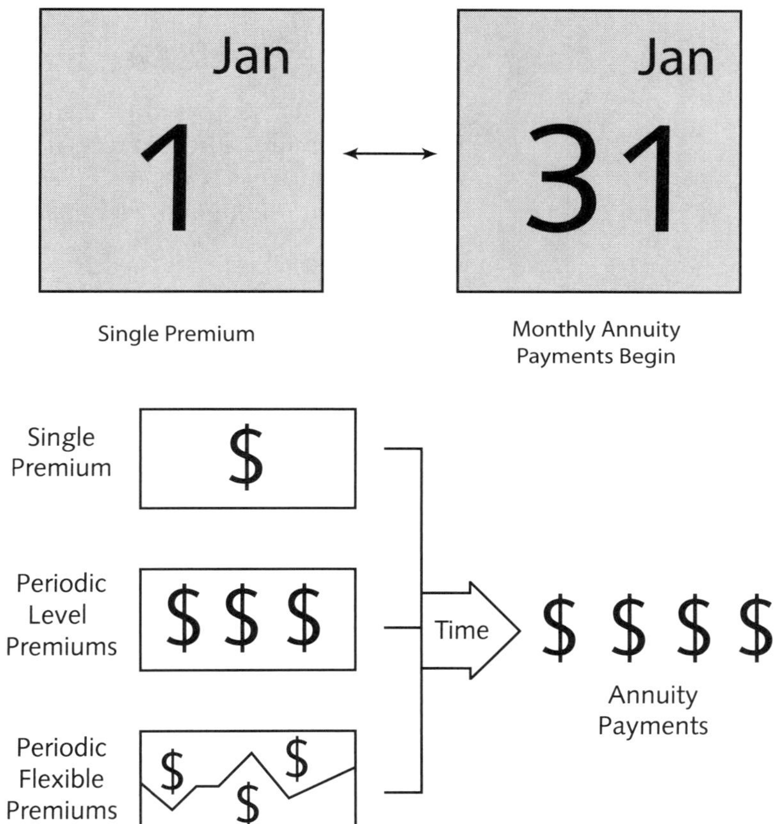

Example

Most of the time, deferred annuity premiums are paid in annual, semiannual, quarterly, or monthly installments over a period of years. With a deferred annuity, the start of income payments is delayed for a specified period—until age 55, 60, 65, or 70. Regardless of premium payment method, with a deferred annuity, income payments to the annuitant begin after the specified period has elapsed after the purchase date.

12. 5 DEFERRED ANNUITY DEATH BENEFITS

When the annuitant dies before the start of annuity payments, some companies return the aggregate, net premiums paid by the purchaser of a deferred annuity and a portion of the interest the money has earned. Others deduct enough money from premiums paid to cover the expense incurred in setting up the contract.

12. 6 ANNUITY PREMIUMS

12. 6. 1 Single Premium

An annuity purchased by a single lump-sum payment is called a single premium annuity. The annuity itself is a contract between the company and the annuitant. For the single premium, the company promises to pay the annuitant an amount each period (monthly, quarterly, semiannually, or annually).

12. 6. 2 Level Premium

Under this arrangement, the premiums are paid in periodic installments over the years before the annuity income begins. Level premiums have a forced savings aspect to them, much like making regular deposits into a passbook savings account. A common level premium arrangement is the annual premium annuity in which the premiums are paid in yearly installments. Premiums also can be paid semiannually, quarterly, or monthly.

12. 6. 3 Flexible Premium

A flexible premium annuity is like the level premium annuity in that annuity premiums are made over time, usually years, until annuity benefits are scheduled to begin. The difference is that with a flexible premium annuity, the purchaser has the option to vary the amount of each premium payment, as long as it falls between a minimum and maximum amount—for example, between $200 and $10,000.

The flexible premium annuity can be advantageous to persons whose incomes may be subject to considerable fluctuation or who, for whatever reason, cannot pay for an annuity all at once or with periodic premiums that are the same amount each time.

There is, however, a disadvantage to a flexible premium annuity. The actual amount of the annuity benefit cannot be determined in advance because there's no way to determine in advance the amount of each premium that will be paid or how much will be paid in total for the annuity. The purchaser of a flexible premium annuity, therefore, must wait until the final premium payment has been made to determine the exact amount of the annuity benefit. Benefits can be projected on the basis of assumptions about premium payments.

12.6.4 Premium Determination

There are five factors used to determine annuity premiums.

- **Annuitant's age** The age at which an annuitant will begin to receive a lifetime income is important because it helps the company determine what premium to charge. An annuitant who will begin to receive $300 per month for life beginning at age 60 will pay a higher premium than an annuitant who will begin to receive $300 per month for life beginning at age 65.
- **Annuitant's sex** Because statistically women live longer than men, a woman will pay higher premiums because she is likely to require more income payments than a man her own age.
- **Assumed interest rate** Life insurance companies invest premiums and earn a rate of return on those investments. When determining premiums, companies estimate an assumed interest rate for those premium dollars.
- **Income amount and payment guarantee** The amount of the periodic income to be paid out also impacts the premium, as do any payment guarantees (such as a 10-year period certain). The higher the amount of periodic income and the longer the guarantee it must be paid, the higher the annuity premium will be.
- **Loading for company expenses** As with life policies, the annuity purchaser helps pay the company's operating expenses. The premiums charged must have an expense, or loading, factor added to them.

12.7 FIXED ANNUITIES

Annuities can be defined according to their investment configuration, which affects the income benefits they pay. The two classifications are *fixed annuities*, which provide a fixed, guaranteed accumulation or payout, and *variable annuities*, which attempt to offset inflation by providing a benefit linked to a variable underlying investment account.

12.7.1 General Account Assets

A **fixed annuity** is a fully guaranteed contract, which is backed by funds invested in the insurer's **general account**. Principal, interest, and the amount of the benefit payments are guaranteed. The general account consists of conservative investments selected by the insurer to match its contractual guarantees and liabilities to the annuitant.

12.7.2 Interest Rate Guarantees

There may be two levels of guaranteed interest: a **current rate** that is guaranteed at the beginning of each calendar year, and a **minimum guaranteed** rate that will be paid if the current rate falls below this level.

Calculating guaranteed interest rates Premiums or payments made during the accumulation period earn a guaranteed return on a tax-deferred basis. There are two ways to calculate guaranteed interest paid on these contributions.

The **current purchase rate** reflects the current interest rates based on current economic conditions. This rate is guaranteed at the beginning of each calendar year and could fluctuate from year to year.

The **guaranteed purchase rate** is the minimum interest rate that is guaranteed for the life of the contract. This will be a fairly modest amount, such as 4–5%. This is the minimum return that will be paid even if the current annual rate falls below the guaranteed rate.

Deferred annuities guarantee a minimum interest rate that contributions will earn. Because the guaranteed rate is often less than prevailing interest rates, the insurer will frequently credit excess interest on the contract. Excess interest calculations are based on how much the insurer has actually earned on its investments.

12. 7. 3 Level Benefit Payment

When converted to a payout mode, fixed annuities provide a guaranteed fixed benefit amount to the annuitant, typically stated in terms of dollars per $1,000 of accumulated value. This is possible because the interest rate payable on the annuity funds is fixed and guaranteed at the point of annuitization. The amount and duration of benefit payments are guaranteed. Because they provide a specified benefit payable for life (or any other period the annuitant desires), fixed annuities offer security and financial peace of mind. However, because the benefit amount is fixed, annuitants may see the purchasing power of their income payments decline over the years due to inflation.

12. 8 VARIABLE ANNUITIES

A **variable annuity**, like variable life insurance, is designed to provide a hedge against inflation through investments in a separate account of the insurer consisting primarily of common stock. A variable annuity is not a fully guaranteed contract.

Variable annuities provide annuitants the opportunity to experience large gains; they may, however, also produce a loss. Thus, variable annuities are characterized by a variable rate of growth and a variable benefit payable to the annuitant.

12. 8. 1 Regulation as Securities

Variable annuities are regulated by both the federal Securities and Exchange Commission (SEC) and state insurance departments. They are considered securities and have to comply with federal securities laws and regulations, with certain limited exemptions. Regulation by state insurance departments includes review and approval of variable annuity contracts that will be offered to the public, examination and licensing companies marketing variable annuities, and licensing of agents who will sell variable annuities. Due to this dual regulation, an agent who wants to sell variable annuities must pass a test and be registered with the Financial Industry Regulatory Authority (FINRA), and the agent must also be licensed to sell life insurance by the state. Some states have additional requirements and require an agent to qualify for a separate variable contracts license.

12. 8. 1. 1 *Separate Account Assets*

Insurers are required to maintain a separate account for equity products, such as variable annuities. This account consists primarily of a portfolio of common stock and other equity investments. Performance of the variable annuity is dependent upon the performance of the funds invested in the separate account. Due to this fact, there is investment risk to the annuitant since there is no guarantee of principal, interest, or investment income associated with the separate account.

A contractholder's equity in a variable annuity is measured in units, and there are two types of unit measurements.

12. 8. 2 Accumulation Units

During the accumulation period, an owner's units are identified as *accumulation units*. Both the number of units and the value of the units will vary in accordance with the amount of premium payments made and the subsequent performance of the separate account.

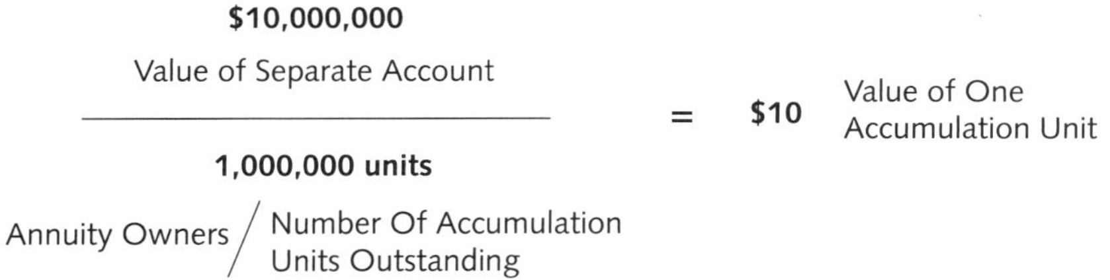

12. 8. 3 Annuity Units

When the annuity period begins, the accumulation units are converted to *annuity units*. The value of the annuity units will vary in accordance with the daily performance of the separate account, and periodic benefit checks will fluctuate accordingly.

Example

Suppose that the annuitant transfers $50,000 from the accumulation account and the table shows a value of $5 per $1,000. The first monthly payment to the annuitant would be 50 × $5, or $250.

Exercise 12.B

Match the terms with the annuity principle that is illustrated by the sentence.

____ 1. This is an account held by an insurer that consists primarily of a portfolio of common stock and other equity investments.

____ 2. The value of these will change based on the daily performance of the separate account, and so will the amount of the benefit checks.

____ 3. This type of annuity provides a hedge against inflation and is not a fully guaranteed contract.

____ 4. This is an account held by an insurer that consists of conservative investments to match its contractual guarantees and liabilities.

____ 5. This is a type of annuity where benefit payments begin within 12 months of purchase.

A. General account

B. Annuity units

C. Variable annuity

D. Immediate annuity

E. Separate account

Answers to the exercise can be found at the end of the Unit 12 answers and rationales.

12. 9 ANNUITY SETTLEMENT OPTIONS

12. 9. 1 Life Annuities

In a **life annuity,** the payout is guaranteed for life. Life annuities may be contrasted with temporary annuities, discussed later.

12. 9. 1. 1 Life Annuity—No Refund

A life only (straight life) option provides for payment of annuity benefits for the life of the annuitant with no further payment following the death of the annuitant. This option will pay the highest amount of monthly income to the annuitant because it is based only on life expectancy, but it creates a risk that the annuitant may die early and forfeit much of the value of the annuity to the insurance company.

12. 9. 2 Guaranteed Minimum Payouts

Many people were not happy knowing that most or all of their investment would be lost if they were to die after receiving just a few payments. This caused insurance companies to start offering some alternatives that provided a minimum guaranteed payout.

12. 9. 2. 1 Refund Life Annuity

A refund life annuity will pay the annuitant for life, but if the annuitant dies too soon after the annuity period begins, there will be a refund of any undistributed principal or cost of the annuity. This option assures that the full purchase price of the annuity will be paid out to someone. This refund may be in the form of continued monthly installments (installment refund) or paid in one lump sum (cash refund), whichever has been elected by the annuitant.

12. 9. 2. 2 Life Annuity Certain

An annuity certain is an option that does not guarantee a lifetime income to the annuitant. It provides an income for a guaranteed period (or for a fixed amount) regardless of whether the annuitant is alive or not. The guaranteed period could be 5, 10, 15, or 20 years. If the annuitant outlives the guaranteed period, the annuity payments cease. If the annuitant dies during the guaranteed period, the payments continue to a survivor until the guaranteed period of time ends.

The **life annuity with period certain** provides a life annuity with an extra guarantee for a certain period of time. This guarantees a lifetime income, but if death occurs within the period certain, annuity payments will be continued to a survivor for the balance of the period certain (which may be specified as 5, 10, 15, or 20 years, or some other period).

12. 9. 3 Joint Life and Survivorship and Joint Life Annuities

A joint and survivorship option provides benefits for the life of the annuitant and the life of a survivor. A stated monthly amount is paid to the annuitant, and upon the annuitant's death the same or a lesser amount (such as two-thirds or one-half) will be paid for the lifetime of the survivor.

A joint life annuity differs from the joint and survivorship annuity option because it covers two or more annuitants and provides monthly income only until the first annuitant dies. After the first annuitant's death, all income benefits cease.

12. 9. 4 Temporary Annuity Certain

A temporary annuity provides annuity payments for a specified period of time (such as 5 or 10 years), or until death of the annuitant—whichever occurs first. It does not necessarily guarantee payment for life or for the specified period of time. It provides for one contingency or the other. The key concept is that the earlier event will terminate benefits.

12.10 TWO-TIERED ANNUITIES

A **two-tiered annuity** is one that has different values available for distribution at maturity depending on whether the value is taken in a lump sum before annuitization or left with the issuer for periodic payments.

These annuities offer relatively high rates, but only if the owner holds the contract for a certain number of years and then annuitizes it.

Agents who sell two-tiered annuities must make sure that clients know how the product works and are prepared to commit themselves and their beneficiaries to the annuity for a lifetime.

12.11 TAX-SHELTERED ANNUITIES

A TSA is a pension plan for employees of nonprofit organizations as specified by the IRS, in accordance with section 501(c)(3) and 403(b) of the Internal Revenue Code. The tax deferment allowed is much like that allowed for contributions a corporate employer makes to a qualified pension or profit-sharing plan.

12.12 RETIREMENT INCOME ANNUITIES

A **retirement income annuity** is an ordinary deferred annuity, but with an additional feature—a decreasing term life insurance rider that provides term life insurance with a face amount that decreases each year the policy is in force. The effect is that if the annuitant reaches retirement age, say 65, the decreasing term insurance death benefit expires and annuity payments begin providing retirement income. If, however, the annuitant dies before retirement, the decreasing term insurance death benefit is combined with the value of the annuity and then paid to the annuitant's beneficiary in any settlement option chosen.

12.13 INDEXED ANNUITIES

An **equity-indexed annuity (EIA)** is a *fixed annuity* (meaning the principal and interest are both guaranteed) with an equity-linked rate of return. Excess interest earnings (above the interest rate guarantees) are calculated using an indexing method that is linked both to the stock market as well as the insurance company's overall investment performance. EIAs are not currently classified as securities and do not require a securities license to sell.

Interest earned is tied to an equity index such as the S&P 500, adjusted yearly to reflect any index increases.

The advantage of an equity-indexed annuity is that it has a guaranteed minimum interest rate and can never decrease in value. It also gives the annuitant the opportunity to beat the rate of inflation.

12. 14 MARKET VALUE-ADJUSTED ANNUITIES

Market value adjusted (MVA) annuities are individual deferred annuity contracts with underlying assets held in a different account. The values are guaranteed if held for a specific period of time, but the nonforfeiture values may fluctuate according to a market value adjustment formula if held for shorter periods. MVA annuities are also known as modified guaranteed annuities. This is a fixed contract, and the interest paid is dependent on the fixed rate and the actual rate of the underlying bonds which are in the General Account.

The interest rate on MVA annuities is guaranteed (fixed) for a specific period of time. An adjustment is only made if the annuity is surrendered. If interest rates rise, surrender charges will be higher due to the adjustment. If interest rates are low, there will not be a surrender charge.

The market value adjustment comes into play only if the annuity owner decides to surrender the annuity contract early. If the owner does decide to do this, a surrender charge and market value adjustment apply. If current interest rates are higher than the contract rate, the annuity owner will receive less. If the current rates are lower than the contract rate, the annuity owner will receive more. This increase or decrease is what is referred to as the "market value adjustment."

12. 15 GROUP VERSUS INDIVIDUAL ANNUITIES

Annuities can benefit groups as well as individuals. Retired employees receiving a stream of income from their former employer are getting an annuity benefit. Small employers often purchase group annuities for employees during their working years. Larger employers often operate their own annuity pool, using a trust fund to hold investment assets and dispense benefits.

12. 16 COMPARISON OF ANNUITIES

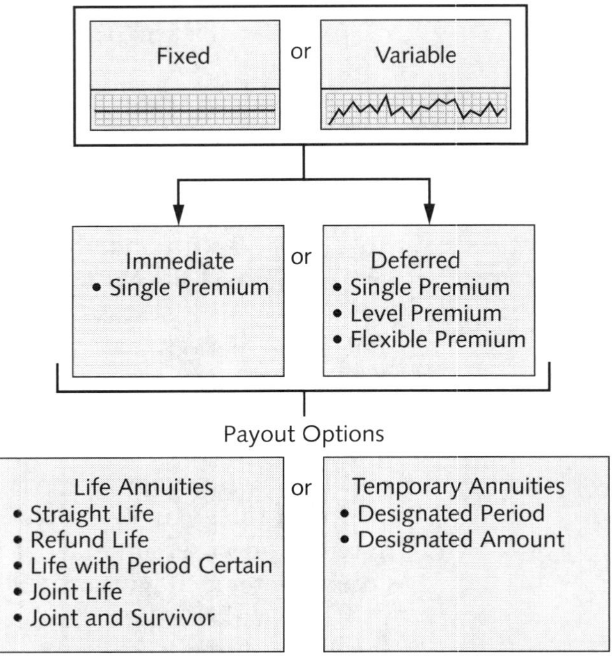

UNIT TEST

1. Annuities exist to
   A. accumulate a sum of money
   B. distribute a lifetime income
   C. both accumulate a sum of money and distribute a lifetime income
   D. neither accumulate a sum of money nor distribute a lifetime income

2. Tracey is paying money into an annuity she hopes will support her in her retirement years. Her contract currently is in which of the following periods?
   A. Accumulation period
   B. Nonforfeiture period
   C. Payout period
   D. Annuity period

3. Liz purchases an immediate annuity. The annuity contract must be
   A. a fixed annuity
   B. a variable annuity
   C. a deferred annuity
   D. a single premium annuity

4. Which type of annuity is most likely to provide death benefits?
   A. Fixed annuity
   B. Variable annuity
   C. Deferred annuity
   D. Immediate annuity

5. Which of the following factors is NOT used to determine annuity premiums?
   A. Annuitant's retirement date
   B. Assumed interest rate
   C. Income amount and payment guarantee
   D. Applicant's sex

6. Which of the following types of annuities are regulated as securities?
   A. Fixed annuities
   B. Flexible annuities
   C. Variable annuities
   D. Structured annuities

7. Which of the following is a purpose of the annuity?
   A. The creation of a fund at the death of an individual
   B. The replacement of earnings upon the disability of an individual
   C. The distribution of a lifetime income
   D. The discounting of a principal sum back to its present value

8. An annuity might be called the flip side of
   A. compounding
   B. life insurance
   C. retirement planning
   D. Social Security

9. Annuities are a mechanism for transferring to an insurance company the risk of
   A. poor investment returns
   B. becoming uninsurable
   C. outliving financial resources
   D. outliving a spouse or child

10. An annuity that guarantees a minimum rate of return is
    A. an immediate annuity
    B. a deferred annuity
    C. a variable annuity
    D. a fixed annuity

11. Devon purchases an annuity that will pay a monthly income for the remainder of his life and then stop making payments. Devon has purchased
    A. a fixed annuity
    B. a straight-life annuity
    C. a variable annuity
    D. a temporary annuity certain

12. Albert has purchased an annuity that will pay him a monthly income for the rest of his life. If Albert dies before the annuity has paid back as much as he put into it, the insurance company has agreed to pay the difference to Albert's daughter. Albert has purchased
    A. a straight-life annuity
    B. a life annuity with period certain
    C. a refund life annuity
    D. a temporary annuity

13. Which type of annuity is most likely to be used to distribute lottery winnings?
    A. Flexible premium, temporary annuity with period certain
    B. Single premium, temporary annuity with amount certain
    C. Single premium life annuity
    D. Flexible premium, temporary annuity with amount certain

14. Marcus purchases an annuity that offers a guaranteed minimum interest rate and a guarantee against loss of principal if the contract is held to term. However, if the Nasdaq moves upward, Marcus's annuity might end up accruing more than the guaranteed minimum interest rate. Marcus has purchased
    A. an equity-indexed annuity
    B. a market value-adjusted annuity
    C. a market value-indexed annuity
    D. an equity-adjusted annuity

15. Eric purchased an annuity with favorable rates. However, because of unforeseen circumstances, he needs to surrender the annuity. If the market has gone up, Eric will need to pay a higher surrender charge than if the market has gone down. Eric owns
    A. an equity-indexed annuity
    B. a market value-adjusted annuity
    C. a market value-indexed annuity
    D. an equity-adjusted annuity

ANSWERS AND RATIONALES TO UNIT TEST

1. **C.** Annuities are useful for both accumulating a sum of money and for distributing a lifetime income.

2. **A.** This annuity is still in the accumulation phase.

3. **D.** An immediate annuity is purchased with a single premium, and annuity payments begin one payout interval later.

4. **C.** A death benefit is paid if the annuitant dies before the annuity payments begin. This is more likely to occur with a deferred annuity.

5. **A.** All of these factors, except the annuitant's retirement date, are used to determine annuity premiums.

6. **C.** Variable annuities are regulated as securities because the contract owner bears the investment risk.

7. **C.** The purpose of an annuity is to fund a lifetime income.

8. **B.** An annuity might be called the flip side of life insurance.

9. **C.** A life annuity provides that payments will be made until the annuitant's death no matter how long the annuitant lives.

10. **D.** A fixed annuity guarantees a minimum rate of return.

11. **B.** A straight-life annuity will pay a monthly income for the remainder of Devon's life and then stop making payments.

12. **C.** Albert has purchased a refund life annuity.

13. **B.** Lottery winnings are most likely distributed through a single premium, temporary annuity with amount certain.

14. **A.** Marcus has purchased an equity-indexed annuity.

15. **B.** Eric owns a market value-adjusted annuity.

UNIT 12 EXERCISE ANSWERS

Exercise 12.A

1. **B**
2. **C**
3. **A**
4. **D**

Exercise 12.B

1. **E**
2. **B**
3. **C**
4. **A**
5. **D**

UNIT

13

Group Life Insurance

13. 1 LEARNING OBJECTIVES

After completing this lesson, you will be able to:

- list and explain the required provisions of group policies;
- list the five main types of group life insurance; and
- list and explain the four characteristics of conversion from group to permanent life insurance.

13. 2 INTRODUCTION

Many employers offer group life insurance as an employee benefit. Group life insurance differs from individual life insurance contracts in both underwriting methods and policy provisions. This life insurance coverage is concerned with the selection of risks by group factors rather than by individuals. Group life insurance protection involves a contract between the insurer and employer. An additional party is also present: the covered employee. Group insurance is usually written as one-year term insurance.

13. 3 LEGAL REQUIREMENTS

All states define a **true group** as having at least 10 people covered under one master contract. Some states make allowance for even smaller groups.

Group life insurance includes the following characteristics.

- Insurance coverage must be incidental to the purpose of the group.
- Beneficiaries are covered under a master contract.
- Beneficiaries receive an individual certificate.
- Plans can be contributory or noncontributory.
- Beneficiaries are underwritten as a group.
- Beneficiaries have the right to conversion privileges.

Group life insurance coverage must be incidental to the purpose for which the group has been formed. This means that a group may not be formed for the specific purpose of providing insurance coverage for its members. For example, a group of sick people would not be considered a legally acceptable group because the main purpose of the group is to purchase insurance. Examples of legally insurable groups include the following:

- Single-employer groups
- Labor unions
- Trade associations

- Creditor and debtor groups
- Fraternal organizations

Group life insurance coverage is generally issued without evidence of insurability being required by the individuals making up the group (though sometimes plans do require such proof).

The employer is the policyowner and pays the premium and receives the master contract. Most group life policies are written as term insurance. The employee does not receive a policy and instead receives a **certificate of coverage** that verifies that life insurance protection is in force.

13. 3. 1 Contributory Versus Noncontributory

Contributory versus noncontributory plans refers to which party or parties will pay the group life insurance premiums. If the employer pays the entire premium, the plan is **noncontributory**. If the employee pays part of the premium (the premium is shared by both the employer and employee), the plan is **contributory**. In a noncontributory plan (non-participating), the group contract must cover 100% of the eligible persons in the group. If the plan is contributory (also known as participating), at least 75% of the eligible employees must be covered before the plan can become effective. For example, if 500 employees are eligible for a contributory group plan, at least 375 would have to enroll in the plan for it to be effective.

Under contributory plans, the period of time during which the employee may enroll and receive coverage without evidence of insurability is known as the **eligibility period**.

Eligibility of Group Members By its very nature, group insurance provides for participation by virtually all members of a given insurance group. Whether or not an individual member chooses to participate usually depends on the amount of premium that individual must pay (if the plan is contributory).

Employers and insurers are allowed some latitude in setting minimum eligibility requirements for employee participants. For example, an employer might decide that employees must be full-time workers and actively at work to be eligible to participate in a group plan.

A probationary period may be required for new employees, which means they must wait a certain period of time (usually one to six months) before they can enroll in the plan.

The probationary period is followed by the enrollment period: the time during which new employees can sign up for the group coverage.

If an employee does not enroll in the plan during the enrollment period (typically 31 days), she may be required to provide evidence of insurability if she wants to enroll later. This is to protect the insurer against adverse selection.

Exercise 13.A

1. A group life insurance plan is considered noncontributory when
   A. the employer pays all of the premium for the plan
   B. the employee pays part or all of the premium for the plan
   C. the third-party administrator pays the premium for the plan
   D. the service organization pays part of the premium

Answers to the exercise can be found at the end of the Unit 13 answers and rationales.

13. 4 STANDARD PROVISIONS

Most states have enacted standard provisions for group policies, including the following:

- Grace period (usually 31 days)
- Incontestability (usually one or two years after the policy becomes effective, two years from the insured's effective date of coverage)
- Entire contract (the application must be attached to and made part of the contract)
- Evidence of insurability (individual insurability must be proven if the employee or member joins the plan after the enrollment period)
- Misstatement of age (premium is adjusted to the correct age; under individual insurance benefits are adjusted)
- Facility of payment (allows partial payment of policy proceeds to a close relative or friend if no beneficiary is named or living to cover final expenses)
- Conversion (the right to convert to an individual policy when the insured's coverage is terminated or the master policy is terminated)
- Individual certificates (issued as evidence of coverage)
- Minimum number (a minimum number of group members is required)

13. 5 CERTIFICATES OF INSURANCE

In group insurance, the policy is evidence of a contract between the insurer and the employer or association (the policyowner). When an employee becomes covered by a group life plan, the employer, as the master policyowner, retains the life insurance policy. As proof of protection, the employee receives a form that certifies the coverage, the benefits under the plan, and the beneficiary's name.

Because it certifies or states all these things, it is called a **certificate of insurance**.

13.6 POLICY FORMS

Five main types of group life insurance are marketed to eligible groups: group term life, group permanent life, group creditor life, group paid-up life, and group survivor income benefit insurance. Group insurance is also written to include the dependents of the group members.

One disadvantage of group life insurance is that it is usually only temporary coverage, and an individual member of the group may lose that coverage when that individual leaves the group.

To lessen this disadvantage, group term policies must include provisions to provide for conversion to individual coverage. They also may include continuation of insurance provisions and waiver of premium provisions. Some employers continue group term insurance at reduced amounts for retired workers.

13.7 DEPENDENT COVERAGE

In most cases, it's possible to include the dependents of employees who are insured under a group life plan. Dependents may be any of the following:

- The insured's spouse
- The insured's children
- The insured's dependent parents
- Any person for whom dependency can be proven

13.8 GROUP CONVERSION OPTION

Group life insurance policies must include a conversion privilege that gives insured members the right to convert to an individual policy upon termination of the master policy, upon the loss of group coverage due to termination of employment, or upon the loss of eligibility on the part of a class of insureds (such as "all part-time employees").

This option guarantees the member that coverage will continue for 31 days after leaving the group. The member can convert to any type of insurance except term insurance; the policy premiums will be based on the attained age of the member.

If the member dies during the conversion period, the insurer will pay the death benefit in full. No proof of insurability is required when a conversion takes place. If the master contract is terminated, every individual who has been covered under the plan for at least five years will be allowed to convert to individual plans. The converted policy must have the same coverage amount as the group policy.

Exercise 13.B

1. In a group life insurance plan, a Certificate of Insurance is provided to
   A. the Insurance Commissioner for approval as to form and content
   B. the employees, in lieu of the master contract
   C. the employer, in lieu of the master contract
   D. the insurer, as evidence that the policy was delivered by the agent

2. For group life insurance policy, the person responsible for applying for the policy, maintaining the policy, and paying the premium is
   A. the union shop steward, on behalf of all covered union members
   B. the company attorney, on behalf of the employees
   C. the insurer who provides the policy
   D. the master policyowner

Answers to the exercise can be found at the end of the Unit 13 answers and rationales.

UNIT TEST

1. A contributory life insurance plan must cover
   A. at least 50% of the eligible employees
   B. at least 75% of the eligible employees
   C. at least 85% of the eligible employees
   D. all of the eligible employees

2. Doris dies 15 days after her group coverage is terminated and before she has the chance to convert her policy to permanent coverage. Doris's beneficiary will receive
   A. the full benefit under the group policy
   B. the full death benefit under an individual policy
   C. the death benefit minus unpaid premium under the group policy
   D. the death benefit minus unpaid premium under the individual policy

3. Which of the following statements about conversion from group life insurance is TRUE?
   A. Coverage must be converted to a term policy
   B. Conversion must be applied for within 6 months of termination
   C. Proof of insurability will be required
   D. Premiums for the new policy will be based on the insured's attained age

ANSWERS AND RATIONALES TO UNIT TEST

1. **B.** A contributory life insurance plan must cover at least 75% of the eligible employees.

2. **A.** Doris's beneficiary will receive the full benefit under the group policy.

3. **D.** In converting from group life insurance, the premiums for the new policy will be based on the insured's attained age.

UNIT 13 EXERCISE ANSWERS

Exercise 13.A

1. **A**

Exercise 13.B

1. **B**
2. **D**

UNIT

14

Social Security and Tax Considerations

14. 1 LEARNING OBJECTIVES

After completing this lesson, you will be able to:

- explain the Social Security system and eligibility requirements for Social Security benefits;
- explain the taxation of insurance and annuity products; and
- explain Section 1035 policy exchanges and the tax benefits provided by them.

14. 2 SOCIAL SECURITY

14. 2. 1 Covered Workers

Social Security (also referred to as OASDI—old age, survivors, and disability insurance) benefits are determined by a formula based on earnings. Nearly 90% of all employed persons are covered by Social Security and pay Social Security taxes. Employees pay 50% of the employment tax. Self-employed persons pay 100% of the tax. The Social Security Administration is responsible for administering benefits and collecting premiums. To receive most Social Security benefits, a person must be fully insured. A worker who has worked 40 quarters is considered **fully insured**. A few of the survivor benefits are payable for **currently insured** persons.

14. 2. 2 Types of Benefits

Social Security provides the following categories of benefits:

- Monthly retirement benefits for retired workers at least age 62
- Monthly benefits for spouses of retired workers
- Monthly survivor benefits for the spouse and certain other survivors of deceased workers
- Monthly disability benefits for disabled workers and their dependents
- A modest lump-sum death benefit payable at a worker's death

14. 2. 3 Eligibility for Social Security

Most workers are covered under Social Security, including common-law employers and employees, most self-employed persons, Armed Forces personnel, and employees of nonprofit organizations.

The main excluded worker groups are railroad workers and federal employees hired before 1984. Federal employees hired after 1984 are covered. Railroad workers contribute to their own railroad retirement system.

In addition, employees of state and local governments are not covered unless the government entity has entered into an agreement with the Social Security Administration or does not have a retirement program.

14. 2. 4 Insured Status

A covered worker becomes qualified for Social Security benefits by attaining either fully, currently, or disability insured status. Insured status depends on how many *quarters of coverage* a worker has earned.

14. 2. 4. 1 Fully Insured

A person becomes fully insured by acquiring a sufficient number of quarters of coverage to meet either of the following two tests.

A person is fully insured after acquiring 40 quarters of coverage (10 years of covered employment). Once a person has acquired 40 quarters of coverage, that person is fully insured for life, even if that person spends no further time in covered employment (or covered self-employment).

A person is fully insured if:

- that person has at least six quarters of coverage; and
- that person has acquired at least as many quarters of coverage as there are years elapsing after 1950 (or, if later, after the year in which the person reaches age 21) and before the year in which that person dies, becomes disabled, or reaches, or will reach age 62, whichever occurs first.

14. 2. 4. 2 Currently Insured

A person is currently insured after acquiring at least six quarters of coverage during the full 13-quarter period ending with the calendar quarter in which the person:

- died;
- most recently became entitled to disability benefits; or
- became entitled to retirement benefits.

14. 2. 4. 3 Disability Insured

A special insured status is required if a worker is eligible for disability benefits under Social Security. This status requires that the worker be fully insured and have earned at least 20 quarters of coverage in the 40 calendar quarter periods ending with the calendar quarter in which the disability begins. This requirement is modified slightly if a covered worker is disabled before age 31.

The individual's insured status determines eligibility for Social Security benefits. A fully insured person and eligible dependents are entitled to all Social Security benefits. A worker who is only currently insured has limited benefits available. If a worker is only currently insured at death, Social Security benefits would be payable only to a dependent child in addition to the lump-sum death benefit of $255.

The insured status required for some of the more important Social Security benefits is summarized in the following table.

Benefit	Insured Status
Retirement at 65	Fully
Disability	Fully or Disability
Lump-sum death benefit	Fully or Currently
Spouse's benefit (worker living)	Fully
Spouse's survivor benefit	Fully
Child's benefit (worker living)	Fully
Child's survivor benefit	Fully or Currently
Parent's survivor benefit	Fully

14. 3 PRIMARY INSURANCE AMOUNT

Social Security benefits are expressed as a percentage of the primary insurance amount (PIA). The PIA for a worker is based on the average level of earnings of that worker and is updated and published annually in tables by the federal government. Most types of Social Security benefits are some percentage of the PIA as set for the year for the worker's earnings level.

14. 4 NORMAL RETIREMENT AGE

To receive full Social Security retirement benefits, a person must wait until normal retirement age. If benefits are taken before this age, the monthly benefit amount is reduced.

The Social Security normal retirement age is currently 65. It will gradually increase to age 67 in accordance with the following table.

Year of Birth	Normal Retirement Age
1937 and before	65 years
1938	65 years, 2 months
1939	65 years, 4 months
1940	65 years, 6 months
1941	65 years, 8 months
1942	65 years, 10 months
1943–1954	66 years
1955	66 years, 2 months
1956	66 years, 4 months
1957	66 years, 6 months
1958	66 years, 8 months
1959	66 years, 10 months
1960 and after	67 years

14. 5 DUAL BENEFIT LIABILITY

Often a person is eligible to receive more than one Social Security benefit. For example, a spouse who has reached age 65 may be eligible to receive a retirement benefit based on her own earnings and also a benefit based on her late husband's earnings. In these cases, the person is entitled to receive only the larger of the two benefit amounts instead of both amounts.

14. 6 RETIREMENT BENEFITS

By working and paying Social Security taxes, individuals earn "credits" toward Social Security benefits. Benefit payments are based on how much was earned over a full working career. Higher lifetime earnings result in higher benefits. Benefit payments are also affected by the age at which you retire. The "full retirement age" is 65 for people who were born before 1938. But because of longer life expectancies, the Social Security law was changed to gradually increase the full retirement age until it reaches age 67. This change affects people born in 1938 and later.

14. 7 SURVIVOR BENEFITS

There are several types of survivor benefits provided under Social Security.

Social Security survivors benefits can be paid to:

- a widow or widower;
- a disabled widow or widower—as early as age 50;
- a widow or widower at any age if that person takes care of the deceased's child who is under age 16 or disabled and receiving Social Security benefits;
- unmarried children under 18 or up to age 19 if they are attending high school full time;
- stepchildren, grandchildren, or adopted children under certain circumstances;
- children at any age who were disabled before age 22 and remain disabled; or
- dependent parents age 62 or older.

Lump-sum death benefit This benefit helps the deceased's survivors to pay for funeral costs. The lump-sum death benefit provided by Social Security may not exceed $255. Payment is made to a surviving spouse who was living with the deceased. If no surviving spouse is present, the benefit may be paid to an eligible child.

Surviving spouse's benefit The eligible surviving spouse of a fully insured worker is entitled, at the spouse's normal retirement age, to a monthly life income equal to the worker's primary insurance amount (PIA) at death. Or, if the spouse wishes to receive these benefits early, the spouse can elect reduced benefits, starting as early as age 60.

If the surviving spouse has a dependent child, and the child was a dependent of the deceased worker, an additional benefit of 75% of the worker's PIA is payable, regardless of the spouse's age, until the child reaches age 16. Disabled children will entitle the surviving spouse to this benefit indefinitely, as long as the child remains disabled and under the care of the surviving spouse.

The **blackout period** is the period of years during which no Social Security benefit is payable to the surviving spouse of a deceased, fully insured worker. It is between the time the youngest child of the worker (in the spouse's case) attains the age of 16 and the spouse's age is 60.

14. 8 DISABILITY BENEFITS

Disability under Social Security has a five-month elimination period and is defined as "the inability to engage in any substantially gainful activity by reason of medically determinable physical or mental impairment that can be expected to result in death or that has continued or can be expected to continue for at least 12 full months."

14. 9 MAXIMUM FAMILY BENEFIT

When several members of a worker's family are entitled to receive benefits, the family may run up against an overall limitation on benefit payments called the maximum family benefit. Like the PIA, a maximum family benefit is established for each level of average earnings and is updated annually.

14. 10 RETIREMENT EARNINGS LIMIT

Once a Social Security retiree reaches normal retirement age, there is no restriction on the amount the retiree may earn from employment (or self-employment) without losing Social Security benefits. Retirees age 64 and under may earn only up to a certain amount without a reduction in benefits.

One earnings limit applies to retirees who have not yet reached their normal retirement age, and a modified limit applies in the year an individual reaches normal retirement age. The dollar amounts are indexed to inflation and change annually. For 2010, for example, a retiree who has not yet reached normal retirement age would face a reduction in retirement benefits of $1 for every $2 earned beyond $14,160.

In the year an individual reaches normal retirement age, $1 in benefits will be deducted for every $3 earned in excess of $37,680 (the limit for 2010).

14.11 SOCIAL SECURITY TAXES

Social Security is a pay-as-you-go program—that is, the Social Security taxes collected from workers are not set aside in an account for each worker but are used to pay benefits to current beneficiaries of the program. Put another way, when someone begins receiving benefits, she is not drawing on a fund of some specific amount that consists of her previous tax deposits plus earnings. Those benefits are financed by the taxes currently collected from covered workers.

Social Security benefits are financed by a payroll tax on employers, employees, and the self-employed. There is no Social Security tax on investment income (e.g., interest or dividends) or any kind of income other than earnings from employment or self-employment.

The rate of tax is a flat amount set by Congress and adjusted upward from time to time. The tax rate for employers and employees is currently set at 6.2% (not counting the additional tax for Medicare). The self-employment tax rate is 12.4%—twice the employee rate—because self-employed individuals pay both the employee and the employer portion of the tax. The tax rate is multiplied by the relevant earnings figure to compute the Social Security tax.

14.11.1 Taxation of Social Security Benefits

A portion (up to 85%) of the Social Security retirement income benefit is includable in the worker's adjusted gross income for tax purposes. Various formulas apply depending on the level of adjusted gross income, whether the taxpayer is married or single, and if married, whether filing separate or joint returns.

Exercise 14.A

1. Alfred was born in 1954. What is his "normal retirement age" according to Social Security?
   A. 62
   B. 65
   C. 66
   D. 67
2. What are the 3 main types of Social Security benefits?
   A. Life insurance, disability, retirement
   B. Retirement, survivors, disability
   C. Retirement, disability, Medicaid
   D. Death benefits, Medicaid, retirement

Answers to the exercises can be found at the end of the Unit 14 answers and rationales.

14. 12 TAX CONSIDERATIONS

14. 12. 1 Individual Life Insurance

Values included in the insured estate With respect to federal estate taxes, life insurance proceeds are subject to inclusion in the deceased's estate for federal estate tax purposes if any of the following apply.

- The estate was the named beneficiary.
- The deceased was the policyowner.
- The deceased transferred the policy to another person within three years of death.

In contrast, many individually owned life insurance policies could be subject to estate taxes because the insured is often the policyowner. However, agents should be aware that because of the federal "unified tax credit," estate taxes should only be a concern for those with significant assets.

Cash surrender value If a policyowner surrenders a policy for its cash value, some of the cash value received may be subject to ordinary income tax if it exceeds the sum of the premiums paid for the policy. Generally, the amount equal to premium payments is not taxable. Any additional amount in excess of the premium payments made would be taxable as income.

Policy loans Policy loans under life insurance policies are not taxable as income because they are treated as a debt against the policy. Under contract terms, policy loans must be paid back with interest in order to maintain policy values. Otherwise, outstanding loans reduce any available death benefit.

14. 12. 1. 1 Modified Endowment Contract

To discourage the use of life insurance contracts with high premiums as investments, federal law subjects all permanent policies to a test. A life insurance policy that fails the test will be considered a **modified endowment contract (MEC),** which makes the policy subject to less favorable tax treatment. A policy that passes the seven-pay test is not an MEC.

Before this test, single premium life policies and other types of limited-pay contracts were taxed the same as other life insurance policies. A policyowner was able to borrow (make withdrawals, and so forth) from the policy's cash value without paying tax.

A modified endowment contract is a life insurance policy with premiums that exceed what would have been paid to fund a similar type of life insurance policy with seven annual premiums (the seven-pay test). For example, if the total aggregate premiums paid at any time during the policy's initial seven years exceed the total premium that would have been paid on a seven-year level annual premium basis for the same period, the contract will not meet the required seven-pay test and will be considered a modified endowment contract.

Modified endowment contract tax treatment makes the utilization of a high premium life policy as a short term investment less attractive because it will be more costly. Funds withdrawn are subject to last-in first-out (LIFO) tax treatment, which assumes that the investment or earnings portion of the contract's values is withdrawn first (making these funds fully taxable as ordinary income) before the insured's *basis* (the total amount of premiums paid; the insured's basis in the contract is always returned without being subject to income taxation).

In addition to paying income tax on withdrawn amounts, a penalty of 10% is imposed on the total withdrawals, basis, and growth made prior to age 59½. Because it is more costly, the return on investment experienced by an MEC policyowner will be less. Like an annuity, the cash value buildup accumulates tax free unless it is withdrawn.

Once a policy is classified as a modified endowment contract, it will remain an MEC forever, and it will also automatically make any policy subsequently received in exchange for it a modified endowment contract, even if the new policy would otherwise pass the seven-pay test.

14. 12. 1. 2 Premiums

Premiums paid for individual life insurance are considered to be a personal expense and are not tax deductible.

When a business buys group term life insurance for its employees, premiums are generally considered a necessary business expense and are tax deductible. However, when a business buys life insurance to perpetuate the business (for example, under a buy-sell agreement), the premiums are considered to be a capital investment and are not tax deductible.

14. 12. 1. 3 Policy Proceeds

Proceeds Life insurance proceeds may or may not be subject to federal income taxes and/or estate taxes. Generally, the following rules apply with respect to federal income taxes:

- **Lump sum settlements** are not taxable as income. This is true whether the policy is an individually owned contract or a business owned policy. Thus, an individual or corporate beneficiary pays no federal income tax on life insurance proceeds.
- **Installment payments** are partially taxable as income. Whenever life insurance proceeds are taken other than in a lump sum, part of the proceeds received will be tax free and part will be taxable. The basic concept is that the principal (the face amount) is returned tax free. However, each installment received is part principal and part interest, and the interest portion of the installment is taxable as income.

14. 12. 1. 4 Accelerated Benefits

Accelerated, or living, benefits paid by a life insurance policy fall into the same category as a policy's death benefits—that is, accelerated benefits are received income tax free as long as they are qualified. **Qualified** means the insured has been certified by a physician as having an illness or physical condition that can reasonably be expected to result in death 24 months or less after the date of the certification. Other stipulations may be applied, but the end result is that those who require access to these benefits may receive the money without having to pay income taxes on it.

14. 12. 1. 5 Dividends and Surrender Values

Dividends paid to participating policyowners are generally not taxable as income. They are considered a return of premium. However, any interest earned on dividends is taxable, so the accumulation at interest dividend option explained earlier would incur income tax liability for the interest earned on the accumulated dividends.

Any dividend of an MEC that the insurer keeps to pay principal or interest on a policy loan is, just like the loan itself, considered to be money taken from the policy.

Generally speaking, when any proceeds are received from a surrendered or matured life insurance policy, the part of the proceeds, if any, that exceeds the cost of the policy is subject to ordinary federal income tax in the year received. Cost is equal to the total premiums paid (not including costs for qualified additional benefits) less the sum of any amounts previously received under the contract that were not includable in gross income.

Suppose Olaf surrenders his whole life policy, and it has a cash value of $25,000. During the time he held the policy, Olaf paid $22,000 in premiums. As a result, $3,000 ($25,000 less $22,000) of the cash surrender value will be subject to federal income tax.

14. 12. 1. 6 Annuity Payments

Like income payments made as a result of a settlement option in a life insurance policy, income payments made from an annuity are only partly subject to federal income taxation. Federal tax law holds that a fixed part of each annuity income payment is designated as a return of capital and as such is nontaxable. The remainder of each annuity income payment is considered to be income and is taxable.

14. 12. 1. 7 Cash Value Accumulation

One of the most significant advantages of life insurance products is their ability to accumulate cash on a tax-deferred basis. Permanent life products, including variable and universal life products, may accumulate cash values that are not taxed unless and until withdrawn. The same is true of annuities, qualified retirement plans, and IRAs. All of a policyholder's current earnings are working for the policyholder, unreduced by a current tax liability.

Note, however, that annuities owned by corporations, for whatever purpose, do not accumulate cash on a tax-deferred basis.

Bank accounts, stocks and bonds, and other kinds of noninsurance investments pay interest or dividends that are taxed currently.

Exercise 14.B

Circle the correct answer for each question below.

1. Lump sum settlements are/are not taxable as income.
2. Accelerated benefits are/are not received income tax free.
3. Dividends are/are not taxable as income.
4. Life insurance proceeds are/are not included in the deceased's estate for federal estate tax purposes.

Answers to the exercises can be found at the end of the Unit 14 answers and rationales.

14. 13 GROUP LIFE INSURANCE

Proceeds from a group life policy, like those from an individual life policy, are not subject to federal income tax when received by the beneficiary as a lump-sum payment.

Premiums for group life insurance policies, whether paid by the employer entirely or shared by employer and employee, are not deductible by the employee, but a company can deduct such premium payments as a business expense.

When all or part of the premiums for group life insurance are paid by the employer, these contributions are generally not considered as income to the employees covered by the group life policy. However, this rule applies only to the first $50,000 of employer-provided coverage. The cost of coverage in excess of $50,000 will be taxed to the employee.

14. 14 DOCTRINE OF ECONOMIC BENEFIT

This rule holds that if an employee receives property or benefit in lieu of income and that property or benefit would have been taxable income if it were received in cash, an economic benefit has been received and will be taxed accordingly.

Nonqualified plans, such as deferred compensation, that are funded with life insurance and aimed at certain key and/or highly compensated employees, may be affected by this rule. Qualified plans containing insurance on the life of the plan participant also may be affected. Care must be taken if those employees are to escape current taxation on such plans.

14.15 FEDERAL ESTATE TAX

Federal estate taxes are imposed on estates that exceed certain amounts. Life insurance proceeds are includable in a deceased insured's gross estate:

- if the proceeds are payable to the estate, either directly or indirectly;
- if the deceased possessed any incidents of ownership in the policy at death (such as the rights to change the beneficiary, to assign the policy, or to borrow against the policy); or
- if the policy was assigned by the insured, other than for full and adequate consideration, within three years of death.

14.16 CHARITABLE USES OF LIFE INSURANCE

There are two basic ways to make charitable gifts of life insurance. The first is to make an outright gift of a policy on the life of the donor. The value of the policy at the time of the gift is generally deductible, with certain restrictions. The charity (the donee) is the beneficiary. The donor may give the charity enough cash each year to pay the premium on the policy; if so, the cash gifts are generally deductible.

When this method of giving is used, it is important that the donee, the charity, be given all the rights of ownership. If the donor retains any control over the policy, the tax advantages (deductions) are lost.

In the second method, the donor can retain ownership of the policy, make the charity the beneficiary, and continue to pay the premiums. In this case, the premium payments are not tax deductible. The amount of the proceeds will be included in the donor's estate but will wash out as a charitable deduction. One advantage of this method is that the donor retains the right to change beneficiaries if this becomes necessary or desirable. The principal disadvantage is that premium payments are not deductible.

14.17 GIFTS OF LIFE INSURANCE

Anyone who makes a gift of a large amount may have to pay a gift tax. Probably the most common method of making a gift of life insurance to someone other than a charity is literally to give a policy to the donee. If this gift involves the transfer of all the incidents of ownership from the donor to the donee, the gift will probably qualify for a present interest gift tax exclusion, and the donor will not incur gift tax liability. This is true unless the replacement value of the policy, which is usually about equal to the cash value, is more than a certain threshold ($13,000 in 2010 or $26,000 for a joint/split gift by a donor and spouse).

The second most common method of making a gift of life insurance is to make a gift of the premiums on the insurance. As long as the amount of premium paid by the donor, plus all other gifts made during the same year to the same donee, is equal to or less than the annual gift tax exclusion, the donor should not incur federal gift tax liability.

A donor (or donors) may continue to make a tax-free gift of insurance premiums of up to $13,000 ($26,000 for donor and spouse) each year as long as desired. The recipient of the gift does not have to pay income tax on the gift.

14. 18 TRANSFER FOR VALUE RULES

Lump sum life insurance proceeds may not be exempt from income taxes if the benefit payment results from a transfer for value. If the benefits were transferred to a person in exchange for valuable consideration (such as money, services, or something else of value), the proceeds would be taxable as income. This section of the tax laws is designed to prevent a tax exemption for benefits that are purchased from another party because the intent of the transaction would be to exchange something of value for tax free income.

Any profit received by the investor would be taxable as income.

Exceptions to the transfer of value rule include an assignment of benefits as collateral security, transfers between a policyholder and an insured, and transfers to a partner or a corporation of the insured.

14. 19 SECTION 1035 (POLICY EXCHANGES)

Under Section 1035(a) of the Internal Revenue Code, certain exchanges of insurance policies and annuities may occur as nontaxable exchanges. Generally, if a policyowner exchanges a life insurance policy for another life policy with the same insured and beneficiary and a gain is realized, it will not be taxed as income under section 1035(a).

Policies that do qualify as a 1035(a) exchange are:

- a cash value life insurance policy to another cash value life insurance policy;
- a cash value life insurance policy to an annuity; and
- an annuity to another annuity.

14. 20 BUSINESS INSURANCE

The premiums paid by companies for life insurance policies used for business purposes are generally not deductible as business expenses, with the exception of group insurance. By the same token, the proceeds from life policies purchased for business purposes are received by the company income tax free.

Policy proceeds are usually not includable in the estate of an individual insured by a business unless the individual possessed some *incident of ownership* in the policy. This is true even if the insured was the owner or one of the owners of the business.

Exercise 14.C

1. Which of the following would NOT qualify as a 1035 exchange?
   A. A cash value life insurance policy to another cash value life insurance policy
   B. A cash value life insurance policy to an annuity
   C. An annuity to cash value life insurance policy
   D. An annuity to another annuity

Answers to the exercises can be found at the end of the Unit 14 answers and rationales.

UNIT TEST

1. How many quarters of coverage does a person need to be fully insured?
   A. 10
   B. 20
   C. 30
   D. 40

2. Carol is eligible for a retirement benefit based on her own earnings and also a benefit based on her late husband's earnings. Carol will receive
   A. both benefits
   B. only the benefit based on her own earnings
   C. only the benefit based on her husband's earnings
   D. only the larger benefit

3. A person who begins receiving retirement benefits at normal retirement age receives what percentage of PIA as a retirement benefit?
   A. 50%
   B. 75%
   C. 100%
   D. 150%

4. At what age can a surviving spouse who is disabled start receiving survivor benefits if the deceased was fully insured?
   A. 50
   B. 55
   C. 60
   D. 65

5. At what age can a surviving spouse who is not disabled start receiving survivor benefits if the deceased was fully insured?
   A. 60
   B. 62
   C. 65
   D. 67

6. Social Security taxes are often shared between the employer and employee. What do self-employed people pay?
   A. Just the employee's portion of the tax
   B. Just the employer's portion of the tax
   C. Both the employer's portion and the employee's portion of the tax
   D. Neither the employer's portion nor the employee's portion of the tax

7. Which of the following people would NOT be eligible for benefits under Social Security?
   A. Steve, 45, who loses his currently insured wife while still raising two young children
   B. Tina, 6, whose fully insured parent is killed in an auto accident
   C. Clarice, 60, whose fully insured son supported her
   D. Alice, 50, who is fully insured when she is disabled by cancer that is expected to kill her before she can return to work

8. At what age is an individual eligible to receive full Social Security retirement benefits?
   A. 65
   B. 67
   C. Nominal retirement age
   D. Normal retirement age

9. Social Security benefits are expressed as a percentage of
   A. the primary insurance amount
   B. the presiding insurance amount
   C. the potential insurance amount
   D. the preferred insurance amount

10. Disability benefits under Social Security require at least
    A. a 3-month waiting period
    B. a 5-month waiting period
    C. a 7-month waiting period
    D. a 12-month waiting period

11. The penalties assessed against MECs primarily affect
    A. the cost basis of the policy
    B. money put into the policy
    C. money taken out of the policy
    D. the death benefits of the policy

12. As a general rule, for federal tax purposes
    A. neither life insurance nor annuity premiums is tax deductible
    B. life insurance premiums are tax deductible but annuity premiums are not
    C. annuity premiums are tax deductible but life insurance premiums are not
    D. both life insurance and annuity premiums are tax deductible

13. Billy is receiving the proceeds of a life insurance policy as an income stream over a period of several years. What part of the money will be subject to tax?
    A. None of it; it is life insurance proceeds
    B. All of it; it is being paid out in an income stream
    C. Only the part that represents income earned on the original death benefit
    D. Only the part that represents the original death benefit and not the income earned on the original death benefit

ANSWERS AND RATIONALES TO UNIT TEST

1. **D.** To be fully insured, a person must have 40 quarters of coverage. A person can accumulate one quarter of coverage each year after their 21st birthday.

2. **D.** A person who is eligible to receive more than one Social Security benefit is entitled to receive only the larger of the two benefit amounts.

3. **C.** A person who retires at normal retirement age receives 100% of PIA as a retirement benefit.

4. **A.** A surviving spouse who is disabled can start receiving survivor benefits at age 50 if the deceased was fully insured.

5. **A.** A surviving spouse who is not disabled can begin receiving survivor benefits at age 60.

6. **C.** Self-employed people pay both the employer's portion and the employee's portion.

7. **C.** Social Security survivors benefits can only be paid to a dependent parent age 62 or older.

8. **D.** An individual is eligible to receive full Social Security retirement benefits when that person reaches normal retirement age.

9. **A.** Social Security benefits are expressed as a percentage of the primary insurance amount.

10. **B.** Disability benefits under Social Security require at least a 5-month waiting period.

11. **C.** The penalties assessed against MECs primarily affect money taken out of the policy.

12. **A.** As a general rule, for federal tax purposes, neither life insurance nor annuity premium is tax deductible.

13. **C.** Only the part that represents income earned on the original death benefit is subject to tax.

UNIT 14 EXERCISE ANSWERS

Exercise 14.A

1. **C.** Individuals born in 1954 have a normal retirement age of 66 years.

2. **B.** The 3 most common types of Social Security benefits are retirement, survivors, and disability benefits.

Exercise 14.B

1. are not
2. are
3. are not
4. are

Exercise 14.C

1. **C.** "Annuity to cash value life insurance" would not qualify as a 1035 exchange.

15

Retirement Plans

15. 1 LEARNING OBJECTIVES

After completing this lesson, you will be able to:

- describe qualified and nonqualified retirement plans;
- list the benefits of qualified retirement plans;
- explain profit-sharing plans, pension plans, and 401(k) plans;
- explain IRAs, SIMPLE plans, and Keogh plans;
- explain who is eligible to establish a tax-deferred annuity arrangement and how such a plan works;
- explain the rules governing plan distributions;
- explain when and how plan benefits are taxed; and
- explain rollovers.

15. 2 QUALIFIED AND NONQUALIFIED RETIREMENT PLANS

Life insurance companies play a major role in retirement planning, as the products and contracts offered provide ideal funding or financing vehicles for both individual plans and employer-sponsored plans. Retirement plans can be divided into two categories:

Non-qualified plan—A non-qualified plan does not meet federal guidelines and is not eligible for certain tax benefits.

Qualified plan—A qualified plan is one that, by design or definition, meets certain requirements established by the federal government and, consequently, receives favorable tax treatment.

Regulation of Qualified Plans The Employee Retirement Income Security Act (ERISA) of 1974 provides much of the regulation for qualified plans. ERISA establishes certain reporting and disclosure requirements for employer sponsored plans. The reporting provisions are based on specific requirements of the US Department of Labor and the Internal Revenue Service. In addition, specific disclosure information is required to be provided to plan participants. These regulations specify eligibility requirements, contribution limitations, tax rules, vesting considerations, and penalties for non-compliance with qualified plan requirements. It should be remembered that laws, especially the tax laws, change periodically. Thus, eligibility or contribution requirements and limitations may change over time, as may the tax status of some of these qualified plans.

General qualification requirements for employer-sponsored retirement plans include the following.

- The plan must be for the exclusive benefit of the employees and their beneficiaries.
- The plan must be communicated to employees in writing and be permanent.

- The plan must be established by the employer.
- The plan must not discriminate in contributions or benefits on the basis of income or sex.
- The plan must have a defined vesting schedule.
- The plan must be approved by the IRS.

Common characteristics of a qualified retirement plan include the following.

- Employer contributions to a qualified retirement plan are considered a deductible business expense, which lowers the business's income taxes.
- The earnings of a qualified plan are exempt from income taxation for the employee and the accumulated values grow tax deferred.
- Employer contributions to a qualified plan are not currently taxable to the employee in the years they are contributed, but these contributions are taxable when they are paid as a benefit (and, typically, when the employee is retired and in a lower tax bracket).
- Contributions to an individual qualified plan, such as an individual retirement account or annuity (IRA), are deductible from income under certain conditions.

If a plan does not meet the specific requirements set forth by the federal government, it is termed a nonqualified plan and, thus, is not eligible for favorable tax treatment.

Within the qualified category are two kinds of overall plans:

- Defined-benefit plans
- Defined-contribution plans

A **defined benefit plan** is a qualified plan in which the employer agrees to make necessary contributions on behalf of eligible employees in order to provide a specific retirement benefit. The amount of the retirement benefit is clearly defined (usually as a percentage of salary), but the amount of the employer's contribution is not specifically known.

A defined benefit plan defines how much a participant can receive at retirement (money-out).

A **defined contribution plan** is a qualified retirement plan in which the employer agrees to make a specific contribution on behalf of all eligible employees, which is usually expressed as a percentage of compensation. The amount of the contribution is clearly specified, but the amount of the retirement benefits to be received is not specified.

A defined contribution plan defines how much a participant can contribute to their plan (money in).

A company has a number of defined-benefit and defined-contribution plans from which it can choose, as shown by the following chart.

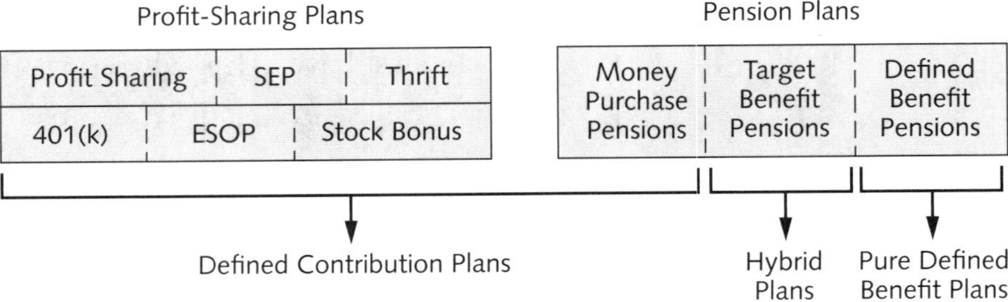

15. 3 VESTING

Corporate plans typically include a **vesting schedule**, which reflects the employee percentage of ownership in benefits resulting from employer contributions.

An employee is always 100% vested in the employee's own contributions. Any funds an employer contributes to a retirement account are only available to the employee after a certain number of years. Vesting is regulated by the IRS.

15. 4 DEFINED BENEFIT PLANS

15. 4. 1 Group Deferred Annuity

Defined benefit plans are designed to provide a specific benefit to an employee upon retirement.

Funding for defined benefit plans can be provided through either a **group deferred annuity** or an individual deferred annuity, among other ways. With a **group deferred annuity**, the employer holds a master contract and certificates of participation are given to the persons covered by the plan. Specified amounts of deferred annuity are purchased each year in order to provide a specified retirement income to an employee.

15. 4. 2 Individual Deferred Annuity

Another means of funding a defined benefit plan is to take out individual deferred annuities on each plan participant. The premium rate is determined individually, on the basis of attained age and sex. Premiums are level to retirement.

15. 5 DEFINED CONTRIBUTION PLANS

15. 5. 1 Profit-Sharing Plans

An employer may elect to establish a qualified profit-sharing plan, under which contributions to the plan are made only if profits are realized. Generally, the contribution consists of a specified proportion of company profits, and the maximum contribution per employee is expressed as a percentage of compensation (such as 10% of salary). However, the contribution is contingent on profitability. If profits are inadequate in a given year, the specified share might only fund a lesser proportion of employee compensation (such as 6%). If there are no profits at all, there would be no contribution for that year.

In contrast to pension plan obligations, a profit-sharing plan is not a fixed liability. Profit-sharing plans frequently require an immediate distribution of each employee's share on an annual basis, in which case the amounts received are taxed as current income to the employees. These plans are not necessarily designed to provide retirement benefits—it is not a requirement. In some cases, they are set up to accumulate the profit-sharing proceeds for the purposes of later paying benefits at retirement.

15. 5. 2 Pension Plans

Pension plans are established and maintained by employers interested in providing systematically for the payment of definitely determinable benefits to retired employees over a period of years—usually for life. Retirement benefits are generally based on such factors as years of service and compensation.

Money purchase plans are considered defined contribution plans with required (as opposed to discretionary) contributions. A money purchase plan states the required contribution percentage. For example, a money purchase plan that has a contribution of 5% of each eligible employee's pay would require the employer to make a contribution of 5% of each eligible employee's pay into each employee's separate account. A participant's benefit is based on the amount of contributions to the account over time and the gains or losses associated with the account at time of retirement.

A target benefit pension plan is a cross between a defined-contribution and defined-benefit plan that works much like a money purchase plan except that a target benefit is specified. This target benefit looks like a defined-benefit plan, but it's only a target and may or may not be reached.

15. 5. 2. 1 401(k) Plans

A type of elective deferral (salary reduction) plan used in larger employee groups is known as a 401(k) plan. The name comes from the section of the tax code that enables these plans. A 401(k) plan allows an employee to reduce his compensation by a stated percentage and have this amount placed in the 401(k) plan on a tax deductible and tax deferred basis. Often the employer will match employee contributions by contributing a percentage or dollar amount, such as $.50 for each $1 contributed by an employee.

15.6 INDIVIDUAL RETIREMENT ACCOUNTS AND ANNUITIES

IRAs are qualified retirement plans available to individuals. IRAs help individuals save money to finance their retirement by allowing them to make pre-tax contributions to the IRA. An IRA allows an individual to contribute 100% of that person's earned income (wages) up to the *limits* (a specific dollar amount) established by the IRS. Almost any individual with *earned income* (wages) who is under the age of 70½ is eligible to open an IRA.

Contributions to an IRA could be tax deductible depending on the income level of the participant and the participant's spouse if married. For example, contributions are tax deductible/or partially tax deductible if the following apply.

IRA contributions are always tax deductible if the participant is not eligible to contribute to an employer sponsored plan, regardless of the participant's income.

IRA contributions are tax deductible to an individual who has a qualified plan only if the individual's income level is below a level set by the IRS.

An individual may still make non-deductible contributions to an IRA account (either in excess of or in lieu of any allowed deduction) and enjoy tax deferred growth on the money. For a married couple, an individual account must be set up for each person, even if only one spouse is working.

Other tax considerations:

- Because an IRA is a qualified plan, the same rule regarding early withdrawal penalties and exceptions apply.
- Distributions must be made by April 1 following the year the participant turns age 70½ or a 50% excise tax will be assessed on the amount that should have been withdrawn.
- If the beneficiary is the spouse, the spouse can collect the interest in an IRA starting no later than December 31 of the year immediately following the owner's death or no later than December 31 of the calendar year in which the owner would have reached age 70½.
- If the beneficiary is anyone other than a spouse, the entire interest must be paid in full on or before December 31 of the calendar year of the fifth anniversary of the owner's death.

15. 6. 1 Income Limits for IRA Deductibility

AGI Phase-Out Levels for Traditional IRA Deductions

Individuals who are actively participating in an employer-sponsored retirement plan will see the deductible portion of their traditional IRA contributions reduced or phased out once their adjusted gross incomes exceed certain threshold levels. Those with AGIs above these levels cannot take any IRA deduction. For 2008, these threshold levels are:

	Full Deduction Allowed	Partial Deduction Allowed	No Deduction Allowed
Filing Status	AGI level	AGI level	AGI level
Single	\$0–\$53,000	\$53,001–\$63,000	\$63,001 and above
Married, filing jointly 2008	\$0–\$85,000	\$85,001–\$105,000	\$105,001 and above

Popular vehicles used to fund an IRA include:

- mutual funds;
- bank, savings and loan, or credit union accounts or CDs;
- bank trust accounts; and
- fixed or variable flexible-premium annuities.

15. 7 ROTH IRAs

A new kind of IRA was phased in January 1, 1998. Roth IRAs are different that a traditional IRA in the fact that contributions to the Roth IRA are not tax deductible but distributions are received tax free (this includes contributions and interest earned). Roth contribution limits are set by the IRS. Interest earned and distributions made are tax free if the IRA is maintained for at least five years and the distribution meets specific qualifications (the attainment of age 59½, death, disability, the purchase of a first home, or qualified higher education expenses). There is no requirement in a Roth IRA for distributions to begin before age 70½.

15. 8 SIMPLE RETIREMENT PLANS

SIMPLE (Savings Incentive Match Plan for Employees) IRA A SIMPLE IRA is a simplified retirement plan for small employers (100 or fewer employees) who do not have another type of retirement plan available to their employees. A SIMPLE plan may be structured as an IRA or a 401(k), and allows for elective contributions by employees as well as matching or nonelective contributions by employers. Plans must meet vesting and participation requirements, but they are generally not subject to the nondiscrimination rules applicable to other qualified plans.

Employee contributions to a SIMPLE IRA may only be made through a qualified salary deduction plan, according to a set percentage of compensation not to exceed a determined amount set by the IRS annually. Employer contributions may be made either as dollar-for-dollar matching contributions (up to 3% of employee compensation), or a nonelective contribution of 2% for each eligible employee.

All contributions must be nonforfeitable and are vested immediately. However, the premature distribution penalty is 25% during the first two years of participation.

IRAs may be funded by individual retirement annuities, mutual funds, trust accounts, or other financial institution accounts.

15. 9 SIMPLIFIED EMPLOYEE PENSIONS (SEPs)

Under a simplified employee pension plan (SEP), a small employer can contribute specific amounts directly into IRA accounts on behalf of eligible employees. This is a simplified method of establishing a pension plan because an IRA is already a qualified plan and it is easier for an employer to establish and administer.

Contributions to the plan are not included in the employee's taxable income for the year made, to the extent that the contribution does not exceed 25% of the employee's compensation or $40,000.

Distributions from the plan will be taxable as current income when received after retirement. Once an SEP is established, the employer must make contributions for each employee who is at least 21 years of age, who has performed services for the employer during the current year, and has performed services for at least three of the previous five years.

15. 10 KEOGH PLANS

The Self-Employed Individuals Tax Retirement Act of 1962, known popularly as the Keogh Act, makes a special type of retirement plan available for non-incorporated businesses. A Keogh plan (or an **HR-10**) is a qualified retirement plan for self-employed individuals and their eligible employees, if any. Examples of self-employed individuals include sole proprietors, partnerships, farmers, or professionals such as doctors and lawyers. In order to be eligible for to participate in a Keogh an employee must:

- be at least 21 years old;
- have worked for the company for at least one year; and
- work 1,000 hours or more in a year.

The exception to this is if someone owns at least 10% of the business, that person is still eligible for a Keogh plan. Under a Keogh plan, an employer must contribute the same percentage to their employees as they contribute to their own plan, As an example, if an employer contributes a specific dollar amount to his own plan, then he must contribute the same dollar amount to his employee's plan. Like all qualified plans, Keogh plans are subject to contribution limits set by the IRS.

15. 11 TAX-DEFERRED ANNUITY ARRANGEMENTS (403(b) ARRANGEMENTS)

Under a 403(b) plan, employees of organizations such as school systems, churches, and hospitals are eligible to set aside portions of their current income by means of a salary reduction or an elective deferral. This elective deferral is not currently taxed, will grow tax deferred, and will be taxed as current income when received at retirement. Salary reduction deferrals by an individual may not exceed $15,000 per year.

15. 12 SECTION 529 PLANS

One of the most powerful vehicles for providing for higher education expenses is a Section 529 plan, named for the tax code that governs it. Although the formal name for such plans is Qualified Tuition Programs (QTPs), they are most often referred to as Section 529 Plans.

There are two types of Section 529 or Qualified Tuition Plans: prepaid tuition plans and college savings plans. *Prepaid tuition plans* allow contributors to prepay college tuition and other fees for a designated beneficiary for a set number of academic periods or course units while locking in current tuition costs. *College savings plans* allow contributors to invest after-tax dollars in professionally managed accounts that contain a mix of stocks, bonds, and other investments. Contributors assume both inflation and investment risk.

Section 529 plans don't restrict eligibility or limit the amount of contribution based on the income of the contributor. State residency also is not a restriction. A contributor can open a Section 529 plan in any state and the beneficiary can use the funds to attend college anywhere.

The beneficiary of a Section 529 plan does not need to report income when withdrawals are used for qualified college costs.

15. 13 PLAN DISTRIBUTIONS

Since qualified plans are designed as retirement plans, a tax penalty is imposed for early withdrawals by an individual—all withdrawals are taxable as current income, but any withdrawal before age 59½ is subject to an additional tax penalty of 10% of the amount withdrawn. However, no early withdrawal penalty is charged for the following exceptions:

- Medical expenses in excess of 10% of adjusted gross income
- Distributions toward the purchase of a first home
- Distributions used toward qualified higher education expenses
- Distributions due to death or disability of the participant

- Distributions to a former spouse or dependent child as a result of a divorce decree
- Distributions which are part of a series of periodic payments under a life annuity arrangement

There is a 6% excess contribution penalty that applies to IRAs. There is also a requirement that distributions from any qualified plan must begin at a certain age. For example, amounts in a traditional IRA must start to be withdrawn by April 1 of the year following the year in which the individual reaches age 70½; the individual must take a distribution from the account or at least begin a plan of distribution. Failure to do so results in a late withdrawal penalty equal to 50% of the amount that should have been received by the participant. Individuals over age 50 are allowed to make an additional contribution per year, called the catch-up provision.

Exercise 15.A
Match the plans with their descriptions.

____ 1. This plan, formally called a "Qualified Tuition Program" helps build funds for higher education.

____ 2. An elective deferral plan for employees of organizations such as school systems, churches, and hospitals

____ 3. A qualified retirement plan for self-employed individuals and their eligible employees

____ 4. A qualified plan in which a small employer contributes specific amounts directly into IRA accounts on behalf of eligible employees

____ 5. A type of IRA where contributions are not tax deductible but distributions are received tax free and where distributions do not have to begin before age 70½

____ 6. A type of elective deferral plan that allows an employee to reduce compensation by a stated percentage on a tax deductible/tax deferred basis; often the employer matches employee contributions

A. 401(k) Plan
B. Roth IRA
C. Section 529 Plan
D. 403(b) Plan
E. Keogh Plan
F. Simplified Employee Pension

Answers to the exercise can be found at the end of the Unit 15 answers and rationales.

15. 14 INCIDENTAL LIMITATIONS

Pension plans and other qualified plans may include incidental life insurance and health insurance benefits, but these must be incidental to the purpose of the plan; the primary purpose of the plan must be to provide retirement benefits.

For term and universal life policies, the death benefit is considered incidental if the aggregate premiums are less than 25% of the aggregate contributions for any participant. (Only the pure insurance portion of a UL premium is used in this calculation.) For whole life policies, the death benefit is incidental if the aggregate premiums are less than 50% of the aggregate contributions for any participant.

Another way to make the incidental determination is the 100-to-1-ratio test, which provides that life insurance is incidental to a qualified plan as long as the death benefit does not exceed 100 times the expected monthly benefit.

A portion of the cost for life insurance provided under a qualified pension or profit-sharing plan may be included as part of an employee's taxable income for the year. However, the employee only pays tax on the cost of that portion of insurance protection that provides an economic benefit to the employee, such as any death benefit payable to the employee's beneficiary or estate. The cost for any benefits that are payable to the plan, trustee, or employer, such as key person life insurance, is not taxable as income to the employee.

To the extent that the cost for incidental life insurance protection is taxable as current income to the employee, the employee only pays tax on the cost for pure protection. For cash value insurance, the taxable cost would be the one-year term rate for the amount of protection at risk (face value minus accumulated cash value), regardless of the premium actually being paid by the plan. For term insurance, the full premium for amounts payable for the employees' benefit is taxable because it represents the cost for pure protection.

15. 15 TAXATION OF PLAN BENEFITS

Now let's look at the tax treatment of funds paid to plan participants at retirement. The only funds that escape taxation at distribution are those that have already been taxed. For example, some plans allow participants to make voluntary, after-tax contributions to their plans. These funds would not be taxed at distribution.

Distributions may be made in the form of annuity installments or, in the case of a defined contribution plan, in a lump sum. Those made in the form of installments may be made partially income tax free. The portion of each payment that represents money that has already been taxed to the recipient, if any, is excluded from gross income. The remainder is taxed as ordinary income in the recipient's tax bracket.

Distributions from a qualified retirement plan may also be triggered by the plan participant's death. Lump-sum distributions of plan benefits upon a participant's death are considered *income in respect of a decedent* and are generally subject to income tax when received by the estate or other beneficiaries, less any amount the plan participant contributed using after-tax dollars. An itemized deduction may be available to the beneficiary for any federal estate taxes paid on income in respect of a decedent, even if the beneficiary is not the one who paid the estate tax.

Tax treatment of benefits received as annuity installments by beneficiaries after the plan participant's death are usually treated like those received by the participant—a portion of the payments may be income tax free if the participant made contributions to the plan with after-tax dollars.

15. 15. 1 Rollovers

There is one major exception to the various annual contribution limitations that have been discussed with respect to qualified plans: permitted rollovers and transfers from one plan to another. The main difference between a rollover and a transfer is the party who receives the qualified plan funds and the tax consequences associated with doing a rollover compared to a transfer.

A **rollover** is a tax free withdrawal of cash or other assets from one retirement program and its reinvestment in another retirement program. The amount rolled over is not counted as current income and is not taxable until later withdrawn. However, a rollover must be completed within 60 days after the distribution is received, or else the full amount becomes taxable as current income.

A **transfer** occurs when amounts in a qualified plan are transferred into another qualified plan. For example, when an employee changes jobs and the new employer's plan allows for acceptance of transferred amounts, a transfer occurs. A transfer is a distribution that goes directly from one qualified plan sponsor to another qualified plan sponsor. The participant is never in possession of the funds.

15. 15. 1. 1 IRS Rules

A participant must complete a rollover to another qualified plan within 60 days or the distribution is considered a nonqualified distribution and is subject to taxes and penalties.

Qualified rollovers must include the total amount that was in the account. This includes the 20% withheld plus 80% received by plan participant or else there will be taxes and penalties on any portion of the total amount that was not reinvested within 60 days.

A plan sponsor must withhold 20% of the distribution in federal taxes on a rollover, and there is no withholding on a transfer. Once the rollover takes place to the new custodian, the remainder of the distribution is made.

15. 16 THE EMPLOYEE RETIREMENT INCOME SECURITY ACT (ERISA)

ERISA was enacted to protect the interests of participants in employee benefit plans as well as the interests of the participants' beneficiaries. Much of the law deals with qualified pension plans, but some sections also apply to group insurance plans.

15. 16. 1 Fiduciary Responsibility

ERISA mandates very detailed standards for fiduciaries and other parties-in-interest of employee welfare benefit plans, including group insurance plans. This means that anyone with control over plan management or plan assets of any kind must discharge that fiduciary duty solely in the interests of the plan participants and their beneficiaries. Strict penalties are imposed on those who do not fulfill this responsibility.

15. 16. 2 Reporting and Disclosure

ERISA requires that certain information concerning any employee welfare benefit plan, including group insurance plans, be made available to plan participants, their beneficiaries, the Department of Labor, and the IRS. Examples of the types of information that must be distributed include:

- a summary plan description to each plan participant and the Department of Labor;
- a summary of material modifications that details changes in any plan description to each plan participant and the Department of Labor;
- an annual return or report (Form 5500 or one of its variations) submitted to the IRS;
- a summary annual report to each plan participant; and
- any terminal report to the IRS.

UNIT TEST

1. Curtis knows that when he retires, he will receive $100 a month for every year of service with his employer. This is an example of
   A. a defined-benefit plan
   B. a defined-contribution plan
   C. a profit-sharing plan
   D. a money purchase plan

2. All of the following statements about profit-sharing plans are correct EXCEPT
   A. such plans are established by employer's so employees can participate in company profits
   B. the amount of annual contributions is set by law
   C. the plan must provide a formula for allocating contributions to the plan among plan participants
   D. plan contributions are held in trust

3. At what age can people begin making catch-up contributions to their retirement plans?
   A. 50
   B. 55
   C. 60
   D. 65

4. Which of the following types of retirement plans does NOT have a mechanism for making catch-up contributions past a certain age?
   A. IRA
   B. Roth IRA
   C. SIMPLE plan
   D. SEP

5. Who may contribute to an IRA?
   A. Anybody with earned income
   B. Only people who don't participate in company retirement plans
   C. Only people who earn less than certain specified amounts
   D. Only people who are self-employed

6. Under which of the following circumstances are qualified plan distributions likely to receive a tax penalty?
   A. Premature distributions only
   B. Late distributions only
   C. Both A and B
   D. Neither A nor B

7. Premature distribution from a qualified plan or an IRA can result in the amount being taxed as income plus a penalty tax of
   A. 5%
   B. 10%
   C. 15%
   D. 25%

8. A rollover from one IRA to another or from a qualified plan to an IRA must be accomplished within how many days if the owner is to avoid an income tax liability on the amount rolled over?
   A. 10
   B. 30
   C. 60
   D. 90

9. At what age is an individual no longer subject to early withdrawal penalties under an IRA?
   A. 55
   B. 55½
   C. 59
   D. 59½

10. Which of the following organizations would be eligible to offer a 403(b) arrangement?
    A. Fire department
    B. Public school system
    C. Any small business
    D. Any corporation

11. Carmen owns a business that provides a retirement plan to its employees whereby the business makes contributions of up to 25% of the total compensation paid to all participating employees to IRA plans owned by the individual employees. Carmen's plan is most likely
    A. a SIMPLE plan
    B. a Keogh plan
    C. a 403(b) plan
    D. an SEP

12. Delbert is self-employed and sets up a retirement plan for himself. Delbert most likely sets up
    A. a SIMPLE plan
    B. a Keogh plan
    C. a 403(b) plan
    D. an SEP

13. Kim is required to take a $2,000 minimum annual distribution from her IRA. She fails to comply and only takes a $1,000 distribution. Because of this failure, Kim will be subject to
    A. a deductible excise tax of $1,000
    B. a nondeductible excise tax of $1,000
    C. a deductible excise tax of $500
    D. a nondeductible excise tax of $500

ANSWERS AND RATIONALES TO UNIT TEST

1. **A.** This is a defined benefit plan because it is designed to provide a specific benefit amount at retirement.

2. **B.** Under a defined contribution plan, the amount of any annual contributions is usually left to the employer's discretion.

3. **A.** People age 50 and up can make additional catch-up contributions.

4. **D.** SEPs do not provide for catch-up contributions.

5. **A.** Anybody with earned income may contribute to an IRA.

6. **C.** Tax penalties may apply to premature and late distributions.

7. **B.** Premature distribution from a qualified plan or an IRA can result in the amount being taxed as income plus a penalty tax of 10%.

8. **C.** A rollover from one IRA to another or from a qualified plan to an IRA must be accomplished within 60 days to avoid an income tax liability on the amount rolled over.

9. **D.** At age 59½ , an individual is no longer subject to early withdrawal penalties under an IRA.

10. **B.** A public school system is eligible to offer a 403(b) arrangement.

11. **D.** Carmen's plan is most likely an SEP.

12. **B.** A self-employed person will most likely set up a Keogh plan.

13. **D.** Kim is subject to a nondeductible excise tax of $500.

UNIT 15 EXERCISE ANSWERS

Exercise 15.A

1. **C**
2. **D**
3. **E**
4. **F**
5. **B**
6. **A**

UNIT

16

Health Insurance Basics

16. 1 INTRODUCTION

Health insurance provides payment of benefits for the loss of income and/or the medical expenses arising from illness or injury. Health insurance is often called accident and sickness insurance or accident and health insurance. Many different kinds of health insurance coverages are available. Health insurance varies according to the methods of underwriting, the injury or illness covered, the types of insurers, the types of benefits and services provided, the types of losses covered, and the amount of benefits available.

The basic perils that are designed to be covered in an accident and health policy are accidents and sicknesses. An accident is defined as bodily injury caused by something that is unexpected, unintentional, and unforeseen. A sickness is defined as a loss due to an illness or a disease. These terms become more defined in Unit 19, Disability Income Insurance.

16. 2 LEARNING OBJECTIVES

After completing this lesson, you will be able to:

- explain the risk that health insurance is designed to protect against;
- explain the difference between reimbursement, fee-for-service, and capitation payment;
- list and describe four typical HMO structures;
- describe the basic characteristics of preferred provider organizations (PPOs);
- list the types of benefits provided by Social Security;
- explain who is eligible for workers' compensation, and list the types of benefits provided under workers' compensation; and
- briefly explain who qualifies for Medicaid, the intent of the program, and how it functions.

16. 3 TYPES OF LOSSES AND BENEFITS

16. 3. 1 Loss of Income from Disability

Disability income insurance, also referred to as loss-of-time insurance, pays a weekly or monthly benefit for disabilities resulting from accident or sickness. The primary purpose of disability income coverage is to replace loss of personal income due to a disability.

Disability income policies are issued on an individual basis or on a group basis through an employer-sponsored plan, labor union, or association. Benefits paid are in accordance with the policy's provisions and, to a degree, the insured's loss of income.

16. 3. 2 Accidental Death and Dismemberment

AD&D policies (or riders) pay the policy's **principal sum** for accidental death in accordance with the policy's provisions and definition of accidental death. The **principal sum** is similar in meaning to a policy's face amount. This same amount is paid if the insured suffers the actual severance of two arms, two legs, or the loss of vision in two eyes due to an accident. This amount is usually identified as the **capital sum** if the policy is paying an accidental dismemberment benefit.

AD&D benefits may be included as riders on life insurance policies, as part of disability income insurance, as part of health insurance, or as a separate policy (a type of limited coverage).

16. 3. 3 Medical Expense Benefits

Medical expense insurance, commonly referred to as hospitalization insurance, provides benefits for expenses incurred as a result of in-hospital medical treatment and surgery as well as certain outpatient expenses such as doctor's visits, lab oratory tests, and diagnostic services. Hospitalization insurance may be issued as an individual policy covering all family members or as a group insurance policy provided through an employer-sponsored program.

When medical expense coverage for proprietors and partners is paid for by the business, the premiums have traditionally been considered tax deductible to the business but includable as income to the individual. There is no limit to the amount of tax-free medical expense benefits the individual can receive.

Medical expense insurance can be differentiated based on who is covered (insured versus subscriber) and who provides coverage (any provider versus limited choice of provider).

16. 3. 4 Dental Expense Benefits

Dental expense benefits are generally sold as part of group health insurance coverage. Most insurers do not provide individual dental policies. Dental benefits are offered for preventive maintenance (cleanings and x-rays), repair (e.g., fillings or root canals), and replacement of teeth.

16. 3. 5 Long-Term Care Insurance

Long-term care (LTC) insurance pays for the care of persons with chronic diseases or disabilities and may include a wide range of health and social services provided under the supervision of medical professionals. LTC insurance often covers nursing home care, home-based care, and respite care.

16. 3. 6 Limited Health Exposures and Insurance Contracts

A variety of special health insurance policies are available that provide limited coverage. To ensure that the insured has sufficient notice that the coverage is limited, every policy that provides limited coverage must, by law, state plainly on the first page of the policy, "THIS IS A LIMITED POLICY." A good way to remember these policies is by using the acronym HIT-ABCD.

Hospital income (hospital indemnity) insurance pays a specified sum on a daily, weekly, or monthly basis while the insured is confined to a hospital. The amount of the benefit is not related to expenses incurred or to wages lost while the insured is hospitalized.

Travel accident insurance provides coverage for death or injury resulting from accidents occurring while the insured is a fare-paying passenger on a common carrier.

Accident only insurance provides coverage for injury from accident and excludes sickness. Benefits may be paid for all or any of the following: death, disability, dismemberment, and hospital and medical expenses.

Blanket insurance is a form of group insurance. Often the individual's name is not known because the individuals come and go. Such groups include students, campers, passengers of a common carrier, volunteer groups, and sports teams. Unlike other group insurance, the individuals are automatically covered under the blanket policy and do not receive certificates of insurance.

Credit insurance is listed here because of the limited nature of its coverage. This policy is issued only to those who are in debt to a creditor. The coverage is limited to the total amount of the debtor's indebtedness.

Specified disease or **dread disease insurance** provides a variety of benefits for only certain diseases, usually cancer or heart disease.

16. 3. 7 Prescription Coverage

Prescription medication coverage is normally provided as an optional benefit under a group medical expense policy. The insured and eligible dependents are provided with a stated cost for any prescription medication required. This specific cost is usually $2, $3, or $5 per prescription. Thus, regardless of the cost of the medication, the insured only pays the stated amount, and the balance of the prescription cost is paid by the insurance company.

16. 3. 8 Vision Care

Relatively new to the array of health care benefits offered to groups is coverage for vision care. In fact, vision care coverage is available only on a group basis.

Although basic, comprehensive, and major medical policies often cover disease and injury to eyes, there is generally no coverage for eye exams and corrections such as eyeglasses or contact lenses. To close this gap, insurers may offer vision care policies, which usually cover:

- eye examinations;
- cost of lenses and frames;
- cost of contact lenses; and
- other corrective items.

Exercise 16.A

Six different common types of limited health policies can be remembered with the acronym HIT-ABCD. List the policies represented by each letter below.

1. H______________ I____________
2. T______________
3. A______________
4. B______________
5. C______________
6. D______________

Answers to the exercise can be found at the end of the Unit 16 answers and rationales.

16. 4 DETERMINING INSURANCE NEEDS

Health insurance is designed to protect the insured from the risk of medical and disability expenses.

Health insurance provides benefits exactly when needed. Disability income insurance can enable the insured to make mortgage payments and cover other necessary family expenses when total disability due to an accident or sickness cuts off the insured's income.

Medical expense insurance provides the insured with necessary funds to cover hospital and physician expenses associated with a serious illness, thus preserving the family's savings and other assets.

The individual's and family's health insurance needs must be identified. These needs are then prioritized in terms of their importance to the family. Other forms of health insurance should be reviewed with regard to this needs analysis. These benefits include:

- workers' compensation benefits for job-related disabilities;
- Social Security disability benefits;
- Medicare, if the individual is eligible;
- work-related benefits through employer-sponsored plans; and
- health coverage under any statutory plans.

Once the individual's total health insurance needs analysis has been completed, meaningful recommendations can be made as to the type and amounts of health insurance required.

16. 5 HEALTH CARE PROVIDER ORGANIZATIONS AND PLANS

Patients have traditionally been seen by physicians in office or hospital environments. Today, physicians also see patients in surgicenters and urgent care centers and at skilled nursing facilities. Surgicenters are health care facilities that are physically or geographically separate from hospitals and that provide surgical services to outpatients who do not require hospitalization. Urgent care centers provide primary and urgent care treatment on a less than 24-hour-per-day basis but are not equipped to treat true medical emergencies, such as heart attack or stroke victims, and do not provide continuity of care. **Skilled nursing facilities** are primarily engaged in providing skilled nursing care, which is nursing care for patients who do not require acute hospital nursing care but who need inpatient supervision by a registered nurse. **Assisted living facilities** are designed to provide limited medical care to patients on an intermittent basis. **Home health care** involves the provision of services by staff of home health agencies in an individual's place of residence on a per-visit or per-hour basis to patients or clients who have or are at risk of an injury, illness, or disabling condition or who are terminally ill and require short- or long-term intervention by health professionals.

The traditional broad health coverage provided by insurance plans provides little incentive for efficient, cost-effective health care delivery. In the past decade, it has become clear that too much money is being spent on health care. One response from insurers and providers has been to reorganize the health care delivery system into a form of managed care. **Managed care** imposes controls on the use of health care services, the providers of health care services, and the amount charged for these services, usually through health maintenance organizations or preferred provider arrangements. Managed care organizations achieve efficiency by increasing beneficiary cost sharing, controlling inpatient admissions and lengths of stay, establishing cost-sharing incentives for outpatient surgery, selectively contracting with health care providers, directly managing high-cost health care cases, and so forth.

The traditional stock and mutual companies and Blue Cross and Blue Shield are not the only insurers of health care. The health maintenance organizations and preferred provider organizations formed by hospitals and physicians also to deliver health care directly to enrollees in their plans.

16. 5. 1 Commercial Insurers

Commercial insurers are stock and mutual life insurers and sometimes casualty companies. Commercial insurers have traditionally provided coverage on a reimbursement basis but have also begun to embrace alternative approaches. **Reimbursement** plans pay benefits directly to the **insured**, who is responsible for paying the providers of medical services.

Commercial insurers offer both individual and group health insurance products. These products include basic medical expense coverage, major medical plans, comprehensive medical plans, disability income policies, and other types of health products.

Recent developments from commercial insurers in response to the need for cost control include the preferred provider organizations (PPOs) and health maintenance organizations (HMOs).

16. 5. 2 Blue Cross and Blue Shield

Blue Cross and Blue Shield are the dominant health insurers of the United States. The nation's Blue Cross and Blue Shield plans are loosely affiliated through the national Blue Cross and Blue Shield Association but are independently managed. Blue Cross and Blue Shield plans are geographically limited and are not available in all states.

16. 5. 2. 1 Differences from Commercial Insurers

Blue Cross and Blue Shield (the Blues) are different than traditional commercial insurers in the following important areas.

- The Blues provide the majority of their benefits on a service basis rather than on a reimbursement basis. This means that the insurer pays the provider directly for the medical treatment given the subscriber, instead of reimbursing the insured.
- The Blues have contractual relationships with the hospitals and doctors. As participating providers, the doctors and hospitals contractually agree to specific costs for the medical services provided to subscribers.

16. 5. 2. 2 Corporate Structure

Blue Cross/Blue Shield organizations, which are often referred to as service organizations, are examples of producers' cooperatives. Physicians and hospitals that sponsor Blue Cross/Blue Shield plans provide the insurance, so they are considered to be the producers in the cooperative.

Traditionally, the Blues have operated as nonprofit organizations, which means any net gain realized from company operations is eventually returned to the subscribers in the form of reduced premiums or increased benefits. A few plans have been allowed to become for-profit companies, or form for-profit subsidiaries, to allow them to raise money for expansion and compete in the health care marketplace.

Blue Cross traditionally has been a hospital service plan and Blue Shield a physician service plan, but these distinctions are becoming blurred. In most states, Blue Cross and Blue Shield have merged, but each group still covers the expenses for which it was first developed: Blue Cross covers hospital expenses and Blue Shield covers medical and surgical expenses. In some states, both Blue Cross and Blue Shield serve as hospital and physician service plans. Under the hospital plan, the contract is between Blue Cross and the hospital providing the hospital care. Under the medical plan, the contract is between Blue Shield and the physicians providing the service. The contract is evidence of their joint cooperation in providing health care to the public. One purpose of these plans was to ensure that health care providers—hospitals and practitioners—received payment for their services. Thus, with occasional exceptions, reimbursements for incurred expenses are made directly to the providers, not to the subscribers.

16. 5. 2. 3 *Enrollment and Premium Rates*

Members of Blue Cross and Blue Shield are known as **subscribers**. Subscribers in either plan can transfer their membership from one Blues organization to another in other areas of town or to other cities or states. Subscribers may also change their coverage from individual to family, from family to group, or any combination of changes they need to make. When transfers or changes are made, the subscriber's coverage continues without interruption.

16. 5. 2. 4 *Types of Coverage and Benefits*

Blue Cross offers broad coverages and pays claims on a service basis. The plan covers hospital daily room and board, outpatient services for minor surgery or accidental injury, medical emergencies, diagnostic testing, physical therapy, kidney dialysis, chemotherapy, and, in some cases, preadmission testing. Family plans may also include coverage for dependent handicapped children.

Blue Shield offers medical coverage for physician services received by plan subscribers. Again, through the contractual arrangement with the providers, Blue Shield normally pays the participating physician a predetermined amount for the specific service provided. Usually, this amount is based on the usual, customary, and reasonable (UCR) fees charged by other physicians in the same geographical area for the same or similar medical procedures.

16. 5. 2. 5 *Blues and Managed Care*

The Blues have also been strongly influenced by managed care. Many Blues subscribers are now covered by a Blues-affiliated HMO or PPO, or **point-of-service (POS) plan**, which is a type of health plan allowing the covered person to choose to receive a service from a participating or a nonparticipating provider, with different benefit levels associated with the use of in-plan and out-of-plan providers.

16. 5. 3 Health Maintenance Organizations

16. 5. 3. 1 *History and Development*

The number of health maintenance organizations (HMOs) has grown rapidly in response to increasing health care costs. The purpose of HMOs is to manage health care and its costs through a program of prepaid care that emphasizes prevention and early treatment. This prepayment, which entitles the health care consumer to a wide range of services, is referred to as a **service-incurred** basis. In contrast, traditional health insurance coverage is handled on a reimbursement basis, with the insured or provider being reimbursed for all or part of medical expenses actually incurred.

The emphasis on prevention means HMOs cover preventive medicine, such as routine physical and well-child examinations and diagnostic screening paid for in advance. This is in sharp contrast to health insurance plans that traditionally did not cover preventive programs, paying only after the fact of disease or injury. Theoretically, the HMOs' focus on prevention ultimately leads to reduced health care costs. At the same time, HMOs provide for hospital, surgical, and medical treatment when such services are needed.

One way HMOs differ from traditional health insurance providers is that HMOs have a dual function not shared by insurance companies. The illustration that follows, which is oversimplified for clarity, shows that under traditional arrangements, consumers receive the health care itself from one group, the medical profession—physicians, hospitals, therapists, and so forth—while the financial coverage comes from a separate entity, the insurance company.

Traditional Health Insurance Arrangement

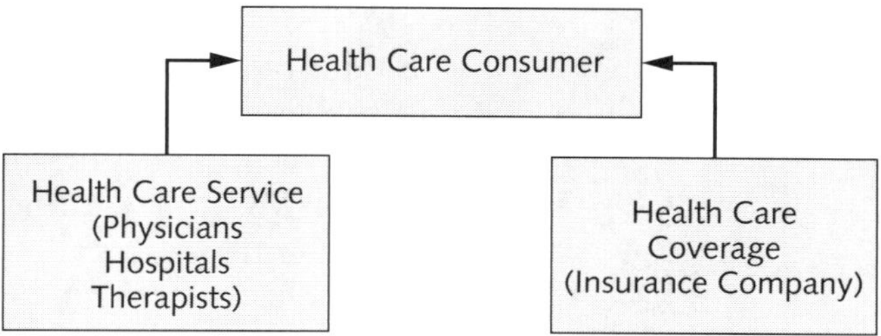

In contrast, as shown in the next illustration, an HMO provides both the health care services and the health care coverage.

Health Maintenance Organization Arrangement

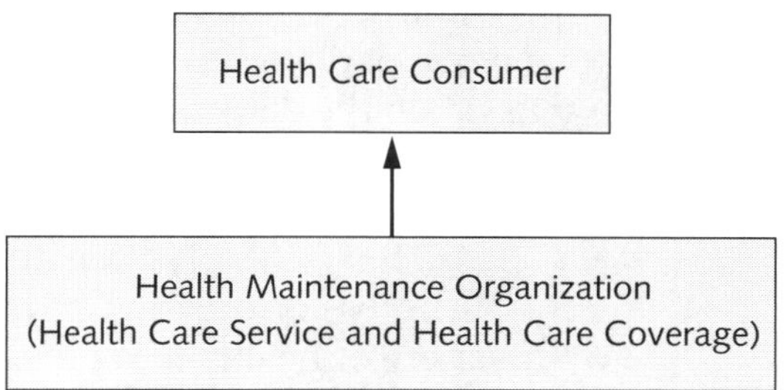

16. 5. 3. 2 *Health Maintenance Organization Arrangement*

These two functions are combined because the HMO comprises a group of medical practitioners who have contracted to provide specified services to HMO members at agreed-upon prices. In return, each consumer who is a member of the HMO agrees to pay the HMO a specified amount in advance to cover required hospital and medical services. Thus, the HMO both handles the financial arrangements and makes available the health care services.

16. 5. 3. 3 *Federal Requirements*

Although the emphasis on prevention and containing costs was a major factor in the development of HMOs, federal HMO laws further encouraged development by two primary means:

- Requiring certain employers who provide health benefits to employees to offer enrollment in an HMO as an option

- Providing for government grants. To receive government grants, HMOs must:
  - maintain certain minimum financial requirements in terms of the net worth of the HMO or reserves to pay health claims;
  - provide a defined package of health services that includes routine preventive care;
  - require no more than nominal use charges or co-payments (in addition to the prepaid amounts) for services actually rendered to individuals; and
  - establish premiums on a community rating basis without considering actual usage of services by individuals.

Once an HMO has met the minimum standards as well as other federal and state requirements, it is allowed to operate in a designated **service area**—often within a certain county or a specified distance surrounding the HMO facilities.

16. 5. 3. 4 HMO Organization

16. 5. 3. 4. 1 Profit Versus Nonprofit

Usually, if the HMO is a producers' cooperative owned and operated by a group of physicians, the HMO is for-profit. If it is a consumers' cooperative in which the doctors are salaried employees of the HMO, it is usually not-for-profit.

16. 5. 3. 4. 2 Typical Structures: Group Model

The basic structure of an HMO involves contractual agreements with a variety of health care providers and facilities to provide services to HMO subscribers. The first of the four models to be discussed is the **group model**.

More than two-thirds of HMOs existing in the late 1980s were based on the **group model**, sometimes called the medical group model or the group practice model. Under this arrangement, the HMO contracts with an independent medical group that specializes in a variety of medical services to provide those services to HMO subscribers. Under the agreement, the HMO pays the medical group entity, not the individual service providers. The medical group itself chooses how to pay its individual physicians, all of whom remain independent of the HMO rather than becoming salaried employees.

Often, the HMO pays the group a **capitation fee**, which is a fixed amount paid monthly for each HMO member. Thus, the medical group can make a profit on those members for whom a fee is paid but who use few or no services. On the other hand, the medical group can lose money on frequent users. The medical group model thus entails some financial risk on the part of the practitioners.

16. 5. 3. 4. 3 Typical Structures: Staff Model

A second type of arrangement is the **staff model**, so named because the contracting physicians are paid employees working on the staff of the HMO.

They generally operate in a clinic setting at the HMO's physical facilities. When hospital services are required, the staff doctors and HMO administration arrange for those services. In some cases, the HMO may even own and operate a hospital. Unlike the group model, practitioners in the staff model are under no financial risk; they are simply employed by the HMO, and it is the HMO corporation that takes the risk.

16. 5. 3. 4. 4 Typical Structures: Network Model

The **network model** operates much like the group model, except the HMO contracts with at least two, and more likely several, medical groups rather than just one. In addition, the HMO may make similar contractual arrangements with independent doctors to provide services in their individual offices. The purpose of a network is to increase accessibility to providers as a convenience for HMO subscribers who might otherwise be required to visit a facility far from their homes or workplaces. Under the network model, medical groups are generally paid a capitation fee, and individual physicians may be paid either a capitation fee or a discounted fee.

16. 5. 3. 4. 5 Typical Structures: Individual Practice Association Model

The fourth and final model is one that gives HMO members the maximum freedom of choice of physicians and locations. The **individual practice association (IPA) model** allows the HMO to contract separately with any combination of individual physicians, medical groups, or physicians' associations. Some HMOs, in fact, have been started by such groups.

In the IPA model, there is no separate HMO facility. Physicians operate out of their own private offices, and their HMO patients may be individuals whom the physicians were already attending. Many people prefer this arrangement because it allows them to continue with their personal doctors. Payment is usually on a fee-for-service basis, whereby the fees have been negotiated in advance.

16. 5. 3. 4. 6 Open- and Closed-Panel Types

Open and closed panels are another way to characterize HMOs. Physicians, hospitals, and other health care providers who have contracts with an HMO are referred to as the HMO's panel. With an **open panel**, any and all providers who want to provide services for the HMO may do so as long as they agree to the HMO's requirements.

In contrast, a **closed panel** is a limited number of health care providers chosen by the HMO. HMO subscribers must receive their health care services from this closed panel of providers to have those services paid for on the prepaid plan. The theory is that, with a closed panel, the HMO is better able to manage costs with fewer providers.

16. 5. 3. 5 Sponsorship and Eligibility

Throughout this section, we've mentioned several types of groups that may sponsor HMOs. Other sponsoring groups include:

- medical schools or associations;
- physicians;

- hospitals;
- employers;
- service organizations (such as Blue Cross/Blue Shield);
- labor unions;
- consumer groups;
- insurance companies; and
- government entities.

Most HMOs, no matter who sponsors them, restrict membership to a specifically defined group. For example, an HMO organized by a labor union might limit enrollment to members of specific unions. An HMO sponsored by a Blue Cross/Blue Shield plan might accept only the employees of organizations within its service area that employ 500 or more individuals. Every rule has its exception, however, and some HMOs solicit individual enrollees from the entire population in the service area.

16. 5. 3. 6 Basic and Supplemental Services

The emphasis of HMOs is prevention, and the benefits offered are broader than those provided by commercial insurers. HMO benefits are not limited to treatment resulting from illness or injury; they also include preventive health care measures such as routine physical examinations.

HMOs are required to provide for certain basic health care services.

- **Inpatient hospital and physician services** must be provided for a period of at least 90 days per calendar year for treatment of illness or injury. A partial list of the hospital services provided include
  - room and board,
  - maternity care,
  - general nursing care,
  - use of operating room and facilities,
  - use of intensive care unit,
  - x-rays, laboratory, and other diagnostic tests,
  - drugs, medications, and anesthesia, and
  - physical, radiation, and inhalation therapy.
- **Outpatient medical services** must be provided when prescribed or supervised by a physician and rendered in a non-hospital-based health care facility (e.g., physician's office, member's home). Outpatient medical services include diagnostic services, treatment services, short-term physical therapy and rehabilitation services, laboratory and x-ray services, and outpatient surgery.

- **Preventive health services** with the goal of protection against and early detection and minimization of the ill effects and causes of disease or disability must be provided. Specifically, this includes well-child care from birth, eye and ear examinations for children age 17 and under, periodic health evaluations, and immunizations.
- **In and out of area emergency services**, including medically necessary ambulance services, must be available on an inpatient or an outpatient basis 24 hours a day, seven days a week.

Many HMOs may provide one or more of the following supplemental health care services:

- Prescription drugs
- Vision care
- Dental care
- Home health care
- Nursing services
- Long-term care
- Substance abuse services

Consumers who want supplemental services that are not already included in their coverage plan may purchase them from the HMO only as an adjunct to the basic health care services the HMO offers.

16. 5. 3. 6. 1 Co-Payments

Members of an HMO may be charged only nominal amounts—**co-payments**—for basic services in addition to the original monthly payment. In many cases, no additional payments are required for services. Any co-payments are described in the certificate of coverage or the evidence of coverage.

On the other hand, HMOs are permitted to require co-payments on supplemental services and to charge an amount that is added to the monthly fee. For example, suppose an HMO makes dental coverage available to members who want to pay for it. The basic package of services might cost $200 per month, and an additional $5 will buy the dental coverage. The HMO then might require the consumer to pay $3 for every routine dental checkup. (All figures are hypothetical.)

16. 5. 3. 6. 2 Exclusions and Limitations

Exclusions and limitations are used either to limit a benefit provided or specifically to exclude a type of coverage, benefit, medical procedure, and so forth. HMOs may not exclude and limit benefits as readily as commercial insurers. This is because the rationale of an HMO is to provide comprehensive health care coverage. Some of the benefits HMOs may (and often do) exclude from coverage include:

- eye examinations and refractions for persons over age 17;
- eyeglasses or contact lenses resulting from an eye examination;

- dental services;
- prescription drugs (other than those administered in a hospital);
- long-term physical therapy (over 90 days); and
- out-of-area services (other than emergency services).

16. 5. 3. 7 *Important Features of HMOs*

16. 5. 3. 7. 1 Gatekeeper System

HMOs often have a gatekeeper system under which the member must select a primary care physician (PCP), who in turn provides or authorizes all care for the particular member. Any referrals, such as referrals to specialists, must be made and authorized by the PCP. Think of this person as opening (or refusing to open) the gate between the member and the health care providers. In emergency situations, the member's needs are covered, but generally the individual must notify the PCP as soon as possible if it wasn't possible to do so when the emergency arose. Members are required to involve the PCP in all service decisions to ensure claims will be paid.

Suppose Ronald knows his PCP can't perform the open-heart surgery he needs. Ronald may not simply select a surgeon of his choice and assume the claim will be paid by his HMO. He must first consult with the gatekeeper, his personal PCP, who will make the referral and authorize treatment.

16. 5. 3. 7. 2 24-Hour Access

As a rule, members have 24-hour access to the HMO. Telephones are answered and referrals and authorizations are made 24 hours a day, seven days a week. Nursing and medical staff, including PCPs, must be willing to respond during nonbusiness hours as well. Therefore, an HMO member who needs to consult with a PCP late at night or on a weekend would likely be able to do so.

16. 5. 3. 7. 3 Open Enrollment

The term **open enrollment** can mean two different things:

- In employer-sponsored group plans, a period each year when employees may choose to enroll or remain enrolled in the HMO or to change health plans
- A period each year when an HMO must advertise availability to the general public on an individual basis

In the first case, open enrollment allows employees who have not yet joined the HMO to do so if they wish. Those who are already HMO subscribers may at this time also choose to continue in the HMO or to change plans if another health care plan is available.

In the second case, open enrollment may be required by state law, permitting all who apply to join. During this period, which usually lasts 30 days, the HMO generally may not reject any applicant for health reasons. However, some laws permit the HMO to refuse enrollment to people who are hospitalized during the enrollment period or who have chronic illnesses or permanent injuries. For the most part, the advantage of open enrollment lies completely with potential enrollees, who may have been rejected for traditional coverage because of their health but who will now be accepted by the HMO. The HMO, on the other hand, is placed at risk because it is more likely to lose money on such subscribers.

Example

Darren has been rejected for health insurance by several insurance companies because of a history of heart attacks. Darren's state requires HMOs to have a period of open enrollment. If Darren applies for HMO coverage during the open enrollment period, chances are he will be accepted even though he might not be able to obtain coverage elsewhere because of his medical history.

16. 5. 3. 7. 4 Nondiscrimination

When HMO coverage is offered to a group, the HMO may not refuse to cover an individual member of the group because of adverse preexisting health conditions, such as a history of heart trouble that predates enrollment in the HMO. This is different from traditional insurers, which generally have the option of refusing to cover certain group members and of excluding preexisting health conditions.

16. 5. 3. 7. 5 Complaints

All HMOs are required to have a complaint system, often called a **grievance procedure**, to resolve written complaints by members. The HMO is required to provide forms for written complaints, including the address and telephone number to which complaints should be directed.

16. 5. 3. 7. 6 Prohibited Practices

HMOs, like traditional commercial insurers, are not allowed to engage in certain types of business practices, policies, and so on. Specifically, HMOs are prohibited from excluding a member's preexisting conditions from coverage, and they are prohibited from unfairly discriminating against a member on the basis of age, sex, health status, race, color, creed, national origin, or marital status. HMOs are also prohibited from terminating a member's coverage for reasons other than nonpayment of premiums or co-payments, fraud or deception in the member's use of services, violation of the terms of the contract, failure to meet or continue to meet eligibility requirements prescribed by the HMO, or a termination of the group contract under which the member was covered.

16. 5. 3. 7. 7 Quality Assurance

Because HMOs provide service benefits rather than reimbursement benefits, they are required to follow guidelines prescribed by the state Insurance Department to ensure quality service to members. These guidelines specify the requirements for reasonable hours of operation, after-hours emergency health care, and standards to ensure that sufficient personnel will be available to attend to members' needs. The guidelines also require adequate arrangements to provide inpatient hospital services for basic health care and that the services of specialists are provided as a basic health care service.

16. 5. 3. 7. 8 Open-Ended Plans

An **open-ended HMO** (also known as a leaky HMO or a point-of-service HMO) is a hybrid arrangement whereby participants may use non-HMO providers at any time and receive indemnity benefits subject to higher deductible and coinsurance amounts. The out-of-pocket cost to the participant (and probably to the employer) is higher, but the arrangement allows participants to remain in control of choosing a health care provider.

16. 5. 3. 7. 9 Open-Access HMOs

Dissatisfaction with the gatekeeper mechanism, delays in receiving care, and problems in obtaining referrals have led many health plans to offer open access. An **open-access HMO** allows members to receive care from network specialists without first going through a primary care physician (gatekeeper) and receiving a referral. Alternatively, a point-of-service plan allows members to seek the care of a specialist outside of the HMO provider network. Because the plan does not control the outside provider, POS plans tend to be more expensive than open-access HMOs.

16. 6 PREFERRED PROVIDER ORGANIZATIONS

Other efforts to reduce medical costs have resulted in **preferred provider organizations (PPOs)**. A PPO is an arrangement under which a selected group of independent hospitals and medical practitioners in a certain area, such as a state, agrees to provide a range of services at a prearranged cost. The contracting agency or organizer of the PPO might be any one of a number of groups, including:

- traditional insurance companies;
- Blue Cross/Blue Shield;
- local groups of hospitals;
- local groups of physicians;
- an existing HMO;
- large employers; and
- trade unions.

The organizers and the providers agree on medical service charges that are generally lower than those the providers would charge patients not associated with the PPO. Unlike most prepaid HMO arrangements, the providers are paid on a fee-for-service basis rather than receiving a flat monthly amount for each user. Providers are willing to enter into this arrangement in return for guaranteed payment from the PPO and a potential increase in the number of patients.

People who receive services choose a preferred provider from a list the PPO distributes. As a general rule, the users have more choices among doctors and hospitals under a PPO than under an HMO arrangement. However, some recent HMO structures offer similar arrangements. PPOs fall somewhere between commercial insurers, wherein the user has unlimited choice of practitioners, and HMOs, wherein the user might be severely restricted. Even with the usually long list of PPO providers from which to choose, people may opt to go to another provider. However, the PPO agrees to pay its full benefits only when a preferred provider is used. If an individual uses a nonpreferred facility, the PPO usually pays a reduced amount and the individual must pay the balance.

Although a PPO generally pays a reduced amount for services performed by a nonpreferred provider, this rule is mitigated for emergency services under most PPO plans. Recognizing that emergencies may require treatment in facilities other than those preferred by the PPO or by providers who have not agreed to the PPO arrangement, PPO plans generally pay in full for emergency treatment regardless of where and by whom it is performed.

Example

Dorian is a member of a PPO in his home town of Topeka, Kansas. While vacationing in Utah, he is injured in an auto accident and is rushed to the nearest hospital in Salt Lake City. Dorian's medical bills in Salt Lake City total $5,600 before he is returned to Topeka. The same treatment with his preferred providers in Topeka would have cost only $4,780. Under these circumstances, Dorian's PPO is likely to pay the full amount to the Salt Lake providers.

PPOs and HMOs are often lumped together and referred to as managed health care systems. Although they do share the concept of saving costs by proper health care management and are similar in many ways, they are distinguishable by the fact that PPOs have no separate physical facility and HMOs generally do. But even this distinction has become blurred somewhat by continuing refinements and variations in the way HMOs operate. Currently, an HMO may operate through a PPO arrangement rather than have its own facility.

A Gatekeeper PPO is a plan that operates as a PPO but requires a primary care physician (also known as a gatekeeper) for referrals.

Exercise 16.B
Match the following health care systems with the appropriate method of payment.

____ 1.	Jerry belongs to an HMO. His primary care physician receives a set amount monthly to provide care for Jerry, regardless of how often the physician sees Jerry.	A. Fee for service
____ 2.	Maryanne belongs to a PPO. Her primary care physician receives a payment every time Maryanne receives care from her.	B. Reimbursement
____ 3.	Harold has a traditional medical expense insurance policy. When he visits his doctor, Harold files a claim. The insurer sends Harold a payment based on the submitted charges.	C. Capitation

Answers to the exercise can be found at the end of the Unit 16 answers and rationales.

16. 7 POINT-OF-SERVICE PLANS

Point-of-service plans are another form of managed care. With POS plans, the subscriber is given a choice of receiving in-network care or out-of-network care. With in-network coverage, the insured receives care through a particular network of doctors and hospitals participating in the plan, and all care is coordinated by the insured's primary care physician. This includes referrals to specialists and arrangements for hospitalization, which must all be approved by the PCP. In-network coverage is the highest level of coverage within the plan, which means the plan will pay more for medical services and the insured won't have to submit claim forms. Out-of-network coverage applies when the insured receives care from a provider who does not participate in the plan's network, and the care is not coordinated by the PCP. An insured receiving out-of-network care usually pays more of the cost than if it had been in-network care (emergencies excepted). Out-of-network care also means that the insured must submit claim forms in order to receive benefits.

Example
Arnold is a member of a point-of-service plan. He develops a heart condition but decides not to follow his PCP's recommendation to see an in-network cardiologist. Instead, he becomes the patient of a famous cardiologist in another city, and this cardiologist is out-of-network. Arnold can expect that his POS plan will pay less than it would pay if had he become the patient of the in-network cardiologist.

16. 7. 1 Exclusive Provider Organizations

Exclusive provider organizations (EPOs) are a type of PPO in which individual members use particular preferred providers instead of choosing among a variety of preferred providers. Providers are not paid a salary but are paid on a fee-for-service basis.

EPOs are characterized by a primary physician who monitors care and makes referrals to a network of providers (the gatekeeper concept), strong utilization management, experience rating, and simplified claims processing. EPOs can serve as an alternative to or companion with HMOs and PPOs.

16. 8 EMPLOYER-ADMINISTERED PLANS

16. 8. 1 Self-Funding

If claim costs are fairly predictable, an employer may consider a self-funded health care plan. With a self-funded plan, an employer, not an insurance company, provides the funds to make claim payments for company employees and their dependents. In the event that claims are higher than predicted, a self-funded health insurance plan can be backed up by a **stop-loss contract**.

A **stop-loss contract** is designed to limit the employer's liability for claims. There are two variations of this coverage. Specific stop-loss coverage begins to apply after an individual's medical expenses exceed a predetermined threshold such as $5,000. Aggregate stop-loss coverage applies when the employer's liability for group insurance claims exceeds a specified amount. The insurer pays all claims after the specified amount is reached.

An employer self-funded plan may be an indemnity program that reimburses covered employees for medical care they have received. Alternatively, the employer may provide benefits through the service plan offered under an HMO or through an insurer's PPO network.

An insurer may also be used for a self-funded employer under an administrative services only contract. Under the **ASO contractual agreement**, the insurer provides claim forms, administers claims, and makes payments to health care providers, but the employer still provides the funds to make claims payments.

16. 8. 1. 1 Advantages of Self-Insurance

Self-insurance has four major advantages.

- The company can save money if actual losses are less than those predicted.
- The expense of carrying insurance may be reduced because of the elimination of administrative costs, agent commissions, brokerage fees, and premium tax.

- Because the company has assumed the entire risk, there may be a greater effort on its part to seek ways to reduce claims and encourage employees to actively participate in wellness programs and improved lifestyles.
- The company has use of the money that normally would be held by the insurance company.

16. 8. 1. 2 *Disadvantages of Self-Insurance*

The main disadvantages of self-insurance are as follows.

- Actual losses may be more than predicted, causing the unexpected loss of funds that were to be used for other purposes.
- Expenses could be higher than expected if additional personnel have to be hired to administer claims, manage risk, or offer employee information.
- Income taxes could be higher because the company will not be able to take premiums paid as a deduction; only the claims paid and operating expenses may be taken as tax deductions.

16. 8. 2 501(c)(9) Trusts

Section 501(c)(9) of the Internal Revenue Code provides for the establishment of **voluntary employees' beneficiary associations**, or **501(c)(9) trusts**, which are funding vehicles for the employee benefits offered to members. Liberalized tax treatment made 501(c)(9) trusts an attractive self-funding employee benefit plan alternative, but restrictive legislation in the Tax Reform Act of 1984 has caused their popularity to diminish.

16. 8. 3 Small Employers

Small employers (usually defined as those with fewer than 25 or 50 employees) have been hit especially hard by increases in health care insurance premiums.

Several states have acted to ensure that health insurance coverages are available at a reasonable cost and under reasonable conditions for small employers. The new requirements include the following:

- Standard benefit plans that must be offered to small employers
- Maximum waiting periods for preexisting conditions
- The insurer may not exclude particular individuals or medical conditions from coverage
- Carriers may cancel or nonrenew small employer plans only for nonpayment of premium, fraud, misrepresentation, or noncompliance with plan provisions

16. 8. 4 Cafeteria Plans

A **cafeteria plan** could be defined as a plan in which employees select health benefits from a variety of coverage options on the basis of their individual and family needs. Cafeteria plans tend to be more complex (and more expensive) than traditional plans, especially with regard to plan administration, and usually make the most sense for larger employers. Benefits are elected in advance of the year in which they will be used (for example, benefits to be used in 2011 would be elected at the end of 2010). Taxation of cafeteria plans is regulated by Section 125 of the Internal Revenue Code.

16. 8. 5 Medical Savings Accounts (MSAs)

Medical savings accounts (MSAs), also known as Archer MSAs, were created to help employees of small employers, as well as self-employed individuals, pay for their medical care expenses. MSAs are tax-free accounts set up with financial institutions such as banks and insurance companies.

To qualify for an MSA, an individual must be one of the following:

- An employee (or spouse) who works for a small employer that maintains an individual or family high-deductible health plan for the employee
- A self-employed person (or spouse) who maintains an individual or family high-deductible health plan

A **small employer** is one that has averaged 50 or fewer employees during either of the last two calendar years. Using 2010 limits, a **high-deductible health plan** is one with an annual deductible between $2,000 and $3,000 for an individual policy, or between $4,050 and $6,050 for a family policy, with a maximum out-of-pocket of $7,400.

As of January, 2006 no new Archer MSAs can be established. Existing accounts continue to allow contributions and can be rolled over into health savings accounts.

16. 8. 6 Flexible Spending Accounts (FSAs)

A variation of the traditional cafeteria plan is the **flexible spending account (FSA)**. The FSA is a cafeteria plan that is funded with employee money by means of a salary reduction. A salary reduction plan is a pretax plan; the employee agrees to a reduction in compensation, and this amount is used to cover certain medical expenses. This naturally results in a lower-cost plan from the employer's perspective, with an employer's expenses usually limited to administrative costs. FSAs typically are for moderate-sized to large employers.

The FSA plan provides the selectivity and flexibility of the regular cafeteria plan. Thus, desired benefits can be chosen by the employee, especially the employee whose spouse works and has a similar benefits package. Because of the coordination of benefits provision found in most group hospitalization policies, duplicate coverage will pay only once. If an employee is contributing toward the cost of the plan, it makes sense that payroll deduction dollars be used for selective benefits instead of duplicate benefits.

The salary reduction method results in the employees funding nontaxable benefits with nontaxed dollars. This also results in a reduced payroll and reduced payroll taxes for the employer.

16. 8. 7 High Deductible Health Plans (HDHP)

A high deductible health plan (HDHP) is a health plan that offers very low premiums but requires the insured to pay a relatively high deductible. For an individual, a qualified high deductible health plan is one with a minimum deductible of $1,200 and a $5,950 cap on out-of-pocket expenses. (These limits are for 2010, but the limits are indexed annually). For a family, a qualified health plan is one with a minimum deductible of $2,400 and a $11,900 cap on out-of-pocket expenses in 2010. These limits are also indexed annually. On its own, an HDHP will require an insured to pay a substantial amount out of pocket before the plan will begin to pay benefits. Most HDHPs are paired with a health savings account which allows the insured or employer to contribute to a savings account that will grow tax free as long as it is used to pay for qualified medical expenses.

16. 8. 8 Health Savings Accounts (HSAs)

Since 2004, individuals under the age of 65 who are enrolled in certain high-deductible health plans have been able to establish **health care savings accounts (HSAs)**. The maximum HSA contribution in 2010 is the amount of the deductible under the taxpayer's high-deductible health plan (up to a limit of $3,050 for individual policies and $6,150 for family policies). People ages 55 to 64 can make an additional catch-up contribution $1,000 in 2009 and thereafter for individual policies. Contributions by individuals are deductible from gross income.

Employers may set up HSAs for their eligible employees and contribute to them, subject to the dollar limits discussed previously. Employer contributions are excluded from employees' taxable income.

HSA distributions are tax free if used to pay qualified medical expenses, which generally include the same kinds of medical expenses that are deductible as itemized deductions. Distributions for any other purposes are subject to income tax; a 10% penalty tax also applies unless the account beneficiary has died, become disabled, or is age 65 or older.

16. 8. 9 Health Reimbursement Accounts (HRAs)

Some employers provide employees with high-deductible medical expense plans and create a tax-favored savings account for each covered employee under which the employee can obtain reimbursement for certain medical expenses that are not covered under a high deductible plan. HRA contributions are made by the employer on a pre-tax basis and can be used to pay deductibles, coinsurance, and co-payments. The employer may restrict the use of the funds in an HRA, and typically the funds roll over from year to year. HRAs are the dominant form of consumer-directed health plans.

16. 8. 10 Consumer-Driven Health Plans (CDHPs)

Consumer driven health plans allow employers combine a high deductible health plan with a spending or reimbursement account, such as an FSA, HSA, or HRA. The employer will contribute a certain amount per year, typically $1,000–$2,000, which usually rolls over year to year. A typical CDHP will focus on personalized wellness and prevention, things that are not usually covered by traditional medical plans.

Exercise 16.C

A variety of tax-favored savings plans have been created to encourage use of higher deductibles and the setting aside of funds for out-of-pocket health care costs. Match the source of funds to the appropriate plan.

___ 1.	Employers	A. Flexible Spending Accounts
___ 2.	Employees	B. Health Savings Accounts
___ 3.	Either Employer or Employee	C. Health Reimbursement Account

Answers to the exercise can be found at the end of the Unit 16 answers and rationales.

16. 8. 11 Multiple Employer Trusts (METs)

Multiple employer trusts (METs) provide health insurance benefits to small businesses through a series of trusts usually established on the basis of specific industries such as manufacturing, sales and service, real estate, and others.

Most states have group-size eligibility requirements for employer groups to qualify for group insurance. Generally, states may require a minimum of 5 to 10 participants for a group to be eligible for group benefits. METs typically have no such requirements, and, in reality, a group of one could be eligible for group benefits.

METs are formed by insurers or third-party administrators called sponsors. The sponsor develops the plan, sets the underwriting rules, and administers the plan. To prevent the possibility of adverse selection, the underwriter must make sure that the sponsor's underwriting rules are adequate and that the sponsor adheres to them. This is necessary because an employer with only two, three, or five employees could elect to join an MET because the employer knows of the poor health condition of one of the employees. The underwriting standards must be able to prevent this from happening.

16. 8. 12 Multiple Employer Welfare Arrangements (MEWAs)

Multiple employer welfare arrangements (MEWAs) are created by small employers who join to provide health insurance benefits for their employees, often on a self-insured basis.

The federal Employee Retirement Income Security Act (ERISA), designed to protect group health insurance plan participants, restricts states' abilities to regulate employee welfare benefit plans while preserving state insurance laws having to do with reserve requirements. A state may regulate insurance but may or may not consider an employee welfare benefit plan an insurance plan for the purpose of regulation.

Some self-funded MEWAs claim they are not subject to Insurance Department regulation and operate under a supposed preemption under ERISA. As a result, many have gone unregulated and have fraudulently collected premiums from small businesses, only to go out of business themselves and leave millions of dollars of unpaid claims.

16. 9 OTHER FORMS OF GROUP INSURANCE

16. 9. 1 Blanket Policies

Many types of groups, such as the students of a single school or a group of campers, are indefinite in number and composition and are constantly changing. These characteristics prevent qualification for group insurance under the usual terms.

However, groups such as these can have health coverage at group rates under a **blanket policy**. Because no employer/employee relationship is involved, the members of such groups are not usually interested in covering themselves for loss of income resulting from their activities as a group. Instead, they usually want only hospital, medical, and surgical coverages.

Example

The dean of a college might make insurance available to all full-time students. The group members are constantly changing as students enroll, graduate, or drop out. By obtaining a blanket policy, the dean can secure student coverage at the same low premium rates as group coverage. However, the members of the group, the students, will not be identified by name. Instead, all who can prove they are enrolled full time will be covered by the insurance blanket.

Gina owns a small business and is the leader of a local Girl Scout troop. Through an insurance company, Gina has established insurance plans for both of these groups.

For her employees, Gina provides group health insurance. Under the group plan, Gina provides the insurance company with each group member's name.

For the scout troop, Gina provides a blanket policy, under which she does not give the insurance company a list of the group's members because they change frequently.

The members of a group insured under a blanket policy may or may not help to pay the premiums for their coverage. In the case of the college students, the school might require that they pay at least part of the premiums. In the case of the scouts, perhaps Gina's scout council pays for the coverage, and the children are not required to pay anything. In any event, blanket policies may be either contributory or noncontributory.

16. 9. 2 Franchise Policies

Group policies require the number of insured persons to remain above a specified minimum. Many small businesses and other groups do not have enough members to qualify. An arrangement that allows very small groups to have some of the benefits of group insurance, especially the lower cost, is called **franchise insurance**.

Franchise insurance works much like group insurance, but it is established differently. There is no master policy. Instead, each member of the group receives an individual insurance policy. This allows group members to make some coverage choices, but they are required to provide health information on their applications, just as they would for individual policies.

Like true group coverage, franchise insurance offers hospital, surgical, medical, and disability income coverage. Plans may be contributory or noncontributory. One premium is paid for the whole group.

One example of franchise insurance is coverage sold by mail to groups, such as the members of a certain association or holders of certain credit cards. Purchasers receive individual policies at group rates, so this is a type of franchise insurance.

16. 10 GOVERNMENT HEALTH INSURANCE

Both the federal and state governments offer statutory health insurance programs. On the federal level, Social Security provides disability income benefits and administers the Medicare program. On the state level, all states have workers' compensation laws and Medicaid or some similar form of state-subsidized health care.

16. 11 SOCIAL SECURITY

Social Security pays four types of benefits:

- Disability income benefits to workers
- Medicare benefits
- Retirement benefits to workers and their dependents
- Survivors benefits to a worker's family

A special insured status is required if a worker is eligible for disability benefits under Social Security. This status requires that the worker be fully insured and have earned at least 20 quarters of coverage in the 40-calendar-quarter period ending with the calendar quarter in which the disability begins. This requirement is modified slightly if a covered worker is disabled before age 31.

A covered worker may be eligible for disability income benefits if the required insured status is achieved and the worker is under age 65 and can satisfy the Social Security definition of total disability.

Social Security defines **total disability** as the inability to engage in any substantial gainful activity because of physical or mental disability that is expected to last for at least 12 months or end in death. *Substantial work activity* means significant mental and/or physical duties for which a person is compensated.

This definition does not refer to the individual's occupation prior to disability or to the level of predisability compensation. A surgeon earning $200,000 annually may be disabled to the degree that the individual could no longer perform surgery. However, a surgeon who could perform other meaningful work duties (e.g., bank employee, school teacher, salesperson), would probably not be eligible for disability benefits because this person could not meet the Social Security definition of total disability.

The amount of the disability benefit is equal to the worker's primary insurance amount (PIA), which in essence is the same as the individual's monthly retirement benefit. Disability benefits are payable only for total disabilities. Disability benefits begin with the sixth full month of disability. This waiting period begins with the first full month of disability. No benefit is paid for a partial disability.

As a result of the disabled person's work record, family members such as the following may also receive disability benefits:

- An unmarried child under age 18, or under 19 if in high school full time
- An unmarried child disabled before age 22
- A spouse caring for a child under age 16 or disabled
- A spouse age 62 or older
- A disabled widow or widower age 50 or older
- A disabled surviving divorced spouse age 50 or older, if the marriage lasted at least 10 years

Exercise 16.D

Social Security benefits are often referred to as OASDI + Med. What does this stand for?

1. O________ A________
2. S______________
3. D__________ I__________
4. Med______________

Answers to the exercise can be found at the end of the Unit 16 answers and rationales.

16. 12 WORKERS' COMPENSATION

Most states require employers to provide workers' compensation benefits for their employees. Workers' compensation is designed to help persons who suffer from loss of income due to injury or sickness that occurs as a result of their occupation.

16. 12. 1 Eligibility

To be eligible for workers' compensation benefits, the disabled worker must:

- work in an occupation that is covered by workers' compensation; and
- have had an accident or sickness that is work related.

16. 12. 2 Benefits

Workers' compensation laws provide for the payment of four types of benefits:

- Medical benefits
- Income benefits
- Death benefits
- Rehabilitation benefits

Medical benefits are provided without limit. An injured or diseased employee is entitled to receive all necessary medical and surgical treatment to cure or relieve the condition. Certain maximums or limits may apply to a type of care or a particular medical item, but overall benefits are unlimited.

Income benefits are paid to employees who suffer work-related disabilities. An elimination period applies before benefits for loss of wages begin. If the disability continues beyond a certain period, retroactive benefits are paid for the initial waiting period. A disability may be total (making employment impossible) or partial (resulting in a reduced ability to work). Either type of disability may be temporary or permanent. For permanent total disability or temporary total disability, the benefit is 66.66% of weekly wages, subject to minimum and maximum weekly limits. However, for permanent total disability, the dollar maximum and the benefit period are greater. (Benefits for permanent total disability often continue for life, while benefits for a temporary total disability are limited.) People with partial disabilities are able to perform some work, so the laws provide a benefit equal to a percentage of the wage loss (the difference between earnings before and after the accident). In addition to benefits for lost wages, the state provides scheduled benefits for specific permanent partial disabilities such as loss of limbs, sight, or hearing. Usually, these benefits are paid in addition to any other income benefits.

Death benefits provide two types of payments. Up to a certain dollar amount is provided as a burial allowance, and the state also provides weekly income payments for a surviving spouse and children. Weekly benefits are

66.66% of the deceased worker's wages, subject to minimum and maximum dollar amounts, a maximum time limit, and an aggregate payment limit. Surviving children generally receive benefits until a certain age.

Rehabilitation benefits are now recognized as a valuable tool for reducing workers' compensation costs and returning disabled employees to their jobs as soon as possible. Rehabilitation may include:

- therapy;
- vocational training;
- devices such as wheelchairs; and
- the costs of travel, lodging, and living expenses while being rehabilitated.

16. 13 MEDICAID

Medicaid provides health care benefits for the financially needy. It is basically a state program with some federal financial support. Medicaid is designed to provide increased assistance to those who are unable to pay for their medical needs. For persons age 65 or over, Medicaid principally supplements Medicare for those who cannot pay the expenses not covered by Medicare. For those who are not eligible for Medicare, it provides medical assistance for certain categories of people who are medically needy: the blind, the disabled, families with dependent children, or medically needy children under age 21.

Medicaid is a federal-state program. The federal government encourages states to increase medical assistance to the indigent, regardless of age, by paying one-half of the administration cost of state medical assistance programs and 50–80% of the fees to the providers of services to the needy. The actual federal matching proposition varies inversely with the state average per capita income; therefore, the poorer states receive larger federal grants.

Generally, Medicaid helps to pay for medical services that the patient cannot pay for. Thus, Medicaid covers such services as hospitalizations, physician's services, diagnostic testing, pregnancies, and others.

In addition, Medicaid also serves as a supplement to Medicare in some situations. For example, Medicare currently offers extremely limited coverage for nursing home care. Often, Medicaid will supplement these limited benefits by paying for nursing home expenses. Other health care expenses not completely covered by Medicare may be paid for by Medicaid.

16. 14 HEALTH CARE REFORM ACT

16. 14. 1 Subsidies

Individuals and families who make between 100–400% of the Federal Poverty Level (FPL) and want to purchase their own health insurance on an exchange are eligible for subsidies. They cannot be eligible for Medicare and Medicaid and cannot be covered by an employer. Eligible buyers receive premium credits, and there is a cap for how much they have to contribute to their premiums on a sliding scale.

This health reform will close the Medicare prescription drug "donut hole" by 2020. Seniors who hit the donut hole by 2010 will receive a $250 rebate.

Beginning in 2011, seniors in the gap will receive a 50% discount on brand name drugs. The bill also includes $500 billion in Medicare cuts over the next decade.

16. 14. 2 Medicaid

In regards to Medicaid, the Health Care Reform Act will:

- expand Medicaid to include 133% of federal poverty level which is $29,327 for a family of four;
- require states to expand Medicaid to include childless adults starting in 2014; and
- require the federal government to pay 100% of costs for covering newly eligible individuals through 2016.

Illegal immigrants are not eligible for Medicaid.

16. 14. 3 Insurance Reforms

The following insurance reforms have occurred as a result of the Health Care Reform Act.

- Six months after enactment, insurance companies could no longer deny children coverage based on a preexisting condition.
- Starting in 2014, insurance companies cannot deny coverage to anyone with preexisting conditions.
- Insurance companies must allow children to stay on their parent's insurance plans until age 26.
- In 2014, everyone must purchase health insurance or face a $695 annual fine. There are some exceptions for low-income people.

16. 14. 4 Employer Mandate

Employers with more than 50 employees must provide health insurance or pay a fine of $2000 per worker each year if any worker receives federal subsidies to purchase health insurance. Fines are applied to entire number of employees, minus some allowances.

UNIT TEST

1. Julia has a policy that will pay any expenses she incurs as the result of in-hospital medical treatment, as well as some of the expenses she incurs on an outpatient basis. Julia probably has
   A. a disability income policy
   B. a medical expense insurance policy
   C. a long-term care policy
   D. a hospital income insurance policy

2. George has a policy that will provide him an income if he is disabled from illness or injury and recuperating at home. George probably has
   A. a disability income policy
   B. a medical expense insurance policy
   C. a long-term care policy
   D. a hospital income insurance policy

3. George's brother, Jerry, has a policy that will provide him an income if he is disabled from illness or injury, but only if he is confined to a hospital. George's brother probably has
   A. a disability income policy
   B. a medical expense insurance policy
   C. a long-term care policy
   D. a hospital income insurance policy

4. Between George and his brother, Jerry, who has the more limited policy?
   A. George
   B. Jerry
   C. Neither; both policies probably have the same limitations
   D. Not possible to tell from the information provided

5. The main difference between traditional health insurance arrangements and HMOs is that
   A. traditional health insurance companies provide both the health care service and the health care financing, but HMOs provide only the health care financing
   B. traditional health care insurance companies provide both the health care service and the health care financing, but HMOs provide only the health care service
   C. HMOs provide both the health care service and the health care financing, but traditional health care insurance companies provide only the financing
   D. HMOs provide both the health care service and the health care financing, but traditional health care insurance companies provide only the service

6. Which of the following types of health care insurers is an example of a producers' cooperative?
   A. Urgent care center
   B. Blue Cross/Blue Shield
   C. Commercial insurer
   D. Skilled nursing facility

7. The Hoosier HMO contracts with an independent medical group that specializes in a variety of medical services in order to provide those services to HMO subscribers. The Hoosier HMO is structured as
   A. a staff model HMO
   B. a network model HMO
   C. a group model HMO
   D. an individual practice association model HMO

8. The Albuquerque HMO's contracting physicians are paid employees working on the staff of the HMO, operating in a clinic setting at the HMO's physical facilities. The Albuquerque HMO operates as
   A. a staff model HMO
   B. a network model HMO
   C. a group model HMO
   D. an individual practice association model HMO

9. Star HMO contracts with 14 medical groups to increase accessibility to providers as a convenience for subscribers. Each of the medical groups is paid on a capitation basis to provide services to Star's subscribers. The Star HMO operates as
   A. a staff model HMO
   B. a network model HMO
   C. a group model HMO
   D. an individual practice association model HMO

10. The Provider's Choice HMO was started by a group of individual physicians, and each physician operates out of his or her own office. The physicians are paid on a fee-for-service basis with the fees negotiated in advance. Provider's Choice HMO operates as
    A. a staff model HMO
    B. a network model HMO
    C. a group model HMO
    D. an individual practice association model HMO

11. Gwyneth's HMO requires that she receive health care services from a specified, limited number of health care providers chosen by the HMO. Gwyneth's HMO is
    A. open panel
    B. closed panel
    C. choice panel
    D. guarded panel

12. All of the following are examples of managed care plans EXCEPT
    A. health maintenance organizations
    B. preferred provider organizations
    C. indemnity arrangements
    D. point-of-service plans

13. A method of payment in which a provider is paid a specific fee monthly for each subscriber is known as
    A. indemnity
    B. fee-for-service
    C. managed care
    D. capitation

14. Calvin is hit by a car while traveling out of state. When the bill for his emergency services arrives, Calvin's HMO will probably
    A. pay for the services, even though they were incurred out of network, because emergency coverage is a basic health care service
    B. deny the claim because the services were out of network
    C. pay the claim only if the HMO had an affiliation agreement with the facility where the services were provided
    D. pay the claim if the HMO had an affiliation agreement with the facility where the services were provided, or if there is no affiliated facility within 50 miles

15. Best Cleaners has a health plan that provides its employees with a high-deductible medical indemnity plan and an account funded by the business, which employees can use to pay for medical expenses throughout the year or withdraw at the end of the year as taxable income. The plan is probably
    A. a cafeteria plan
    B. a medical savings account
    C. a multiple employer trust
    D. a third-party administrator

16. Bob's Balloons has a plan in which its employees can select benefits from a variety of coverage options based on individual and family needs. The plan is probably
    A. a cafeteria plan
    B. a medical savings account
    C. a multiple employer trust
    D. a third-party administrator

17. The Gargantuan Garage company funds its own claims but uses another company to make sure the plan is run correctly, acting as a liaison between the insurer and the employer. This arrangement is probably
    A. a cafeteria plan
    B. a medical savings account
    C. a multiple employer trust
    D. a third-party administrator

18. Which of the following individuals would probably qualify for Social Security disability benefits?
    A. George, a ski instructor who breaks his leg
    B. Carl, who becomes ill with a viral infection and is not expected to be able to work for the next 6 months
    C. Mike, a mechanic who loses his dominant hand in an accident
    D. John, who experiences serious early-onset Alzheimer's and is unable to remember how to get to work

19. Under workers' compensation, the permanent total disability benefit, while subject to minimum and maximum dollar amounts, is generally
    A. 50% of weekly wages
    B. 66.66% of weekly wages
    C. 70.5% of weekly wages
    D. 75% of weekly wages

20. Under workers' compensation, individuals with partial disabilities who are able to perform some work are eligible to receive
    A. no benefits
    B. 66.66% of weekly wages, subject to minimum and maximum dollar amounts
    C. the entire wage loss, subject to minimum and maximum dollar amounts
    D. a percentage of the wage loss, subject to minimum and maximum dollar amounts

ANSWERS AND RATIONALES TO UNIT TEST

1. **B.** A medical expense insurance policy pays for inpatient treatment and some outpatient expenses.

2. **A.** A disability income policy provides income to an individual disabled by illness or injury.

3. **D.** A hospital income insurance policy provides income to an individual who is disabled by illness or injury and confined to a hospital.

4. **B.** Jerry's policy pays only if he is confined to a hospital.

5. **C.** HMOs provide both health care service and health care financing.

6. **B.** Blue Cross/Blue Shield is an example of a producers' cooperative.

7. **C.** A group model HMO contracts with an independent medical group to provide services to its subscribers.

8. **A.** A staff model HMO hires the doctors as employees and owns their own facilities.

9. **B.** A network model HMO contracts with medical groups, which it pays to provide services to its subscribers.

10. **D.** An individual practice association model HMO consists of individual physicians operating out of their own offices.

11. **B.** A closed-panel HMO specifies a limited number of health care providers from which its subscribers may receive services.

12. **C.** Indemnity arrangements are not managed care plans.

13. **D.** A method of payment in which a provider is paid a specific fee monthly for each subscriber is known as capitation.

14. **A.** Calvin's HMO will probably pay for the services, even though they were incurred out of network because emergency coverage is a basic health care service.

15. **B.** A medical savings account is funded by an employer and can be used to pay for medical expenses or withdrawn at the end of the year.

16. **A.** A cafeteria plan provides a variety of coverage options based on individual and family needs.

17. **D.** A third-party administrator funds its own claims but uses another company to make sure the plan is run correctly.

18. **D.** Social Security disability benefits are payable only to a totally disabled person who will not be able to return to work.

19. **B.** Under workers' compensation, the permanent total disability benefit, although subject to minimum and maximum dollar amounts, is generally 66.66% of weekly wages.

20. **D.** Under workers' compensation, individuals with partial disabilities who are able to perform some work are eligible to receive a percentage of the wage loss, subject to minimum and maximum dollar amounts.

UNIT 16 EXERCISE ANSWERS

Exercise 16.A

1. Hospital Income
2. Travel accident
3. Accident only
4. Blanket
5. Credit
6. Dread disease

Exercise 16.B

1. **C**
2. **A**
3. **B**

Exercise 16.C

1. **C**
2. **A**
3. **B**

Exercise 16.D

1. Old Age
2. Survivors
3. Disability Income
4. Medicare

UNIT

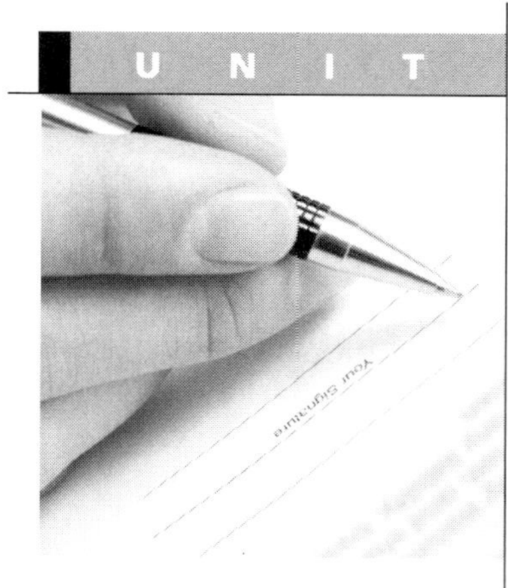

17

Policy Underwriting, Issuance, and Delivery

17. 1 UNDERWRITING OBJECTIVES

Health insurance underwriting is the process of selecting, classifying, and rating risks. Most companies offering health policies have a variety of policies available, and underwriting standards for each policy are usually established. Low-limit policies with limited coverages do not require the underwriting that broad coverage policies with high limits do; the greater the company's exposure, the more careful the underwriter must be.

17. 2 LEARNING OBJECTIVES

After completing this lesson, you will be able to:

- explain the underwriting objectives applicable to health insurance;
- list possible payment modes for health insurance, and explain which is used most frequently and which results in the highest overall cost to the insured;
- explain when health insurance policies go into effect;
- define replacement and the advantages and disadvantages of replacing health insurance policies; and
- define *fiduciary* and explain how it applies to health insurance producers.

17. 3 PREMIUM PAYMENTS

17. 3. 1 Definition of Premium

The premium is a sum of money the insured pays the insurer in exchange for or in consideration of the benefits or indemnities provided in the policy.

Because a premium is paid in consideration of the benefits provided in the policy, it is frequently called just that: a consideration. So the premium is the consideration paid for the benefits provided by the policy.

17. 3. 2 Earned and Unearned Premium

Premium payment frequency varies, but regardless of frequency, the insured is always paying for the upcoming period. That is, insurance premiums are paid in advance.

Suppose Kathryn's health insurance premium is $500 per year, which she pays in full on January 1. Because the $500 covers an entire year, the insurer earns the premium as the time passes, having both earned and unearned premium on hand during the policy term.

17. 3. 3 Payment Modes

In the insurance industry, **mode** of premium payment refers to the frequency with which premiums are paid. Payments may be made in five ways:

- Annually—once a year
- Semiannually—twice a year
- Quarterly—once every three months
- Monthly—once a month
- Weekly—once a week

Of these five modes, the least-used frequency for individual policies is weekly and is very rarely used.

Insurers generally calculate premiums on an annual basis. If the insured wants to pay by any of the other modes, the premium increases slightly as the frequency increases.

So, for example, a monthly premium mode results in a premium that is somewhat higher than a semiannual mode. An annual premium mode also results in a premium that is somewhat lower than a quarterly mode.

Exercise 17.A

Arrange the premium modes shown in order from the least expensive to the most expensive based on annual cost.

Monthly
Semiannually
Annually
Quarterly

1. ________________ (least expensive)
2. ________________
3. ________________
4. ________________ (most expensive)

Answers to the exercise can be found at the end of the Unit 17 answers and rationales.

17. 3. 4 Initial Premium

The **initial premium**, as the name implies, is the first premium the applicant pays to place the policy into effect. A health insurance policy goes into force when:

- the initial premium has been paid; and
- the policy is delivered to the insured.

If the initial premium was paid with the application and the applicant satisfies all of the conditions of the conditional receipt, coverage takes effect just as if the policy had already been issued.

A producer should always try to obtain the initial premium with an application and submit the entire package for underwriting. This affords faster protection to applicants, and applicants are less likely to change their minds about purchasing policies once they have money invested in them.

The important thing to remember is that coverage never applies until the insured has paid for it. If the initial premium does not accompany the application, the premium must be collected at policy delivery along with a signed statement that the insured continues to be in good health. The policy is then effective as of the date stated in the policy.

When the policy is delivered, the producer should explain the provisions, point out any exclusions, and—very importantly—go over any significant rating that affects the insured's coverage and premium payments.

17. 3. 5 Policy Effective Date

Although it is generally true that a policy is effective when the initial premium has been paid and the policy is delivered (or under the conditions of a conditional receipt), there is a better way for a producer to respond when asked when a particular policy takes effect.

The best approach is to state that the policy takes effect on the date specified in the policy as the effective date.

Remember that accident coverages usually take effect immediately when the policy is issued, whereas sickness coverages may require a probationary period. Therefore, different coverages under the same policy might have different effective dates.

17. 3. 6 Policy Term

Once a health insurance policy becomes effective, it will stay in force for the period for which the premium has been paid, unless the insurer or the insured cancels it. In other words, the policy will stay in force for a specified period or term.

The length of the term is governed by the length of time for which coverage is purchased by the premium payment. If a policy calls for annual premium payment, for example, one year is the term of the policy. If premiums are paid semiannually, the term extends for each six-month period for which the premium is paid.

17. 3. 7 Policy Fee

When a policy is issued, some companies charge a **policy fee**, which is generally a flat amount that helps defray such expenses as acquisition costs, producer commissions, administration, and maintenance of the policy. Usually, the policy fee is added to the premium and paid annually. Some companies, on the other hand, may charge a policy fee only once—at the time the policy is issued.

17. 4 DELIVERING THE POLICY

The surest way to be certain the policy is delivered is to do it personally. In addition to knowing the policy has been delivered, the producer has the following opportunities.

- The producer can explain the policy. It is important in health insurance for the policyowner to have basic understanding of what is and is not covered. With today's high health care costs, it is extremely important for the insured to know what the policy limitations are on the different types of medical expenses covered. Sometimes, policy premiums are higher than standard (rated up) because the insured does not meet certain basic health requirements or is involved in extra hazardous hobbies or avocations. These facts should be explained to avoid future misunderstandings and dissatisfaction. If the premium was not collected with the application, the company may require the producer to obtain a statement of good health from the insured at the time the policy is delivered and the premium is paid.
- The producer can reinforce the relationship and good will that have been established with the client.
- The producer can explain the possible need for additional health or other coverages.

Legally, the policy is considered delivered when it is mailed or turned over to the policyowner or someone acting on the policyowner's behalf. Some companies mail policies directly to policyowners; however, many prefer that the producer make a personal delivery. In some cases, a **constructive delivery** is deemed to occur when the insurer mails a policy to its producer for actual delivery to the policyowner, because the insurer has issued the policy and released it for delivery. However, a legal delivery has not yet occurred if the insurer requires personal delivery for verification of good health at the time of delivery, or if the policy is being provided to the applicant merely to review and inspect at that time and not necessarily to buy.

17. 5 SERVICING THE POLICY

In many industries, closing the sale means the end of the producer/consumer transaction. However, this is not so in insurance. Insurance policies require ongoing customer service throughout the policy period. Competition in the industry is another incentive to provide good customer service because it can make all the difference at renewal time. Good customer service makes insureds feel more comfortable doing business with you and makes them more likely to renew with your agency. Proper service of insurance policies also results in referrals, additional coverage, good public relations, and reduced errors and omissions exposure.

17. 6 REPLACEMENT

Producers attempting to replace the insured's current policy with a new policy need to take special care not to mislead the insured or provide coverage that is to the insured's detriment. Of particular concern is the fact that health conditions covered under an insured's existing policy may not be covered under a replacement policy because of the exclusion of preexisting conditions, or new waiting periods may be established.

A producer recommending replacement should give special attention to the exclusions and limitations in the proposed policy, compared with the existing policy. Not all policies cover the same things. If the contracts are different, the replacement policy might not provide the same coverages or the same level of benefits as the existing policy.

Some states have passed **no loss/no gain** legislation, which requires that when health insurance is replaced, ongoing claims under the former policy must continue to be paid under the new policy, thereby overriding any preexisting conditions exclusion. In replacing group health coverage, a transfer of benefits statement ensures that benefits provided under the old policy continue under the new policy.

Because the elderly are extremely vulnerable and often victimized insurance prospects, and they are most susceptible to being penalized by preexisting conditions limitations, producers should be aware that there are often more-restrictive regulations for replacing Medicare supplement policies.

Certainly, there are legitimate circumstances when replacement of a policy makes sense and should be recommended—for example, when broader coverage or higher benefits can be obtained at a lower rate and preexisting conditions and waiting periods are not issues.

However, a producer needs to be very careful in recommending a change in policies or carriers when any potential factors could lead to an uninsured loss that might otherwise have been covered. Producers need to be aware of their own errors and omissions liability, particularly in the area of replacement. Replacement is not illegal, but it is heavily regulated.

17. 7 PROFESSIONALISM AND ETHICS

All business transactions are based to a certain extent on trust. When it comes to insurance, the trust factor is especially significant. When asked what factors matter most in a financial advisor, consumers choose ethical performance more than twice as often as financial performance. Ethics and professionalism are critical components of a successful career as an insurance producer.

Ethics means setting a standard of conduct or behavior based on established values. Insurance producers and other industry employees have long sought to distinguish themselves as professionals. A professional is defined as a person in an occupation requiring an advanced level of training, knowledge, or skill. *Professionals* enjoy privileges commensurate with their skills, but they also have higher responsibilities in caring for others because of the title of professional. *Professionals* relate to their clients in a way that reflects well on the entire industry. The highest standard of service is provided by preparing for new clients long before even meeting them.

17. 7. 1 Fiduciary Responsibility

Insurance producers have a **fiduciary** duty to just about any person or organization with whom they come into contact as a part of the day-to-day business of transacting insurance. By definition, a **fiduciary** is a person in a position of financial trust. Attorneys, accountants, trust officers, and insurance producers are all considered fiduciaries.

As a fiduciary, producers have an obligation to act in the best interest of the insured. The producer must be knowledgeable about the features and provisions of various insurance policies and know the use of these insurance contracts. The producer must be able to explain the important features of these policies to the insured. The producer must recognize the importance of dealing with the general public's financial needs and problems and offering solutions to these problems through the purchase of insurance products.

As a fiduciary, the producer must know and comply with the state's insurance laws. Many of these laws are for consumer protection. It is the producer's duty to comply with these laws and protect the interest of the insured at all times.

Exercise 17.B

Match the item to the phrase that best describes it.

____ 1.	Acting in a position of financial trust	A. No loss/no gain
____ 2.	Causing a policy to be lapsed, surrendered, or forfeited to obtain another	B. Replacement
____ 3.	Continuing to pay on-going claims from a previous policy under a new contract	C. Fiduciary

Answers to the exercise can be found at the end of the Unit 17 answers and rationales.

17. 7. 2 Summary of the Producer's Responsibilities

The insurance producer is a key person in the process of marketing, underwriting, and delivering insurance policies. As a marketing representative of the insurer, the producer has a responsibility to represent and market the insurer's products in an ethical and professional manner. This requires knowledge of various insurance products, awareness of a prospect's insurance needs and problems, and the ability to solve these needs with the proper insurance products.

UNIT TEST

1. The sum of money the insured pays the insurer in exchange for the benefits provided in the policy is
   A. the co-payment
   B. the premium
   C. the indemnity
   D. the capitation

2. Ally pays for her health insurance monthly. Her identical twin, Georgia, has the same policy, but pays annually. Which of them probably pays more for her policy?
   A. Ally probably pays more.
   B. Georgia probably pays more.
   C. They probably pay the same.
   D. It is not possible to determine from the information provided.

3. Health insurance coverage never applies until
   A. the policy is delivered
   B. an underwriting decision is made
   C. the application is reviewed by underwriting
   D. the insured has paid for the policy

4. Once a health insurance policy becomes effective, unless it is canceled, it will stay in force for
   A. 1 year
   B. 6 months
   C. the length of the term
   D. an indefinite period

5. Legally, the policy is considered delivered in all of the following situations EXCEPT
   A. when the policy is approved by the company
   B. when the policy is mailed to the policyowner
   C. when the policy is turned over to the policyowner
   D. when the policy is turned over to someone acting on behalf of the policyowner

6. An insurer might require personal delivery
   A. to ensure the policy goes to the right person
   B. for verification of the continued good health of the insured at the time of delivery
   C. to ensure the correct policy is delivered
   D. to verify information listed on the application

7. No loss/no gain legislation requires a replacing policy to
   A. have exactly the same premium as the policy it replaces
   B. have exactly the same limits of coverage as the policy it replaces
   C. continue to pay claims ongoing under the policy it replaces
   D. continue to use the same producer to manage the policy as the policy it replaces

8. A statement that ensures benefits provided under the old policy will continue under the new policy is
   A. a transfer of benefits statement
   B. a continuation of benefits statement
   C. a preexisting conditions coverage statement
   D. a replacement statement

9. Restrictions applying to the replacement of Medicare supplement policies are
   A. often less restrictive than regulations applying to the replacement of other policies
   B. generally the same as regulations applying to the replacement of other policies
   C. often more restrictive than regulations applying to the replacement of other policies
   D. prohibited entirely by federal law

ANSWERS AND RATIONALES TO UNIT TEST

1. **B.** The insured pays a premium to the insurer in exchange for the policy.

2. **A.** Ally probably pays more because premiums increase as frequency increases.

3. **D.** Health insurance coverage never applies until the insured has paid for the policy.

4. **C.** A health insurance contract remains in force for the length of the term as specified in the contract.

5. **A.** The policy is not considered delivered when the policy is approved by the company.

6. **B.** An insurer might require personal delivery for verification of the continued good health of the insured at the time of delivery.

7. **C.** No loss/no gain legislation requires a replacing policy to continue to pay claims ongoing under the policy it replaces.

8. **A.** A statement ensuring that benefits provided under the old policy will continue under the new policy is a transfer of benefits statement.

9. **C.** Restrictions applying to the replacement of Medicare supplement policies are often more restrictive than regulations applying to the replacement of other policies.

UNIT 17 EXERCISE ANSWERS

Exercise 17.A

1. Annually
2. Semiannually
3. Quarterly
4. Monthly

Exercise 17.B

1. **C**
2. **B**
3. **A**

UNIT

18

Policy Provisions

18. 1 INTRODUCTION

Because both state insurance laws and insurance policies vary greatly, an attempt has been made to make health insurance policies conform to certain standard regulations. To accomplish this, all states have adopted the Uniform Individual Accident and Sickness Policy Provisions Law. Nearly every state has modified the law to some extent, but all have adopted it in principle.

The law includes 12 mandatory provisions that must be included in individual health insurance policies and 11 optional provisions. Each of the mandatory provisions must be included in each policy, usually in a section of the policy titled "Mandatory or Required Provisions." Insurance companies need not use the exact wording of the provisions, but any variations must be at least as favorable to the insured as the original statutory wording. Provisions may also be referred to as clauses. There is no additional cost attached to a provision or clause.

18. 2 LEARNING OBJECTIVES

After completing this lesson, you will be able to do the following:

- describe and explain the purpose of the mandatory policy provisions;
- describe and explain the purpose of the optional policy provisions; and
- describe and explain the purpose of the other standard policy provisions.

18. 3 TWELVE MANDATORY (REQUIRED) POLICY PROVISIONS

18. 3. 1 Entire Contract

Here is the exact wording of the provision.

This policy, including the endorsements and the attached papers, if any, constitutes the entire contract of insurance. No change in this policy shall be valid until approved by an executive officer of the insurer and unless such approval be endorsed hereon or attached hereto. No agent has authority to change this policy or to waive any of its provisions.

This provision defines the scope of an **entire contract** as:

- the insurance policy provisions;
- a copy of the application;
- riders, if any; and
- attachments or amendments, if any.

In order for something to be included in the contract, it must be attached, and it must be in writing. Nothing else is part of the contract.

An agent or producer may not change a policy or waive any of its provisions, but changes may be made if they are approved by an executive officer of the insurance company. Any changes requested by the owner and approved by the company will be added in the form of an amendment. The insured will be aware of any such changes because the insured will be endorsed on or attached to the policy.

18. 3. 2 Time Limit on Certain Defenses (Incontestability)

Here is the exact wording of the provision.

A. After two years from the date of issue of this policy, no misstatements, except fraudulent misstatements, made by the applicant in the application for such policy shall be used to void the policy or to deny a claim for loss incurred or disability (as defined in the policy) commencing after the expiration of such two-year period.

B. No claim for loss incurred or disability (as defined in the policy) commencing after two years from the date of issue of this policy shall be reduced or denied on the ground that a disease or physical condition, not excluded from coverage by name or specific description effective on the date of loss, had existed prior to the effective date of coverage of this policy.

Unless an insured's misstatements are fraudulent, after two years from the date the policy is issued, the policy becomes incontestable. Part A says that no material misstatements in the application (except for fraud) can be used to void the policy or deny a claim after two years have passed (three years in some states). Fraud can void the health insurance contract whenever it is found and can be proven by the health insurer.

Part B states that after two years, the policy cannot be voided, a claim may not be denied, and benefits may not be reduced on the grounds that an illness or a condition was preexisting. This does not prevent an insurer from specifically excluding coverage for a certain condition, but to be excluded, the condition must be named or specifically described in the policy when it is written and is referred to as an impairment waiver or rider.

18. 3. 3 Grace Period

Here is the exact wording of the provision.

A grace period of __ days (the period varies according to premium payment frequency: 7 days for weekly premium policies; 10 days for monthly premium policies; 31 days for all other policies) will be granted for the payment of each premium falling due after the first premium, during which grace period the policy shall continue in force.

A policy that contains a cancellation provision may add, at the end of the above provision, "*subject to the right of the insurer to cancel in accordance with the cancellation provision hereof*."

A policy in which the insurer reserves the right to refuse any renewal shall state, at the beginning of the above provision, the following: "*unless not less than five days prior to the premium due date the insurer has delivered to the insured, or has mailed to the last address as shown by the records of the insurer, written notice of its intention not to renew this policy beyond the period for which the premium has been accepted.*"

The required grace period depends on how often the insured pays the policy premiums, as illustrated.

Required Grace Period, by Payment Frequency

Weekly Premium Policies Require a 7-day Grace Period

JANUARY						
S	M	T	W	T	F	S
		1	2	3	4	5
6	7	8	9	10	11	12
13	14	15	16	17	18	19
20	21	22	23	24	25	26
27	28	29	30	31		

Monthly Premium Policies Require a 10-day Grace Period

JANUARY						
S	M	T	W	T	F	S
		1	2	3	4	5
6	7	8	9	10	11	12
13	14	15	16	17	18	19
20	21	22	23	24	25	26
27	28	29	30	31		

All Other Policies Require a 31-day Grace Period

JANUARY						
S	M	T	W	T	F	S
		1	2	3	4	5
6	7	8	9	10	11	12
13	14	15	16	17	18	19
20	21	22	23	24	25	26
27	28	29	30	31		

Insurers must allow the insured a period of grace for premium payment. This is a specified time following the premium due date during which coverage remains intact. During a grace period, the company continues coverage in full force and will accept the premium from the policyowner just as if it were not late.

Exercise 18.A

Match the number of days in a grace period with the premium mode.

____1. 7 days — A. Annually

____2. 10 days — B. Weekly

____3. 31 days — C. Monthly

Answers to the exercise can be found at the end of the Unit 18 answers and rationales.

18. 3. 4 Reinstatement

The insured, unlike the insurer, may cancel a policy at any time. In addition, the insured can simply refuse or fail to pay the premium when it is next due. When this occurs, we say that the policy has lapsed. Whether the policy is canceled by the insured or if it lapses unintentionally, the end result is the same: the coverage terminates.

Because this provision is quite long, we'll cover it in two parts. Here is the first portion.

> *If any renewal premium is not paid within the time granted the insured for payment, a subsequent acceptance of premium by the insurer or by any agent duly authorized by the insurer to accept such premium, without requiring in connection therewith an application for reinstatement, shall reinstate the policy; provided, however, that if the insurer or such agent requires an application for reinstatement and issues a conditional receipt for the premium tendered, the policy will be reinstated upon approval of such application by the insurer or, lacking such approval, upon the 45th day following the date of such conditional receipt unless the insurer has previously notified the insured in writing of its disapproval of such application.*

According to this part of the provision, with certain exceptions, a lapsed policy is reinstated when either the company or the company's authorized agent accepts subsequent premiums.

However, an application for reinstatement might be required, and a conditional receipt could be issued to the insured for any premium payment. The insurer will then generally notify the applicant whether or not the policy has been reinstated, but if the insurer does not so notify the applicant, the policy is automatically reinstated on the 45th day after the date of the receipt.

Here is the second portion of the reinstatement provision.

> *The reinstated policy shall cover only loss resulting from such accidental injury as may be sustained after the date of reinstatement and loss due to such sickness as may begin more than 10 days after such date. In all other respects, the insured and insurer shall have the same rights thereunder as they had under the policy immediately before the due date of the defaulted premium, subject to any provisions endorsed hereon or attached hereto in connection with the reinstatement. Any premium accepted in connection with the reinstatement shall be applied to a period for which premium has not been previously paid, but not to any period more than 60 days prior to the date of reinstatement.*

Once the policy is reinstated, there is:

- a 10-day waiting period for sickness coverages; and
- no waiting period for accident coverages.

Otherwise, both the insurer and the insured have all the same rights each had the day before the policy lapsed, subject to any endorsements or riders attached at the time of reinstatement.

Exercise 18.B

There are two important time frames connected with reinstatement of a health policy. Fill in the correct number of days in each of the following sentences.

1. A policy must automatically be considered reinstated by an insurer ____ days after submitting any required application and/or premium.
2. Coverage for sickness by a reinstated policy will begin after a waiting period of ____ days.

Answers to the exercise can be found at the end of the Unit 18 answers and rationales.

18. 3. 5 Notice of Claim

Here is the exact wording of the provision.

> *Written notice of claim must be given to the insurer within 20 days after occurrence or commencement of any loss covered by the policy, or as soon thereafter as is reasonably possible. Notice given by or in behalf of the insured or the beneficiary to the insurer at __________ (insert the location of such office as the insurer may designate for the purpose), or to any authorized agent of the insurer, with information sufficient to identify the insured, shall be deemed notice to the insurer.*

When a claim arises, certain stipulations apply. If reasonably possible, the insured must give written notice of claim to the insurer within 20 days after the loss occurs. The insured may send the notice either to the address the insurer provides or to the agent.

Although the term *reasonably* is not defined, an example will illustrate one possibility. An insured is injured in an accident and remains in a coma for five weeks, thus failing to provide written notice of claim within the required 20 days. The company is still liable for the claim because it could not reasonably have required the claim to be filed during the time the insured was in a coma.

Policies providing loss-of-time benefits payable for at least two years will include the following statement.

> *Subject to the qualifications set forth below, if the insured suffers loss of time on account of disability for which indemnity may be payable for at least two years, he shall, at least once in every six months after having given notice of claim, give to the insurer notice of continuance of said disability, except in the event of legal incapacity. The period of six months following any filing of proof by the insured or any payment by the insurer on account of such claim or any denial of liability in whole or in part by the insurer shall be excluded in applying this provision. Delay in the giving of such notice shall not impair the insured's right to any indemnity which would otherwise have accrued during the period of six months preceding the date on which such notice is actually given.*

The essence of this provision is that if the policy provides disability income for an extended period, the insurer can require that the insured provide, every six months, written notice that the claim is continuing. This provision does not apply when the insured suffers a legal incapacity.

18. 3. 6 Claim Forms

Here is the exact wording of the provision.

> *The insurer, upon receipt of a notice of claim, will furnish to the claimant such forms as are usually furnished by it for filing proofs of loss. If such forms are not furnished within 15 days after the giving of such notice, the claimant shall be deemed to have complied with the requirements of this policy as to proof of loss upon submitting, within the time fixed in the policy for filing proofs of loss, written proof covering the occurrence, the character and the extent of the loss for which claim is made.*

When an insurer receives a notice of claim, it should furnish the insured with forms to provide proof of loss within 15 days. If the insurer fails to do so, however, the insured is required to act to protect the claim by filing written proof of loss detailing the occurrence, the character, and the extent of the loss.

18. 3. 7 Proof of Loss

Here is the exact wording of the provision.

> *Written proof of loss must be furnished to the insurer at its said office in case of claim for loss for which this policy provides any periodic payment contingent upon continuing loss within 90 days after the termination of the period for which the insurer is liable, and in case of claims for any other loss within 90 days after the date of such loss. Failure to furnish such proof within the time required shall not invalidate nor reduce any claim if it was not reasonably possible to give such proof within such time, provided such proof is furnished as soon as reasonably possible and in no event, except in the absence of legal capacity, later than one year from the time proof is otherwise required.*

The next illustration shows the difference between filing a proof of loss when benefits are paid periodically versus filing proof for a one-time, nonperiodic loss as provided in the provision.

Filing Proof of Loss

Insured Xavier	Insured Yvonne
Receives periodic payments of disability income from May 1 through October 11.	Submits a claim for hospital expenses after an accident at home on April 25.
Must file proofs of loss within 90 days after October 11—the date the insurer's liability for payment has ended.	Must file proofs of loss within 90 days after April 25—the date of the loss since no periodic benefits are involved.
Both Insureds	
Have up to a year following the required filing dates to file proofs of loss if they cannot reasonably do so earlier. Legal incapacity excuses this limit.	

Normally, written proofs of loss must be furnished within 90 days after the date of loss. However, when the claim involves periodic payments because of a continuing loss, proofs must be furnished within 90 days after the end of the period for which the company is liable.

If it was not reasonably possible for the insured to provide proofs of loss within the time required, the claim is not invalidated. Nevertheless, unless the insured suffers legal incapacity, proofs of loss must be furnished no later than one year from the date they were otherwise due.

18. 3. 8 Time of Payment of Claims

Here is the exact wording of the provision.

> *Indemnities payable under this policy for any loss other than loss for which this policy provides any periodic payment will be paid immediately upon receipt of due written proof of such loss. Subject to due written proof of loss, all accrued indemnities for loss for which this policy provides periodic payment will be paid ________ (insert period for payment which must not be less frequently than monthly), and any balance remaining unpaid upon the termination of liability will be paid immediately upon receipt of due written proof.*

According to this provision, except for claims involving periodic payments over a specified time span, the insurer must make the payment immediately after receiving proof of loss.

Payment of periodic indemnities (for disability, for instance) must be made at least monthly.

Let's look at an example of how this provision works.

Example

Serena has been receiving $700 a month for a total disability, but she is able to return to work two weeks after her most recent indemnity payment. She has two more weeks' benefits coming. She files a final proof of loss, including statements from her doctor (that she has been released) and her employer (that she has returned to work). Upon receipt of this final proof of loss, the insurer must pay the final two weeks' indemnity immediately.

Notice that, in every case, the insured must provide written proof of loss to the insurer.

18. 3. 9 Payment of Claims

This long provision actually contains both a required portion and two optional paragraphs. Here is the required section.

> *Indemnity for loss of life will be payable in accordance with the beneficiary designation and the provisions respecting such payment which may be prescribed herein and effective at the time of payment. If no such designation or provision is then effective, such indemnity shall be payable to the estate of the insured. Any other accrued indemnities unpaid at the insured's death may, at the option of the insurer, be paid either to such beneficiary or to such estate. All other indemnities will be payable to the insured.*

This required portion of the provision states that:

- death benefits will be paid to the named beneficiary;
- if there is no beneficiary designated, the company will pay the benefit to the insured's estate;
- if the insured was receiving monthly indemnities under the policy and some accrued benefits remain at the time of death, the company may pay these accruals to either the beneficiary or the insured's estate; and
- while the insured is alive, all other benefits are paid to the insured unless otherwise specifically designated in the policy.

Here is the first of the two optional paragraphs that are included in the payment-of-claims provision.

> *If any indemnity of this policy shall be payable to the estate of the insured, or to an insured or beneficiary who is a minor or otherwise not competent to give a valid release, the insurer may pay such indemnity, up to an amount not exceeding $_____ (insert an amount which shall not exceed $1,000), to any relative by blood or connection by marriage of the insured or beneficiary who is deemed by the insurer to be equitably entitled thereto. Any payment made by the insurer in good faith pursuant to this provision shall fully discharge the insurer to the extent of such payment.*

This first optional paragraph is often called the **facility of payment** clause because it makes claim payment easier under the circumstances described. It stipulates two things.

- If the insured or the beneficiary cannot legally release the company from further liability, as when the insured or beneficiary is a minor or is legally incapacitated, the company may pay the benefits to any relative by blood or marriage who is deemed to be entitled to the money.
- The amount paid to this person cannot exceed $1,000.

If a claim is paid under this provision, the payment absolves the company of further liability.

Here is the second of the optional paragraphs that may be included with the payment-of-claims provision.

> *Subject to any written direction of the insured in the application or otherwise, all or a portion of any indemnities provided by this policy on account of hospital, nursing, medical, or surgical services may, at the insurer's option, and unless the insured requests otherwise in writing not later than the time of filing proofs of such loss, be paid directly to the hospital or person rendering such services, but it is not required that the service be rendered by a particular hospital or person.*

According to this second optional paragraph, unless the insured specifically directs otherwise, the company may pay benefits to a hospital or person rendering medical or surgical services. However, the company may not require that the insured enter a specific hospital or see a particular doctor.

18. 3. 10 Physical Examination and Autopsy

Here is the exact wording of the provision.

> *The insurer at its own expense shall have the right and opportunity to examine the person of the insured when and as often as it may reasonably require during the pendency of a claim hereunder and to make an autopsy in case of death where it is not forbidden by law.*

According to this provision, while the insured is alive and receiving benefits, the insurer may require that the insured submit to physical examinations.

If an insured has died, apparently accidentally, the insurer may have an autopsy performed to determine the exact cause of death. However, any applicable state laws that might prevent such an autopsy take precedence.

The insurer is required to pay for examinations or autopsies and may require only reasonable examinations.

18. 3. 11 Legal Actions

Here is the exact wording of the provision.

> *No action at law or in equity shall be brought to recover on this policy prior to the expiration of 60 days after written proof of loss has been furnished in accordance with the requirements of this policy. No such action shall be brought after the expiration of three years after the time written proof of loss is required to be furnished.*

When written proof of loss has been submitted, the company needs time to investigate the claim and make certain it is valid. To provide the insurer with this time, this provision prohibits the insured from suing the insurer for at least 60 days after filing a written proof of loss.

The maximum time during which suit can be filed is three years after written proof of loss is furnished.

18. 3. 12 Change of Beneficiary

Here is the exact wording of the provision.

> *Unless the insured makes an irrevocable designation of beneficiary, the right to change of beneficiary is reserved to the insured and the consent of the beneficiary or beneficiaries shall not be requisite to surrender or assignment of this policy or to any change of beneficiary or beneficiaries, or to any other changes in this policy.*

The policyowner, who is usually the insured, may name a beneficiary either **revocably**, which means that the insured can change the beneficiary later, or **irrevocably**, which means the beneficiary designation may not be changed.

In other words, the right to change the beneficiary or dispose of the policy or its benefits in any manner one chooses is reserved to the insured unless the insured has named an irrevocable beneficiary.

Example

Ben has named his spouse the beneficiary of the accidental death benefit of his health insurance policy, and he has relinquished his right to change that designation. Now he wants to obtain a large loan, and the lender agrees to make the loan if Ben assigns any payments under his policy to the lender. Ben may assign the policy only with his spouse's permission because she is the irrevocable beneficiary. Ben would not need this permission if his spouse were a revocable beneficiary.

Exercise 18.C

Fill in the blanks to help remember six of the 12 Mandatory Provisions.

> Barbara had a terrible skiing accident resulting in a badly broken leg which required her to be hospitalized. She had an individual Hospital Expense policy that provided reimbursement for covered expenses. In accordance with the Mandatory Provisions of her policy, Barbara had ____ days to give Notice of Claim. The insurer then had ____ days to provide her with Claim Forms. She had a total of ____ days after her accident to provide Proof of Loss. The Payment of Claims provision directs the insurer to pay the benefits to the ____ and the Time Payment of Claims provision tells them to pay____________. If the insurer fails to pay her claim, Barbara may take Legal Action no sooner than ____ days and no later than ____ years after filing her Proof of Loss.

Answers to the exercise can be found at the end of the Unit 18 answers and rationales.

18. 4 ELEVEN OPTIONAL POLICY PROVISIONS

The optional provisions are not required to be included in the policy, but if the subject of any of them is contained in the policy, it must be worded in accordance with the wording of the appropriate optional provision. An insurer may reword any of the optional provisions so long as the new wording is not less favorable to the insured or the beneficiary.

18. 4. 1 Change of Occupation

Here is the first optional provision.

> *If the insured be injured or contract sickness after having changed his or her occupation to one classified by the insurer as more hazardous than that stated in this policy, or while doing for compensation anything pertaining to an occupation so classified, the insurer will pay only such portion of the indemnities provided in this policy as the premium paid would have purchased at the rates and within limits fixed by the insurer for a more hazardous occupation. If the insured changes an occupation to one classified by the insurer as less hazardous than that stated in this policy, the insurer, upon receipt of proof of such change of occupation, will reduce the premium rate accordingly, and will return the excess pro rata unearned premium from the date of change of occupation or from the policy anniversary date immediately preceding receipt of such proof, whichever is the more recent. In applying this provision, the classification of occupational risk and the premium rates shall be such as have been last filed by the insurer prior to the occurrence of the loss for which the insurer is liable, or prior to date of proof of change in occupation with the state official having supervision of insurance in the state where the insured resided at the time this policy was issued; but if such filing was not required, then the classification of occupational risk and the premium rates shall be those last made effective by the insurer in such state prior to the occurrence of the loss or prior to the date of proof of change in occupation.*

This provision relieves the insurer from paying benefits not anticipated when the premium was established. If an insured's occupation is more hazardous than the insurer knew, and resulted in injury or illness, the insurer might be required to pay a larger benefit than the premium warrants. Here's an example of how this provision works.

Example

If Max, the insured, had continued at the occupation he had when he purchased his disability income policy, disability from an accidental injury would have resulted in a benefit of $1,600 per month based on the premium Max paid. However, Max changed to a more hazardous occupation without notifying the insurer, and then suffered a disabling injury on the job. The insurer will pay only the amount of benefit that Max would have been able to purchase, with the premium already paid, for the more hazardous job, so Max's benefit is reduced.

Suppose Max had changed to a less hazardous occupation but paid premiums based on the more hazardous occupation. In this case, Max sends proof that he changed occupations to the insurer, the premium rate is reduced accordingly, and the insurer returns the excess premium to Max on a pro rata (proportionate) basis.

When calculating how much of the extra premium to return, the company uses the more recent of:

- the date the occupation changed; or
- the policy anniversary date immediately preceding receipt of the proof of change.

18. 4. 2 Misstatement of Age

Here is the exact wording of the provision.

> *If the age of the insured has been misstated, all amounts payable under this policy shall be such as the premium paid would have purchased at the correct age.*

When an insured is younger, a premium dollar buys a certain amount of insurance. As the insured ages, the same premium dollar buys less insurance. This provision is similar to the previous provision regarding a more hazardous occupation. If the insured has misstated his age on the application, the company may adjust benefits to the amount the premiums paid would have bought had the insured's correct age been known.

If an insured overstated his age—stated an older age than he actually was—when applying for the coverage, the insured has been paying a premium that is too high. Under this provision, the insurer could increase any benefits to the amount the premium paid for.

Or, if the insured had understated his age, the company would pay the insured (or a beneficiary, in the event of accidental death) a smaller benefit.

Whether the insured misstated his age intentionally or unintentionally, the company simply adjusts benefits accordingly.

18. 4. 3 Other Insurance with This Insurer

Here is the exact wording of the provision.

> *If an accident or sickness policy or policies previously issued by the insurer to the insured be in force concurrently herewith, making the aggregate indemnity for ___________ (insert type of coverage or coverages) in excess of $_______ (insert maximum limit of indemnity or indemnities), the excess insurance shall be void and all premiums paid for such excess shall be returned to the insured or to the estate.*

Or,

> *Insurance effective at any one time on the insured under a like policy or policies in this insurer is limited to one such policy elected by the insured, his or her beneficiary or estate, as the case may be, and the insurer will return all premiums paid for all other such policies.*

This provision deals with insurance of the same type with the same insurer.

If an individual has so much insurance that it is more profitable to see a doctor, enter a hospital, or stay home from work, there might be some temptation to do just that rather than to have a quick recovery. Such an individual is **overinsured**—a situation insurers try to avoid.

This optional provision allows an insurer to control overinsurance through its own policies. The company can establish maximum amounts payable to any one insured for certain coverages—disability income insurance being the most common—so no matter how many policies an insured has with this particular company, there is a limit on the amount of benefits that will be paid.

Either of the two provisions may be included in the policy. If the insurer chooses the first paragraph, it is the insurer's responsibility to decide on the maximum indemnity that will be paid and the type of coverage to which the provision applies. When these limitations are included in the policy, any amount of like insurance over the specified maximum is considered void, and the insurer will return premiums paid for these void benefits to the insured or to the insured's estate.

If the insurer uses the second paragraph, coverage is limited to one policy as selected by the insured, the beneficiary, or the administrator of the insured's estate. When the second optional provision is used, the premiums paid for the other policy or policies are refunded.

18. 4. 4 Insurance with Other Insurers

Although the previous optional provision concerned overinsurance with the same insurer, the next two deal with other insurers. Because they are closely related, they are presented together.

Part 1

If there be other valid coverage, not with this insurer, providing benefits for the same loss on a provision-of-service basis or on a expense-incurred basis and of which this insurer has not been given written notice prior to the occurrence or commencement of loss, the only liability under any expense-incurred coverage of this policy shall be for such proportion of the loss as the amount which would otherwise have been payable hereunder plus the total of the like amounts under all such other valid coverages for the same loss, and for the return of such portion of the premiums paid as shall exceed the pro rata portion of the amount so determined. For the purpose of applying this provision when other coverage is on a provision of service basis, the like amount of such other coverage shall be taken as the amount which the services rendered would have cost in the absence of such coverage.

Part 2

If there be other valid coverage, not with this insurer, providing benefits for the same loss on other than an expense-incurred basis and of which the insurer has not been given written notice prior to the occurrence or commencement of loss, the only liability for such benefits under this policy shall be for such proportion of the indemnities of which the insurer had notice (including the indemnities under this policy) bear to the total amount of all like indemnities for such loss, and for the return of such portion of the premium paid as shall exceed the pro rata portion for the indemnities thus determined.

The essence of these provisions is this: if an insured has two or more policies from different companies that cover the same expenses, and if the insurers were not notified that the other coverage existed, each insurer will pay a proportionate share of any claim. This prevents the insured from receiving benefits greater than the loss.

When both of these optional provisions appear in the same policy, **Part 1** must be captioned *expense-incurred benefits* as it deals with losses to be reimbursed on that basis. Likewise, **Part 2** must be captioned *other benefits* as it deals with overinsurance for losses reimbursed on any basis other than expense incurred.

18. 4. 5 Relation of Earnings to Insurance—Average Earnings Clause

This provision specifically concerns loss of time, or disability income, coverage.

If the total monthly amount of loss of time benefits promised for the same loss under all valid loss of time coverage upon the insured, whether payable on a weekly or monthly basis, shall exceed the monthly earnings of the insured at the time disability commenced, or the average monthly earnings for the period of two years immediately preceding a disability for which claim is made, whichever is greater, the insurer will be liable only for such proportionate amount of such benefits under this policy as the amount of such monthly earnings or such average monthly earnings of the insured bears to the total amount of monthly benefits for the same loss under all such coverage upon the insured at the time such disability commences, and for the return of such part of the premiums paid during such two years as shall exceed the pro rata amount of the premiums for the benefits actually paid hereunder; but this shall not operate to reduce the total monthly amount of benefits payable under all such coverage upon the insured below the sum of $200 or the sum of the monthly benefits specified in such coverages, whichever is the lesser, nor shall it operate to reduce benefits other than those payable for loss of time.

This optional provision is also designed to prevent malingering—remaining disabled in order to collect insurance. The provision specifically addresses the relationship between what the insured actually has been earning on the job and the amount of insurance available by failing to return to work. The illustration gives an example of how insurance might pay more than the insured earns.

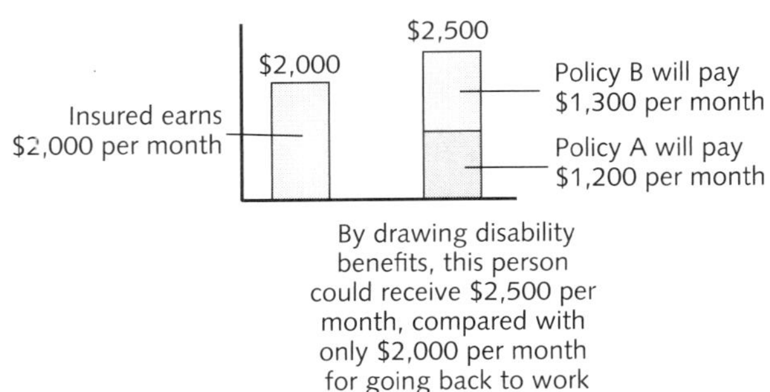

According to this provision, if the total monthly benefits from all policies are more than the insured's monthly income, each insurer will pay a proportionate share of the lost income. This will prevent the insured from receiving benefits greater than the loss. Because the insured paid for more coverage than can be collected, each company must refund a proportionate share of the excess premiums.

18. 4. 6 Unpaid Premium

Upon the payment of a claim under this policy, any premium then due and unpaid or covered by any note or written order may be deducted therefrom. Here is the exact wording of the provision.

This very simple optional provision allows an insurer to deduct premiums that are due or past due as part of settling a claim. Some companies will also accept a promissory note from an insured, indicating the insured will pay at a stipulated time in the future. In return, the company agrees to continue coverage in force as if the premium had already been paid. When a company holds such a note and a claim is made, this provision allows the insurer to deduct the amount of the premium before paying the indemnity. With or without a promissory note, here is how this provision would operate.

Example

Frederick sends his insurer a claim for $1,800 to cover hospital and medical expenses from an illness.

CLAIM $1,800

The insurer notes that Frederick owes a past-due premium of $300, which the insurer deducts from the claim…

UNPAID PREMIUM – $300

…then pays the $1,500 balance:

AMOUNT OF CLAIM PAID $1,500

18. 4. 7 Cancellation

Let's break this optional provision into two parts. Here is the first part.

> *The insurer may cancel this policy at any time by written notice delivered to the insured or mailed to the last address as shown by the records of the insurer, stating when, not less than five days thereafter, such cancellation shall be effective; and after the policy has been continued beyond its original term, the insured may cancel this policy at any time by written notice delivered or mailed to the insurer, effective upon receipt or on such later date as may be specified in such notice.*

Although this provision may not be used in noncancelable policies, in policies that may be canceled, the insurer may do so by delivering (usually by mail) written notice to the insured UNPAID PREMIUM – $300's last known address. Cancellation is effective no fewer than five days after the date of notice.

Here is the remainder of the optional provision regarding cancellation.

> *In the event of cancellation, the insurer will return promptly the unearned portion of any premium paid. If the insured cancels, the earned premium shall be computed by the use of the short rate table last filed with the state official having supervision of insurance in the state where the insured resided when the policy was issued. If the insurer cancels, the earned premium shall be computed pro rata. Cancellation shall be without prejudice to any claim originating prior to the effective date of cancellation.*

When a policy is canceled before its expiration date, some of the prepaid premium is **unearned**—that is, the insurance company has not yet earned the premium because the period of time it was intended to cover has not yet passed. The way in which unearned premium is returned to the insured depends on who canceled the policy: the insurance company or the insured. The explanations and illustrations that follow show what happens to a premium dollar.

When the insurance company cancels, the portion of the premium dollar the insurer has already earned is kept by the insurer and the entire unearned portion is returned to the insured. This is a **pro rata** return.

Pro Rata Return of Premium

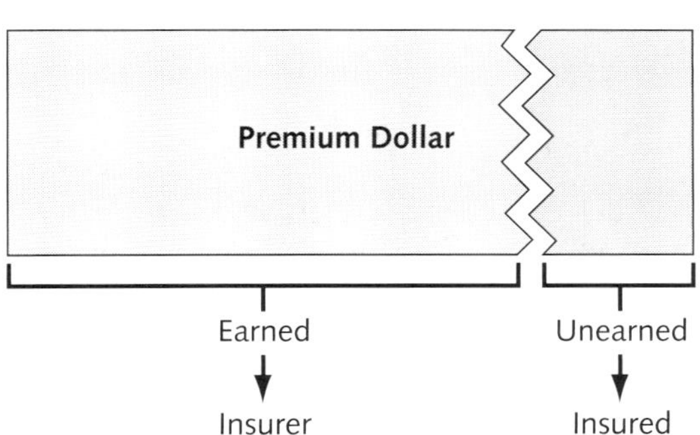

When the insured cancels, the insurance company is allowed to retain a portion of premium over and above that which it has earned. So the insurer keeps earned premium and a portion of **unearned** premium, returning the balance of unearned premium to the insured. This is a **short-rate** return.

Short Rate Return of Premium

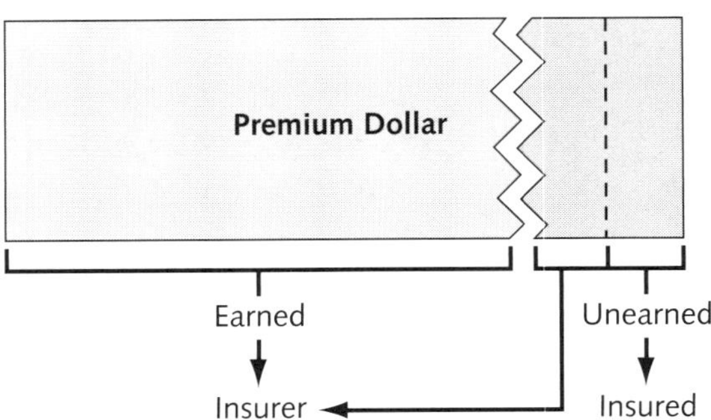

18. 4. 8 Conformity with State Statutes

Here is the exact wording of the provision.

> *Any provision of this policy which, on its effective date, is in conflict with the statutes of the state in which the insured resides on such date is hereby amended to conform to minimum requirements of such statutes.*

Although this provision is usually optional, some states insist that it be included in all policies; therefore, in some states, this provision is required.

Not only does the provision help insurers avoid issuing policies that conflict with existing state laws, it also can prevent reissuing policies that are in conflict with any ruling enacted during the time a policy is being or is about to be issued.

The provision applies to the laws of the insured's state of residence.

18. 4. 9 Illegal Occupation

Here is the exact wording of the provision.

> *The insurer shall not be liable for any loss to which a contributing cause was the insured's commission of or attempt to commit a felony or to which a contributing cause was the insured's being engaged in an illegal occupation.*

In our discussion of common exclusions, you learned that most companies exclude coverage for injuries or accidental death suffered while the insured is committing or attempting to commit a felony. Therefore, you can assume that most policies do include the illegal occupation provision.

Example

Dan's policy contains this provision. Dan's application stated that he is the proprietor of a small newsstand. After Dan was severely beaten one night by someone who apparently was trying to rob him, he applied for benefits under the hospital and medical provisions of his policy. Upon investigating the incident, police discover that Dan was using his newsstand simply as a front. His real employment is fencing stolen goods, and the beating he suffered was the result of a quarrel with other criminals. Since Dan was engaged in an illegal occupation that contributed to his injury, the insurer will not pay his claim.

If Dan's injury had resulted from an auto accident instead of a beating, a complete investigation might not have been made, nor his illegal occupation discovered. If this had been the case, the insurer probably would have paid the claim.

18. 4. 10 Narcotics

Here is the exact wording of the provision.

> *The insurer shall not be liable for any loss sustained or contracted in consequence of the insured's being under the influence of any narcotic unless administered on the advice of a physician.*

As with of the illegal occupation provision, many insurers include this optional provision. Injuries or death resulting while the insured is under the influence of either alcohol or narcotics is commonly excluded. Following are two examples of how this provision works.

Example

If Oliver wrecks his car and is injured while returning home from a party at which he used cocaine, even though this was his first experience with drugs, the insurance company will not pay any resulting claims.

Example

Because Amy was in great pain when she visited her doctor, the doctor prescribed a prescription containing morphine. Later, under the influence of the drug, Amy fell down the stairs in her home. In this case, because Amy was using a drug administered by her physician, the insurer will likely reimburse her for any resultant medical expenses.

18. 5 OTHER HEALTH INSURANCE PROVISIONS (STANDARD)

18. 5. 1 The Policy Face

The face of the policy is a standard printed form containing the name of the insurance company and providing enough information to give the insured a capsule summary of what type of policy and what type of coverage are provided by the contract. The policy face identifies the insured and states the term of the policy (when it goes into effect and when coverage expires). The policy face also states how the policy can be renewed.

The policy face usually gives a brief statement of the type or types of benefits. However, it is essential to examine the benefit provisions within the body of the contract to obtain a complete understanding of the coverage provided.

18. 5. 2 Free Look (Right to Examine Clause)

Many states require that health policies contain a **free-look** provision, allowing individuals to look over the policy for a specified period with the right to refuse it. Usually, this is a 10-day trial period, and in some states, may be a 15- or 20-day period, beginning on the day the individual receives the policy. If the individual decides to return the policy by the end of the trial period, that individual receives a full refund of the prepaid premium.

This free-look provision permits applicants to inspect the policy at their leisure and make a final decision about whether it meets their needs. If the individual cancels during the trial period, the insurance company is not liable for any claims originating during that period.

Example

Sheila receives a new health policy on March 11. On March 16, she is involved in an auto accident but suffers no apparent injury. On March 18, she exercises her 10-day free-look right and notifies the insurer, BBB Health Company, to cancel the policy. On March 20, she is hospitalized with a neck problem that her doctor says is the result of the March 16 auto accident. Sheila has not received a premium refund from BBB, so she files a claim for medical expenses related to the accident. Since she has returned the policy under the free-look provision, the insurer is not required to pay the claim but must fully refund the premium Sheila has already paid.

Under a free-look provision, the policy usually may be returned either to the insurer or to its agent within the time specified. Check your state laws and your health policies to see if a free-look provision is required. Your company may include such a provision even if it isn't required by state law.

18. 5. 3 Insuring Clause

The **insuring clause** is usually the initial policy clause. In general, it represents the insurer's promise to pay under the conditions stipulated in the policy. The insuring clause performs these functions:

- Describes the general scope of coverage
- Provides any definitions required
- Sets forth the conditions under which benefits will be paid

This clause is often viewed as the foundation of a health policy in terms of the insurer's general agreement to provide coverage. An example of such a case would be as follows:

"The insurer, ABC Mutual, agrees to pay disability income benefits to the insured upon receipt of proof of loss, and the timely payment of premiums by the insured. All benefits will be paid in accordance with the policy's provisions contained herein."

18. 5. 4 Consideration Clause

In legal terms, **consideration** is an exchange of something of value on which a contract is based. When both parties exchange consideration, the contract is validated.

In health insurance, the insurance company exchanges the promises in the policy for a two-part consideration from the insured. A health insurance contract is valid only if the insured provides consideration in the form of:

- the full minimum premium required; and
- the statements made in the application.

Example

If Joan completes an application but does not pay the first premium due, she does not have a valid contract even if the policy is issued. On the other hand, if she pays the first premium and the policy is issued as applied for, the contract is valid because she provided the correct consideration.

In health policies, the consideration clause not only defines consideration but also states:

- the date coverage begins; and
- the length of the initial coverage period.

This clause may be stated separately, or it may be part of a renewability clause in the policy.

18. 5. 5 Renewability Clause

18. 5. 5. 1 Cancelable Policies

With a **cancelable policy**, the insurer may cancel coverage at any time, provided it returns any unearned premiums to the insured. Cancellation does not relieve the insurer from paying valid existing claims.

Cancelable policies are not common and, obviously, are not advantageous to the insured. Unless the policy contains a clause that permits the company to cancel on other than a premium due date, it simply cannot be canceled. The company may refuse to renew the policy on a premium payment date, but, unless specifically stated in the policy, health insurance policies usually are not cancelable by the insurer.

When canceling a cancelable policy, the company must notify the insured in writing, mailing the notice and the unearned premium to the insured's last known address. In most states, cancellation is effective not less than five days from the date of the notice.

Example

An insurer decides to cancel Anthony's cancelable health policy. The company mails a notice of cancellation and a refund check for the amount of unearned premium to Anthony's last known address. A few months later, Anthony files suit to collect benefits for a claim that did not exist at the time the notice was mailed.

Anthony bases his suit upon the fact that he had moved and did not receive the notice of cancellation. Assuming the company has an accurate record of the transaction on file, including a copy of the cancellation notice and evidence that the unearned premium check was issued, the insurer is not liable for the claim because it followed proper cancellation procedures. However, if the claim had existed before the insurer canceled, the insurer would be liable.

18. 5. 5. 2 Optionally and Conditionally Renewable Policies

To remain in force, health policies must be renewed periodically, that is, the coverage remains in force only for the length of time for which premiums have been paid. When the premium is due again, the policy may be renewed or it may expire. Both the policyowner and the insurer have a role in the renewal process.

A policyowner has the option of canceling a policy at any time by notifying the insurer, or of allowing it to lapse at a premium due date by not paying the premium.

Health policies also include specific provisions that determine whether the insurance company may refuse to renew a policy. When the insurer has the option to refuse to renew, the policy may be one of two types:

- **Optionally renewable**, which means the insurer may elect not to renew for any reason or for no reason but may exercise that right only on the policy anniversary date or a premium due date
- **Conditionally renewable**, which means the insurer may elect not to renew only under conditions specified in the policy

Health status is not a condition used when determining renewability. If an insured moves outside the service area, for example, the insured may no longer meet the conditions of the policy, and that would determine if the policy will be renewable at the anniversary date. Upon renewal, the company can modify the premiums on an anniversary date based on classification only.

To protect the insured when a valid claim is being paid or is eligible for payment at the time the premium is due, the insurer may not prejudice that claim. That is, the claim will be paid even if the insurer elects not to renew the policy.

18. 5. 5. 3 Guaranteed Renewable Policies

In some policies, the insurer relinquishes its rights to cancel at any time and to refuse renewal at a premium due date. This type of policy is called **guaranteed renewable**, and it includes several important features.

- Renewal is guaranteed as long as the insured pays the premium.
- The insurer may not cancel unless the insured fails to pay the premium.
- Premiums may not be increased on an individual basis.

- Premiums may be increased on the basis of an entire classification, such as occupation.
- The guarantee to renew ends at a specified age.

Nonpayment of premium is the only reason an insurer may cancel or refuse to renew a guaranteed renewable policy. Furthermore, the insurer is not permitted to increase the premiums on the basis of individual insured's experience. It may, however, increase the premiums on a class basis.

18. 5. 5. 4 Noncancelable Policies

The terms ***noncancelable*** and ***noncancelable and guaranteed renewable*** are often used interchangeably to describe a noncancelable policy. As the name implies, an insurer may not cancel or refuse to renew a noncancelable policy. Although this appears to be the same as a guaranteed renewable policy, there is one important difference. With a guaranteed renewable policy, the insurer may increase the premiums by classifications. With a noncancelable policy, however, the insurer may only increase premiums based on the terms of the policy. For example, a noncanceleable policy would have to include a premium increase in the contract at the time it is issued.

18. 5. 6 Benefit Payment Clause

Health insurance benefits are paid differently depending on the type of policy. How benefits will be paid is set out in the policy's **benefits provision**. Typically, benefits are paid in the form of:

- periodic income under disability policies;
- lump-sum reimbursements for expenses incurred under hospital, medical, surgical, and major medical policies; or
- lump-sum indemnity payments for death or dismemberment under accidental death and dismemberment policies.

Suppose the benefits provision of Mitchell's policy indicates that if he is unable to work under certain conditions, he will be paid a specified amount monthly. This is known as a **periodic income** payment under his disability income policy.

On the other hand, Tom's medical expenses resulting from hospitalization for surgery will be paid under his major medical policy in the form of a lump-sum reimbursement.

According to the benefits provision of Carla's policy, she will receive \$10,000 if one of her limbs is accidentally amputated. This is an example of a lump-sum indemnity payment under an accidental death and dismemberment policy.

18. 5. 7 Exclusions and Reductions

These provisions limit the insurer's obligation to pay. An **exclusion or exception** is a provision that entirely eliminates coverage for a specified risk. A **reduction** is a decrease in benefits as a result of specified conditions.

Most health insurance policies exclude war and acts of war, self-inflicted injuries, aviation, military service, and overseas residence. Benefits will not be provided if the cause of a loss is due to military service, a war or civil disorder, a self-inflicted injury such as an attempted suicide, or if the loss is due to aviation as a pilot.

In general, coverage is temporarily suspended if an individual resides in a foreign country for a specified period of time or if the individual is serving in the military. Coverage is reinstated or reactivated when the insured returns to the United States or no longer is serving in the military.

18. 5. 8 Preexisting Conditions

Preexisting conditions can be excluded from coverage under a health insurance policy. This exclusion may be permanent or temporary. By definition, a preexisting condition is any condition for which the insured sought treatment or advice before the effective date of the policy.

Furthermore, a preexisting condition can also be defined as any symptom that would cause a reasonable and prudent person to seek diagnosis and medical treatment. This concept prevents an applicant who suspects that he may have a serious medical problem from buying health insurance and then going to a doctor for diagnosis and treatment.

Preexisting conditions may be covered by the insurer if they are indicated on the application. The insurer will then review the medical information and, depending on the condition, may elect to cover the problem or exclude it. Usually, only serious or chronic conditions will be excluded.

18. 5. 9 Nonoccupational Coverage

Some people work in occupations that are considered extremely hazardous, such as railroad switchers or steeplejacks. Many insurance companies won't assume the risk of covering such people for the hazards involved in their occupations. To provide these individuals with general accident and sickness or disability income coverage, some companies issue policies that contain a provision excluding job-related injuries.

Since policies with this provision do not cover occupational hazards, they are usually called **nonoccupational policies**. Without the exposure to everyday work hazards, the insurer takes a lesser risk, so the premiums are generally lower than for policies that cover occupational hazards. Remember, though, nonoccupational policies do not provide full coverage, either—for both on- and off-the-job injuries.

Occupational coverage is basically full coverage. If the health policy provides 24-hour coverage, occupational losses will be covered as well as any other type of loss.

18. 5. 10 Case Management Provisions

To control the costs associated with medical care, many insurers are instituting methods to reduce costs while giving the insured options for health care. As health care costs have risen, more and more policies provide for some type of administrative oversight in an attempt to contain costs. These provisions are variously called case management, managed care, claims control, cost containment, or similar terms.

The **second surgical opinion** is a provision that can be included in policies that offer surgical expense benefits. This coverage allows the insured to consult a doctor, other than the attending physician, to determine alternative methods of treatment. Although the use of this provision is sometimes optional, it is more often mandatory for certain procedures, such as tonsillectomy, cataract surgery, coronary bypass, mastectomy, and varicose veins. Some insurance companies have medical examiners review claims, and the examiner's decision to approve or deny a claim is considered the required second opinion.

One cost control mechanism being used by insurers and employers is utilization review. **Utilization review** consists of an evaluation of the appropriateness, necessity, and quality of health care and may include preadmission certification and concurrent review.

Under the **precertification provision** (also known as precertification authorization or prospective review), the physician can submit claim information before providing treatment to know in advance whether the procedure is covered under the insured's plan and at what rate it will be paid. This way both the physician and the insured know in advance what the benefit will be and can plan accordingly. This provision allows the insurance company to evaluate the appropriateness of the procedure and the length of the hospital stay.

Under the **concurrent review** process, the insurer monitors the insured's hospital stay to make sure that everything is proceeding according to schedule and that the insured will be released from the hospital as planned.

Recent evidence has shown that many treatments can be satisfactorily provided without the need for a hospital stay. **Ambulatory outpatient care** is the alternative to the costly inpatient diagnostic testing and treatment. Today, ambulatory care is best known to operate in hospital outpatient departments. However, this care can be provided by special ambulatory care health centers, group medical services, hospital emergency rooms, multispecialty group medical practices, and health care corporations. These ambulatory facilities provide, in addition to diagnosis and treatment, preventive care, health education, family planning, and dental and vision care.

18. 5. 11 Waiver of Premium

Under this provision, the insurer waives premium payments after the insured has been totally disabled (as defined in the policy) for a specified period, usually three or six months. If the insured remains totally disabled, no further premium payments will be required from the insured. If the insured recovers from the disability, the insured will resume paying the premiums.

UNIT TEST

1. According to the entire contract provision, the entire contract includes all of the following EXCEPT
   A. the insurance policy
   B. the premium payment
   C. any endorsements
   D. any attachments

2. In most states, the policy becomes incontestable after
   A. 2 years
   B. 3 years
   C. 4 years
   D. 5 years

3. All insurance policies may be canceled at any time by
   A. the insurer only
   B. the insured only
   C. neither the insurer or the insured
   D. neither the insurer nor the insured

4. Normally, written proofs of loss must be furnished within how many days after the loss?
   A. 15
   B. 45
   C. 60
   D. 90

5. If there is no beneficiary listed on a policy, benefits will be paid to
   A. the state
   B. the insured's estate
   C. the insured's nearest blood relative
   D. the insured's nearest relative by marriage or blood

6. The insurer may generally require an autopsy at its own expense unless
   A. the deceased requests in writing that an autopsy not be performed
   B. the deceased's relatives request that an autopsy not be performed
   C. the deceased's relatives have proven religious objections to an autopsy being performed
   D. the state has an applicable law that forbids autopsy

7. When Betty purchased her insurance policy, her age was recorded as 32 when she was actually 34. Assuming her policy includes the misstatement of age provision and the insurance company discovers this 4 years later, Betty's policy
   A. will be canceled for misrepresentation
   B. will be unchanged because the incontestable period has expired
   C. limits will be lowered
   D. limits will be raised

8. The optional provisions that deal with multiple insurance policies of the same type on a single insured deal with the problem of
   A. underinsurance
   B. overinsurance
   C. inappropriate insurance
   D. incorrect insurance

9. If a policyholder has two or more policies from different companies that cover the same expenses and the insurers were not notified that the other coverage existed, each insurer will
   A. have the option to cancel the policyholder's policy without notice
   B. have the option to cancel the policyholder's policy with appropriate notice
   C. pay the claim regardless, as long as the premiums have been paid
   D. pay a proportionate share of any claim

10. If a policy includes the provision on conformity with state statutes, and the state changes the law to be in conflict with another provision of the policy
    A. the policy will automatically be void
    B. the provision will be automatically grandfathered and able to stay the same
    C. the insurer will be able to apply for a grandfather provision for those policies already in force
    D. the provision will automatically be amended to conform to the minimum requirement of the statutes

11. A pro rata return is one in which the insurer returns
    A. all of the unearned premium
    B. some of the unearned premium
    C. both earned and unearned premium
    D. neither earned nor unearned premium

12. The grace period varies according to
    A. premium payment frequency
    B. premium payment amount
    C. method of premium payment
    D. type of policy

13. Mike allows his policy to lapse, then applies for reinstatement using the company's required application. The company does not inform Mike either that the policy has been accepted or that the policy is being rejected. At what point can Mike consider the policy reinstated?
    A. Not until the insurer notifies him that it has been reinstated
    B. As soon as the application has been submitted
    C. After 45 days
    D. After 90 days

14. A reinstated policy will cover
    A. sickness immediately and accidents after 10 days
    B. both sickness and accidents after 10 days
    C. accidents after 10 days and sickness after 30 days
    D. accidents immediately and sickness after 10 days

15. If an insured is disabled for at least 2 years, the insurer may require proof of continuance of disability every
    A. month
    B. 2 months
    C. 6 months
    D. year

16. Because the insurer needs time to respond to a claim, the law provides the insurer with a window during which the insured cannot sue to recover under a claim. This window lasts for
    A. 30 days
    B. 60 days
    C. 90 days
    D. 120 days

17. The maximum time during which suit can be filed is how many years after written proof of loss is furnished?
    A. 1
    B. 2
    C. 3
    D. 4

18. A revocable beneficiary
    A. has the right to refuse assignment of the policy
    B. may stop the policyowner from disposing of the policy
    C. may be changed without the beneficiary's consent
    D. is assigned for life

19. Which of the following is NOT a required provision under the Uniform Provisions Model Act?
    A. Grace period
    B. Change of occupation
    C. Time of payment of claims
    D. Proof of loss

20. Which of the following is an optional provision under the Uniform Provisions Model Act?
    A. Cancellation
    B. Physical examination and autopsy
    C. Legal actions
    D. Reinstatement

21. Julia worked as a race car driver until recently, when she took a job in the promotions office handling media inquiries. If she has the same health insurance, her premiums are likely to
    A. stay the same
    B. go up
    C. go down
    D. stop because the policy will be canceled

22. Joe took out a disability policy while working as a very successful stockbroker. A few years later, he decides to take a less stressful job at a not-for-profit organization, writing about financial issues. He loves his new job and doesn't mind the fact that he makes a lot less money. When he becomes disabled 3 years later, his disability benefit is more than he has made in salary in 3 years. If the policy contains an average earnings clause, Joe's benefit will be
    A. the same as listed in the policy
    B. the lesser of Joe's monthly earnings at the time the disability started, or the average monthly earnings for the period of 2 years immediately preceding his disability
    C. the greater of Joe's monthly earnings at the time the disability started, or the average monthly earnings for the period of 2 years immediately preceding his disability
    D. the greater of Joe's monthly earnings at the time the disability started, or the average monthly earnings for the period of 2 years immediately preceding his disability. In addition, the insurer will return some of the excess premiums that paid for the benefit Joe is not eligible to receive.

23. Cindy has a claim for $2,000 and a past due premium of $200. The insurer will
    A. refuse to pay the claim until the past due premium is paid
    B. pay the claim minus the past due premium
    C. pay the claim and forgive the past due premium
    D. pay the claim and bill Cindy for the past due premium

24. If Lois cancels her health insurance policy, the insurer will issue
    A. a pro rata refund of all of the unearned premium
    B. a pro rata refund of most of the unearned premium
    C. a short-rate refund of all of the unearned premium
    D. a short-rate refund of most of the unearned premium

25. Joel is hit by a car while crossing the street against the light. If Joel's policy contains the illegal occupation provision, the insurer
    A. is not liable for the claim because Joel was engaged in illegal activity at the time of the accident
    B. is not liable for the claim because Joel's illegal activity was the direct cause of the accident
    C. will pay the claim because crossing the street against the light is not a felony or a regular occupation
    D. may or may not pay the claim, depending on Joel's occupation

26. Carmen gets her health insurance policy on May 1, and on May 3 she decides she doesn't want it and returns it to the company. On May 6, she is hit by a car. The company will
    A. pay any resulting claim because she was injured within the 10-day free-look period
    B. pay any resulting claim only if the premium has not yet been returned to Carmen
    C. pay any resulting claim minus the amount of the returned premium
    D. only return any premium Carmen has paid and not any resulting claim

27. The insuring clause does all of the following EXCEPT
    A. describe the insured
    B. describe the general scope of coverage
    C. provide any definitions required
    D. set forth the conditions under which benefits will be paid

28. Consideration for a health policy includes
    A. the premium only
    B. the statements made in the application only
    C. the statements made in the application and the insuring clause
    D. the statements made in the application and the premium

29. Jennifer takes out an optionally renewable health policy with an annual premium due on June 14. The insurer decides it no longer wants to insure people with first names longer than five letters. The insurer may
    A. not cancel the policy because it does not have a good reason
    B. not cancel the policy unless the number of letters in the first name is a condition specified in the policy
    C. cancel the policy, but only on June 14 of the next year
    D. cancel the policy whenever it wants to

30. CeeCee's policy is guaranteed renewable. Which of the following may the insurer NOT do?
    A. Refuse to renew the policy if CeeCee fails to pay the premium
    B. Increase the premiums on all members of CeeCee's class
    C. Increase the premiums on CeeCee's policy only
    D. Refuse to renew the policy when CeeCee reaches a specified age

31. George has a noncancelable policy. Which of the following may the insurer do?
    A. Cancel the policy if George fails to pay premiums
    B. Increase the premiums on all members of George's class
    C. Increase the premiums on George's policy only
    D. Cancel the policy if the insurer chooses no longer to do business in George's state

32. Which of the following statements is TRUE?
    A. An exclusion is a provision that eliminates coverage for a specified condition; a reduction is a provision that decreases benefits as a result of a specified condition.
    B. A reduction is a provision that eliminates coverage for a specified condition; an exclusion is a provision that decreases benefits as a result of a specified condition.
    C. A reduction is a provision that eliminates coverage for a specified condition; an exception is a provision that decreases benefits as a result of a specified condition.
    D. A reduction is another term for an exception.

ANSWERS AND RATIONALES TO UNIT TEST

1. **B.** The entire contract clause specifies what is included in the contract and that all parts must be in writing and attached. The premium is not part of the entire contract.

2. **A.** In most states, the policy becomes incontestable after 2 years.

3. **B.** All insurance policies may be canceled at any time by the insured only.

4. **D.** The written proof of loss must be furnished within 90 days of the date of loss.

5. **B.** If there is no beneficiary listed on a policy, benefits will be paid to the estate.

6. **D.** The insurer may generally require an autopsy at its own expense unless the state has an applicable law that forbids autopsy.

7. **C.** Because her age was understated, her limits will be lowered.

8. **B.** The optional provisions that deal with multiple insurance policies of the same type on a single insured deal with the problem of overinsurance.

9. **D.** If a policyholder has two or more policies from different companies that cover the same expenses and if the insurers were not notified that the other coverage existed, each insurer will pay a proportionate share of any claim.

10. **D.** If a policy includes the provision on conformity with state statutes, and if the state changes the law to be in conflict with another provision of the policy, the provision will automatically be amended to conform to the minimum requirement of the statutes.

11. **A.** A pro rata return is one in which the insurer returns all of the unearned premium.

12. **A.** The grace period is determined by the premium payment mode or frequency.

13. **C.** Mike can consider the policy reinstated after 45 days.

14. **D.** A reinstated policy will cover accidents immediately and sickness after 10 days.

15. **C.** If an insured is disabled for at least 2 years, the insurer may require proof of continuance of disability every 6 months.

16. **B.** The window lasts for 60 days.

17. **C.** The maximum time during which suit can be filed is 3 years after written proof of loss is furnished.

18. **C.** A revocable beneficiary may be changed without the beneficiary's consent.

19. **B.** Change of occupation is not a required provision under the Uniform Provisions Model Act.

20. **A.** Cancellation is an optional provision under the Uniform Provisions Model Act.

21. **C.** Her premiums are likely to go down because of a change of occupation provision.

22. **D.** If the policy contains an average earnings clause, Joe's benefit will be the greater of Joe's monthly earnings at the onset of disability, or the average monthly earnings for the period of 2 years immediately preceding the onset of disability. In addition, the insurer will return some of the excess premiums that were paid for the benefit Joe is not eligible to receive.

23. **B.** The insurer will pay the claim minus the past due premium.

24. **D.** The insurer will issue a short-rate refund of most of the unearned premium.

25. **C.** If Joel's policy contains the illegal occupation provision, the insurer will pay the claim because crossing the street against the light is not a felony or a regular occupation.

26. **D.** The company will only return any premium Carmen has paid and not any resulting claim.

27. **A.** The insuring clause does not describe the insured.

28. **D.** Consideration for a health policy includes the statements made in the application and the premium.

29. **C.** The insurer may cancel the policy, but only on June 14 of the next year.

30. **C.** The insurer may not increase the premiums on CeeCee's policy only.

31. **A.** The insurer may cancel the policy if George fails to pay premiums.

32. **A.** An exclusion is a provision that eliminates coverage for a specified condition; a reduction is a provision that decreases benefits as a result of a specified condition.

UNIT 18 EXERCISE ANSWERS

Exercise 18.A

1. **B**
2. **C**
3. **A**

Exercise 18.B

1. 45
2. 10

Exercise 18.C

1. 20 days (Notice of Claim)
2. 15 days (Claim Form)
3. 90 days (Proof of Loss)
4. Insured (Payment of Claims)
5. Immediately (Time of Payment of Claims)
6. 60 days (Legal Action)
7. 3 years (Legal Action)

UNIT

19

Disability Income Insurance

19. 1 INTRODUCTION

When people are disabled and unable to work, the chances are high their income will stop sooner or later. Unfortunately, even when income stops, the costs of day-to-day living continue. That's why disability is often called the "living death." Earning power, in a sense, dies while life goes on—expenses continue and may even increase.

Disability income insurance is available to continue a portion of earnings while an insured is disabled. Too few people consider the possibility that they will be unable to continue earning an income by working. However, it is a fact that a person who is 25 years old today has better than a 50% chance of being disabled for more than 90 days before reaching age 65, while the likelihood of dying before age 65 is much less. Yet people are likely to insure with life insurance and to buy health insurance to cover medical expenses, while ignoring the need for disability insurance.

Disability income insurance, sometimes referred to as **loss of time coverage**, is designed to protect an individual's most important asset: the ability to earn an income.

19. 1. 1 Financial Planning Considerations

The importance of disability income protection cannot be overestimated as it relates to the overall planning of family finances. No matter what other safeguards may have been taken, the family's future is at stake when the ability to work is in peril. The following are some practical considerations in determining disability income needs.

- Establish the minimum income that would be required if income stopped because of disability.
- Consider the need for retirement plan maintenance if the individual has such a plan that would be disrupted in the event of long-term disability.
- After establishing the insured's total needs, allow for any benefits that would be provided by Social Security and workers' compensation.
- Include enough long-term disability coverage for both occupational and nonoccupational sickness or injury as well as short-term disability coverage to provide income during the Social Security waiting period or to supplement workers' compensation.

19. 1. 2 Alternatives to Disability Income Insurance

When people consider purchasing disability income insurance, they may ask about other alternatives that would allow them to use money they would devote to premiums differently. Listed are some other options people might consider if they develop a disability, along with the consequences of each option:

- **Using savings**. According to one source, if an individual saved 5% of income each year, 6 months of total disability could wipe out 10 years of savings—savings that may have been designated for another purpose such as retirement or children's education.

- **Borrowing**. The problem is, who will lend money to someone who can't work?
- **Depending on spouse's income**. Will it be enough? If two incomes were needed before, one income may be insufficient.
- **Liquidating assets**. Can the individual get a fair market price when forced to liquidate? By their very nature, disabilities are unexpected, and the market may be down for the stocks, real estate, or other assets to be liquidated.

19. 2 LEARNING OBJECTIVES

After completing this lesson, you will be able to:

- explain the importance of the elimination period and how it affects benefits;
- explain when the benefit period begins, and list some typical benefit periods;
- explain the factors that go into determining total disability and how it is defined in each policy;
- explain the difference between own occupation and any occupation when determining total disability; and
- explain the difference between occupational and nonoccupational disability.

19. 3 DEFINITIONS AND BENEFITS

Disability income insurance can be defined as a contract that normally pays a monthly benefit, following the elimination period, for total disability due to accident or sickness. Disability benefits may also be paid for partial or residual disability as well as total disability. An understanding of each of these terms is important because as a producer, you must be able to explain to insureds how this policy will work if they become disabled. Benefits will be paid in accordance with the policy's terms and conditions.

19. 3. 1 Probationary Period

A **probationary** or **qualification period** may be found in some disability income policies. It is a period that begins when a policy goes into effect. During this period, no benefits will be paid under the policy. The period is often 15 or 30 days, or even 60 days for long-term policies. This probationary period generally applies to sickness, but not to accidents. Its major purpose is to relieve the insurance company from paying benefits for **preexisting conditions**—health problems that existed before the policy's inception—but its effective result is that no benefits are paid for any otherwise covered events during the stipulated period.

19. 3. 2 Elimination Period

An **elimination period** is the period for which an insured person must be disabled before benefits begin. The elimination period may be thought of as a time deductible rather a dollar deductible because benefits are not payable for the elimination period. Benefits begin only after this period of time is satisfied. For example, if an insured has an elimination period of 30 days and is totally disabled for 75 days, benefits would be payable only for the 45 days in excess of the elimination period.

The elimination period may be 30, 60, 90, or 180 days or longer, depending on the period elected by the insured. The longer the elimination period, the smaller the insurance premium, because the insured is willing to go without benefits for a longer period of time and the insurer will not have to pay for short-term claims.

19. 3. 3 Benefit Period

After the elimination period has been satisfied and monthly disability benefits begin, they will be paid for a specific period, provided the insured remains totally disabled. This period is the **benefit period**. Typical benefit periods are one year, two years, five years, and to age 65.

Thus, if an insured has a disability income policy with a monthly benefit of $1,000 payable after a 30-day elimination period with a benefit period of five years, the insured would be entitled to five full years of benefits following the elimination period for each total disability (assuming that the insured continues to be totally disabled throughout the benefit period).

The longer the benefit period, the higher will be the policy's premium.

Important Disability Policy Periods

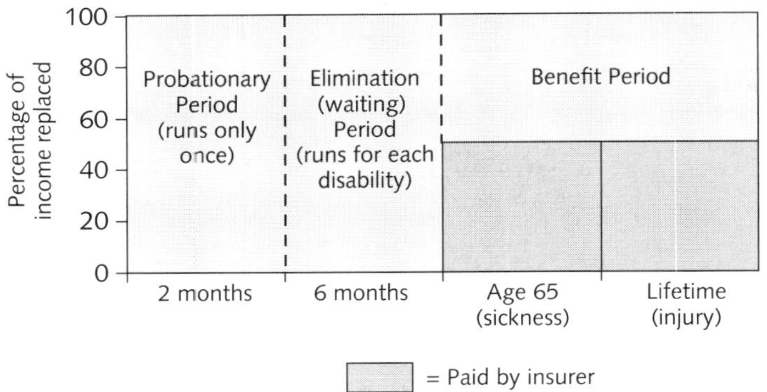

= Paid by insurer

19. 3. 4 Defining Total Disability

Because the major purpose of disability income policies is to provide income when the insured is totally disabled and unable to work, the meaning of total disability is important. **Total disability** is always defined in the policy, and different companies may use different definitions. These definitions are based on work activity, and insurers look at work activity in terms of two dimensions: the insured's own occupation and any occupation the insured may be qualified to perform.

19. 3. 4. 1 Own Occupation

The first way total disability might be defined concerns the occupation in which the particular individual is normally engaged. In this case, total disability is defined as an insured's inability to perform any or all of the duties of the insured's own occupation.

This refers to the insured's own occupation at the time disability begins. Suppose Lee, who is a word-processing typist, is involved in an accident in which three fingers on one hand and four on the other are severed. Using the definition given, Lee has a total disability because he is unable to use the keyboard—a primary duty of his occupation.

19. 3. 4. 2 Any Occupation

An alternative and more restrictive definition of total disability is an insured's inability to perform the duties of any occupation for which the insured is reasonably qualified by education, training, or experience.

Again, consider Lee, the word-processing typist whose fingers were severed. Under the first definition, he was totally disabled because he was unable to perform the duties of his own occupation. Suppose, however, that Lee is qualified to teach word processing. Under this second definition, Lee is not totally disabled because he can work as an instructor, an occupation for which he is qualified by training and experience.

The own-occupation definition, which is less restrictive and therefore more favorable to the insured, is used more commonly than the any-occupation definition.

Later in this unit, we'll talk about both short- and long-term disability income policies. Long-term policies generally use both definitions to cover different periods during the insured's disability. The own-occupation definition generally is used for the initial period of disability, which might extend from two to five years as stated in the policy. Then the any-occupation definition applies to disability continuing beyond the initial period.

Once again, remember Lee, the word-processing typist. Suppose Lee's policy includes both of these provisions, and it identifies the initial period as two years. If Lee performed no work at all during the two years following the loss of his fingers, he could collect total disability benefits under the own-occupation definition.

Suppose Lee wants neither to be a word-processing instructor nor to do any other kind of work except his previous occupation, which he is now unable to do. After two years, he could no longer claim total disability and continue receiving benefits because the any-occupation definition becomes effective. Because he is qualified and able to perform other work, he is no longer classified as totally disabled.

19. 3. 4. 3 Loss of Earnings

Between these two definitions of **total disability**, there are several variations. In fact, some policies use a two-tier definition that refers to the insured's own occupation during an initial period of disability and then shifts to any occupation. These policies usually define **total disability** as the inability to perform the duties of the insured's own occupation for a period of two to five years, and thereafter the inability to perform the duties of any occupation for which the insured is suited by reason of education, training, experience, or prior economic status. This is known as the **loss of earnings** test for disability.

19. 3. 4. 4 Injury Versus Sickness

Total disability is occasionally further defined in terms of its cause. For example, some policies may cover only, or cover differently, disability caused by accidental injury, and some may cover only disability caused by sickness. In these cases, the terms *total accident (or injury) disability* and *total sickness disability* might be used.

If you see these terms, you know that total accident disability is disability caused by an accident, and total sickness disability is caused by sickness.

19. 3. 4. 5 Occupational Versus Nonoccupational

Although short-term policies often cover only nonoccupational disability, most long-term plans cover both occupational and nonoccupational sickness and accidents. When occupational benefits are provided, they are often reduced by benefits received from workers' compensation and Social Security.

19. 3. 4. 6 Medically Defined

Some older policies also require that in addition to meeting the definition of total disability, the insured must also be confined to the house and under the treatment of a doctor. This is called **medically defined** disability.

19. 3. 5 Presumptive Disability

Aside from the occupational considerations, many disability income policies have another criterion by which total disability may be classified. This is called **presumptive disability**, which is a condition that automatically qualifies insureds for total disability classification, whether or not they can work. Conditions generally considered to be presumptive disabilities include:

- loss of use of any two limbs;
- total and permanent blindness; and
- loss of speech and hearing.

Under these criteria, if Bruce's right arm and leg are severed in an accident, he is presumptively disabled. However, if Allen's left leg is amputated, he is not because only one limb is involved.

Presumptive disability may also be determined using a loss of earnings test. The insured's level of earnings before disability is compared to the level of earnings after disability. If postdisability earnings fall below predisability earnings by a given percentage, the insured is considered totally disabled and eligible for a full benefit even if some level of earnings remains.

19. 3. 6 Partial Disability

Although total disability is the insured's inability to perform any duties of the insured's own occupation, not every disability is total. Some people may suffer a less than total disability. The earliest form of less than total disability is partial disability. Partial disability means the person cannot perform every duty of the occupation but can perform one or more important duties of the occupation.

Example

Bob works in a warehouse where his duties involve moving materials both with a mechanical lift-truck and by hand. Bob injures his back and is unable to perform the part of his job that involves moving heavy materials by hand, but he can use the lift-truck. Because Bob is able to perform some of the duties of his occupation, but not all of them, he is partially disabled.

The usual partial disability indemnity is 50% of the monthly or weekly indemnity for total disability. If a policy pays, for example, $3,000 per month for total disability, it will probably pay $1,500 for partial disability. These benefits are usually paid for a relatively short period—commonly three or six months.

An insured might receive both total and partial disability benefits as the result of a single accident. For example, a person might be totally disabled for three months, then be able to return to work but able to perform only a few of the usual duties for some time—let's say two months. If the policy so stipulates, the individual described would be eligible to receive total disability benefits during the first three months and partial disability benefits for the next two months.

19. 3. 7 Residual Disability

Many recent policies have replaced the partial disability provision with a **residual disability** provision. A **residual disability** benefit is usually a percentage of the total disability benefit for periods when the insured is unable to perform some of the duties of her own occupation, which results in a loss of income.

This benefit focuses more on the loss of earnings than the physical limitations of the disability. Earnings during partial disability must be at least a stated percentage less than earnings before disability—20% less, for example. For instance, if earnings before disability were $2,000 per month and the policy required earnings during partial disability to be reduced at least 20% to receive residual benefits, a partially disabled person could earn no more than $1,600 per month.

The percentage of reduction in earnings is multiplied by the normal benefit to determine the residual benefit. So, if in the previous example, the normal benefits were $1,000 per month, the residual benefit would be $200: 20% (reduction in earnings) × $1,000 (normal benefit). If the reduction in earnings is not at least the minimum stated percentage, no benefits are payable under this option.

Benefits can be paid if the insured returns to work either full-time or part-time and will continue to receive benefits throughout the benefit period, as long as the insured qualifies under the definition of the policy.

19. 3. 8 Recurrent Disability

Occasionally, after a period of disability appears to be over, the disability will recur as a result of the same illness or accident. A second period of disability from the same or a related cause of a prior disability is a **recurrent disability**.

Most disability income policies stipulate that if the insured returns to work for a specified period of time after the original disability, a recurrence must be handled as a new claim for a new period of disability, requiring a new elimination period, rather than as a continuation of a prior claim. Usually, the specified period is 90 days, although some insurers permit six months.

Assume a policy specifies that no new elimination period is required if the disability recurs within 90 days. The insured suffers a disability as the result of an accident, returns to work for six months, and then suffers the same type of disability. In this situation, the disability claim would be treated as a new event rather than a recurrent disability because more than 90 days have passed. Had the insured returned to work for only two months before the disability recurred, no new elimination period would have been required.

Exercise 19.A

Match the following disability definitions to the appropriate terms.

____ 1. The period of time at the start of the policy when disability benefits for sickness are not paid

____ 2. Totally disabled and unable to perform the duties of current job

____ 3. Unable to perform some but not all the duties of your job and benefits equal 50% of total disability benefits for up to six months

____ 4. A benefit that does not require a new elimination period for a second period of disability occurring within six months of recovery

____ 5. A waiting period after a disability occurs before payments begin

____ 6. Unable to perform some but not all the duties of a job and benefits are proportionate to loss of income and payable for the full policy term

____ 7. Totally disabled and unable to perform the duties of any job for which you are suited by education, training, or work experience

____ 8. Totally disabled based on loss of eyesight or more than one limb

A. Recurrent disability

B. Residual disability

C. Any occupation

D. Probation

E. Presumptive disability

F. Partial disability

G. Own occupation

H. Elimination

Answers to the exercises can be found at the end of the Unit 19 answers and rationales.

19. 3. 9 Permanent Disability

Disability is usually defined as permanent or temporary, in addition to total or partial. A permanent disability is one that reduces or eliminates the insured's ability to work for the rest of the insured's life. Permanent disability results from any injury from which the insured is not expected to recover, such as loss of sight or one or more limbs.

19. 3. 10 Temporary Disability

A temporary disability occurs when an insured is unable to work while recovering from an illness or injury but is expected to fully recover from that illness or injury. Examples would be a broken leg or a sprained back.

19. 3. 11 Confining Versus Nonconfining Disability

Some policies may include a provision that differentiates between disabilities in still another way: whether the disability is confining or nonconfining.

A total, **confining disability** is a condition that requires the individual to stay indoors, perhaps in the hospital or at home except for visits to the doctor.

Example

Lana is at home recuperating from tuberculosis. If she may not leave her home until she is completely recovered, she has a total, confining disability.

A total, **nonconfining disability** refers to a condition that disables but does not require the individual to remain confined indoors.

Example

While Warren was recovering at home from a serious illness, his doctor encouraged him to take a short walk each day. Warren's is a total, nonconfining disability.

You should be aware of this terminology, but unless a policy specifically includes this provision, the absence or presence of confinement does not affect the total disability classification.

19. 3. 12 Accidental Means

Of the terms used to define accident, the two that will be discussed here are **accidental bodily injury** and **accidental means**.

A policy that includes the "accidental means" wording is more restrictive than one that refers simply to accidental bodily injury. To help you understand the restrictive nature of accidental means, let's look at an example.

Example

Mary is carrying a heavy bag of groceries and strains her back. This accident would be defined as accidental bodily injury because Mary did not intentionally strain her back. However, while the injury was caused by accident, it could not be defined as accidental means because the cause of the accident was foreseeable. That is, using reasonable judgment, Mary could foresee that carrying too heavy a load could produce problems, such as the bag breaking and the contents spilling out and injuring her foot, or, as in this example, the heavy load creating a strain on her back. If the policy under which Mary was covered defined accident in terms of accidental means, she would not receive benefits.

Example

On the other hand, if while carrying this same heavy bag of groceries, a dog runs in Mary's path, causing her to fall and break her arm, she would be covered under the definition of accidental means. This is because the injury was caused by circumstances that could not reasonably be foreseen. Mary could not possibly foresee that a dog would run in her path; that in running in front of her, the dog would cause her to fall; and that in falling, she would break her arm. There are too many contingencies to be planned for. Also, the cause of the fall was not based on any action taken by Mary or by any activity in which Mary was engaged.

19. 3. 13 Definition of Sickness

Sickness or **illness** may not be defined in any manner that is more restrictive than "sickness or disease that first manifests itself after the effective date of the policy." If a policy provides nonoccupational coverage only, the definition of sickness may exclude work-related disabilities.

Example

Susan applies for and is issued a disability income policy with an effective date of May 1, 2008. Approximately one month later, she begins to have a digestive problem, which is diagnosed on August 15, 2008, as a gall bladder problem requiring surgery. Medically, her symptoms first appeared after the effective date of the policy and, thus, this sickness claim would be honored by the insurer.

Example

On the other hand, let's assume that Susan begins to have the digestive problem on May 1, 2008. She contacts her doctor, and he suggests that she take some antacid medication, which she purchases from her local drug store. By June 1, the problem appears to be no better, but Susan does nothing about it. Susan purchases some disability income insurance with an effective coverage date of July 1, 2008. One month later, she consults with her doctor who, after conducting some tests, diagnoses her gall bladder problem. Even though the diagnosis occurred after the effective date of the disability income policy, the symptoms appeared before the effective date of the policy. Should a claim arise and all the facts become known, the insurer could determine that the gall bladder problem preexisted the effective date of the insurance and deny the claim.

The definition of sickness is very important because it could be used to permanently exclude benefits for conditions that existed prior to the effective date of coverage.

19. 4 BENEFIT CALCULATIONS

Following are some sample benefit calculations that use the concepts discussed thus far.

Beth has a disability income policy with a 30-day elimination period, a $2,000 monthly income benefit for total disability, and a benefit period to age 65. Beth becomes totally disabled on January 1 and is unable to work for three months. She returns to work on a part-time basis on April 1 and is able to earn 40% of her predisability compensation during April. In May, she earns 60% of her predisability income. By June 1, she is working full time, earning 100% of her predisability income. Let's consider how Beth's benefits would differ under a policy that provides total and residual disability benefits and a policy that provides total disability benefits only.

It can be seen in the benefit calculation that a policy that pays residual disability benefits provides an incentive for the insured to return to work because it pays proportional benefits. A more traditional "total disability only" policy implies that an insured cannot return to work for any length of time without losing all benefits. While it appears that the insurance company in the example would pay less (by terminating benefits as soon as Beth returned to work part time in April), it might actually end up paying as much or more than the policy providing residual benefits (because without partial benefits, Beth might not return to work until she is fully recovered in June, and she might claim total disability benefits for two additional months).

Benefit Calculation

Month	Income Loss	Total and Residual Benefit Policy	Total Disability Only Policy
January	100%	None—satisfying the elimination period	None—satisfying the elimination period
February	100%	$2,000—100% of the total disability benefit	$2,000—total disability benefit
March	100%	$2,000—100% of the total disability benefit	$2,000—total disability benefit
April	60%	$1,200—60% of the total disability benefit	None—performing occupational duties
May	40%	$800—40% of the total disability benefit	None—performing occupational duties
June	0	None—no loss of income	None—performing occupational duties

19. 5 TYPES OF DISABILITY BENEFITS AND EXCLUSIONS

19. 5. 1 Short-Term Disability

Most short-term policies provide for short elimination periods (usually 30 days or less) and short benefit periods. The benefit period is normally for six months but not longer than one year (although it is possible to have a short term benefit payable for up to two years, it is not very common). The benefit amount is limited to a percentage of compensation, such as 60 or 70%.

One of the rationales for short-term disability has been that the worker presumably is eligible for Social Security disability benefits after the five-month Social Security waiting period. In reality, this may or may not be true, depending on whether the worker can qualify for Social Security disability benefits. In addition, if the person does qualify for benefits, the first benefit check will likely not be received before one year from the onset of disability.

In any event, short-term disability benefits were designed to fill the gap until Social Security began paying benefits to the claimant.

19. 5. 2 Long-Term Disability (LTD)

LTD policies provide for longer elimination and benefit periods than do short-term policies. Typically, the elimination period is 90 days or six months, with benefits provided for two or five years or to age 65. Most often, LTD policies provide benefits to age 65.

The amount of the long-term benefit is limited to a percentage of the workers' compensation, such as 60 or 70%. As with short-term policies, LTD coverage may be occupational or nonoccupational.

Additionally, LTD policies usually provide for integration of plan benefits with other disability income benefits payable to the insured. The LTD benefit may be offset by any of the following:

- Any benefits provided by another formal employer plan
- Benefits payable under workers' compensation or any similar statutory program
- Any benefits payable under Social Security

The purpose for having integration with these other sources of disability income is to prevent overinsurance on the part of the insured.

19. 5. 3 Lump-Sum Benefits

Lump-sum payments under disability policies were once paid more often than they are today. Modern safety measures and enforcement, coupled with advancements in medical technology, have made total and permanent disabilities less common. Although lump-sum benefits may be paid for presumptive disability or under special disability policies covering business buy-sell agreements, it is more common for disability income benefits to be received in the form of installment payments.

19. 6 EXCLUSIONS

Common exclusions found in disability income policies are losses arising from war, military service, attempted suicide, overseas residence, aviation under certain circumstances (pilot or crew of aircraft), and losses that result when an insured is injured while committing a felony.

19. 7 OPTIONAL BENEFITS AND RIDERS

19. 7. 1 Rehabilitation Benefit

Because of disability, insureds may not be able to return to their normal occupation but still be able to work at some kind of job. The rehabilitation benefit facilitates vocational training to prepare insureds for a new occupation.

The rehabilitation benefit applies when the insured is totally disabled and receiving benefits. If that is the case and the insured chooses to participate in a vocational rehabilitation program approved by the insurer, then total disability benefits will continue as long as the insured actively participates in the training program and remains totally disabled.

Some insurers may provide a lump-sum benefit for vocational training. Whether a lump-sum or a monthly disability benefit, this benefit enables the insured to take positive steps toward returning to work, even though it may be in another occupation. Thus, this option benefits both insureds and the insurer.

19. 7. 2 Future Increase Option

This option also may be referred to as the **guaranteed insurability option** or **guaranteed purchase option** because it enables the insured to purchase additional disability income protection, regardless of insurability, at specified future dates. However, the rate for this additional coverage will be at the insured's attained age at the time of purchase, not the age when the policy was originally issued.

This benefit has some limitations. The insured will be able to purchase only a specified, predetermined amount of disability income insurance at each option date. To guard against overinsurance, the insurer will usually limit the amount of additional coverage to possibly $500 or less on each option date. Also, the insured's earned income must warrant additional coverage. That is, it is assumed that every few years, the insured's earned income will increase substantially, thus leaving room for additional disability insurance.

Another limitation is the number of option dates on which the insured may purchase additional coverage. Usually, these option dates will be every three years from ages 25 to 50.

19. 7. 3 Cost-of-Living Benefit

The purchasing power of fixed disability benefits may be eroded because of inflation and increases in the cost of living. To protect against these trends, most insurers will offer an optional cost-of-living benefit.

Under the provisions of this option, the insured's monthly disability benefit (total or residual) will be increased automatically once the insured is on claim (receiving disability income benefits). Typically, this increase will occur after the insured is on claim for 12 months and each 12-month period thereafter as long as the insured remains on claim.

19. 7. 4 Lifetime Benefits

This option extends the benefit period from age 65 to lifetime. This extension may apply to accident-only benefits or to accident and sickness benefits. Normally, if the total disability is due to an accident and it occurs before age 65, benefits will be paid for the lifetime of the insured, provided the insured remains totally disabled.

Most companies will place some time limitations for the lifetime sickness benefit. That is, the disabling sickness must begin before a specified age. A policy providing lifetime sickness benefits may stipulate that if the sickness begins at age 55 or earlier, then 100% of the total disability benefit will be provided for the lifetime of the insured. However, if the disability begins after age 55 but before age 65, a reduced benefit will be paid for life.

19. 7. 5 Social Security Rider

The Social Security Administration defines **total disability** as the "inability to perform any substantial gainful work which may exist in the national economy." In addition, the disability must be expected to last at least 12 months or end in death. This is a very rigid and ultraconservative definition of total disability. As a result, many disabled people do not qualify for Social Security disability benefits. In fact, the Social Security Administration denies about two-thirds of all disability claims.

Even when Social Security benefits are payable, there is a five-month waiting period, and benefits do not begin until the sixth month of disability. When a Social Security rider is added to an individual's disability income policy, an additional monthly benefit is payable during the waiting period.

The rider may or may not continue to pay benefits after Social Security benefits begin. There are two different methods by which this type of rider may provide benefits.

- **All or nothing rider**. Under this approach, the insured will be paid a benefit only if Social Security pays nothing. Conversely, if Social Security provides any benefit, then the rider pays nothing.
- **Offset rider**. Under this approach, the benefit provided by the rider will be reduced, or offset, by the amount of any benefit provided by Social Security.

19. 7. 6 Social Insurance Supplements

Some insurers offer social insurance supplements designed to fill gaps left by various government benefit programs. The concept is similar to the Social Security rider, except that this coverage also may mesh with workers' compensation benefits and benefits provided by state disability funds. These supplemental benefits may be included as part of the disability income policy or may be added to the policy by rider. The benefits are usually payable during any waiting periods for social insurance benefits or if the social insurance benefits are denied. Benefits will be paid monthly until government benefits begin. If, for any reason, the government benefits stop, the insurer will step in and begin the monthly payments again. However, the benefits are only payable during the benefit period specified in the contract and only while the insured remains disabled.

19. 7. 7 Additional Monthly Benefit (AMB) Riders

Most insurers offer short-term riders to provide additional benefits during the first 6 or 12 months of a claim. Some companies may call these Social Security riders because the benefit is payable during the Social Security waiting period, although the rider itself may not even refer to Social Security benefits. More commonly, the term *additional monthly benefit rider* is used. The additional benefits during the early months of disability may be used to supplement government benefits or short-term disability benefits provided by an employer, or they may be used to help pay extra transitional expenses that might be incurred when an insured is first disabled.

19. 7. 8 Hospital Confinement Rider

This optional benefit results in the elimination period being waived when the insured is hospitalized as an inpatient. The payment of any disability benefits usually requires satisfying the elimination period. The hospital confinement benefit pays the regular total disability benefit during the elimination period when the insured is hospitalized.

The factor that triggers the payment of the benefit is any period of hospitalization during the elimination period. Benefits will be paid only as long as the insured is hospitalized.

Example

An insured has a disability income policy with a 30-day elimination period and a $1,000 per month benefit for total disability, payable to age 65. The insured also has the hospital confinement option and is hospitalized for minor surgery for two days. Following the hospitalization, the insured returns to work within three days. Total disability benefits will be paid for the two days. The amount paid will be 2/30 (1/15) of $1,000, or $67.

19. 7. 9 Impairment Rider

When an applicant for insurance has an existing medical problem or chronic condition, an insurer might attach an **impairment rider** to the standard policy. This rider excludes coverage for a specific ailment or condition that otherwise would be covered. Because the condition currently exists, the insurance company will be unlikely to take the risk, so will normally refuse coverage. Using the impairment rider to exclude this specific condition, however, benefits both the applicant and the insurer in the following ways.

- The applicant is able to obtain coverage that might not otherwise be available for other health care needs.
- The insurance company is able to protect itself from undue risk from this particular condition and is still able to provide health coverage.

Impairment riders are written on an individual basis for a specific person's medical condition, such as heart disease, cancer, or diabetes. The exclusion in the rider applies only to the person with the impairment and not to any other insureds, such as family members covered by the same policy.

19. 7. 10 Nondisabling Injury Rider

This benefit does not pay a disability benefit but rather provides for the payment of medical expenses incurred as the result of injury that does not result in total disability.

19. 7. 11 Waiver of Premium (with Disability Income)

This rider specifies that in the event of disability, premiums will be waived retroactively to the beginning of the disability. The definition is usually permanent and total disability. Again, however, a few companies have gone to a definition in terms of occupation, as previously discussed.

19. 7. 12 Accidental Death and Dismemberment (AD&D)

Accidental death policies or riders include a death benefit that is payable in the event of death resulting from accidental bodily injury. A companion coverage is provided for loss of limbs or sight, often called dismemberment coverage.

A schedule is made a part of the policy that lists various dismemberments and losses of sight for which a specified sum will be paid to the insured. In policies with weekly disability income benefits, the sum payable is usually expressed as a multiple of the weekly indemnity. In policies without weekly disability income benefits, the sums payable are usually expressed as percentages of the death benefit limit or sometimes as percentages of a limit in the policy known as the **capital sum**. The capital sum might be $20,000 and the death benefit is usually the same amount ($20,000).

Sample Schedule

Loss Of	Sum Equal To Weekly Indemnity For
Both hands, or feet, or sight of both eyes	200 weeks
One hand and one foot	200 weeks
Either hand or foot and sight of one eye	200 weeks
Either hand or foot	100 weeks
Sight of one eye	65 weeks
Thumb and index finger of either hand	50 weeks

The intent of the dismemberment feature is to provide insureds with a lump sum that will help them over the period when they go through rehabilitation and, probably, training for work other than that for which they previously were qualified. If the policy has a disability income feature, once a dismemberment sum is paid, the disability income payments stop. In some cases, the insured might be disabled for a while and, during the disability, suffer one of the losses listed above. In that event, the insured would be paid disability income up to the time of the loss of limb or sight only.

Most company policies provide that, even if the insured is not disabled after an accident, if a loss of limb or sight occurs within 90 days of the date of the accident, the sums in the schedule will be paid.

Accidental death and dismemberment coverage provides both a life insurance and a health insurance benefit. However, the life insurance benefit applies only to accidental death and is not paid for death by natural causes.

19. 7. 13 Other Provisions

Although disability income policies do not typically accumulate cash value or have a life insurance component, it is possible to purchase riders to the policy that provide benefits similar to those of life insurance policies. Thus, an **annual renewable term** life insurance feature may be attached to a disability income policy, providing a death benefit as well as disability income coverage.

Similarly, a **return of premium rider** may be attached to a disability income policy. This rider provides for the return of a percentage of premiums paid (usually 80%) during a specific term period (usually every 10 years) minus the claims paid during the term period. The refund is made every 10 years and at age 65 or as of the date of death. Essentially, for an additional premium, the policyholder gets 80% of the money back either in claims, premium refunds, or a combination of both. Various settlement options are offered for receiving the premium refund. Amounts left on deposit with the insurance company earn interest and constitute cash value or may be applied toward future premium payments.

Exercise 19.B

Match the following definitions to the appropriate terms.

____1.	Provides income or lump sum benefits for vocational training	A. Social insurance supplement
____2.	Provides for annual increases in the disability benefit to offset inflation	B. Waiver of Premium
____3.	Provides for policy premiums to be suspended after the insured has been disabled for a specific amount of time, such as 3 months	C. Future increase option
____4.	Provides for the insured to be able to purchase additional amounts of disability income periodically without proving insurability	D. Cost of living
____5.	Provides additional disability benefits equal to government benefits payable during any application or waiting period or if benefits are denied	E. Rehabilitation benefit
____6.	Provides additional lump sum benefits to the insured or beneficiary if the insured loses limbs or dies as the direct result of an accidental injury	F. Accidental death and dismemberment

Answers to the exercises can be found at the end of the Unit 19 answers and rationales.

19. 8 BUSINESS USES

Disability income insurance is designed to protect an individual's most important asset:the ability to earn an income. By protecting against the loss of income during periods of disability, this type of coverage enables the disabled insured to continue to provide for the basic necessities of life. The application and use of disability income coverage is not confined to individuals but also is very relevant in business situations.

The life insurance section of this book identifies business uses of life insurance—that is, to fund buy-sell agreements, key person insurance, and so on. Life insurance benefits are paid to the business upon the death of a key person or the businessowner so that the business may continue. A similar concept applies for the business with regard to the disability of a key person or the businessowner. The living death of disability can have a serious impact on the continued existence and profitability of a business.

19. 8. 1 Business Overhead Expense (BOE)

The BOE policy is designed for the small business owner. Its purpose is to cover certain overhead expenses that continue when the businessowner is disabled. Most insurers will limit the BOE policy to relatively small businesses.

Example

General Motors would not be eligible for a BOE policy, but a small firm consisting of the owner and three to four employees could purchase a BOE policy.

The policy will indemnify the business (not the owner) for such business expenses as rent, taxes, insurance premiums, utility bills, employees' compensation (not the owner's salary), and so forth. By covering these expenses when the owner is disabled, the business is able to keep its doors open and continue to operate.

Naturally, the overall concept is that the small business owner is so important to the profitability of the business that when the business owner becomes totally disabled, the business will suffer economically and may even be forced to close. An example of such a situation would be a dentist. Typically, if the dentist cannot practice, business income will eventually be impaired and the few employees working in the dentist's office may lose their jobs. As the business income slows, the bills still have to be paid, as do the employees. The BOE policy will solve this problem.

Generally, BOE policies have elimination periods of 15 or 30 days and benefit periods of one or two years. The benefit amount will be determined by the average eligible overhead expenses of the business. If the businessowner becomes disabled, after the elimination period is satisfied, the business will receive benefits equal to the actual overhead expenses incurred during the owner's disability.

BOE premiums are tax deductible to the business. The disability benefits received are thus taxable to the business. However, these taxable benefits are then used to pay tax-deductible business expenses.

19. 8. 2 Key Person Disability Insurance

Just as key person life insurance indemnifies the business for the lost services of a key person, so does a key person disability income policy. This type of coverage pays a monthly benefit to a business to cover expenses for additional help or outside services when an essential person is disabled. The key person could be a partner or working stockholder of the business. The key person could also be a management person who is personally responsible for some very important functions, such as a sales manager.

The key person's economic value to the business is determined in terms of the potential loss of business income that could occur, as well as the expense of hiring and training a replacement for the key person. The key person's value then becomes the disability benefit that will be paid to the business.

The benefit amount may be paid in a lump sum or in monthly installments. Generally, the policy's elimination period will be 30 to 90 days, and the benefit period will be one or two years.

The business is the owner and premium payor of the policy. Benefits are received by the business tax free because the premium paid is not tax deductible.

19. 8. 3 Disability Buyout Insurance

When there is a buy-sell agreement funded with life insurance to buy out the interest of a deceased owner or partner, there should also be a provision in the agreement for the buyout of the owner's business interest in the event of disability. Naturally, this disability provision should be funded with buyout disability income insurance. This is set up much like the buy-sell agreement used in life insurance.

One of the critical considerations with reference to the disability buyout policy is the elimination period. Once the elimination period is satisfied, benefits will begin to be made to the business for the purpose of buying out the interest of the disabled owner or partner. Generally, once the buyout begins, it cannot be stopped. Thus, for example, a disabled partner does not want to be bought too soon and then possibly recover from the disability and find that he has no job and no business interest.

For this reason, the elimination period for disability buyout insurance will normally be one or two years. The buyout agreement will specify the value or a method of determining the value of the owner's business interest. This value will be paid to the business following the elimination period. The benefits may be paid in a lump sum or in monthly installments. If the policy provides a monthly benefit, usually the benefit period will not exceed five years. The business, of course, uses the policy proceeds to buy out the interest of the disabled person.

Usually, the business is the owner and premium payor for the policy or policies. The premiums are not deductible, but the benefits are received by the business tax free.

Exercise 19.C

Fill in the blanks with the appropriate business disability policy.

1. A disability income policy that indemnifies a business for the loss of the services of an employee is called _______ ________.

2. A disability policy that would pay a lump sum to a business to facilitate buy-sell agreement of a disabled owner is known as _______ ______ _______.

3. A ________ _________ __________ policy is designed to indemnify a business for any routine expenses incurred in the event the owner of a business becomes disabled.

Answers to the exercises can be found at the end of the Unit 19 answers and rationales.

UNIT TEST

1. To receive benefits from a disability income policy for disability due to sickness, the insured must be
   A. totally disabled
   B. partially disabled
   C. either totally or partially disabled
   D. deceased

2. All of the following define a disability EXCEPT
   A. partial disability
   B. recurrent disability
   C. residual disability
   D. accidental death and dismemberment

3. The benefit that enables a disabled insured to learn to work in another occupation is known as
   A. the cost-of-living benefit
   B. the rehabilitation benefit
   C. the guaranteed insurability option
   D. the lifetime benefit option

4. The benefit that protects against the erosion of purchasing power for fixed disability benefits is known as
   A. the cost-of-living benefit
   B. the rehabilitation benefit
   C. the offset rider
   D. the lifetime benefit

5. The rider that provides more benefits during the first 6 months or year of a claim is known as
   A. the cost-of-living rider
   B. the rehabilitation rider
   C. the additional monthly benefit rider
   D. the lifetime benefit rider

6. The benefit that pays the regular total disability benefit during the elimination period when the insured is hospitalized is known as
   A. the hospital confinement rider
   B. the rehabilitation benefit
   C. the nondisabling injury rider
   D. the offset rider

7. The option that allows an insured to purchase additional amounts of disability income protection is known as
   A. the lifetime benefit option
   B. the additional monthly benefit option
   C. the all or nothing option
   D. the future increase option

8. Social insurance supplements provide disability income
   A. before workers' compensation and Social Security begin payments
   B. after workers' compensation and Social Security end payments
   C. both A and B
   D. neither A nor B

9. The elimination period may be thought of as
   A. a dollar amount deductible
   B. a time deductible
   C. a dollar amount co-payment
   D. a time co-payment

10. The longer the benefit period
    A. the higher the policy's premium
    B. the lower the policy's premium
    C. the higher the policy's benefits
    D. the lower the policy's benefits

11. Which definition of total disability is more favorable to the insured?
    A. Own occupation
    B. Any occupation
    C. They are the same in terms of benefits to the insured
    D. There is no way to determine from the information provided

12. Occupational disability benefits are often reduced by benefits received
    A. from Social Security only
    B. from workers' compensation only
    C. from either Social Security or workers' compensation
    D. before the end of the elimination period only

13. Which of the following generally is NOT considered to be a presumptive disability?
    A. Loss of the dominant hand
    B. Loss of use of any two limbs
    C. Total and permanent blindness
    D. Loss of speech and hearing

14. Which of the following statements about partial disability is NOT true?
    A. The person is not able to perform every duty of the prior occupation.
    B. The person is able to perform one or more important duties of the occupation.
    C. Sickness disability is more likely to be partial than accident disability.
    D. An insured might receive both total and partial disability benefits as the result of a single accident.

15. Some policies have replaced the partial disability provision with
    A. a reduced disability provision
    B. a redundant disability provision
    C. a recurrent disability provision
    D. a residual disability provision

16. Brandon injures his back working at a warehouse. Six months later, he is well enough to go back to work lifting boxes. Two weeks into working, however, he strains his back again and has to go back on bed rest. This is an example of
    A. a redundant disability
    B. a residual disability
    C. a recurrent disability
    D. a reduced disability

17. Lee is helping a friend move his pool table when he strains his back, causing a disability. The insurer declines coverage, saying the injury was not accidental under the terms of Lee's policy. Lee's policy must include
    A. an accidental bodily injury definition of accidental
    B. an accidental means definition of accidental
    C. a confining definition of accidental
    D. a nonconfining definition of accidental

18. Most often, LTD policies provide benefits
    A. for 2 years
    B. for 5 years
    C. to age 60
    D. to age 65

19. Common exclusions under disability policies include all of the following EXCEPT
    A. disability caused by flying as a passenger on a commercial aircraft
    B. disability resulting when an insured is injured while committing a felony
    C. disability caused by self-inflicted injury
    D. disability caused by an act of war

20. Which of the following statements regarding the future increase option rider is NOT true?
    A. The rate for additional coverage will be at the insured's attained age at the time of purchase.
    B. The rider guarantees the ability to increase coverage to a predetermined limit regardless of change in the insured's income.
    C. The rider generally limits the number of option dates on which the insured may purchase additional coverage.
    D. The rider usually limits the amount of additional coverage available at each option date.

21. Disability benefits will generally be paid for the lifetime of the insured if total disability due to sickness begins at age
    A. 45 or earlier
    B. 50 or earlier
    C. 55 or earlier
    D. 65 or earlier

22. Which of the following statements regarding Social Security disability benefits is TRUE?
    A. For benefits to be paid, the disability must be permanent and expected to end in death.
    B. For benefits to be paid, the disability must prevent the individual from being able to perform any substantial gainful work existing in the national economy.
    C. Most of the people who apply for disability under Social Security are able to get benefits.
    D. Social Security provides a fairly liberal definition of total disability in order to keep individuals able to spend and support the national economy.

23. Which of the following statements about accidental death and dismemberment coverage is NOT true?
    A. A schedule listing various dismemberments and the sums that will be paid for them will be listed in the policy.
    B. The sums payable are generally expressed as percentages of the death benefit limit or the capital sum.
    C. If the policy has a disability income feature, the disability income payments continue even after the dismemberment sum is paid.
    D. Even if the insured is not disabled after an accident, if a loss of limb or sight occurs within 90 days of the date of the accident, the sums in the schedule will be paid.

24. Which of the following organizations would be most likely to be eligible for business overhead expense insurance?
    A. A law firm with 15 partners
    B. A doctor's office
    C. A major multinational corporation
    D. A public library

25. To protect the businessowner, the elimination period for disability buyout insurance normally is
    A. 1 to 2 weeks
    B. 3 to 6 months
    C. 6 months to 1 year
    D. 1 to 2 years

ANSWERS AND RATIONALES TO UNIT TEST

1. **A.** To receive benefits from a disability income policy for disability due to sickness, the insured must be totally disabled.

2. **D.** Accidental death and dismemberment is a rider that can provide additional benefits, but it does not define a disability.

3. **B.** The rehabilitation benefit pays for the insured to train for a new occupation.

4. **A.** The benefit that protects against the erosion of purchasing power for fixed disability benefits is known as the cost-of-living benefit.

5. **C.** The rider that provides more benefits during the first 6 months or year of a claim is known as the additional monthly benefit rider.

6. **A.** The benefit that pays the regular total disability benefit during the elimination period when the insured is hospitalized is known as the hospital confinement rider.

7. **D.** The option that allows an insured to purchase additional amounts of disability income protection is known as the future increase option.

8. **C.** Social insurance supplements provide disability income before workers' compensation and Social Security begin payments and after workers' compensation and Social Security end payments.

9. **B.** The elimination period is the time period before the benefits will pay after a disability occurs.

10. **A.** The longer the benefit period, the higher the policy's premium.

11. **A.** The own occupation definition of total disability is more favorable to the insured.

12. **C.** Occupational disability benefits are often reduced by benefits received from either Social Security or workers' compensation.

13. **A.** Loss of the dominant hand is not considered to be a presumptive disability.

14. **C.** Sickness disability is less likely to be partial than accident disability.

15. **D.** Some policies have replaced the partial disability provision with a residual disability provision.

16. **C.** A recurrent disability is when a second period of disability arises from the same or a related cause of a prior disability.

17. **B.** An accidental means definition of accidental means that the accident is completely unforeseen and unintended.

18. **D.** Most often, LTD policies provide benefits to age 65.

19. **A.** Disability caused by flying as a passenger on a commercial aircraft is not a common exclusion under disability policies.

20. **B.** The rider does not guarantee the ability to increase coverage to a predetermined limit regardless of change in the insured's income.

21. **C.** Disability benefits will generally be paid for the lifetime of the insured if total disability due to sickness begins at age 55 or earlier.

22. **B.** For benefits to be paid, the disability must prevent the individual from being able to perform any substantial gainful work existing in the national economy.

23. **C.** If the policy has a disability income feature, the disability income payments do not continue even after the dismemberment sum is paid.

24. **B.** A doctor's office would be most likely to be eligible for business overhead expense insurance.

25. **D.** To protect the businessowner, the elimination period for disability buy-sell insurance normally is 1 to 2 years.

UNIT 19 EXERCISE ANSWERS

Exercise 19.A

1. **D**
2. **G**
3. **F**
4. **A**
5. **H**
6. **B**
7. **C**
8. **E**

Exercise 19.B

1. **E**
2. **D**
3. **B**
4. **C**
5. **A**
6. **F**

Exercise 19.C

1. Key person
2. Disability buy-out
3. Business overhead expense

20

Medical Expense Insurance

20. 1 INTRODUCTION

Medical expense insurance provides benefits for medical care. Contracts may provide for payment of medical expenses incurred on a reimbursement basis (by paying benefits to the policyowner), payment on a service basis (by paying those who provide the services directly), or payment of an indemnity (by paying a set amount regardless of the amount charged for medical expenses). Medical expense or hospitalization insurance may be written on an individual or group basis. Benefits provided cover the individual and eligible dependents.

Although there are many types of benefits available, medical expense insurance can generally be categorized as basic medical expense insurance, major medical insurance, comprehensive medical insurance, and special policies. Note that these products have largely been replaced by managed care alternatives and are no longer sold as stand-alone coverages. These types of plans have been modified and replaced in response to changes in the health care field relative to cost containment and market competition. However, an understanding of basic medical, hospital, and surgical plans can serve as a foundation for understanding the hybrid plans currently being marketed.

20. 2 LEARNING OBJECTIVES

After completing this lesson, you will be able to:

- explain the purpose of medical expense insurance;
- explain the difference between basic and major medical expense policies; and
- explain the function of deductibles, coinsurance, stop-loss limits, and maximum benefits.

20. 3 BASIC MEDICAL EXPENSE

Basic coverages provided by an individual medical expense policy include hospital expense, surgical expense, and medical expense. These three basic coverages may be sold together or separately. Frequently this is written as "first dollar" coverage, which means it does not have a deductible.

20. 3. 1 Hospital Expense Benefits

As the name implies, **hospital expense** coverage provides benefits for expenses incurred during hospitalization. Hospital indemnities are usually classified into two broad groups:

- Room and board, including nursing care and special diets
- Miscellaneous medical expenses, including x-rays, laboratory fees, medications, medical supplies, and operating and treatment rooms

In some cases, surgical benefits may be included for certain types of surgery and associated costs.

20. 3. 1. 1 Room and Board Benefit

Hospital expense coverage provides benefits for daily hospital room and board and miscellaneous hospital expenses (not including telephone and television) while the insured person is confined to the hospital. The policy may provide for a certain dollar amount for the daily hospital room and board benefit, although the trend is toward coverage of not more than the semiprivate room rate unless a private room is medically necessary.

The room and board benefit may be paid on either an indemnity basis or a reimbursement basis, depending on the particular policy.

When room and board are covered on an indemnity basis, the insurer pays a specified, preestablished amount per day, as shown in a schedule in the policy, for a stated maximum number of days.

Indemnity policies are sometimes called dollar amount plans. Room and board rates vary by geographic location, but it is not unusual to find room and board rates ranging from $300 to $500 per day or more. Typically, the maximum number of days is from 90 to 365.

More commonly, room and board expenses are paid on a **reimbursement** basis. This is also referred to as an expenses-incurred basis. Under this arrangement, the policy will pay in one of two ways.

- The actual charges for a semiprivate room are covered.
- A percentage of the actual charges is paid, with no specific dollar limit.

Under the first reimbursement option—actual charges—the insurer will pay the full actual semiprivate room rate, regardless of what it is, as indicated in the illustration that follows.

Actual Charges/Option A

Insurer pays full actual charges for each

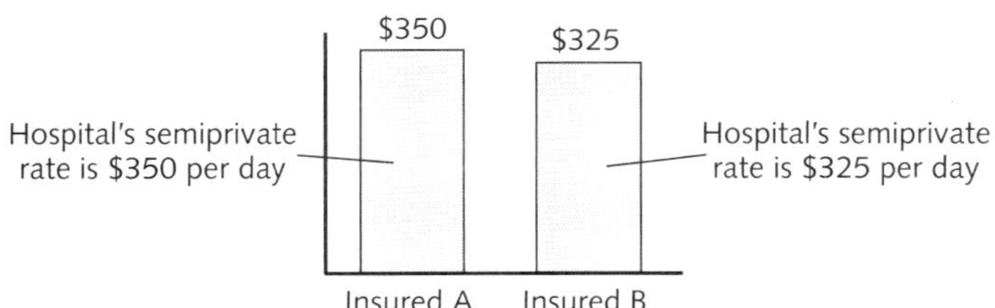

Under this same arrangement, however, the insurer still pays only the semiprivate room rate if the insured must be in a private room, as indicated in the following chart.

Option B

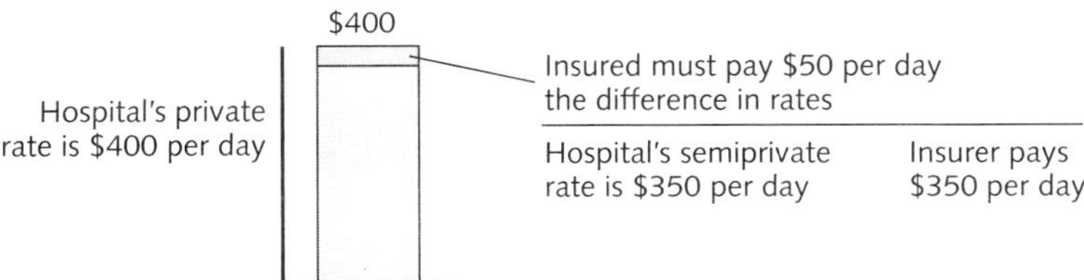

Under the second reimbursement option—payment of a percentage of the actual charges—the insurance company pays a specified percentage, regardless of what the actual charges are. A common percentage is 80%. Here is how it would apply to Insureds A and B from the previous illustration.

Pecentage of Actual Charges

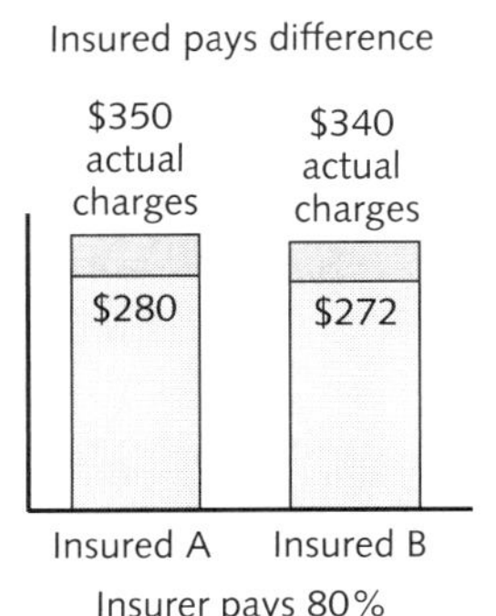

To summarize, under the actual charges type of reimbursement plan, the policy will pay the actual amount charged for a semiprivate room without regard to a specific dollar limit. Under the percentage type of reimbursement plan, the policy will pay a specified percentage of the actual charges.

Some room and board benefits include intensive care, which may be paid in full or in part. Hospital plans with this provision generally provide for a maximum intensive care benefit of some multiple of the room and board maximum—usually two or three times. For example, if the room and board maximum is $400 per day, the plan might pay twice that amount, or $800 per day, for intensive care. A limit might also be placed on the number of days for which this benefit will be paid.

20. 3. 1. 2 Miscellaneous Medical Expenses Benefit

Benefits for miscellaneous medical expenses are generally stated as a limit separate from the room and board benefits. Usually, the limit is expressed as some multiple of the per-day limit for room and board—such as 10 or 20 times—for each period of hospital confinement. For example, a policy might state that it will pay 10 times the semiprivate room rate. If the semiprivate rate is $500 per day, a total of $5,000 (10 × $500) is available for miscellaneous expenses during this single stay in the hospital. If, a year later, the rate has increased to $550 per day, $5,500 will be available.

20. 3. 2 Surgical Expense Benefits

20. 3. 2. 1 Scheduled Plan

Surgical expense policies pay surgeons' fees and related costs incurred when the insured has an operation. Related costs might include fees for an assistant surgeon, an anesthesiologist, and even the operating room, when it is not covered as a miscellaneous medical item.

Basic surgical coverage is often included in the same policy as basic hospital and medical expense. Benefit amounts are included in a schedule that lists major commonly performed operations and benefits payable for each. The fact that a particular type of surgery is not listed in the schedule does not mean that no benefit is available to cover it. Instead, insurers indemnify on the basis of the absolute value and the relative value of each surgical procedure.

In some cases, the schedule itself may be referred to in terms of the maximum benefit paid for the most costly procedure, with all other surgical benefits paid as a percentage of that maximum. For example, under a $10,000 schedule, that amount might be paid for open-heart surgery. A less complex procedure, such as a tonsillectomy, might trigger a benefit equal to 10% of that, or $1,000.

20. 3. 2. 2 Nonscheduled Plan

When surgical benefits (and sometimes other benefits) are not listed by a specific dollar amount in a schedule, a policy will pay on the basis of what is considered **usual, customary, and reasonable (UCR)** in a certain geographic area. This type of indemnity is found more often in the major medical and comprehensive policies discussed later in this unit.

Under this type of arrangement, the definition of UCR is based on the amount physicians in the area usually charge for the same or similar procedures. These nonscheduled plans allow policies to stay apace of inflation and to avoid policy restructuring every time medical costs increase. The insurer still reserves the right to agree or disagree that a particular charge is usual, customary, and reasonable.

20. 3. 3 Regular Medical Expense Benefits

Another category, regular medical expense benefits, is sometimes called physicians' nonsurgical expense. Remember that some states refer to this particular category as basic medical expense. Coverage is for nonsurgical services a physician provides. Sometimes, it is narrowly applied to physician visits to patients confined in the hospital. If so, the benefit will usually pay for:

- a specified maximum number of visits per day;
- a specified maximum dollar amount per visit; and
- a specified maximum number of days that coverage applies.

For example, this type of limited benefit might pay for up to three visits per day at $10 per visit for no more than 30 days.

In other policies, the benefit might be for nonsurgical services a physician performs whether or not the patient is in the hospital. Again there are limits, such as $25 per visit for up to 50 visits a year.

Exercise 20.A

Fill in the blanks with the appropriate basic medical expense insurance policy type.

1. An MEI policy that pays a certain amount per visit for non-surgical physician visits either in their office or in a hospital is known as __________ __________ __________.
2. An MEI policy that pays a certain amount from a schedule or on a usual, customary, and reasonable basis to cover the physicians' charges (surgeon and anesthesiologist) related to a surgical procedure is known as __________ __________.
3. An MEI policy that pays a certain amount per day or reimburses charges related to room and board plus certain miscellaneous charges when the insured is admitted to a hospital is known as __________ __________.

Answers to the exercises can be found at the end of the Unit 20 answers and rationales.

20. 3. 4 Other Medical Expense Benefits

In addition to the hospital, surgical, and medical benefits just discussed, there are other benefits that might be included andmay be added at the insured's option, or for which separate policies might be written. Different insurers may include different options as part of their standard policies, so each policy must be considered individually. Some coverage options are:

- maternity;
- convalescent/nursing home;
- emergency first aid;
- home health care;
- mental infirmity;
- hospice care;
- prescription drugs;
- dread disease;
- outpatient treatment;
- dental;
- private-duty nursing; and
- vision.

We will discuss the most common options here, and in another lesson you'll learn about those that are more typically written as separate policies.

20. 3. 4. 1 *In-Hospital Physician Visits*

Frequently, a basic medical expense policy will include a daily benefit for expenses incurred when the insured's physician visits him in the hospital. This benefit is limited to a dollar amount such as $25 or $30 per day. This amount would be paid for any charges made by the doctor for visiting the patient.

20. 3. 4. 2 *Maternity Benefits*

Some policies provide maternity benefits subject to certain conditions and limitations—the most usual of which is a 10-month waiting period designed to prevent purchase of health insurance solely to cover pregnancy and childbirth expenses. You should be aware, however, that group policies for employee groups of 15 or more are required by law to provide maternity benefits on the same basis as nonmaternity benefits. Thus, under a group plan with 15 or more employees, a 10-month waiting period would not apply unless nonmaternity benefits also required a 10-month waiting period.

Note: Since June 1, 1997, pregnancy may not be subject to a waiting period if the worker has already met the waiting period required by the group coverage of a previous employer.

Aside from group plans as described, many policies exclude maternity benefits but make them available at extra cost. Often, a maternity benefit is a lump sum paid for normal childbirth. The actual amount might be:

- usual, customary, and reasonable charges;
- a specified amount; or
- a multiple of the daily hospital benefit.

The benefit generally includes routine newborn care while the mother is hospitalized.

Other benefits that might be available under the same maternity coverage but scheduled at amounts different from the benefit for normal childbirth include:

- cesarean deliveries;
- natural abortions; and
- elective abortions.

20. 3. 4. 3 *Emergency First Aid Coverage*

An accident may require immediate first aid on the scene. When a medical professional who happens upon an accident provides first aid service, that person might bill the insured. Sometimes such treatment must be performed without the insured's knowledge or assent. Some policies offer coverage for such contingencies by including emergency first aid coverage for treatment expenses incurred within a very short time after an accident. This length of time is specified in the policy.

20. 3. 4. 4 Emergency Accident Benefits

A basic plan may include a specific benefit for expenses incurred as the result of an accident when the insured is taken to the emergency room of a hospital as an outpatient. Typically, this benefit is stated as $300 or possibly $500. The benefit is to cover the cost of treatment in the emergency room including physician expenses, x-rays, stitches, and other services.

20. 3. 4. 5 Mental Infirmity

Although some policies exclude coverage for mental infirmities, more policies now include this coverage than before. Typically, the benefits will be lower than for physical infirmities, usually a stated percentage of the benefit paid for other types of medical care. For example, the physical infirmity benefit might be $100,000, and the mental infirmity benefit 70% of that amount.

Alternatively, a policy might specify a particular dollar amount for mental infirmity that is different from the amount for physical infirmity, such as $50,000 for physical infirmity and $25,000 for mental infirmity.

Suppose Brad's policy will pay a maximum benefit of $100,000 for any one hospitalization but only 60% of the maximum benefit if the impairment is mental. The most Brad could receive under his particular policy if he is hospitalized for mental infirmity is $60,000, which is 60% of $100,000.

20. 3. 4. 6 Hospice Care

Most states require that any hospitalization policy (individual or group) include benefits for hospice expenses. The hospice is a facility designed to control pain and suffering of terminally ill patients until their death. It does not treat diseases, nor does it attempt to cure. In addition, the hospice also provides counseling for the patient and the family of the terminally ill. Expenses covered include room and board, medication, and outpatient services and expenses.

20. 3. 4. 7 Home Health Care

This is usually an optional benefit that provides for reimbursement of expenses incurred by the insured for the services of a visiting nurse, a therapist, or some other support-type person who, because of a medical necessity, visits the insured in the home and provides necessary medical services.

20. 3. 4. 8 Outpatient Care

Outpatient care refers to expenses incurred by the insured for doctor's office visits and out-of-the-hospital diagnostic services, such as laboratory work and x-rays. Often a basic medical expense policy only covers in-hospital expenses (inpatient) whereby treatment is provided to the patient who has been assigned a room and a bed and is staying in the hospital for some period of time. Basic plans may add coverage for certain medical services provided to the insured as an outpatient.

20. 3. 5 Common Exclusions and Limitations

Both disability income and medical expense policies exclude or limit coverage for certain types of injuries and illnesses. One example of a limitation is the smaller benefit for mental infirmity just discussed. Exclusions, on the other hand, are conditions that are completely omitted from coverage.

Items a policy might exclude or limit are represented in the list that follows. Many policies will, in fact, include benefits for all or part of some of the items in the list. It is important for you to be aware of your own state laws and your company's policies regarding each of the following items:

- Preexisting conditions, as defined in the policy and according to state law (however, some states have no loss/no gain laws that require a replacing health insurance policy to cover any conditions for which there are ongoing claims under existing coverage, thus overriding the preexisting conditions exclusion in the replacing policy)
- Hernia, although the trend is to cover this condition
- Self-inflicted injuries
- Suicide
- War or acts of war resulting in death or injury, whether or not war is officially declared
- Military duty, usually a suspension of the policy that ends when the insured is released from such duty
- Noncommercial air travel, which is any air travel other than as a scheduled airline passenger
- Injury while committing a felony
- Injury, illness, or death while under the influence of intoxicants or narcotics
- Cosmetic surgery, except for surgery required as the result of an accidental injury or a congenital defect
- Dental expense, although some policies cover such expenses resulting from accidental injury
- Vision correction, such as eye exams and eyeglasses
- Care provided in a government facility, normally paid by the Veterans Administration or by workers' compensation
- Sexually transmitted diseases
- Experimental procedures
- Organ transplants
- Infertility services
- Alcohol or drug abuse treatment

Here are some examples of situations that would be excluded by most policies.

- The insured is severely cut while breaking the plate glass window of a jewelry store from which he intends to steal gems (injury while committing a felony).
- When the insured is injured in an auto accident, the police administer an alcohol test and discover he is legally intoxicated (injury while under the influence of intoxicants).
- The insured is injured by shellfire while touring another country torn by guerrilla fighting (injury caused by an act of war).

In summary, it is quite evident that basic medical expense plans definitely have time and/or benefit amount limitations. Thus, the insured may well expect to have to pay a considerable amount out of pocket for medical expenses. The solution to this problem is another type of hospitalization coverage referred to as major medical insurance.

Exercise 20.B

An acronym, WAPSOC, can help you to remember the primary exclusions for medical expense insurance. Complete the following words.

1. W ____
2. A ____________
3. P ____ ____________
4. S ______ __________
5. O ____________
6. C _________ ____ _____ _______

Answers to the exercises can be found at the end of the Unit 20 answers and rationales.

20. 4 MAJOR MEDICAL INSURANCE

We have discussed basic benefits designed to cover even some hospital, medical, and surgical costs that are considered relatively minor. When these basic benefits are purchased piecemeal, the total benefits provided can be substantially less than the actual expenses incurred. Providing more complete coverage with fewer gaps, **major medical insurance** covers a much broader range of medical expenses with generally higher individual benefits and policy maximums.

These more extensive health policies are divided roughly into two groups:

- **Comprehensive** major medical expense, in which the more traditional basic coverages and essentially any other type of medical expense are combined into a single comprehensive policy

- **Supplemental** major medical expense, in which coverage begins with a traditional basic policy, which pays first, and the major medical coverage is added to pick up expenses not covered by the basic policy

20. 4. 1 Comprehensive Major Medical Benefits

20. 4. 1. 1 Deductibles

Most major medical benefits begin to be paid after the deductible is satisfied. The policy's deductible is considered satisfied as long as the insured can show evidence of having incurred the necessary expense.

There are essentially two types of comprehensive major medical plans: one with first dollar coverage and one without.

First dollar coverage means that as soon as covered medical expenses are incurred, the policy begins to pay. Policies with first dollar coverage effectively have a deductible of zero. Without first dollar coverage, the insured must pay a specified deductible amount first, and when that amount of expenses incurred has been paid by the insured, the policy starts reimbursing. Deductibles are generally an important feature of major medical policies.

For example, before Jim's major medical policy will pay benefits, Jim must pay the first $400 of medical expenses each year. He does not have first dollar coverage; that is, he must pay a deductible. On the other hand, as soon as Rona was hospitalized, her major medical policy began reimbursing her for expenses. She has first dollar coverage.

20. 4. 1. 2 Coinsurance

Another important feature of major medical coverage is coinsurance. **Coinsurance** means that the insurer and the insured share any expenses above the deductible amount. The insurer always carries the bulk of the expense, usually paying 80% of covered expenses compared with 20% for the insured. Other proportions, such as 75/25%, may be used, so it is important to read the policy. In some areas, coinsurance is referred to as percentage participation.

Here's an example of how coinsurance works. An insured's major medical policy includes a $200 deductible and 80/20% coinsurance. The insured incurs medical expenses totaling $1,200. The insured will pay $400 of this amount—the initial $200 deductible—leaving $1,000 to be shared 80/20, of which the insured pays 20%, or an additional $200. The insurance company will pay $800 of the $1,200 total. This is 80% of the $1,000 remaining after the insured has paid the deductible.

20. 4. 1. 3 Stop-Loss Limit and Maximum Benefits

More and more major medical policies include a **stop-loss limit**, which is a dollar amount beyond which the insured no longer participates in payment of the expenses. The stop-loss limit is sometimes known as the out-of-pocket limit. After the insured's total coinsurance and deductible payments reach that amount, the insurer picks up the entire cost of remaining expenses, up to a stated **maximum benefit**. Currently, the lifetime maximum limits on health policies might range from $100,000 to $1,000,000, and some policies even have unlimited benefits.

Just as the maximum benefit varies considerably, so does the amount of the stop loss limit, depending on the insurer. The next illustration shows how the stop-loss limit and the maximum benefits limit work, assuming a $5,000 stop loss and S1,000,000 lifetime maximum.

Stop-Loss Limit and Maximum Benefits

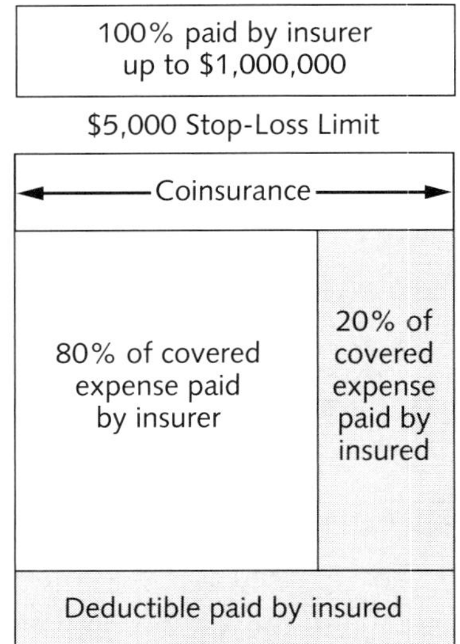

Assume an insured has the comprehensive plan illustrated, with a $300 deductible. Following a severe injury, the insured incurs covered medical expenses totaling $28,000. The insured will pay a total of $5,000, which is the stop-loss limit. The insurance company will pay $23,000, the balance remaining after the insured has paid up to the stop-loss limit.

Exercise 20.C

Comprehensive Major Medical policies have three major components that must be understood. Complete the following sentences by inserting the appropriate component title.

1. Major medical benefits usually begin after the insured has incurred an initial annual amount of out-of-pocket expense called a ____________.
2. Once this initial amount has been paid, the insurer and the insured share the next portion of the bill on some basis, typically 80%/20%. This shared portion is called ________________.
3. Many Major Medical plans limit the amount paid by the insured to some dollar amount. Beyond this amount, called a _____ _____ ______, the insurer pays 100% of covered charges up to the policy maximum benefit.

Answers to the exercises can be found at the end of the Unit 20 answers and rationales.

20. 4. 2 Supplemental Major Medical Benefits

Supplemental Major Medical

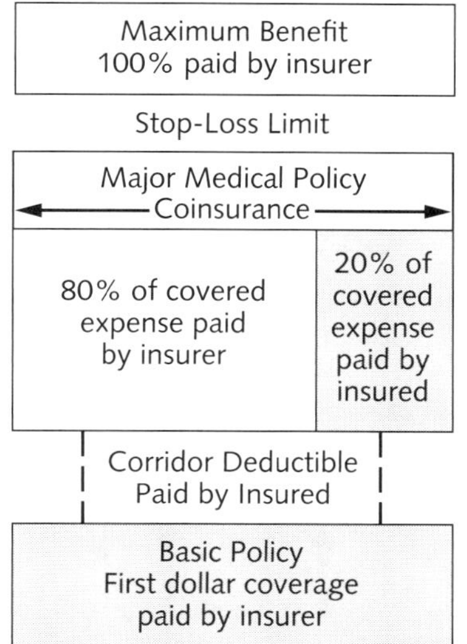

When major medical benefits are provided through a **supplemental policy**, the major medical portion supplements a basic policy that includes hospital, surgical, and medical coverage with an additional policy covering the broader range of medical expenses.

Generally, the basic plan will pay covered medical expenses with no deductible, up to the policy limit. Above that limit, the supplemental policy operates identically to a comprehensive policy that provides no other first dollar coverage. That is, after the basic policy limits are exhausted, the insured must pay a deductible, after which the major medical coverage begins. Because the deductible comes between the basic policy and the major medical policy, it is often called a **corridor** deductible.

Like the comprehensive major medical policy, a supplemental plan is likely to include a stop-loss limit and a maximum benefit limit. Here is how a supplemental major medical plan looks.

20. 4. 2. 1 Supplemental Major Medical

Suppose Jill has a supplemental major medical policy. The basic policy will pay $500 for her scheduled surgery. The corridor deductible is $250, and the plan includes an 80/20% coinsurance provision above the base plan, up to a stop-loss level of $5,000. The policy will pay 100% of covered expenses above the $5,000 limit, up to a limit of $1 million. Jill has covered medical expenses of $4,750 following an illness. Here is how these expenses are paid:

	Insurance Pays	Jill Pays
First $500 of expenses	$500	$0
Deductible	$0	$250
Remaining expenses = $4,000 at 80/20%	$3,200	$800
Total insurance payment	$3,700	$1,050

Let's change the scenario slightly. If Jill's expenses had totaled over $5,000, she would pay nothing over that amount because the insurer pays 100% of covered expenses over the stop-loss limit, which is $5,000 in Jill's policy.

Here's another possibility. If Jill's expenses had totaled only $400 for benefits the basic policy provides, she would have paid nothing because her basic policy provides first dollar coverage.

20. 4. 2. 2 Covered Expenses

Major medical policies, whether supplemental or comprehensive, cover a wide range of medical expenses. The precise services covered may vary somewhat from policy to policy, but many of the following will be included in most major medical plans:

- Hospital inpatient room and board, including intensive and cardiac care
- Hospital medical and surgical services and supplies
- Physicians' diagnostic, medical, and surgical services
- Other medical practitioners' services
- Nursing services, including private-duty service outside a hospital
- Anesthesia and anesthetist services
- Outpatient services
- Ambulance service to and from a hospital
- X-rays and other diagnostic and laboratory tests
- Radiological and other types of therapy
- Prescription drugs
- Blood and blood plasma
- Oxygen and its administration
- Dental services resulting from injury to natural teeth
- Convalescent nursing home care
- Home health care services
- Prosthetic devices when initially purchased
- Casts, splints, trusses, braces, and crutches
- Rental of durable equipment such as hospital-type beds and wheelchairs

Expenses that are excluded from major medical policies generally parallel the exclusions listed previously in this unit. Covered expenses are also known as eligible expenses.

Exercise 20.D

Fill in the term that best completes the following description.

1. In a Supplemental Major Medical policy, the deductible that occurs between basic policy benefits and major medical benefits is called a _______.

Answers to the exercises can be found at the end of the Unit 20 answers and rationales.

20. 4. 3 Other Major Medical Concepts

20. 4. 3. 1 Deductible Features

There are a number of ways deductibles might be handled in major medical policies. Some policies include a **per-cause**—injury or sickness—deductible, whereas others may have an **all-cause** deductible, which is also referred to as a cumulative, or calendar year, deductible.

With a **per-cause** deductible, the insured pays one deductible for all expenses incurred for the same injury or illness. The benefit period for each cause begins when the deductible for that particular injury or illness has been satisfied and may run for one or two years. It works like this: Yu-Long suffered a major illness early in the year that required his incurring continuing medical expenses through mid-year. Then, in September, he was injured in an auto accident that hospitalized him for two weeks. Yu-Long had to pay a separate deductible for each of these incidents because his policy has a per-cause deductible.

On the other hand, with an **all-cause** deductible, expenses for any number of different or the same type of illness or accidents are accumulated to meet the deductible during a single calendar year. Once enough expenses have been paid by the insured to meet the stated deductible, all other covered charges are paid during the remainder of the calendar year.

Under the all-cause deductible arrangement, there is also usually a **carryover provision** that permits expenses incurred during the last three months of the calendar year to be carried over into the new year if needed to satisfy the deductible for the next year. For example, suppose Laura had no medical expenses until November and December. Her illness continued into January. Laura will be able to count the expenses in November and December toward her deductible in the new year.

Policies that cover entire families usually have a **family deductible** rather than individual deductibles. For example, although a policy's individual deductible might be $200, the family deductible amount might be $400. Thus, even a family with six members would pay no more than a $400 deductible as opposed to the $1,200 that would be required if each member had to meet the $200 deductible.

Another deductible provision that can be advantageous to families is the **common injury or illness provision**. Under this provision, only one deductible must be paid when two or more members of the same family are injured in a common accident or become ill concurrently from the same sickness. Suppose Myra and Rick, wife and husband, are riding in Rick's car when they are both injured in an accident on the freeway. The deductible for each person under their health policy is $200, but their policy requires them to pay only $200 in this case.

20. 4. 3. 2 *Benefit Periods and Inside Limits*

The times during which benefits are paid, known as **benefit periods**, are generally tied to the deductible and to any inside or internal limits included in the major medical policy.

When a deductible must be paid, the benefit period might begin either on the first day of the accident or illness or on the date the insured has satisfied the deductible (if later than the date of the event) and may extend for up to two years. In other cases, the benefit period ceases at the end of the calendar year and begins anew with the new deductible.

Inside or **internal limits** are benefit limitations placed on specified coverages in a major medical policy. For example, the policy might limit both the room and board benefit and the number of days benefits will be paid. In this case, the benefit period for hospital room and board would be the number of days specified. Other examples of internal limits might be restrictions placed on convalescent care days, mental health care, x-rays per claim, and similar items.

20. 4. 3. 3 *Restoration of Benefits*

Since lifetime maximums on major medical policies have increased dramatically to $1 million and more, the restoration or reinstatement of plan benefits is not as important as in the past when maximums were much lower. However, some policies in force today carry fairly low maximums, and most major medical policies still include a provision that allows restoration of the maximum to the original level.

For example, a lifetime level might be $100,000. An insured with a severe injury or illness could easily use half or more of that in a single year, leaving only $50,000 for the rest of the insured's life. Generally, a policy allows the maximum to be restored after a certain amount of benefits are used, though sometimes the insured must prove insurability again. Many policies have an automatic reinstatement provision that restores a specified number of dollars each January 1, or after a given period elapses, without requiring the insured to prove insurability.

20. 4. 4 Medical Expense Limitations

Reimbursement-type medical expense policies frequently provide limited coverage or benefits for certain medical conditions. Many plans will include limitations on the benefits to be provided for the following:

- Rehabilitation and skilled nursing/extended care facilities care
- Home health care
- Hospice care

- Ambulance services
- Outpatient treatment
- Medical equipment and supplies
- Reconstructive cosmetic surgery
- Treatment of AIDS
- Infertility and sterilization
- Maternity/complications of pregnancy/well-baby care
- Psychiatric conditions
- Substance abuse
- Organ transplants
- Preexisting conditions
- Reimbursement for nonphysician services

20. 4. 4. 1 Mental or Emotional Disorders

Lifetime benefit amounts are limited for outpatient treatment of these disorders. For example, a major medical policy may have a lifetime maximum of $1 million, but the policy may limit coverage for outpatient treatment of mental or emotional disorders to a lifetime benefit of $25,000. In addition, frequently there may be a limitation with regard to the number of outpatient psychiatric visits per calendar year (such as a maximum of 26 visits per year) or the benefit amount paid per visit (such as a maximum benefit of $50 per visit or coverage for no more than 50% of the actual charges). These limits would not apply to inpatient treatment of mental or emotional disorders.

Note: New federal laws effective in 1997 removed these limitations for group coverage.

20. 4. 4. 2 Maternity

As previously discussed, maternity benefits are often optional. When elected, the amount of the maternity benefit is often limited. This limitation is frequently the result of the high cost of a maternity claim and the corresponding high premium charged for the benefit.

For example, a maternity benefit may be limited to a total benefit of $1,000 regardless of the actual expenses incurred. Usually, the only time additional benefits are paid is when there are certain complications during the pregnancy or at the time of delivery. A very liberal maternity benefit (and a costly one) would be that maternity is treated as an illness and thus a full range of benefits are payable.

20. 4. 4. 3 Substance Abuse

Outpatient treatment for drug or alcohol problems is usually limited in much the same way that coverage for nervous or emotional disorders is limited. Usually, if the insured is hospitalized as an inpatient for treatment of the substance abuse problem, then regular medical expense benefits are payable.

20. 4. 4. 4 Chiropractic Services

The treatment rendered by a chiropractor is normally a covered expense subject to a limitation with regard to total benefits (e.g., $10,000 lifetime) or a limitation with regard to the number of visits that will be covered in a given year and/or the amount that may be paid per visit.

20. 4. 4. 5 Preexisting Conditions

Generally, a preexisting condition is any condition for which the insured sought treatment or advice before the effective date of coverage. Many policies contain a preexisting conditions limitation that excludes coverage for unspecified conditions for a certain period (usually six months). If an insurer wants to permanently exclude a preexisting condition, it usually has to specify the condition by name in the issued policy. Depending on the severity of the condition, it may be permanently excluded or temporarily excluded (i.e., the first 12 months following the effective date of coverage). Seldom is a preexisting condition covered by means of limited benefit amounts. Generally, it is either excluded or covered in full as any other condition.

20. 5 BENEFITS FOR OTHER PRACTITIONERS

In past years, many health insurance contracts placed limitations on the kind of provider who could perform covered treatments and services. In many cases, coverage was limited to treatment rendered by a physician. In effect, this eliminated coverage for treatments rendered by chiropractors, midwives, and other nontraditional healers.

In recent years, it has become recognized that many alternative providers who are subject to state licensing and/or standards of conduct imposed by professional organizations are qualified health care providers. Use of alternative providers can help to minimize health care costs and reduce the demand on hospitals and doctors. Under current laws in many states, policies must provide benefits for services given by various providers if benefits would be payable for the same services when given by a physician, as long as the providers are properly qualified and are acting within the scope of their profession. As a result, benefits for various services are often provided and may not be excluded when performed by the following types of health care professionals, if they are practicing within the scope of their license when rendering treatment:

- Chiropractors
- Optometrists

- Opticians
- Psychologists
- Podiatrists
- Clinical social workers
- Dentists
- Physical therapists
- Professional counselors

20. 6 MEDICAL EXPENSE EXCLUSIONS

Medical expense policies contain many exclusions that are found in all health and disability policies: preexisting conditions, war, intentionally self-inflicted injuries, and active military duty. Medical expense policies also commonly exclude the following:

- Workers' compensation
- Government plans (care in government facilities)
- Well-baby care
- Cosmetic surgery
- Dental care
- Eyeglasses
- Hearing aids
- Custodial care
- Routine physicals and medical care

Workers' compensation and other government plans are excluded to prevent overpayment of claims or overinsurance. If an injured employee will have a claim covered by workers' compensation because the injury was work-related, individual or group medical expense plans will not pay the same claim. The same concept applies if, for example, an individual's medical care is to be provided by a veterans' administration facility.

Some plans exclude well-baby care because the purpose of medical expense coverage is to indemnify an individual who sustains a loss due to an accident or an illness. If a newborn baby is normal and healthy (a well baby) following delivery, then no benefits will be paid for any hospital claim while the child is in the hospital's nursery pending discharge of the mother. If the newborn has a medical problem following birth, normal benefits will be paid.

Cosmetic surgery is usually excluded unless the reason for the surgery is a medical necessity, such as an accident or a disease that disfigures a person. Cosmetic surgery is viewed as voluntary and thus not covered.

Routine dental care is usually excluded with individual medical expense policies but is frequently offered as an optional benefit under a group contract. Again, if a person is injured, such as in an automobile accident, and needs dental surgery for repair of damaged teeth, this type of care is normally covered.

Eyeglasses and hearing aids are normally excluded unless there is a medical reason for acquiring these devices such as injury that causes loss of hearing or vision. Reduced hearing or vision due to age and similar factors are not covered.

Custodial care is care provided to assist the individual in the activities of daily living that does not contribute to the improvement of a medical condition and that can be performed by a person who does not have medical training. Coverage for these types of services may be excluded by a medical expense policy.

Routine physicals are normally also excluded from coverage. Routine physicals include a person's annual check-up when the reason for the physical is simply that it has been a year since the individual had a physical. Also excluded would be preemployment physicals or a child's school physical. There must be a medical reason for the physical before it is considered a covered expense.

Routine medical care such as immunizations is usually excluded. On the other hand, if an insured is injured and requires a tetanus shot as a result of an accident, the immunization is covered. If a doctor simply told a patient to have a tetanus shot because it has been 10 years since the patient's last shot, it would not be covered.

It should be noted that some insurers offer coverage for routine physicals and medical care because it is generally recognized that these preventive health care measures benefit the insured and the insurer. A routine physical exam could result in the diagnosis of a potential major medical problem before it develops into a large claim for the insurer.

20. 7 OPTIONAL FEATURES AND BENEFITS

20. 7. 1 Prescription Drugs

The prescription drug benefit is most often found in group health insurance policies. Some individual health insurance policies offer this benefit as a rider. Different policies offer different prescription card benefits. For example, some policies will cover birth control pills as part of the benefit, and in other policies, birth control pills are specifically excluded. Usually prescription drug coverage requires a small deductible, typically $2, $3, or $5.

A prescription drug benefit generally works one of two ways. Either insureds can be reimbursed for their prescription drug expenses using standard claim forms, or a prescription drug card can be issued. A prescription drug card allows prescriptions to be received by paying only the deductible with each prescription purchase. The pharmacy bills the insurer issuing the card directly for the prescription.

For example, Sally has a prescription drug card as part of her group medical plan, which has a $5 deductible per prescription. Her doctor prescribes two medications for a serious cold. Each of these medications would cost Sally $5. The balance of the prescription cost will be billed to the insurer by the pharmacy.

20. 7. 2 Vision Care

Vision care includes eye examinations (refractions) and eyeglasses. It is usually offered as an optional benefit under group health insurance. Generally, this option will pay a specific amount or the entire cost of an annual eye examination. It normally also covers all or part of the cost of prescribed eyeglasses once in every two-year period.

20. 7. 3 Hospital Indemnity Rider

A hospital indemnity benefit provides for the payment of a daily benefit for each day that the insured is hospitalized as an inpatient. Available amounts are usually $50 to $100 per day or possibly slightly higher. In addition to any other medical benefits paid to the insured, the hospital indemnity benefit will pay the daily amount as long as the insured is hospitalized, usually for a benefit period of one or two years.

20. 7. 4 Nursing or Convalescent Home

Under this benefit, a daily maximum amount is paid for each day the insured is confined to a nursing or convalescent home after a hospital stay. Benefits are paid generally for as short as one month or up to one year.

20. 7. 5 Organ Transplants

More insurers are offering this coverage as it becomes less experimental and more commonplace. To provide coverage, many insurers require that a transplant be performed only in life-threatening situations. Some of the more commonly covered transplants include bone marrow and kidney.

UNIT TEST

1. Lauren's policy covers hospital expenses by paying a specified, predetermined amount per day, as shown in a schedule in the policy. Lauren's policy pays on
   A. a reimbursement choice
   B. an expenses-incurred basis
   C. an indemnity basis
   D. a capitation basis

2. Intensive care benefits under hospital plans are
   A. never included
   B. generally provided at the same level as the room and board maximum
   C. generally provided at some multiple of the room and board maximum
   D. generally provided without limit based on the need of the insured

3. When benefits are not listed by a specific dollar amount in a schedule, a policy will generally pay
   A. the usual, customary, and reasonable charge for the procedure
   B. the universal, customary, and reasonable charge for the procedure
   C. the usual, capitated, and reasonable charge for the procedure
   D. the usually charged rate for the procedure

4. The out-of-pocket limit is also known as
   A. the deductible
   B. the co-payment
   C. the stop-loss limit
   D. the maximum benefit

5. Which of the following is least likely to be covered by a major medical policy?
   A. Outpatient services
   B. Dental care
   C. Prescription drugs
   D. Blood and blood plasma

6. Which of the following is least likely to be covered by a major medical policy?
   A. Surgery performed on an outpatient basis
   B. Replacement of an artificial limb
   C. Nursing home care for a month following release from a hospital
   D. Purchase of blood for transfusion during an operation

7. Carmen falls and breaks her leg, incurring $2,000 in medical expenses. Her policy pays the entire amount. Carmen has
   A. a major medical policy
   B. a hospital income policy
   C. a comprehensive major medical policy
   D. a policy with first dollar coverage

8. A hospital room and board benefit may be paid
   A. on an indemnity basis
   B. on a reimbursement basis
   C. on either an indemnity basis or a reimbursement basis
   D. on neither an indemnity basis nor a reimbursement basis

9. The type of health insurance providing high maximum coverage for medical care is
   A. a basic medical expense policy
   B. a major medical expense policy
   C. a comprehensive medical expense policy
   D. a supplemental medical expense policy

10. The type of policy that has a major medical portion that provides benefits once the basic policy limits are exhausted and a deductible has been paid is
    A. a basic medical expense policy
    B. a major medical expense policy
    C. a comprehensive medical expense policy
    D. a supplemental medical expense policy

11. A combination of basic medical expense coverage and major medical expense coverage is
    A. a basic medical expense policy
    B. a major medical expense policy
    C. a comprehensive medical expense policy
    D. a supplemental medical expense policy

12. The type of policy covering doctor visits while the insured is in the hospital is
    A. a basic medical expense policy
    B. a major medical expense policy
    C. a comprehensive medical expense policy
    D. a supplemental medical expense policy

13. Maternity benefits must be provided on the same basis as nonmaternity benefits
    A. in all cases
    B. only if the insurer chooses to do so
    C. if the policy covers an employee group of 15 or more people
    D. if the policy provides disability income coverage

14. Among individual policies that include coverage for mental infirmities, the benefit will generally be
    A. lower than the benefit for physical infirmities
    B. higher than the benefit for physical infirmities
    C. unlimited
    D. the same as the benefit for physical infirmities

15. A hospice works
    A. to treat diseases only, not accident-related medical issues
    B. to control pain and suffering as well as to treat illness
    C. alleviate pain and suffering for terminally ill patients until death, but does not attempt to cure
    D. with medical professionals when they become ill, to provide treatment in a private setting away from lay patients

16. No loss/no gain laws require
    A. replacing health insurance policies to cover any conditions for which there are ongoing claims under existing coverage
    B. replacing health insurance to remove preexisting condition exclusions from all policies replaced
    C. existing insurers to continue to cover ongoing claims after a policy has been replaced
    D. existing insurers to remove preexisting condition exclusions from all policies being replaced

17. Purchasing basic benefits on an individual basis usually
    A. provides a broader range of coverage than a single major medical policy
    B. provides less-complete coverage with more gaps than a major medical policy
    C. provides exactly the same coverage as a major medical policy
    D. is prohibited by state law

18. The dollar limit beyond which the insured no longer participates in payment of expenses is
    A. the deductible
    B. the coinsurance
    C. the stop-loss limit
    D. the maximum benefit

19. The dollar limit beyond which the insurer no longer participates in payment of expenses is
    A. the deductible
    B. the coinsurance
    C. the stop-loss limit
    D. the maximum benefit

20. The expense that must be incurred before major medical benefits begin to be paid is
    A. the deductible
    B. the coinsurance
    C. the stop-loss limit
    D. the maximum benefit

21. The sharing of expenses between the insured and the insurer is an example of
    A. the deductible
    B. the coinsurance
    C. the stop-loss limit
    D. the maximum benefit

22. A deductible that runs between the first dollar coverage of a basic policy and the comprehensive coverage of a supplemental policy is known as
    A. a stop-loss deductible
    B. a capitated deductible
    C. a corridor deductible
    D. a limited deductible

23. Which of the following would most likely be covered under a medical expense policy?
    A. Gertrude steps on a rusty nail and requires a tetanus shot.
    B. Carmelita decides to get a flu shot this year.
    C. Gary goes to the doctor each year for an annual check-up.
    D. Earl requires some help getting dressed in the morning.

ANSWERS AND RATIONALES TO UNIT TEST

1. **C.** An indemnity policy pays a specified daily benefit, regardless of the amount of the loss.

2. **C.** Intensive care benefits under hospital plans are generally provided at some multiple of the room and board maximum.

3. **A.** When benefits are not listed by a specific dollar amount in a schedule, a policy will generally pay the usual, customary, and reasonable charge for the procedure.

4. **C.** The out-of-pocket limit is also known as the stop-loss limit.

5. **B.** Dental care is typically excluded from coverage.

6. **B.** Replacement of an artificial limb is least likely to be covered by a major medical policy.

7. **D.** First dollar coverage means no deductible is applied.

8. **C.** A hospital room and board benefit may be paid on either an indemnity basis or a reimbursement basis.

9. **B.** A major medical expense policy provides high maximum coverage for medical care.

10. **D.** A supplemental medical expense policy has a major medical portion that provides benefits once the basic policy limits are exhausted and a deductible has been paid.

11. **C.** A comprehensive medical expense policy is a combination of basic medical expense coverage and major medical expense coverage.

12. **A.** A basic medical expense policy covers doctor visits while the insured is in the hospital.

13. **C.** Maternity benefits must be provided on the same basis as nonmaternity benefits if the policy covers an employee group of 15 or more people.

14. **A.** Among individual policies that include coverage for mental infirmities, the benefit will generally be lower than the benefit for physical infirmities.

15. **C.** A hospice works to alleviate pain and suffering for terminally ill patients until death, but does not attempt to cure.

16. **A.** No loss/no gain laws require replacing health insurance policies to cover any conditions for which there are ongoing claims under existing coverage.

17. **B.** Purchasing basic benefits on an individual basis usually provides less-complete coverage with more gaps than a major medical policy.

18. **C.** The stop-loss limit is the dollar limit beyond which the insured no longer participates in payment of expenses.

19. **D.** The maximum benefit is the dollar limit beyond which the insurer no longer participates in payment of expenses.

20. **A.** The deductible must be incurred before major medical benefits begin to be paid.

21. **B.** The sharing of expenses between the insured and the insurer is an example of coinsurance.

22. **C.** A corridor deductible runs between the first dollar coverage of a basic policy and the comprehensive coverage of a supplemental policy.

23. **A.** Gertrude would most likely be covered under a medical expense policy.

UNIT 20 EXERCISE ANSWERS

Exercise 20.A

1. Regular medical expense
2. Surgical expense
3. Hospital expense

Exercise 20.B

1. War
2. Aviation
3. Preexisting
4. Self-inflicted
5. Occupational (when covered by workers' compensation)
6. Cosmetic and well care (non-injury dental and vision care)

Exercise 20.C

1. Deductible
2. Coinsurance
3. Stop Loss Limit

Exercise 20.D

1. Corridor deductible

UNIT

21

Special Types of Medical Expense Policies

21. 1 INTRODUCTION

In this lesson, we will discuss several special types of health insurance plans that are designed for very specific and limited insurance needs, including the following:

- dental care policies;
- limited policies, including dread disease, travel accident, hospital income, vision care, and long-term care; and
- credit insurance policies.

In each case, a special type of policy is one that covers a limited number of situations as described in the policy itself.

21. 2 LEARNING OBJECTIVES

After completing this lesson, you will be able to:

- describe how special policies differ from other types of policies;
- list six common exclusion or limitations;
- explain how prepaid dental plans differ from traditional plans;
- describe the function of limited policies;
- explain what is covered by the following types of policies: dread disease, travel accident, hospital income, vision care, and prescription drug; and
- explain the purpose of credit insurance.

21. 3 DENTAL CARE INSURANCE

21. 3. 1 Traditional Dental Coverages

The number of companies offering dental care insurance is increasing rapidly, as coverage for dental care is being offered more frequently as part of group health plans. Occasionally, dental insurance is part of a health benefits package with a single deductible called an integrated deductible, applying to both medical and dental coverages. More often, dental coverage and dental claims are handled separately (though they may be part of a larger package) with a separate deductible for health insurance coverage and for dental insurance coverage. There also may be a probationary period in group dental insurance to help hold down coverage for preexisting conditions.

Some dental policies are scheduled; that is, benefits are limited to specified maximums per procedure, with first dollar coverage. Most, however, are comprehensive policies that work in much the same way as comprehensive medical expense coverage.

In addition to deductibles, coinsurance and maximums may also affect the level of benefits payable under a dental plan. Coinsurance percentages may apply to reimbursements that are either the reasonable and customary (R&C) type or the scheduled type. A plan based on R&C will apply coinsurance percentages to the dentist's usual and customary fee, provided it is reasonable. This type of plan is also known as usual, customary, and reasonable (UCR) or usual and prevailing (U&P). A plan that is scheduled will apply coinsurance percentages to a schedule or list of fixed-dollar amounts for each covered benefit. Scheduled benefits are generally lower than R&C allowances.

Comprehensive dental plans usually provide routine dental care services without deductibles or coinsurance to encourage preventive dental care. Generally, there is a specified maximum dollar amount payable per year and, sometimes, per family member covered. There also may be a lifetime maximum per individual.

Nonroutine dental care includes the following:

- Restorative—repairing or restoring dental work that has been damaged in some way
- Oral surgery—surgery performed in the oral cavity, for example, the removal of wisdom teeth
- Endodontics—treatment of the pulp (the soft tissue substance located in the center of each tooth)
- Periodontics—treatment of the supporting structures of the teeth
- Prosthodontics—artificial replacements
- Pediatric dentistry—patient management and preventive and restorative techniques particularly suited to children and adolescents
- Oral pathology—microscopic analysis of tissue biopsy material for diagnosis of oral diseases including oral cancer
- Orthodontics—correction of irregularities of the teeth; most commonly, braces

For nonroutine treatments, a comprehensive policy pays a percentage, such as 80%, of the reasonable and customary charges. The patient pays an annual deductible and whatever expense remains. Typically, the deductible is per person or per family, and most policies limit benefits to stated maximums per year.

Policies that provide for orthodontic care generally have separate limits and deductibles for orthodontia. The coinsurance percentage is likely to be 50% rather than the higher 75% or 80% that applies to other types of nonroutine dental care.

Many plans offer a selection of providers from which plan participants must choose. In some plans, if a course of treatment is expected to exceed a certain amount, say $200, a report must be submitted to the insurer by the dentist. The report describes the proposed treatment and itemizes the expected charges. The insurer reviews and evaluates this report and sends the dentist an estimate of benefits to be paid.

Benefits may be on a fixed prepaid basis rather than a fee-for-service plan in which the plan participant is reimbursed. Such plans often provide 100% coverage for:

- routine visits to the dentist;
- protective fluoride treatments;
- diagnostic x-rays;
- dental exams and diagnosis;
- local anesthetics;
- teeth cleanings (usually once every six months); and
- preventive care.

Exercise 21.A

Dental insurance usually combines full coverage for basic services with coinsurance (i.e., 80/20) for non-routine services. For the following list of dental services, put **100%** next to those that would be considered basic and **80%** next to the others.

____ 1. Restorative

____ 2. Oral surgery

____ 3. Routine dental visits

____ 4. Endodontics

____ 5. Fluoride treatments

____ 6. Periodontics

____ 7. Teeth x-rays

____ 8. Pediatric dentistry

____ 9. Exams and diagnosis

Answers to the exercises can be found at the end of the Unit 21 answers and rationales.

21. 3. 2 Exclusions and Limitations

An insurer will often reduce its liability for payment of dental expenses by contractual provisions that state what a plan does and does not cover. A closed list is a method of defining which procedures are covered. If an unlisted procedure is performed, coverage is either denied or paid on the basis of the most similar procedure included on the list. The following are examples of common exclusions and limitations.

- The cosmetic exclusion stipulates that benefits are not payable for dental work that is not necessary for sound dental health.

- The missing tooth provision excludes coverage for teeth that are missing at the time coverage becomes effective.
- The five-year replacement exclusion does not allow replacement of prosthetic appliances (such as retainers or spacers) for five years after a benefit is paid.
- The vertical dimension, splinting, and restoring occlusion exclusion limits liability for exotic and highly optional procedures.
- Expenses for oral hygiene instructions and plaque control programs are often limited or excluded.
- Some plans may offer members coverage up to a certain amount for emergency dental treatment required when outside the service area.

21. 3. 3 Minimizing Adverse Selection

Because the nature of dental coverage is quite different from that of medical coverage, the underwriting of dental coverage requires a few special considerations. There are three circumstances that make dental coverage unique.

- Patients have wider choices in treatment options. For instance, a patient can choose bridgework that is fixed or removable and inlays that are gold or nongold. These choices represent a wide range in treatment costs.
- A person who needs dental work can often postpone treatment until an insurance plan becomes effective, causing the insurer to be liable for larger benefits than it would otherwise expect to pay. (For this reason, few individual dental plans exist; most plans are sold on a group basis to further offset this type of adverse selection.)
- Many dental expenses are cosmetic; therefore, underwriting must often limit benefits for cosmetic procedures in order to avoid paying excessive claims.

21. 3. 4 Prepaid Dental Plans

Another increasingly popular way to offer dental insurance is a through a prepaid dental plan. A **prepaid dental plan** is a corporation, partnership, or other entity that, in return for a prepayment, provides or arranges for the provision of dental care services to enrollees or subscribers. The plan may be owned by a corporation, partnership, association trust, or other entity and operated by a board of directors or trustees, executive committee, or principal officers.

Prepaid dental plans operate in much the same way as health maintenance organizations. They offer services based on capitation, or fixed per-member per-month payments whereby the provider assumes the full risk for the cost of contracted services without regard to the type, value, or frequency of the services provided.

21. 3. 5 Dentist Access to Membership

A prepaid dental plan must provide that any licensed dentist may participate as a provider in the prepaid dental plan.

21. 3. 6 Benefits

Individual group contracts, evidence of coverage, and solicitation materials must provide a statement of the services and benefits each member may receive. Reasonable exclusions, limitations, co-payments, and deductibles may be included, provided they are clearly disclosed in contracts, evidence of coverage, and solicitation documents.

21. 3. 7 Member Choice of Provider

Subscribers must have the right to select any participating dentist as a provider. If a prepaid dental plan would restrict an enrollee's ability to receive services from a class of providers, the limitations must be described in the evidence of coverage and in all solicitation documents.

21. 3. 8 Provider Contracts

The prepaid plan may contract with licensed dentists to provide dental care to subscribers in a specific service area or geographic location.

The dentists are paid (other than the co-payment or deductible) by the prepaid dental plan. Provider contracts are subject to state laws designed to protect enrollees from becoming liable for services the prepaid dental plan fails to pay because of insolvency.

In an open-panel system, dentists render services to both prepaid dental plan subscribers and to nonmembers. In a closed-panel system, services are provided only to subscribers of the prepaid dental plan. The plan must publish a list of participating providers, and enrollees are asked to choose a primary provider.

Under the precertification or prior authorization requirement, when the enrollee's dentist prescribes any course of treatment expected to exceed a specific amount (such as $200), the treatment must be outlined on a precertification form and submitted to the insurer for review and approval before it may be undertaken.

21. 3. 9 Evidence of Coverage

All enrollees must be issued an evidence of coverage describing the dental services covered, limitations on those services (including deductibles and co-payments), how to obtain services and information, and methods for resolving complaints.

21. 3. 10 Complaint Procedure

The complaint system must establish reasonable procedures for resolving written complaints from both enrollees and providers. The organization must respond promptly to written complaints. Responses to written complaints regarding quality or appropriateness of care must include a statement that the complainant may have the complaint reviewed by a consulting dentist and may submit the complaint to a professional peer review organization. Copies of complaints and responses must be maintained for three years.

21. 3. 11 Service Area—Geographic Location

Subscribers must have reliable access to qualified providers in the geographic area served by the prepaid dental plan. They also must have access to short-term emergency dental care services within the areas served, and the plan must pay for services when a dental emergency occurs outside the service area.

21. 3. 12 Quality Assurance Program

Each prepaid dental plan must provide appropriate, necessary, cost-effective, and professional services. Prepaid dental plans must have a quality assurance program to evaluate the quality of care given to enrollees and provide for ways to correct deficiencies in provider or organizational performance. Provider contracts must give disincentives (including termination) for providers rendering inappropriate, unnecessary, excessively costly, or low quality care.

21. 3. 13 Underwriting

The underwriting procedures for group dental insurance are similar to those that apply to other types of group health insurance. Generally, when a group dental plan is initially effective, all employees or members must be covered or eligible for coverage. Under a contributory plan in which the employee pays all or part of the premium, each eligible employee must elect to be covered. To minimize adverse selection, a probationary period usually applies to new employees who join the group after the effective date. Limitations on benefits may also be imposed on any employees who do not choose to be covered when first eligible in order to avoid premium payments, but who elect coverage at a later date when they know they need dental treatment.

Because dental coverage is usually available only on a group basis, most plans do not include a conversion privilege. Members cannot convert to individual insurance when their membership in the group ends or the group plan is terminated.

21. 3. 14 Integrated Deductible Versus Stand-Alone Plan

As noted before, dental insurance may be part of a health benefits package with a single deductible, called an integrated deductible, which applies to both medical and dental coverages. In most cases, however, dental coverage and dental claims are treated separately with a separate deductible for health insurance coverage and for dental insurance coverage.

21.4 LIMITED POLICIES

21.4.1 Dread Disease

In this section, we will look at a series of policies, each of which covers only a limited, specified risk. Collectively, they are called limited policies, and the first of these is often referred to as a dread disease policy.

Dread disease policies can be purchased to cover specific diseases as named in the policy, such as heart disease or cancer. Generally, these policies cover illnesses that do not occur frequently but incur significant costs when they do occur. Because of the low frequency of the disease covered, these policies are often fairly inexpensive in comparison to full health coverage.

Insurance regulatory bodies do not always look favorably upon these policies because less sophisticated insurance buyers have sometimes purchased them believing the coverage was much broader, when major medical coverage was actually needed instead. Dread disease policies are also known as critical illness policies.

21.4.2 Travel Accident Insurance

Special policies can be purchased to cover loss from travel accidents. Travel accident insurance may be offered as a benefit of either an individual or a group accidental death and dismemberment policy. Benefits are limited to losses caused by accidents while traveling, usually by common carriers such as airlines or bus lines.

A frequent use of such coverage under a group policy limits benefits to losses suffered while traveling on business for one's employer. Air travel insurance purchased at airports for individual, one-time coverage is probably the best known type of travel accident policy.

21.4.3 Hospital Income (Indemnity) Insurance

A policy that pays a specific amount of insurance for each day an individual is hospitalized is called hospital income or hospital indemnity coverage. These policies pay an indemnity directly to the insured, not to the hospital. They are not intended to cover expenses for hospitalization but to provide a flow of income that begins when the insured is confined to the hospital and ends on the final day of hospitalization. Some individuals use this kind of policy to meet the deductible and coinsurance requirements of their medical expense policies.

Limitations may apply. Some hospital indemnity policies include an elimination period, in which case coverage does not begin on the first day of confinement. Limits also may be placed on benefits paid for preexisting conditions.

Usually, the amount of insurance available is indicated as a monthly amount for a specified number of months. For example, Ben has a policy that pays $3,000 per month for up to 12 months. However, Ben will be indemnified only for actual continuous days in the hospital, and the monthly amount is the aggregate of a daily amount times 30 days. Ben's $3,000 policy, then, pays $100 for each day the insured is hospitalized.

Because these policies provide a fixed number of dollars, they should be updated periodically to stay apace of inflation.

21. 4. 4 Vision Care Insurance

Although basic, comprehensive, and major medical policies often cover disease and injury to eyes, there is generally no coverage for eye exams and corrections such as eyeglasses or contact lenses. To close this gap, insurers may offer vision care policies, which usually cover:

- eye examinations;
- cost of lenses and frames;
- cost of contact lenses; and
- other corrective items.

Typically, vision care policies operate with a network of eye doctors and providers of eyeglasses, which the policyholder must use to receive benefits. Co-payments will vary according to the type of plan. The plan member simply presents the vision care card to the provider and is told the amount of the co-payment. Individual and family coverage is generally available.

Limitations normally apply. For example, the policy may pay for only one eye exam and one set of lenses per year. Common exclusions are:

- replacement frames or lenses required because of loss or breakage;
- sunglasses and safety glasses; and
- medical and surgical costs of the type covered by basic and major medical policies.

21. 4. 5 Prescription Drug Policies

Prescription drug policies can be described as discount plans for members. Very often, an individual health policy does not cover prescription drugs. For an annual fee or premium, an individual can join a plan that provides discounts of one degree or another for doctor-prescribed drugs. Prescription drug plans operate with a network of pharmacies that members must use in order to receive benefits. Sometimes a mail order service may be provided for drugs used on a regular basis. Plan members receive cards that must be presented to the pharmacy when a prescription is filled. There is a co-payment. Usually generic drugs are dispensed. Some drugs may be excluded, such as fertility drugs, vitamins, experimental drugs, or drugs covered by other programs. There is a dispensing limit such as 34 days' worth or 100 units, whichever is larger. Premiums are guaranteed for one year. Individual and family coverage is generally available.

Exercise 21.B

Match the policy description with the appropriate limited policy title.

_____ 1. A policy that pays an indemnity directly to the insured for each day the insured is admitted to a hospital, regardless of any other coverage the insured may have

_____ 2. A policy that pays a lump sum benefit for death or dismemberment occurring while traveling, typically by common carrier

_____ 3. A policy that pays when expenses are incurred related to a specified illness, such as cancer or heart disease

A. Dread disease insurance

B. Travel accident insurance

C. Hospital indemnity insurance

Answers to the exercises can be found at the end of the Unit 21 answers and rationales.

21. 5 CREDIT INSURANCE

Credit health insurance covers a debtor, with the creditor receiving the benefits to pay off the debt if the debtor is disabled or dies accidentally. Credit insurance may be written as an individual policy covering a single debtor, or it can be sold to a master policyowner on a group basis to cover more than one debtor.

Individual credit health insurance is handled in essentially the same way as any other individual health insurance policy. The applicant applies for the policy and receives it on the basis of individual selection. In this case, the policyowner is the debtor and he names the creditor as the recipient of the policy's benefits.

The most common type of credit health insurance is group coverage sold as a master policy to a creditor that acquires many new debtors each year. For example, an auto dealership that provides financing for the vehicles it sells might have a group credit policy to cover all clients who finance their cars through the dealership.

Group credit health insurance is somewhat more complicated than individual coverage. In most states, a creditor must have a minimum number of debtors per year, often 100, before it qualifies for group credit insurance. Check your own state laws to determine minimum group size requirements.

Group credit health insurance has many of the same features as any other group coverage. No individual selection occurs, so no evidence of insurability is required. Group credit coverage is nearly always contributory, and a high percentage, usually 75%, of those to whom it is offered must want the coverage.

21. 5. 1 Limits on Coverage Amounts

The objective of credit insurance is to ensure that the outstanding indebtedness will be paid if the insured is disabled or dies accidentally before the loan is repaid. Therefore, the accidental death benefit may not exceed the total amount of indebtedness at any given point, nor may the monthly disability benefit exceed the amount of the monthly payment on the loan. Consider this situation.

Raoul has a loan for which he makes payments of $340 a month. His creditor provides group credit health insurance. The monthly disability indemnities covering Raoul under this policy must be no more than $340, the amount of the monthly loan payment.

Now suppose the policy that covers Raoul contains accidental death benefits. Raoul's original loan was for $13,500. Raoul is accidentally killed when the balance due is $7,180. The benefit payable to the creditor is $7,180 because at any given time the death benefit may be no more than the total outstanding loan at the time of death.

Debtors usually pay for group credit health insurance as a portion of the monthly loan payment. Some lending institutions have their own or affiliated insurance companies through which they would like to write all of their credit insurance. However, a debtor is not required to carry insurance through the company suggested by the creditor.

In some states, and under certain conditions, a creditor can insist that the debtor have some type of insurance to help secure the loan. Even so, the debtor, not the creditor, has the option of selecting the insurer.

Suppose Joan finances her car through the Friendly Loan Company. Friendly Loan has its own wholly owned subsidiary insurance company. In Joan's state, a lender may require the debtor to purchase credit insurance, and Friendly Loan would like Joan to purchase coverage from its subsidiary. As a prerequisite to financing the car, Friendly Loan may insist that Joan buy the coverage, but it may not require that she buy coverage from Friendly's subsidiary.

21. 5. 2 Notice of Proposed Insurance

When the loan is closed, the creditor must inform the debtor that he may be covered by the group plan if desired. Even if the creditor pays the full cost of the coverage, the debtor must be notified. Creditors are not permitted to place insurance on debtors without telling them about it.

The notification to a debtor that he will be covered under a credit health policy is called a notice of proposed insurance. This notice takes the place of the certificate of insurance until the certificate can be prepared by the insurer and forwarded to the debtor.

Exercise 21.C

Mark the following statements regarding credit health insurance as true (T) or false (F).

____ 1. Credit health insurance covers a debtor, with the creditor receiving the benefits to pay off a debit if the debtor is unable to pay the debt due to disability or death.

____ 2. The most common type of credit health insurance is an individual policy requiring debtors to be individually underwritten.

____ 3. Credit health insurance may be written without notice to the debtor if the creditor is paying the premiums.

Answers to the exercises can be found at the end of the Unit 21 answers and rationales.

UNIT TEST

1. Scheduled benefits are generally
   A. lower than reasonable and customary allowances
   B. higher than reasonable and customary allowances
   C. the same as reasonable and customary allowances
   D. paid in addition to reasonable and customary allowances

2. Which of the following is NOT a common exclusion or limitation of dental policies?
   A. Benefits are generally not payable for dental work that is not necessary for sound dental health.
   B. Teeth that are knocked out in an accident will generally not be replaced under a dental policy.
   C. Oral hygiene instructions and plaque control programs are often limited or excluded.
   D. Prosthetic appliances generally may not be replaced for 5 years after a benefit is paid.

3. The ability of an individual to wait until covered by dental insurance before seeking treatment for dental issues is an example of
   A. improper insurance
   B. improper selection
   C. adverse selection
   D. adverse insurance

4. Prepaid dental plans offer services based on
   A. capitulation
   B. captive member selection
   C. concentration
   D. capitation

5. Sin Lan has a hospital income policy that will pay $1,500 per month for up to 12 months. There is no elimination period. If Sin Lan is hospitalized, to whom will the insurer make payments?
   A. The hospital
   B. Sin Lan
   C. The doctor
   D. The beneficiary

6. Sin Lan has a hospital income policy that will pay $1,500 per month for up to 12 months. There is no elimination period. If Sin Lan is hospitalized for 10 days, how much will the policy pay?
   A. $50
   B. $500
   C. $1,000
   D. $1,500

7. Which of the following drugs may be excluded from a prescription drug policy?
   A. Ginseng
   B. Fertility drugs
   C. Rogaine
   D. All of these

8. A special type of policy tends to cover
   A. more areas than basic medical expense
   B. a broad number of situations as described in the policy itself
   C. a limited number of situations as described in the policy itself
   D. whatever the insured wants to be covered

9. Comprehensive dental policies
   A. limit benefits to specified maximums per procedure
   B. work in much the same way as comprehensive medical expense coverage
   C. never require deductibles
   D. seldom require coinsurance

10. Which of the following is NOT likely to be considered nonroutine dental care?
    A. Treatment of the soft tissue substance located in the center of each tooth
    B. Microscopic analysis of tissue biopsy material for diagnosis of oral diseases including oral cancer
    C. Annual checkups and cleaning of teeth, including x-rays to check the health of the teeth
    D. Repairing or restoring dental work that has been damaged in some way

11. For nonroutine treatments, a comprehensive policy generally pays
    A. the full amount
    B. a percentage of the reasonable and customary charges from the first dollar
    C. a percentage of the reasonable and customary charges after a deductible
    D. nothing

12. Which of the following is NOT a common way dental insurance programs work to minimize adverse selection?
    A. Increasing the maximum annual benefit to encourage the insured to maintain dental health for the long term
    B. Lowering the coinsurance percentage for optional expenses
    C. Basing the benefit on the least costly treatment option
    D. Graduating the coinsurance percentage to increase each plan year

13. What is the main difference between a prepaid dental plan and a comprehensive dental plan?
    A. Comprehensive dental plans pay on the basis of reasonable and customary charges, whereas prepaid dental plans pay on a capitation basis.
    B. Comprehensive dental plans pay on a capitation basis, whereas prepaid dental plans pay based on reasonable and customary charges.
    C. Comprehensive dental plans cover routine services, whereas prepaid dental plans do not.
    D. Comprehensive dental plans do not cover routine services that are covered by prepaid dental plans.

14. A prepaid dental plan that wants to restrict an enrollee's ability to receive services from a class of providers
    A. is out of luck because such limitations are prohibited by law
    B. must request permission from the Insurance Commissioner for the limitations
    C. must request permission from the federal Department of Insurance for the limitations
    D. must describe the limitations in the evidence of coverage and in all solicitation documents

15. Dread disease policies
    A. are purchased to cover a variety of conditions that fall under the category of dread diseases
    B. cover any disease defined by the ADA as a dread disease
    C. cover specific diseases as named in the policy, such as heart disease or cancer
    D. are a good replacement for general health insurance

16. Benefits of travel accident insurance are limited to
    A. losses caused by accidents while traveling, usually by common carriers such as airlines or bus lines
    B. losses caused while in transit, generally in personal vehicles such as cars or vans
    C. accident losses caused while outside of the state of residence
    D. accident or illness losses caused while outside of the state of residence

17. Hospital indemnity insurance pays
    A. medical costs only while the insured is confined to the hospital
    B. supplemental costs, such as television or phone charges, while the insured is confined to the hospital
    C. an income for each day the insured is confined to the hospital
    D. an income for each month the insured spends partially confined to the hospital

18. Vision care insurance is generally needed to cover all of the following EXCEPT
    A. injury to the eye
    B. eye examinations
    C. costs of contact lenses
    D. costs of prescription lenses

19. Prescription drug policies generally exclude
    A. any narcotic substance
    B. any drugs not covered by other programs
    C. experimental drugs
    D. drugs for ongoing medical conditions

20. Credit health insurance covers
    A. a creditor
    B. a debtor
    C. either a creditor or a debtor
    D. neither a creditor nor a debtor

21. The amount of coverage available under a credit insurance policy is generally limited to
    A. the total amount of indebtedness at any given point
    B. the total amount of the loan covered
    C. the amount the policy is written for
    D. the amount of the debt plus the cost of the premium

22. The creditor must notify the debtor that she may be covered by the group insurance plan
    A. only if the debtor is to be charged the full premium for the insurance
    B. if the debtor is to be charged more than half the premium amount
    C. even if the creditor pays the full cost of the coverage
    D. only if the creditor chooses to make the disclosure

ANSWERS AND RATIONALES TO UNIT TEST

1. **A.** Scheduled benefits are lower than reasonable and customary, and the insured may have some out-of-pocket costs.

2. **B.** Teeth that are knocked out in an accident will generally be replaced under a dental policy; this is not a common exclusion or limitation of dental policies.

3. **C.** The ability of an individual to wait until covered by dental insurance before seeking treatment for dental issues is an example of adverse selection.

4. **D.** Prepaid dental plans offer services based on capitation.

5. **B.** A hospital income policy will pay the insured.

6. **B.** The daily amount is $50, or $1,500 ÷ 30 days. The total payment will equal $50 per day for 10 days, or $500.

7. **D.** All of the listed drugs may be excluded from a prescription drug policy.

8. **C.** Special policies are limited in coverage.

9. **B.** Comprehensive dental policies work in much the same way as comprehensive medical expense coverage.

10. **C.** Annual checkups and cleaning of teeth, including x-rays to check the health of the teeth, are not likely to be considered nonroutine dental care.

11. **C.** For nonroutine treatments, a comprehensive policy generally pays a percentage of the reasonable and customary charges after a deductible.

12. **A.** Dental insurance programs do not increase the maximum annual benefit to encourage the insured to maintain dental health for the long term.

13. **A.** The main difference between prepaid dental plans and comprehensive dental plans is that comprehensive dental plans pay on the basis of reasonable and customary charges, whereas prepaid dental plans pay on a capitation basis.

14. **D.** A prepaid dental plan that wants to restrict an enrollee's ability to receive services from a class of providers must describe the limitations in the evidence of coverage and in all solicitation documents.

15. **C.** Dread disease policies cover specific diseases, such as heart disease or cancer, as named in the policy.

16. **A.** Benefits of travel accident insurance are limited to losses caused by accidents while traveling, usually by common carriers such as airlines or bus lines.

17. **C.** Hospital indemnity insurance pays an income for each day the insured is confined to the hospital.

18. **A.** Vision care insurance generally does not cover injury to the eye.

19. **C.** Prescription drug policies generally exclude experimental drugs.

20. **B.** Credit health insurance covers a debtor.

21. **A.** The amount of coverage available under a credit insurance policy is generally limited to the total amount of indebtedness at any given point.

22. **C.** The creditor must notify the debtor that she may be covered by the group insurance plan even if the creditor pays the full cost of the coverage.

UNIT 21 EXERCISE ANSWERS

Exercise 21.A

1. 80%
2. 80%
3. 100%
4. 80%
5. 100%
6. 80%
7. 100%
8. 80%
9. 100%

Exercise 21.B

1. **C.**
2. **B.**
3. **A.**

Exercise 21.C

1. **T**
2. **F**
3. **F**

UNIT

22

Group Health Insurance

22. 1 INTRODUCTION

Most people have at least a superficial acquaintance with group insurance because the most common type of group coverage is provided through employment. Many employers make health insurance available to their employees—either by paying the premiums for the employees, sharing in premium payment, or deducting the premiums from employees' paychecks.

22. 2 LEARNING OBJECTIVES

After completing this lesson, you will be able to:

- list the events that generally trigger an employee's conversion privilege;
- explain who qualifies as a dependent under group coverage and how dependency is legally determined;
- explain how the coordination of benefits rule determines which insurer is primary and what each insurer pays; and
- explain how the coordination of benefits rule determines which parent's insurance plan is primary for covered children.

22. 3 POLICY TYPES

Group health plans may include any of the several types of insurance discussed earlier, so this section will serve as a review of those individual coverages. Group plans need not include all coverages, but most will include at least two or more. In addition, disability income coverage may be offered under a group arrangement, but it is usually offered separately from hospital, medical, and surgical coverage.

The first possible group coverage, then, pays benefits for lost earnings resulting from accident or sickness disability, and it is commonly called disability income insurance.

Another common type of group coverage deals with accidental loss of life and accidental loss of one or more limbs or of eyesight. You'll recall that accidental loss of life is referred to as accidental death, and accidental loss of one or more limbs or of eyesight is known as dismemberment.

Still another type of group coverage is hospital expense. These policies can pay for hospital expenses whether treatment is on an inpatient or resident basis, whereby the insured is admitted to the hospital, or on an outpatient basis, whereby the insured is not admitted for an overnight stay but is treated and released the same day. The fees of an attending physician during hospital treatment may also be covered.

Example

Eloise's employer provides a group insurance plan covering expenses incurred for hospital care of any type. Eloise is involved in an auto accident on her way home from work, and she is rushed to the hospital for emergency treatment. She is not admitted to the hospital but does receive emergency room treatment. In this particular case, Eloise is an outpatient.

If Eloise's group insurance covers only situations such as the one described and does not provide disability income or any other benefits, the coverage is strictly a hospital expense policy.

If Eloise's group coverage provides a separate benefit in the event Eloise loses her sight in an accident, this type of benefit is called accidental dismemberment.

Some group policies might cover only surgical expenses. Suppose Paul is hospitalized to have his appendix removed. His group policy specifies that the surgeon who performs an appendectomy will receive $450. The hospital charges are not paid. Although this would be fairly unusual today, such policies do exist, and in this situation, Paul's group policy covers only reimbursement for surgical expenses.

Group health policies frequently provide coverage for medical expenses involving physician or nursing services, but no surgical expense. If Mihail becomes ill and must see his physician regularly as well as remain under the care of a private nurse for several weeks, any health care reimbursement for these expenses is considered medical expense coverage.

We've now mentioned five forms of group health coverage, all of which have counterparts in individual policies. They are:

- disability income;
- accidental death and dismemberment;
- hospital expense;
- surgical expense; and
- medical expense.

22. 4 GROUP COVERAGE PROVISIONS

Several provisions apply solely or primarily to group policies. They are provisions that:

- describe who is eligible for the group plan;
- describe when individuals become eligible for the plan;
- specify the minimum number of individuals and the minimum participation by eligible people required to sustain the plan;
- specify the amounts of insurance to which individual group members are entitled; and
- describe the responsibilities of the master policyowner.

As was mentioned, not all members of a group are necessarily eligible for coverage under a group plan. An employer may establish certain eligibility requirements, such as limiting coverage to people who have been employed for a specified period.

Often, an employee becomes eligible for coverage after working with a company for a given period, commonly 90 days. The employee is then eligible to apply for coverage during another period, usually 31 days, within which no medical examination will be required. This is the eligibility period discussed previously.

Any such qualifications or limitations must be indicated in the policy.

22. 4. 1 Conversion Privilege

The conversion privilege allows the insured to convert group coverage to individual coverage without evidence of insurability. This privilege goes into effect only when the insured is no longer eligible for group coverage because of the following circumstances.

- The insured's employment is terminated.
- The insured becomes ineligible for coverage because the class he was insured under is no longer eligible for coverage. (For example, to save expenses, a company that formerly provided coverage for all employees working not less than 20 hours per week may now only provide coverage to the class of employees who do not work less than 40 hours per week.)
- The insured's dependent child reaches the age specified in the policy as the age of terminating dependent coverage.

The insured has 31 days from the time of ineligibility to convert to the new plan of insurance. The new plan of insurance is an individual plan, normally a hospitalization policy, which will not provide the same benefits that the group plan did. Usually, the group medical expense benefits are more liberal than the converted policy's benefits. Often, those who elect to exercise this conversion privilege do so because frequently they may have insurability problems. To limit adverse selection against the company, the insurer typically offers this conversion plan with reduced or limited benefits.

Exercise 22.A

Mark which of the following statements are true (T) and which are false (F) regarding conversion of group health.

____ 1. Conversion is permitted with evidence of insurability within 2 years of leaving employment if already under the care of a physician.

____ 2. Conversion is only allowed if the insured's employment is terminated.

____ 3. The insured typically has 31 days to convert to individual from group.

____ 4. A converted plan is typically issued with reduced or limited benefits.

____ 5. Typically an individual plan has higher premiums than group, but the coverage is usually better.

Answers to exercises can be found at the end of the Unit 22 answers and rationales.

22. 4. 2 Dependent Coverage

Life or health insurance benefits may be extended to the primary insured's dependents. Dependents may be any of the following individuals:

- The insured's spouse
- The insured's children
- The insured's dependent parents
- Any other person who is dependent on the insured

The insured's children can be stepchildren, foster children, or adopted children. Dependent children must be younger than a specified age (usually age 19, or up to 25 if attending school full time). The law further requires that any other person dependent on the insured is eligible for coverage. Such dependency is proved by the relationship to the insured, residency in the home, or being listed on the insured's income tax return as a dependent.

A child may be a dependent beyond the ages of 19 or 25 if that child is permanently mentally or physically disabled before the specified age.

Also, a dependent child may be offered coverage beyond the limiting age of 19 if that child is a full-time college student in an accredited college. Usually, dependent coverage for a student will be extended until age 21 up to age 25.

22. 4. 3 Coordination of Benefits Provision

Many working couples are doubly covered by group health insurance. Both husband and wife often have employer-provided group coverage, and each is covered as a dependent by the other's plan. This type of double coverage can result in individuals being **overinsured**, creating the temptation to realize a profit from being ill.

To avoid this situation, a special provision is required by law in most states. The **coordination of benefits provision** is designed to give insureds as much coverage as possible while eliminating overinsurance. Here is an example of how it works.

In double coverage situations, the insurer covering the employee who has the claim is called the **primary** insurance company. The primary company must pay as much of the claim as the policy limits permit.

Basil and Kendra, a married couple, work at different companies. Both are covered by group plans that extend to dependents, so they have double coverage. Let's assume that Basil has $2,200 in medical bills resulting from an illness. Basil's policy is primary. Basil has major medical coverage and a $200 deductible, so the primary insurer (Basil's insurance company) first deducts that amount from the $2,200 bill, leaving $2,000.

The primary insurer then pays 80% of $2,000, which is $1,600, leaving $600 unpaid—the $200 deductible plus $400, which is Basil's share of the other $2,000.

Kendra's company also covers Basil. For Basil's claim (because he is covered as a dependent of Kendra's), her company is called the **secondary** or **excess** insurer. The secondary company will pay whatever the primary company will not pay, up to its own limits.

Therefore, assuming the remaining $600 is within the limits, Kendra's company pays the full additional $600, which is Basil's percentage participation (20% of $2,000, or $400) plus his deductible ($200). Because double coverage existed, Basil's expenses were fully covered. However, he did not receive more than his actual expenses.

To restate the coordination of benefits rule: the primary company pays the claim as if there were no double coverage, and the secondary company pays whatever the primary company will not pay, within its policy limits.

When a working couple is doubly covered by group insurance, any children they support will also be doubly covered. The birth months and days of the parents are often used to decide which plan is primary. The plan of the parent whose birthday comes first during the year is primary. The other parent's plan is secondary. That is, if Sue's birthday is March 4 and her spouse's is March 8, Sue's plan is primary.

If parents are separated or divorced, the plan of the parent with custody is primary, barring any other legal arrangements.

If it is discovered that an insured is covered by another policy that is responsible for a loss, an insurer may try to recover part or all of their losses from another policy. This is known as subrogation.

22. 4. 4 Records and Recordkeeping

This provision contains information as to whether the insurer or the policyholder will maintain records on the insureds. It provides for the policyholder to furnish the insurance company with necessary information to determine premiums and administer coverage.

22. 4. 4. 1 Clerical Error

A clerical error provision provides that if there is an error or omission in the administration of a group policy, the person's insurance is considered to be what it would be if there had been no error or omission.

For example, an employer has the responsibility to send group enrollment forms for newly hired employees to the insurer. Sean is a new employee, and through an administrative error, his enrollment form is never forwarded to the insurance company. A few months later, he submits a medical expense claim to the insurer and is told that they have no record of his coverage.

This recordkeeping and clerical error provision protects the new employee in this type of situation. Usually, the insurer would accept an enrollment form and all of the past due premium and proceed to pay the medical claim.

22. 5 FEDERAL AND STATE REGULATIONS AFFECTING GROUP POLICIES

A number of federal regulations enacted over the past 20 years affect group life and health insurance policies. These are known by the acronyms COBRA, OBRA, TEFRA, and ERISA. Also, the health reform package, HIPAA, passed in 1996, has major implications for group health insurance policies.

22. 5. 1 Health Insurance Portability and Accountability Act (HIPAA)

The **Health Insurance Portability and Accountability Act (HIPAA)**, which took effect July 1, 1997, ensures portability of group insurance coverage and includes various mandated benefits that affect small employers, the self-employed, pregnant women, and the mentally ill.

22. 5. 1. 1 Portability

The new law makes it easier for individuals to change jobs and still maintain continuous health coverage. If an employer offers health benefits to its employees, the employer now must make full health care coverage available immediately to newly hired employees who were previously covered at another job (the individual must have had coverage for at least 18 months). Before this change, coverage for preexisting conditions could be delayed for six months to one year, and new hires were subject to a waiting period before being eligible for health insurance. If the worker goes without health insurance for more than 63 days between jobs, the waiting period can be reinstated.

Also, an individual with group health insurance who leaves to become self-employed cannot be denied coverage (although the premium charged may be higher).

Group plans cannot impose more than a 12-month preexisting conditions exclusion for a person who sought medical advice, diagnosis, or treatment within the previous six months. However, this exclusion cannot be applied in the case of newborns, adopted children, or pregnancies existing on the effective date of coverage.

22. 5. 1. 2 *Mandated Benefits*

The law guarantees coverage for a 48-hour hospital stay for new mothers and their babies after a regular delivery (96 hours for a cesarean section birth). Also, it expands coverage for mental illness by requiring similar coverage for treatment of mental and physical conditions. The law eliminates the special limitations included in many policies, such as lifetime spending limits and annual limits applied only to mental health coverage.

Small employers (those with 2–50 employees) now cannot be denied group health insurance coverage because one or more employees are in poor health.

22. 5. 2 Continuation of Benefits

The **Consolidated Omnibus Budget Reconciliation Act (COBRA)** is a federal law that requires employers with 20 or more employees to provide former employees and their families a continuation of benefits under the employer's group health insurance plan. Coverage may be continued for 18 to 36 months. Employees and other qualified family members who would otherwise lose their coverage because of a qualifying event are allowed by COBRA to continue their coverage at their own expense at specified group rates. COBRA specifies the rates, coverage, qualifying events, qualifying beneficiaries, notification of eligibility procedures, and time of payment requirements for the continuation of insurance. Here are the terms and concepts most important to the understanding of COBRA and its limitations.

22. 5. 2. 1 *Qualifying Event*

A **qualifying event** is an occurrence that triggers an insured's protection under COBRA. Qualifying events include the death of a covered employee, termination or reduction of work hours of the covered employee, Medicare eligibility for the covered employee, divorce or legal separation of the covered employee from the covered employee's spouse, the termination of a child's dependent status under the terms of the group insurance plan, and the bankruptcy of the employer. Termination of employment is not a qualifying event if it is the result of gross misconduct by the covered employee. In short, a qualifying event occurs when the employee, spouse, or dependent child becomes ineligible for coverage under the group insurance contract.

22. 5. 2. 2 *Qualified Beneficiary*

A **qualified beneficiary** is any individual covered under an employer-maintained group health plan on the day before a qualifying event. Usually this includes the covered employee, the spouse of the covered employee, and dependent children of the employee. Changes made in 1996 amend the definition of *qualified beneficiary* to include children born or adopted during the 18-month coverage period.

22. 5. 2. 3 Notification Statements

Employers are obligated to provide notification statements to individuals eligible for COBRA continuation. This notification must be provided under the following circumstances:

- When a plan becomes subject to COBRA
- When an employee is covered by a plan subject to COBRA
- When a qualifying event occurs

In addition to notifying current employees, the company must also notify new employees when they are informed of other employee benefits. Initial notification made to the spouse of an employee or to the employee's dependents must be made in writing and sent to the last known address of the spouse or dependent.

Following the notification of eligibility for continuation of benefits, an individual has 60 days in which to elect continuation. If continued coverage is not elected within 60 days, the option to do so is forfeited.

22. 5. 2. 4 Duration of Coverage

An employer is not required to make continuation coverage available indefinitely. The rationale behind COBRA is to provide transitional health care coverage until the employee or family member can obtain coverage or employment elsewhere. The maximum period of coverage continuation for termination of employment or a reduction in hours of employment is 18 months. For all other qualifying events, the maximum period of coverage continuation is 36 months. There are also certain disqualifying events that can result in a termination of coverage before the specified time periods. The dates of these events are as follows:

- The first day for which timely payment is not made
- The date the employer ceases to maintain any group health plan
- The first date on which the individual is covered by another group plan (even if coverage is less)
- The date the individual becomes eligible for Medicare

It should be remembered that COBRA deals with continuation of the exact same group coverage that the employee had as a covered employee. This distinction is important so as not to confuse this provision with the conversion of group coverage to a lesser amount of insurance as part of an individual plan.

Not only is the type of coverage the same the insured had while employed, the premium is also the same, except now the terminated employee pays the entire premium to the employer for the privilege of continuing the group benefits. To cover any administrative expense that the employer may incur, the terminated individual may also pay an additional amount each month not to exceed 2% of the premium. Only the health benefits can be continued under COBRA. Any group life insurance under the plan may not be continued. It can, of course, be converted.

Recent amendments to COBRA require the continuation of coverage if a preexisting condition limitation is included in the new group health coverage. However, the new group health coverage is primary, and the continuation coverage is secondary.

22. 5. 2. 5 Plan Termination

In most states, if an employer discontinues its group insurance plan, employees must have the opportunity to convert to individual insurance without a medical exam or other evidence of insurability.

Suppose Giovanni has been employed by the same company for 15 years. He is now 53 years of age and has battled a number of skin cancers during the last four years. Giovanni's employer terminates its group health plan but offers employees the opportunity to convert to individual coverage. To get this coverage, it is likely that Giovanni will not be required to have a physical examination or otherwise show that he is insurable. Giovanni is fortunate; he otherwise might not be able to get health insurance at standard rates.

22. 5. 3 Omnibus Budget Reconciliation Act (OBRA)

The **Omnibus Budget Reconciliation Act of 1989 (OBRA)** extended the minimum COBRA continuation of coverage period from 18 to 29 months for qualified beneficiaries disabled at the time of termination or reduction in hours. The disability must meet the Social Security definition of disability, and the covered employee's termination must not have been for gross misconduct. Changes to COBRA in 1996 permit individuals who become disabled during the first 60 days of the 18-month coverage period to extend their coverage to 29 months, so as to extend coverage until the person would become eligible for Medicare (the 5 month waiting period plus 24 months of eligibility for Social Security disability benefits).

Under OBRA 1989, an employer may terminate COBRA coverage because of coverage under another health plan, provided the other plan does not limit or exclude benefits for a beneficiary's preexisting conditions.

OBRA 1989 also clarifies that COBRA coverage may be terminated only because of Medicare entitlement, not merely eligibility. Before terminating COBRA coverage for beneficiaries at age 65, an employer must first be certain that the individual has actually enrolled under Medicare. Also, 36 months of COBRA coverage must be provided for the spouse and dependent children of a covered employee whose group insurance terminates because of entitlement to Medicare.

22. 5. 4 Tax Equity and Fiscal Responsibility Act (TEFRA)

The **Tax Equity and Fiscal Responsibility Act of 1982 (TEFRA)** is intended to prevent group term life insurance plans (usually part of group health insurance programs) from discriminating in favor of **key employees**. Key employees include officers, the top 10 interest-holders in the employer, individuals owning 5% or more of the employer, or individuals owning more than 1% who are compensated annually at $150,000 or more.

TEFRA amends the Social Security Act to make Medicare secondary to group health plans. TEFRA applies to employers of 20 or more employees and to active employees and their spouses between ages 65 and 69. TEFRA also amends the Age Discrimination in Employment Act (ADEA) to require employers to offer these employees and their dependents the same coverage available to younger employees.

22. 5. 5 Employee Retirement and Income Security Act (ERISA)

The **Employee Retirement Income Security Act of 1974** was intended to accomplish pension equality, but it also protects group insurance plan participants. ERISA includes stringent reporting and disclosure requirements for establishing and maintaining group health insurance and other qualified plans. Summary plan descriptions must be filed with the Department of Labor, and an annual financial report must be filed with the IRS. For other qualified plans, legal documentation of the trust agreement, plan instrument, plan description, plan amendments, claim and benefit denials, enrollment forms, certificates of participation, annual statements, plan funding, and administrative records must all be maintained.

22. 5. 6 Age Discrimination in Employment Act (ADEA)

This act applies to employers with 20 or more employees and is directed toward employees age 40 or older. In general, this act prohibits compulsory retirement, except for those in executive or high policymaking positions. Employee benefits, which in the past usually ceased or were severely limited when an employee turned 65, must be continued for older workers, although some reductions in benefits may be allowed. Some states have even stricter laws with regard to retirement and benefits.

22. 5. 7 Americans with Disabilities Act (ADA)

This act has a widespread impact on almost all facets of American life. With respect to group insurance, it makes it unlawful for employers with 15 or more employees to discriminate on the basis of disability against a qualified individual with respect to any term, condition, or privilege of employment. Employees with disabilities must be given equal access to whatever health insurance coverage the employer provides to other employees, although certain coverage limitations may be acceptable for mental and nervous conditions as opposed to physical conditions, as long as such limitations apply to employees without disabilities as well those with disabilities.

Among other things, the law forbids exclusion or limitation of benefits for:

- specific disabilities such as deafness or AIDS;
- individually distinct groups of afflictions, such as cancer, muscular dystrophy, or kidney disease; and
- disability in general.

Exercise 22.B

There are a number of federal statutes that impact group health insurance. Match the appropriate law with its description.

_____ 1. Employee Retirement and Income Security Act (ERISA) 1974	A. Extends COBRA benefits for disabled employees from 18 to 29 months and provides spouses and dependent children up to 36 months of benefits if they lose COBRA benefits
_____ 2. Tax Equity and Fiscal Responsibility Act (TEFRA) 1982	B. Prevents employers from discriminating in benefit plans in favor of key employees and makes Medicare a secondary payor to group insurance for working employees even above age 65
_____ 3. Consolidated Omnibus Budget Reconciliation Act (COBRA) 1985	C. Establishes stringent reporting and disclosure requirements for establishing and maintaining group health insurance and qualified employer retirement plans
_____ 4. Omnibus Budget Reconciliation Act (OBRA) 1989	D. Ensures portability of group health coverage and includes various benefits affecting small employers, the self-employed, pregnant women and the mentally ill
_____ 5. Health Insurance Portability and Accountability Act (HIPAA) 1997	E. Requires employers with 20 or more employees to provide continuation of health benefits for employees and their families when they leave the plan

Answers to the exercise can be found at the end of the Unit 22 answers and rationales.

22. 5. 8 Pregnancy Discrimination

In the past, pregnancy was treated differently from other medical conditions under both individual and group health policies. However, an amendment to the Civil Rights Act requires that women affected by pregnancy, childbirth, or related medical conditions be treated the same for employment-related purposes as other persons who are not affected in the same way but are in similar positions. This includes receiving benefits under an employee benefit plan, such as group health insurance. Although the federal law applies only to employers who have 15 or more employees, various state laws may affect employers with fewer than 15 employees.

22. 5. 9 Experience Rating Versus Community Rating

In general, premiums for group insurance are based on experience rating. This is a method of establishing the premium for a group based on the group's previous claims experience. The larger and more homogenous the group, the closer it comes to reflecting standard mortality and morbidity rates.

In contrast, the practice of community rating sets premiums by using the same rate structure for all subscribers to a medical expense plan, regardless of their past or potential loss experience, and regardless of whether coverage is written on an individual or a group basis.

22. 5. 10 State Regulation

Many states have some form of mandated group health benefits. These commonly include required coverage for adopted or newborn children, continued coverage for handicapped dependents, coverage for treatment of alcoholism or drug abuse, and coverage for mammograms and pap smears.

Some state statutes mandate continuation of coverage for individuals whose group insurance has terminated. Most often, COBRA satisfies the state continuation of coverage requirements. In instances where the state requirements are more generous than COBRA, the employer must follow the more generous plan.

Extension of benefits is similar to continuation of coverage. In this case, benefits that began to be paid while a health insurance policy was in force continue, or are extended, after the insurance contract is terminated. Some states require group policies to provide for extension of benefits for a covered member who is totally disabled at the time of policy discontinuance.

States often regulate the marketing and advertising of accident and health insurance policies to ensure truthful and full disclosure of pertinent information when selling these policies. As a rule, the insurer is held responsible for the content of advertisements of its policies. Advertisements cannot be misleading or obscure, many not use deceptive illustrations, and must clearly outline all policy coverages as well as exclusions or limitations on coverage (such as preexisting condition limitations).

22. 6 INDIVIDUAL VERSUS GROUP INSURANCE

The chart that follows summarizes how individual and group plans differ.

Comparison of Individual and Group Plans

Individual	Group
Anyone can apply for coverage.	Only group members are covered. Group must meet size and purpose definitions.
Each person has a policy.	There is one master contract.
Individual selects coverage options.	Benefits are essentially the same for all group members.
Individual's health is evaluated.	Group as a whole is evaluated; no individual underwriting.
Coverage renewable at option of the insured, sometimes insurer.	Coverage stops when insured leaves the group.
All accidents are covered.	Only off-the-job accidents are generally covered.

Exercise 22.C

Apply what you have previously learned by indicating which of the following apply to individual insurance (I) and which apply to group insurance (G).

____ 1. Anyone may apply for coverage.

____ 2. There is one master contract.

____ 3. Covers both occupational and non-occupational accidents and sickness.

____ 4. Each person has a policy.

____ 5. Organization must precede insurance.

UNIT TEST

1. The conversion privilege allows the insured to continue group coverage without
   A. paying individual premiums
   B. filling out an application
   C. providing proof of termination of employment
   D. providing evidence of insurability

2. All of the following could be considered dependents except the insured's
   A. adopted children
   B. parents
   C. 25-year-old child who became physically disabled at 24
   D. 21-year-old child who is attending college full time

3. The coordination of benefits provision provides that when a person is covered under more than one plan, the total benefits cannot exceed
   A. the greater of the benefits provided
   B. the lesser of the benefits provided
   C. both of the benefits combined
   D. the total medical expenses or loss of wages

4. An individual is NOT eligible for the conversion privilege if
   A. the insured's employment is terminated
   B. the insured becomes ineligible for coverage because the insured's class is no longer eligible for coverage
   C. the insured fails to make the conversion within 31 days
   D. the insured's dependent child reaches the age specified in the policy as the age of terminating dependent coverage

5. Which of the following is NOT part of the qualification process for legal dependency?
   A. Relationship to the insured
   B. Residency in the home
   C. Eligibility for insurance
   D. Listing on the insured's tax return as a dependent

6. When both parents have employer-provided group coverage, the children are covered under
   A. the father's plan
   B. the mother's plan
   C. the plan of the parent whose birthday falls closest to the child's birthday
   D. the plan of the parent whose birthday falls closest to the start of the calendar year

7. Under the coordination of benefits rule, the primary company pays
   A. if there is no other coverage
   B. as if there were no other coverage
   C. whatever the other coverage does not pay, up to the policy limits
   D. only if the other coverage refuses the claim

8. Under the coordination of benefits rule, the secondary company pays
   A. if there is no other coverage
   B. as if there were no other coverage
   C. whatever the other coverage does not pay, up to the policy limits
   D. only if the other coverage refuses the claim

9. Carla enrolls in group insurance when she is eligible under her employer's plan. Because of an administrative error, her enrollment form is never sent to the company. When she later has a claim, the insurer will
   A. deny the claim because it has no record of her policy
   B. force the employer to pay the claim because it was the employer's error
   C. pay the claim only if the insurer is proven to have made an error
   D. accept the enrollment form and all of the past due premium and pay the medical claim

10. Which federal law requires employers with more than 20 employees to include in their group insurance plan a continuation of benefits provision for all eligible employees?
    A. COBRA
    B. OBRA
    C. ERISA
    D. TEFRA

11. Which federal law is intended to prevent group term life plans from discriminating in favor of key employees?
    A. COBRA
    B. OBRA
    C. ERISA
    D. TEFRA

12. Which federal law extends the minimum continuation of coverage period from 18 to 29 months for qualified beneficiaries disabled at the time of termination or reduction in hours?
    A. COBRA
    B. OBRA
    C. ERISA
    D. TEFRA

13. Which federal law is intended to accomplish pension equity but also protects group insurance plan participants?
    A. COBRA
    B. OBRA
    C. ERISA
    D. TEFRA

14. Which of the following provisions is NOT a part of HIPAA?
    A. Employers must make full health care coverage available immediately to newly hired employees who were previously covered for at least 18 months.
    B. New mothers and their babies must be allowed to stay in the hospital for at least 48 hours after a regular delivery.
    C. Small employers may not be denied group health insurance coverage because one or more employees is in poor health.
    D. Annual limits and lifetime spending limits may be applied to mental health coverage.

15. Which of the following is considered a disqualifying event under COBRA?
    A. The employer ceases to maintain any group health plan.
    B. The employee is no longer eligible for the group health plan because of a change in the covered classes.
    C. The employee voluntarily leaves employment with the employer.
    D. The employee's employment is terminated by the employer.

16. Under OBRA, an employer may terminate COBRA coverage because of coverage under another health plan
    A. as soon as the coverage is in force
    B. as long as the other health plan does not limit benefits for the insured's preexisting conditions
    C. as long as the other health plan limits benefits for the insured's preexisting conditions
    D. only if the premiums for the new plan are paid entirely by the insured's new employer

17. The Age Discrimination in Employment Act applies to employees age
    A. 40 or older
    B. 45 or older
    C. 50 or older
    D. 55 or older

18. The Americans with Disabilities Act
    A. does not apply to acquired diseases such as AIDS
    B. permits exclusion of benefits for individual distinct groups of afflictions, such as cancer, muscular dystrophy, or kidney disease
    C. applies to all employers with 25 or more employees
    D. requires that employees with disabilities be given equal access to whatever health insurance is provided to other employees

ANSWERS AND RATIONALES TO UNIT TEST

1. **D.** The conversion privilege allows the insured to continue group coverage without providing evidence of insurability.

2. **C.** The insured's 25-year-old child who becomes physically disabled at age 24 cannot be considered a dependent.

3. **D.** The coordination of benefits provision provides that when a person is covered under more than one plan, the total benefits cannot exceed the total medical expenses or loss of wages.

4. **C.** The conversion period is 31 days.

5. **C.** Eligibility for insurance is not part of the qualification process for legal dependency.

6. **D.** When both parents have employer-provided group coverage, the children are covered under the plan of the parent whose birthday falls closest to the start of the calendar year.

7. **B.** Under the coordination of benefits rule, the primary company pays as if there were no other coverage.

8. **C.** Under the coordination of benefits rule, the secondary company pays whatever the other coverage does not pay, up to the policy limits.

9. **D.** In case of an administrative error, the insurer will accept the enrollment form and all of the past due premium and pay the medical claim.

10. **A.** COBRA requires employers with more than 20 employees to include in their group insurance plan a continuation of benefits provision for all eligible employees.

11. **D.** TEFRA is intended to prevent group term life plans from discriminating in favor of key employees.

12. **B.** OBRA extends the minimum continuation of coverage period from 18 to 29 months for qualified beneficiaries disabled at the time of termination or reduction in hours.

13. **C.** ERISA is intended to accomplish pension equity but also protects group insurance plan participants.

14. **D.** Applying annual limits and lifetime spending limits to mental health coverage is not a part of HIPAA.

15. **A.** Ceasing to maintain any group health plan is considered a disqualifying event for an employer under COBRA.

16. **B.** Under OBRA, an employer may terminate COBRA coverage because of coverage under another health plan as long as the other health plan does not limit benefits for the insured's preexisting conditions.

17. **A.** The Age Discrimination in Employment Act applies to employees age 40 or older.

18. **D.** The Americans with Disabilities Act requires that employees with disabilities be given equal access to whatever health insurance is provided to other employees.

UNIT 22 EXERCISE ANSWERS

Exercise 22.A

1. **F**
2. **F**
3. **T**
4. **T**
5. **F**

Exercise 22.B

1. **C.**
2. **B.**
3. **E.**
4. **A.**
5. **D.**

Exercise 22.C

1. **I**
2. **G**
3. **I**
4. **I**
5. **G**

UNIT

23

Social Health Insurance

23. 1 INTRODUCTION

The term *social health insurance* refers to health coverages subsidized and implemented through government administration of tax money and social programs. We will look at four types of social health insurance:

- Medicare and associated private coverages
- Medicaid
- Social Security
- Workers' compensation

23. 2 LEARNING OBJECTIVES

After completing this lesson, you will be able to:

- explain who is eligible for Medicare and how individuals can enroll;
- explain the benefits provided under the Original Medicare Plan: Medicare Parts A and B;
- explain the purpose of Medicare supplement insurance;
- list and describe the core benefits available in Medicare supplement policies;
- describe Medicare Plans C and D;
- describe the Medicaid program, its purpose, and its administration; and
- describe the Social Security program, its purpose, and its administration.

23. 3 MEDICARE PARTS A AND B

23. 3. 1 Medicare

Medicare is the US version of national health insurance, at least as far as the elderly and disabled are concerned. It was originally enacted by Congress in 1965 and has been modified many times since. Medicare is a federal program. It is administered by the Centers for Medicare and Medicaid Services (CMS), a division within the US cabinet-level Department of Health and Human Services.

To make Medicare benefit payments, the US government enters into contracts with selected private insurance companies. The insurance companies that make coverage and payment decisions with respect to services provided by hospitals, skilled nursing facilities, home health agencies, and hospices are called **intermediaries**. The insurance companies that handle claims with respect to services provided by physicians and other providers are called **carriers**.

23. 3. 2 Eligibility

Eligibility for Medicare benefits is not determined by financial need. Practically everyone age 65 or older, as well as many people classified as disabled, are eligible for Medicare Part A and Medicare Part B. A person is eligible for Medicare benefits who:

- is age 65 or over and has qualified for Social Security or Railroad Retirement monthly cash benefits;
- is entitled to benefits under the Social Security program for 24 months as a disabled worker, disabled widow(er), or as a child age 18 or over who was disabled before age 22;
- is diagnosed as having permanent kidney failure and requiring dialysis or a kidney transplant; or
- was born before 1929 and has few or no quarters of coverage under the Social Security system.

Medicare Eligibility

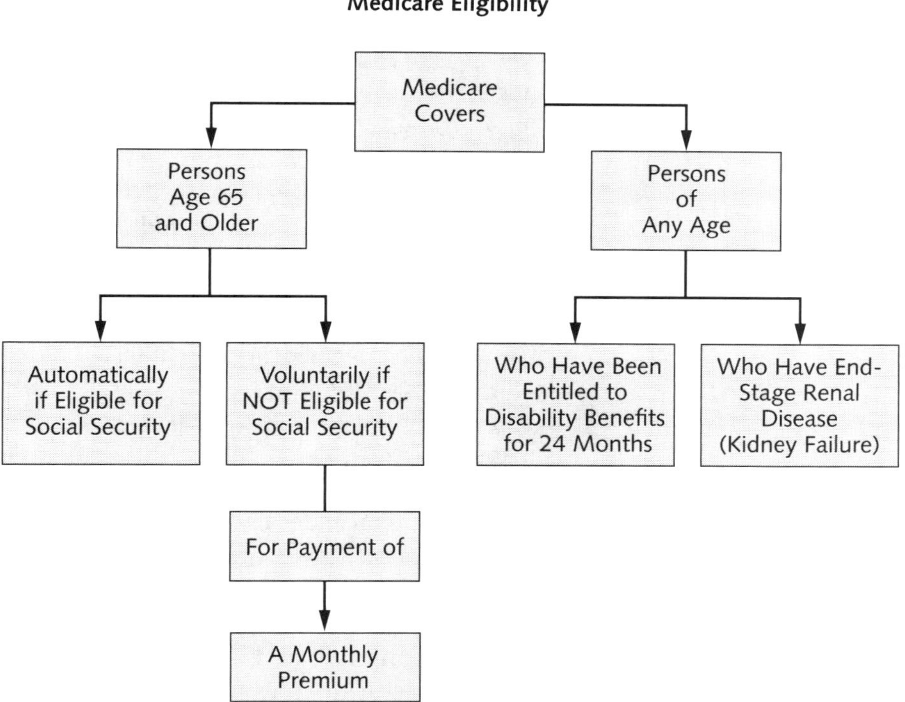

Survivors and dependents of these individuals may also qualify for Medicare coverage under certain circumstances. A common example is the surviving spouse of an individual who qualified for Social Security before the individual's death. A survivor who is at least age 65 can qualify for Medicare after the spouse's death. Other restrictions apply in other situations.

Here are just a few examples of people who would be eligible for Medicare:

- Chris, age 65, the surviving spouse of Stacy, who was age 68 and eligible for Social Security at the time of death
- Orlando, age 49, who is suffering from kidney failure
- Harry, age 85, who was born in 1921 and has few quarters of coverage under Social Security

23. 3. 3 Overview

Medicare covers inpatient care in hospitals (Part A), doctors' services, outpatient care, and some other medical services (Part B), as well as prescription drug coverage (Part D). Medicare also offers what are called Medicare Advantage plans (Part C). Medicare Advantage plans include Medicare managed care plans, such as HMOs, Medicare preferred provider organization plans (PPOs), Medicare private fee-for-service (PFFS) plans, and Medicare special needs plans.

What the Original Medicare Plan Covers

Part A	Part B
Inpatient hospital services, including semiprivate room and board and nursing services	Physicians' and surgeons' services, whether in a hospital, clinic, or elsewhere
Posthospital skilled nursing care, in an accredited care facility	Medical and health services, such as x-rays, diagnostic lab tests, ambulance services, medical supplies, medical equipment rental, and physical and occupational therapy
Posthospital home health services, including nursing care, therapy, and part-time home health aides	
Hospice benefits for the care of terminally ill patients (to the exclusion of all other Medicare benefits, except for physician services)	
Inpatient psychiatric care, on a limited basis	

Medicare provides basic health insurance protection to approximately 42 million Americans. Contrary to popular belief, Medicare does not cover all medical expenses. To control costs, Medicare limits the scope of its coverage and its benefit amounts, thus making the consumer and the service provider more cost conscious and less likely to overuse or overcharge the program. For example, Medicare does not pay for most routine physicals, eye and hearing exams, dental care, and many other medical products and services. In addition, many long-term health problems requiring custodial or private nursing care (such as Alzheimer's disease) are not covered. Medicare coverage is also subject to deductibles, co-payments, and limitations.

23. 4 THE ORIGINAL MEDICARE PLAN

The Original Medicare Plan has two parts: Hospital Insurance (Part A) and Medical Insurance (Part B). Part A covers inpatient care in hospitals and skilled nursing facilities, and it covers care provided in a hospice and some care provided at home. Part B provides medical insurance for required doctors' services, outpatient services and medical supplies, and many services not covered by Part A hospitalization coverage.

23. 4. 1 Enrollment

Enrollment in Part A is free and automatic for individuals entitled to Social Security benefits. These persons are eligible for Part A benefits as of the first day of the month in which they reach age 65. It should be noted that individuals who are not eligible for premium-free Part A may be able to purchase it under certain circumstances.

Enrollment in Part B, on the other hand, is voluntary and requires payment of a monthly premium. When individuals become eligible for the hospital insurance coverage under Part A, they are enrolled and their premium payment is established for Part B coverage also, unless they sign a form indicating they do not want the Part B coverage.

If individuals enroll before the month in which they reach age 65, Part B coverage begins as of the first day of the month when they are 65, just as it does for Part A. If enrollment takes place later, coverage also begins later.

High-income beneficiaries pay higher premiums for Medicare Part B coverage. Premiums are tied to income levels.

People who choose not to enroll in Part B during their initial enrollment period may do so later. A **general enrollment period** occurs each year from January 1 through March 31. When enrollment occurs during this period, coverage begins on the following July 1.

23. 4. 2 Benefits Under the Original Medicare Plan: Medicare Part A

Part A provides coverage for four different kinds of care:

- Inpatient hospital care
- Skilled nursing facility care
- Home health care
- Hospice care

The services covered under each of these arrangements are subject to certain limitations that we will discuss later.

Examples of the four types of care follow.

- An individual who is hospitalized with pneumonia is receiving **inpatient hospital care.**

- An individual receives skilled nursing services in a facility designed for that purpose. **Skilled nursing care** is for patients whose professional nursing needs do not require acute hospital nursing care but who need inpatient supervision by a registered nurse.
- An individual receives assistance several days a week at home following major surgery. This is **home health care**.
- An individual with a terminal illness who will spend the remainder of his life in a hospice receives **hospice care**.

23. 4. 2. 1 Inpatient Hospital Care

Medicare's inpatient hospital care benefit helps pay the reasonable charges that result from hospitalization in a semiprivate room for medically necessary care. This includes meals, regular nursing services, special care units, drugs taken in the hospital, tests, medical supplies, operating room, and many other supplies and services.

For each benefit period, Medicare will pay the full cost of up to 60 days' of inpatient hospital care, after the patient pays a deductible, which changes annually. From the 61st through 90th days of hospitalization, Medicare pays all but a specified coinsurance amount per day. This figure also changes annually. For a stay over 90 days, the patient may draw upon 60 lifetime reserve days, which may be used only once in a lifetime. The patient's daily co-payment amount increases substantially when these reserve days are used.

A benefit period begins upon admission and ends 60 days after hospital discharge. A readmission during these 60 days is considered part of the same benefit period; a readmission after the 60 days run out is the beginning of a new benefit period.

23. 4. 2. 2 Skilled Nursing Facility Care

Medicare will share the cost of skilled nursing facility (SNF) care for up to 100 days in each benefit period.

The patient must pay a specified dollar amount (coinsurance) for the 21st through 100th days of confinement. This amount changes annually. Medicare pays all reasonable charges for the first 20 days.

Medicare defines the skilled nursing facility benefit quite narrowly. The patient must be receiving medically necessary services provided by a highly skilled staff in a Medicare-approved facility, following a prior hospital stay of at least three days. The care must be of a type that can be performed only by or under the supervision of licensed nursing personnel, and only as the result of a doctor's orders.

Any type of intermediate or custodial, as opposed to skilled, nursing care is not covered. Custodial care includes board, room, and nonmedical personal assistance services, such as help performing activities of daily living (e.g., dressing, eating, and bathing).

23. 4. 2. 3 *Home Health Care*

If a patient is confined at home, the home health care benefit provides for certain services performed by a participating home health agency. This is a public or private agency that provides skilled nursing or therapeutic services in the home. Eligible expenses include:

- intermittent part-time nursing care;
- physical, occupational, or speech therapy;
- home health aides;
- medical social services;
- medical supplies; and
- 80% of certain durable medical equipment, such as wheelchairs or hospital beds.

No benefits will be paid for housekeeping services, meal preparation or delivery, shopping, full-time nursing care, blood transfusions, drugs, or biologicals.

The home health care benefit pays for an unlimited number of home visits as medically necessary, provided they are intermittent rather than constant or full time. Note that this is not the same benefit that is found in long-term care policies.

23. 4. 2. 4 *Hospice Care*

A hospice is organized primarily for the purpose of providing support services to terminally ill patients and their families. For terminally ill patients, the hospice care benefit provides inpatient and outpatient hospice care. Payments are made for pain relief and symptom management but not for curative or other types of treatment.

It is possible for Medicare to cover hospice care for an unlimited period, as long as a physician certifies need.

Medicare pays virtually all costs for hospice treatment, with no deductible. Only two services require co-payments:

- Prescription drugs, for which patients must pay 5% or $5 per prescription, whichever is less
- Respite care, for which patients must pay 5% of the Medicare-approved rate up to a specified dollar amount, which changes annually

The **respite care** benefit covers temporary care in a hospice for a patient who is normally cared for in the home. The respite is for the usual caregivers and may last no more than five consecutive days.

Example

Ellis is admitted to a hospice in March. Medicare begins paying covered charges immediately, with no deductible required from Ellis.

In July and again in October, Ellis is recertified as being terminally ill. Medicare continues to pay hospice benefits for Ellis.

During this time, Ellis receives experimental medical treatments that could conceivably halt the progress of his illness. Medicare will not cover these treatments, so Ellis must find other funding to pay for them.

Now let's suppose that Ellis is instead being cared for at home by his brother, Bradley, who needs some time off from the responsibility of caring for Ellis. If Bradley wants to take Ellis to a hospice for several days, Medicare will pay for five consecutive days of respite care.

23. 4. 3 What Part A Does Not Cover

Hospital insurance under Medicare does not cover:

- private-duty nursing;
- charges for a private room, unless medically necessary;
- conveniences, such as a telephone or television in an insured's room; and
- the first three pints of blood received during a calendar year (unless replaced by a blood plan).

23. 4. 4 Benefits Under the Original Medicare Plan: Medicare Part B

Medicare Part B provides coverage for three general kinds of medical services:

- Doctors' services
- Home health care (if not covered by Part A)
- Outpatient medical services and supplies

Part B is an optional program of medical insurance designed to supplement Part A. Persons who enroll in Part A are automatically enrolled in Part B unless they request otherwise. Part B requires payment of a monthly premium, which many people simply have deducted from their Social Security or Railroad Retirement checks.

23. 4. 4. 1 Common Deductible and Co-Payment

Medicare Part B requires cost-sharing by the patient. There is an annual deductible and a coinsurance percentage that applies to all Part B covered services across the board. This contrasts with Part A, in which each benefit provided has its own unique co-payment requirements for the patient.

Under Part B, a patient is always responsible for these costs:

- An annual deductible amount
- 20% of all reasonable charges for covered, medically necessary services
- The first three pints of blood

The deductible can be met by any combination of expenses covered under Part B. The patient does not have to meet a separate deductible for each type of covered service.

Medicare determines what is a reasonable charge for a particular service. If the actual charge is more than that, the patient must pay the difference, unless the doctor or supplier agrees to accept assignment. **Assignment** means that the doctor or supplier will accept Medicare's approved amounts as full payment and cannot legally bill the patient for anything above that amount. Doctors and suppliers are not required to accept assignment, but many will.

If Medicare decides that an expense is medically unnecessary, the patient must pay the entire cost. Neither Medicare nor most private insurance policies will provide benefits.

23. 4. 4. 2 Doctors' Services

Part B covers most physicians', surgeons', and osteopaths' services and supplies furnished as part of such services. It does not matter where such services are provided—in a hospital, in a skilled nursing facility, in a clinic, at the doctor's office, at the patient's home, or anywhere else in the United States.

Some of the specific services covered are:

- medical and surgical services, including anesthesia;
- office visits, house calls, and hospital calls;
- radiological and pathological services provided by a physician;
- medical supplies furnished as part of a physician's professional services;
- second opinions before surgery;
- diagnostic tests that are part of the patient's treatment;
- x-rays;
- services of the doctor's office nurse;
- physical, occupational, and speech therapy services;
- blood transfusions; and
- drugs and biologicals that cannot be self-administered.

Specifically excluded from Part B coverage are physicians' services for:

- routine physical exams (note: Part B does cover one physical examination within the first six months of enrollment);

- routine foot care, treatment of flat feet, and treatment for subluxations of the foot;
- eye exams and fitting of eyeglasses or contact lenses;
- hearing exams and fitting of hearing aids;
- most types of dental care;
- most immunizations; and
- cosmetic surgery (unless needed to repair an accidental injury or to correct a malformed body part).

23. 4. 4. 3 *Preventive Care*

Medicare Part B covers the following preventive services:

- Bone mass measurements for qualified individuals
- Screening blood tests, including cholesterol, lipid, and triglyceride levels, for early detection of cardiovascular disease
- Colorectal cancer screenings
- Diabetes screening tests for enrollees who are at risk for diabetes
- Glaucoma testing once every 12 months
- Pap tests, pelvic examinations, and clinical breast exams for women
- Annual prostate cancer screenings for men age 50 and over
- Annual screening mammograms for women age 40 and over

23. 4. 4. 4 *Home Health Care Services*

Recall that Medicare Part A covers home health care services. For persons who participate in Part B but not Part A, Part B pays the full cost of medically necessary home health visits for patients requiring home nursing care. The patient pays no deductible or coinsurance, except for 20% of the cost of durable medical equipment, provided under the home health care benefit (e.g., wheelchairs and hospital beds).

The home health care expenses of persons with Part A are paid under Part A.

23. 4. 4. 5 *Outpatient Medical Services and Supplies*

Medicare Part B will help pay for certain services received as an outpatient from a Medicare-certified hospital for the diagnosis or treatment of an illness or injury.

The following is a relatively comprehensive list of some of the outpatient medical services and supplies covered under Medicare Part B:

- Outpatient clinic services

- Emergency room services
- X-rays, whether for therapy or diagnosis billed by the hospital
- Medically necessary ambulance services
- Purchase or rental of durable medical equipment used in the patient's home
- Artificial limbs and eyes
- Artificial replacements for internal organs (e.g., colostomy bags and supplies)
- Braces for neck, back, or limbs
- Casts, splints, and surgical dressings
- Blood transfusions (after the first three pints) furnished to an outpatient
- Outpatient physical, occupational, and speech therapy provided in a therapist's office, as an outpatient, or in the patient's home
- Drugs and biologicals that cannot be self-administered
- Mammograms, Pap smears, and colorectal screenings
- Diabetes glucose monitoring and education
- Flu shots

Outpatient services not covered by Part B are:

- routine physical exams (other than the one-time exam mentioned earlier);
- eye exams, fitting of eyeglasses or contact lenses;
- hearing exams and fitting of hearing aids;
- most immunizations; and
- routine foot care.

23. 4. 5 What Part B Does Not Cover

Medical insurance under Medicare Part B does not cover:

- private-duty nursing;
- skilled nursing home care costs over 100 days per benefit period;
- intermediate nursing home care;
- physician charges above Medicare's approved amount;
- most outpatient prescription drugs;

- care received outside the United States (limited coverage for Canada and Mexico);
- custodial care received in the home;
- dental care, routine physicals and immunizations, cosmetic surgery, eyeglasses, hearing aids, orthopedic shoes, and acupuncture expenses; and
- expenses incurred as a result of war or act of war.

23. 4. 6 Claims and Appeals

If a doctor has not accepted a Medicare assignment, the doctor sends the bill directly to the patient. The patient fills out a Medicare claim form and attaches itemized bills from the doctor including date of treatment, place of treatment, description of treatment, doctor's name, and charge for service. The form and accompanying documents are sent to the Medicare carrier (also known as a fiscal intermediary—a private insurance company) in the patient's area. Upon receiving the claim, the carrier sends a form called **Explanation of Medicare Benefits**. This form shows which services are covered and the amounts approved for each service.

23. 5 MEDICARE SUPPLEMENT INSURANCE

As we have seen, the Original Medicare Plan provides substantial hospital and other medical benefits for beneficiaries of the program. However, even after Medicare pays its share, the patient may still owe large amounts because of:

- deductibles;
- coinsurance;
- noncovered services; and
- actual charges by service providers in excess of the approved amount that Medicare will pay.

Several methods are available to supplement Medicare and cover most of the remaining expenses.

- Medicaid, discussed later in this unit, covers expenses not paid by Medicare for eligible low-income people. In other words, these people do not need supplemental insurance.
- Many employers offer their retiring employees an opportunity to continue their group insurance coverage or to convert it to Medicare supplement coverage. For those who continue to work after age 65, Medicare may become the secondary payer to an employer group health care plan. This means that the employer plan will pay first on hospital and medical bills. If the employer plan does not pay all expenses, Medicare may pay secondary benefits for Medicare-covered services to supplement the

amount paid by the employer group health care plan. Medicare is also the secondary payer to employer plans for beneficiaries who have Medicare because of a qualified disability or permanent kidney failure.

- Associations and groups may offer supplemental Medicare coverage to their members who are age 65 and over.
- More often, a Medicare supplement policy is purchased from a private insurer to help cover the costs not paid by Medicare. This may also be referred to as a Medigap policy.

This section concentrates on the last option: Medicare supplement policies purchased from private insurers.

Some kind of supplement to Medicare is needed by almost everyone covered by Medicare except those whose income is low enough to qualify for help from Medicaid.

23. 5. 1 Medicare Supplement Plans

A **Medigap** policy is a Medicare supplement insurance policy sold by private insurance companies to fill "gaps" in Medicare Parts A and B. Medigap policies do not pay costs for Medicare Parts C and D. A person who has a Medicare Advantage plan does not need a Medigap policy because these plans generally cover many of the same benefits that a Medigap policy would cover. In fact, it is illegal for anyone to sell a Medigap policy to a person who is in a Medicare Advantage plan.

Prior to June 1, 2010, there were 12 standardized Medigap plans labeled Plan A through Plan L. Some of these plans have been eliminated, and two new plans have been added. Plans purchased before June of 2010 will remain in force and are renewable for life.

As of June, 2010 there are 10 standardized Medigap plans. Each of the 10 plans has a letter designation of A, B, C, D, F, G, K, L, M, or N. These policies were standardized by the National Association of Insurance Commissioners (NAIC) to help consumers understand and compare them and thus make informed buying decisions. These standards can be found in NAIC's Medicare Supplement Insurance Minimum Standards Model Act. The benefits in each plan may not be altered by insurers, nor may the letter designation be changed (although insurers may add names or titles to the letter designations).

Medigap Plan A covers basic benefits. Medigap Plans B, C, D,F, G, M, and N include the Plan A basic benefits and some extra benefits. Plans K and L offer different benefits than the other Medigap Plans and have lower premiums than those plans. However, Plans K and L require higher out-of-pocket costs from beneficiaries because these plans were designed to give beneficiaries an incentive to control costs. Although Plans K and L are similar, they differ in the percentage of coverage for claims and in the maximum amount of out-of-pocket costs. Note that insurance companies that sell Medigap policies don't have to offer every Medigap plan. Each insurance company decides which Medigap policies it wants to sell. The front of each Medigap policy must state that it is Medicare supplement insurance.

Three states—Massachusetts, Minnesota, and Wisconsin—are referred to as waiver states because they are permitted by statute to have different standardized Medigap plans.

23. 5. 2 Basic Benefits

Each standardized Medigap policy must cover basic benefits. Plans A B, C, D, F, G, M, and N have one set of basic benefits, and Plans K and L have different benefits.

The basic benefits policy covers 100% of the Part A hospital coinsurance amount for each day used from the 61st through the 90th day in any Medicare benefit period. It also covers:

- 100% of the Part A hospital coinsurance amount for each Medicare lifetime inpatient reserve day used from the 91st through the 150th day in any Medicare benefit period;
- 100% of the Part A-eligible hospital expenses for 365 additional days after all hospital benefits are exhausted;
- Part B coinsurance amount (generally 20% of Medicare-approved expenses) after the annual deductible is met; and
- the cost of the first three pints of blood each year and hospice Part A coinsurance.

The basic benefits under Plans K and L provide for different cost sharing for items and services than Plans A through J. Plan K pays:

- 100% of Part A hospitalization coinsurance plus coverage for 365 days after Medicare benefits end;
- 50% of hospice cost-sharing, 50% of Medicare-eligible expenses for the first three pints of blood; and
- 50% of Part B coinsurance, except for 100% coinsurance for Part B preventive services.

Plan L pays:

- 100% of Part A hospitalization coinsurance plus coverage for 365 days after Medicare benefits end;
- 75% of hospice cost sharing;
- 75% of Medicare-eligible expenses for the first three pints of blood; and
- 75% of Part B coinsurance, except for 100% coinsurance for Part B preventive services.

10 Standard Medigap Plans

A	B	C	D	E	F**	G	H	I	J	K	L
Basic benefits*	Basic benefits*	Basic benefits*	Basic benefits*	*	Basic benefits*	Basic benefits*	Basic benefits *	Basic benefits		Basic benefits***	Basic benefits***
	Part A deductible	Part A deductible	Part A deductible		Part A deductible	Part A deductible	50% coinsurance on Part A deductible			50% Part A deductible	75% Part A deductible
		Skilled nursing coinsurance	Skilled nursing coinsurance		Skilled nursing coinsurance	Skilled nursing coinsurance				50% Skilled nursing coinsurance	75% Skilled nursing coinsurance
		Part B deductible			Part B deductible			Part B deductible less $20 per physician visit and $50 emergency room visit		50% Part B deductible	75% Part B deductible
					Part B Excess (80%)	Part B Excess (80%)					
		Foreign travel emergency	Foreign travel emergency		Foreign travel emergency	Foreign travel emergency					
			At-Home recovery			At-Home recovery					
										Out of pocket $4,620	Out of pocket $2,310
					Annual deductible **				Annual deductible **	Annual deductible ****	Annual deductible ****

* The Basic Benefits policy covers 100% of the Part A hospital coinsurance amount for each day used from the 61st through the 90th day in any Medicare benefit period and 100% of the Part A hospital coinsurance amount for each Medicare lifetime inpatient reserve day used from the 91st through the 150th day in any Medicare benefit period; 100% of the Part A-eligible hospital expenses for 365 additional days after all hospital benefits are exhausted; Part B coinsurance amount (generally 20% of Medicare-approved expenses) after the annual deductible is met, and the cost of the first three pints of blood each year and hospice Part A coinsurance.

** Plans F and J also have a high deductible plan option option that pays the same benefits as Plans F and J after one has paid a calendar year deductible. Benefits from high deductible Plans F and J will not begin until out-of-pocket expenses exceed the deductible. Out-of-pocket expenses for this deductible are expenses that would ordinarily be paid by the policy. These expenses include the Medicare deductible for Part A and Part B, but do not include the plan's separate foreign travel emergency deductibleThis high deductible plan pays the same benefits as Plan F after one has paid a calendar year deductible ($1900) Benefits from high deductible Plan F will not begin until the out-of-pocket expenses exceed $1900. Out-of-pocket expenses for this deductible are expenses that would ordinarily be paid by the policy. These expenses include the Medicare deductibles for Part A and Part B, but do not include the plans separate foreign travel emergency deductible.

*** The basic benefits under Plans K and L provide for different costsharing for items and services than Plans A through J. Plan K pays 100% of Part A hospitalization coinsurance plus coverage for 365 days after Medicare benefits end, 50% of hospice cost-sharing, 50% of Medicare-eligible expenses for the first three pints of blood, and 50% of Part B coinsurance, except 100% coinsurance for Part B preventive services. Plan L pays 100% of Part A hospitalization coinsurance plus coverage for 365 days after Medicare benefits end, 75% of hospice costsharing, 75% of Medicare-eligible expenses for the first three pints of blood, and 75% of Part B coinsurance, except 100% coinsurance for Part B preventive services.

Once a person reaches the annual limit, the plan pays 100% of the Medicare copayments, coinsurance, and deductibles for the rest of the calendar years. The out-of-pocket annual limit does not include charges from a provider and that exceed Medicare-approved amounts. Such charges are called "excess charges," and the policyowner is responsible for paying them.

**** These out-of-pocket annual limits increase each year for inflation.

As long as a person pays the premium, a Medigap policy is automatically renewed each year. No provision of any Medicare supplement plan duplicates benefits provided under Medicare—instead, each plan provides supplemental coverage.

23. 5. 2. 1 Medicare SELECT

Medicare SELECT is another version of the standard Medigap policies we have been discussing. It offers the same 12 plans with the same coverages. The only difference between Medicare SELECT and standard Medigap insurance is that Medicare SELECT is operated on a **preferred provider** basis. Each insurer has a list of doctors and hospitals from which the insured must make a choice for treatment to receive benefits. As a result of this requirement, Medicare SELECT policies generally have lower premiums than standard Medigap policies.

23. 6 MEDICARE PART C: MEDICARE ADVANTAGE PLANS

The Original Medicare Plan as adopted in the 1960s allows beneficiaries to receive health care from any physician who accepts Medicare patients. No referrals are necessary. Under this plan, Medicare pays for medically necessary, Medicare-approved services, and the patient is responsible for the remaining expenses. This plan is known as the **original fee-for-service plan**.

The Balanced Budget Act of 1997 (BBA) authorized the use of alternative health care plans, including some types of managed care plans, to provide Medicare benefits. The goals were twofold: to give Medicare beneficiaries more options in choosing a health care plan and to help control Medicare costs, which were beginning to increase at an alarming pace. The alternative health care program authorized by the BBA was known as **Medicare+Choice**, or **Medicare Part C**.

23. 6. 1 Medicare Part C: Medicare Advantage Plans

The Medicare Prescription Drug, Improvement, and Modernization Act of 2003 made additional refinements to the Medicare+Choice program and renamed it **Medicare Advantage**. Plans available under the Medicare Advantage program include the following:

- Medicare private fee-for-service plans
- Medicare managed care plans
- Medicare preferred provider organization plans
- Medicare specialty plans

The original fee-for-service plan is still available to all Medicare beneficiaries nationwide. Beneficiaries who are happy with the original plan are not required to change to a Medicare Advantage plan. They will remain enrolled under the original plan unless they choose to enroll in a Medicare Advantage plan.

To enroll in a Medicare Advantage plan, a person must be enrolled in Medicare Part A and Part B. The enrollee must still pay the monthly Part B premium and also may have to pay an additional premium to the Medicare Advantage plan. People who are enrolled in a Medicare Advantage plan don't need a Medicare supplement policy because Medicare Advantage plans usually provide most of the same benefits provided by Medicare supplements.

23. 6. 2 Medicare Private Fee-for-Service Plans

Medicare private fee-for-service (PFFS) plans are similar to the Medicare original fee-for-service plan, except that they are offered by private companies. They allow beneficiaries to receive care from any Medicare-approved provider who is willing to accept the terms of the plan's payment schedule. But the private company, rather than Medicare, negotiates with providers to determine how much the plan will pay and what enrollees must pay for the services they receive.

Enrollees may have to pay a premium to join the plan and may have to pay other costs, such as co-payments, for some services. These costs may be different from the costs under the Original Medicare Plan. In exchange, however, enrollees often get extra benefits that are not provided under the Original Medicare Plan, such as extra days in the hospital.

23. 6. 3 Medicare Managed Care Plans

Medicare managed care plans share many of the same features found in managed care plans provided under employer-sponsored health plans. They often take the form of **Medicare health maintenance organizations (HMOs).** In these HMOs, enrollees are usually limited to using network providers except for emergencies and may be required to choose a primary care physician. Enrollees who want to see a specialist typically must obtain a referral from their primary care physician.

In most Medicare managed care HMOs, enrollees who go outside the plan for nonemergency services must pay the entire bill out of their own pockets. Some Medicare managed care plans offer a **point-of-service (POS)** option, which allows enrollees to use out-of-network providers but requires them to pay a greater portion of the provider's charges if they do.

Medicare HMOs generally charge enrollees a monthly premium, which must be paid in addition to the usual Medicare Part B premium. They often charge a small co-payment each time an enrollee uses a service, such as $5 for a doctor's visit, but there are usually no additional charges. Enrollees do not have to pay the Medicare deductibles and coinsurance amounts, and they often receive coverage for services the original Medicare fee-for-service plan doesn't cover, such as routine physical exams and dental care.

23. 6. 4 Medicare Preferred Provider Organization Plans

Medicare preferred provider organization (PPO) plans are similar to Medicare managed health care plans but have the following differences.

- Enrollees generally aren't required to name a primary care physician and can see any doctor or provider that accepts Medicare, but they may pay more if they use providers who aren't part of the plan's network.
- Enrollees don't need referrals to see a specialist, although they may need plan approval for certain services.

Since 2006, the Medicare Advantage program includes regional PPOs designed to bring the benefits of Medicare Advantage to rural areas. Medicare beneficiaries in many rural areas did not have access to the Medicare+Choice plans authorized by the Balanced Budget Act of 1997 and were limited to the original Medicare fee-for-service plan. The Medicare Prescription Drug, Improvement, and Modernization Act of 2003 provides additional financial incentives for providers who establish regional PPOs that serve those areas.

23. 6. 5 Medicare Specialty Plans

Medicare specialty plans provide more focused health care for people with specific conditions. A person who joins one of these plans gets health care services as well as more-focused care to manage a specific disease or condition. The goal is to provide quality health care as efficiently and effectively as possible.

23. 7 MEDICARE PART D: MEDICARE PRESCRIPTION DRUG PLANS

The Medicare Prescription Drug and Modernization Act of 2003 established a new Medicare Part D prescription drug benefit. Since January 2006, Medicare offers insurance coverage for prescription drugs to anyone who has Medicare Part A or Part B. Prescription drug coverage is needed because medical practice today relies on drug therapies to treat chronic conditions. As a result, most Medicare beneficiaries sooner or later will need prescription drugs to stay healthy.

Under the standard benefit plan for 2010, Medicare beneficiaries pay a monthly premium of $30 and a $310 annual deductible. Beneficiaries then pay 25% of the first $2,830 of prescription drug costs, and Medicare pays the other 75%. Coverage then stops completely. However, once a beneficiary's total out-of-pocket prescription drug expenses reach $4,550 (2010), then catastrophic coverage starts and beneficiaries pay co-payments of $2.50 for generic drugs and $6.30 for brand name drugs or 5% of total costs, whichever is higher. (These dollar thresholds are scheduled to increase each year.) Although companies have considerable flexibility in designing their own plans, the overall value of the drug coverage offered must be the same or greater than the basic plan. Of course, companies that offer more benefits can charge higher premiums.

Coverage is available only through private plans that are either stand-alone prescription drug plans (PDPs) or Medicare private plans such as HMOs, PPOs, or PFFSs. A stand-alone plan only offers prescription drug benefits. People in these plans get other medical services through the Original Medicare Plan. Most Medicare private plans provide all Medicare-covered services, including prescription drug coverage. Individuals in private fee-for-service plans that don't offer drug coverage can enroll in a stand-alone prescription drug plan. However, individuals in HMOs or PPOs must receive all of their medical and drug coverage through these plans.

The law provides federal subsidy payments to employers and unions that sponsor qualified retiree prescription drug plans.

Exercise 23.A

Match the benefit to the appropriate part of Medicare.

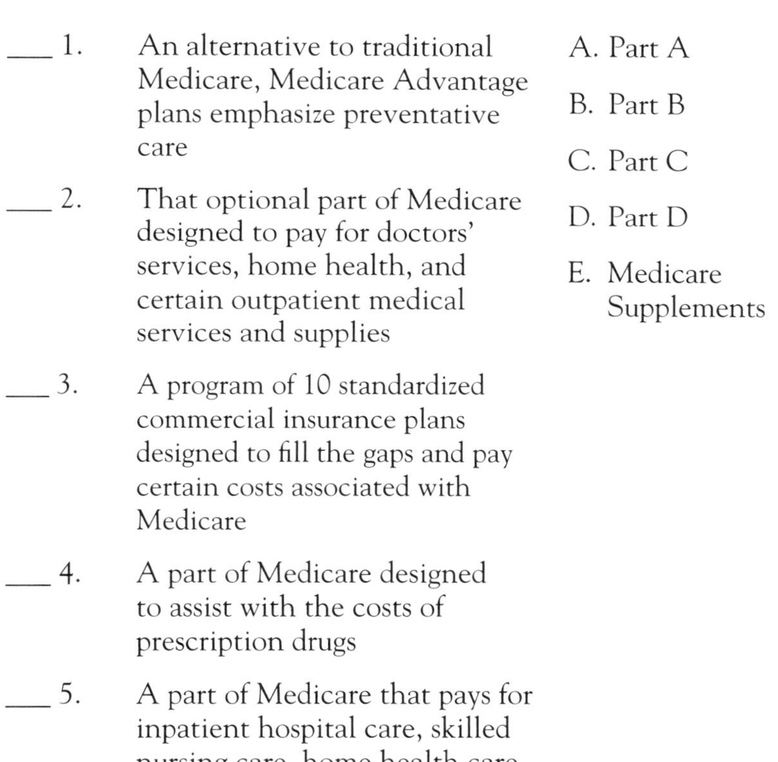

___ 1. An alternative to traditional Medicare, Medicare Advantage plans emphasize preventative care

___ 2. That optional part of Medicare designed to pay for doctors' services, home health, and certain outpatient medical services and supplies

___ 3. A program of 10 standardized commercial insurance plans designed to fill the gaps and pay certain costs associated with Medicare

___ 4. A part of Medicare designed to assist with the costs of prescription drugs

___ 5. A part of Medicare that pays for inpatient hospital care, skilled nursing care, home health care, and hospice care

A. Part A

B. Part B

C. Part C

D. Part D

E. Medicare Supplements

Answers to the exercise can be found at the end of the Unit 23 answers and rationales.

23.8 MEDICARE AND EMPLOYER COVERAGE

Many individuals continue working beyond the age of 65 or have spouses who are working. In such cases, Medicare beneficiaries may be covered by their own or their spouse's employer group health plan. When this occurs, Medicare may be the secondary payer to any group health plan provided by an employer with 20 or more employees. This means that the group health plan pays first on hospital and medical bills. If the plan does not pay all of the expenses incurred, Medicare may pay secondary benefits for Medicare-covered services to supplement the amount paid by the group health plan.

Note that employers with 20 or more employees must offer the same health benefits to employees age 65 or older, as well as to their spouses who are age 65 or older, as they offer to younger employees and spouses. The older employee has the option of rejecting such group health coverage, in which case Medicare becomes the primary payer for Medicare-covered health services.

Medicare may also be a secondary payer to employer-provided group health coverage for certain individuals under age 65 who are entitled to Medicare on the basis of their disability. To be the primary payer, the group health plan must generally be that of an employer or employee organization that covers the employees of at least one employer with 100 or more employees. Such plans are known as large group health plans (LGHPs). An LGHP may not treat disabled employees differently from other employees because of their disability.

23.9 MEDICAID

Medicaid is a welfare health care program for indigent persons. It was established by the federal government but is administered by the states. The eligibility requirements for Medicaid vary somewhat from state to state. Generally, to be eligible for Medicaid, a person must qualify for either (1) Aid for Families with Dependent Children (also known as public assistance or welfare) or (2) Supplemental Security Income, an assistance program under Social Security for indigent persons who are age 65 or over, blind, or disabled. For those who do qualify, Medicaid covers most health care costs, including hospital and doctor bills and nursing home care.

23.9.1 Financial Tests

Each state establishes its own limit on the income and financial resources that a Medicaid recipient may have and still qualify for Medicaid. The recipient must spend down or exhaust income and resources to a minimum amount before Medicaid becomes available.

The recipient—an individual, couple, or family—is permitted to retain a small amount of monthly income plus certain assets (or what the law refers to as resources). The recipient is allowed to keep his home. Within important limits, the recipient may also be able to keep some personal property.

23. 9. 2 Spousal Impoverishment Rule

In the case of a married couple, suppose that only one spouse requires nursing home care. Without some relief in the law, the institutionalized spouse would have to impoverish the other spouse to qualify for Medicaid. The law now provides that the spouse who is not institutionalized is permitted to keep a portion of the couple's resources, as determined by state and federal guidelines.

The law also allows the noninstitutionalized spouse to retain some of the couple's assets or to receive a transfer of assets from the institutionalized spouse to bring assets up to a specified minimum level that is adjusted annually.

If the institutionalized spouse has any resources remaining after making a transfer to the spouse, they are applied toward the nursing home bill. Medicaid then pays only the difference between the actual bill from the nursing home and the institutionalized spouse's contribution toward that bill out of his income and resources.

Exercise 23.B

Mark which of the following statements are true (T) and which are false (F) regarding Medicaid.

____ 1. Medicaid is a welfare health program intended for the indigent.

____ 2. Eligibility for Medicaid is set by federal statute.

____ 3. Medicaid covers most health care costs, including those associated with Medicare, if appropriate.

____ 4. Medicaid excludes custodial or nursing home care, like Medicare.

Answers to the exercise can be found at the end of the Unit 23 answers and rationales.

23. 9. 3 Medicare Cost Assistance

Medicaid is required by law to pay the following Medicare costs of indigent Medicare patients:

- Medicare deductibles
- Part B premium
- Medicare co-payments
- Part A premiums (when required)

The Medicare Secondary Payer Statute (MSP) reduces Medicare costs by making parties responsible for a Medicare beneficiary's injury or illness pay the costs of the injury or illness. Medicare does not cover an injury or illness if the costs were, or can be, paid under workers' compensation, an automobile or liability insurance policy, or under no fault insurance. If the responsible party cannot pay, Medicare will cover the cost. However, these conditional payments are subject to reimbursement from the responsible party. The Centers for Medicare and Medicaid Services (CMS) pursue recovery from the responsible party through subrogation.

23. 10 SOCIAL SECURITY DISABILITY

The Social Security program in the United States provides death benefits, survivor benefits, retirement benefits, and disability benefits, the last of which is a type of social health insurance. Social Security disability benefits are available to people who meet these requirements:

- Total and permanent disability for at least five months
- Disability expected to last for at least 12 months or end in death
- **Fully insured** and **disability insured** as defined under Social Security regulations

Fully insured means the individual has been credited with the appropriate number of quarters of coverage required by Social Security laws.

Disability insured means the individual is fully insured, has the required quarters of coverage, and meets the first two qualifications in the list above.

On the basis of these definitions, here are examples of two people who could qualify for Social Security benefits. Bill, who was totally and permanently disabled in an auto accident, is fully and disability insured. Mary has been totally and permanently disabled for six months and is not expected to live.

On the other hand, here are examples of two people who do not qualify for Social Security benefits. Lionel is 50% disabled from a military wound. Iona is fully and disability insured and disabled, but she expects to return to work after a nine-month recuperation period.

Benefits available are equal to 100% of the individual's **primary insurance amount (PIA)**, which is the amount the person would normally receive as a retirement benefit. After being entitled to disability benefits for two years, an individual may also receive Medicare benefits.

Social Security disability benefits are based on the level of a worker's earnings up to the time of disability. However, they are not designed to replace the entire amount of a worker's earnings. A worker's average earnings are reduced by a formula to calculate primary insurance amount. Benefit amounts are based on the PIA as follows.

- A disabled worker receives a benefit equal to 100% of PIA.
- A spouse caring for the worker's unmarried child who is under age 16 or was disabled before age 22 also receives a benefit, equal to 50% of the worker's PIA.
- Each unmarried child under age 18 (19 if in high school) or disabled before age 22 receives a benefit equal to 50% of the worker's PIA.

The total dollar amount a family may receive is capped by a maximum family benefit amount that is also based on the worker's average earnings. If the total amount a family is eligible for would exceed the maximum family benefit, the disabled worker receives the full amount for which the worker is eligible, but dependents' benefits are scaled back proportionately until the total amount equals the maximum family benefit. Social Security disability payments generally continue as long as the recipient cannot engage in any substantial gainful activity. This is essentially the same as the any-occupation definition discussed in a previous lesson.

Suppose that Lavonia, formerly a professional dance instructor, was disabled for 34 months. At the end of that period, she was well enough to work at a telephone answering service to pay her bills and fixed expenses. However, she will never again be able to teach dance. Even if Lavonia had qualified for Social Security disability payments previously, it is unlikely she will continue to qualify because she is able to engage in a substantial gainful activity. Whether she can resume her former occupation is not an issue in making this determination.

Exercise 23.C

Fill in the blanks in the following definition of Social Security Disability Income.

> Social Security disability benefits are available for workers who are _(1)_ disabled, who are considered __(2)__ under the rules of Social Security, whose disability is expected to last at least __(3)__ months or end in __(4)__, after a waiting period of __(5)__months.

1. ______ and ______
2. ______ _______
3. _____
4. _____
5. _____

Answers to the exercise can be found at the end of the Unit 23 answers and rationales.

23. 11 TRICARE

TRICARE is a regionally managed health care program for active duty and retired members of the military uniformed services and their families as well as survivors who are not eligible for Medicare. Participants choose among three health care options: TRICARE Standard, a fee-for-service plan; TRICARE Extra, a preferred provider plan; and TRICARE Prime, for those who seek care at military treatment facilities (MTFs).

23. 12 WORKERS' COMPENSATION

23. 12. 1 Types of Benefits

All state workers' compensation laws incorporate four categories of benefits:

- Disability (loss of income) benefits
- Medical benefits
- Survivor (death) benefits
- Rehabilitation benefits

Disability benefits compensate for loss of income or earning capacity suffered by individuals injured in their occupation. How and in what amounts benefits are paid depend on the severity and permanency of the injury.

Payments may be made on a weekly basis, a lump-sum basis, or some combination. For example, an employee temporarily off work with a broken leg will probably receive a weekly payment based on a percentage of regular wages, subject to an upper limit.

On the other hand, an employee who suffers a permanent loss, such as amputation of a limb, will probably receive a flat lump-sum payment based on a predetermined schedule in the state's workers' compensation law.

Some state laws prescribe both methods of payment for permanent injuries. It is important to be aware of your own state's workers' compensation provisions.

Medical benefits compensate for the cost of medical treatment resulting from job-related injury. In most cases, workers' compensation will pay for the full cost of this treatment.

Suppose an employee of Spaulding Mattress Manufacturers breaks a leg while on the job and is taken to a hospital to have it casted. The resulting hospital bills will be payable under workers' compensation medical benefits because the employee was injured on the job.

If this same employee had broken a leg in an accident while driving home from work, workers' compensation medical benefits would not apply because the injury was not job-related.

Survivor benefits attempt to compensate the widowed spouse or other survivor of an employee whose death results from a job-related injury. The amount of the benefit depends on:

- the deceased's earnings, subject to fixed minimums and maximums; and
- the number of surviving dependents.

A fixed amount is also available for burial expenses. Benefits normally extend until the spouse remarries or until the children become adults.

Rehabilitation benefits are not specifically named in some state workers' compensation acts. However, rehabilitation is provided in every state because all states accept the provisions of the Federal Vocational Rehabilitation Act, which provides federal aid toward the costs incurred.

Diligent rehabilitation and determination on the part of the disabled employee can make the difference between a partial disability and a total one. Rehabilitation for gainful employment serves to reduce insurance losses while restoring the injured worker's dignity. Therefore, rehabilitation is considered worthy of federal help.

Exercise 23.D

Match the definition to the title for the four principal benefits of workers' compensation.

____ 1. Compensates the widow or other dependent family member of an employee whose death results from a work-related injury

____ 2. Compensates for the cost of medical treatment resulting from a work-related injury

____ 3. Serves to reduce insurance losses while restoring the injured worker' dignity by preparing the worker to resume gainful employment

____ 4. Compensates for the loss of income or earning capacity suffered by individuals injured in their occupation

A. Disability income benefits

B. Medical benefits

C. Survivor benefits

D. Rehabilitation benefits

Answers to the exercise can be found at the end of the Unit 23 answers and rationales.

23. 12. 2 Compensable Injuries

To be considered compensable, as interpreted in workers' compensation law, an injury must meet three basic criteria.

- It must be accidental.
- It must arise out of the individual's employment.
- It must arise in the course of the individual's employment.

Accidental means that the injury was not intended to happen as far as the injured person is concerned. For example, injury resulting from falling from a loading dock would meet the criteria, whereas injury resulting from deliberately jumping from the loading dock would not.

The second requirement for a compensable injury is that it must arise out of employment. This means the employment must be the source of the accident. If Bud is a welder and is injured while welding on the job, the injury is compensable, provided the third criterion is also met.

The third criterion is that the injury must arise in the course of employment. The time, place, and circumstances of the accident are important in determining whether it results from the employment. If Bud from the previous paragraph were injured while welding at his place of employment but the injury occurred after hours while Bud was welding for his personal use, the injury would not be compensable.

23. 12. 3 Occupational Diseases

To be classified as an occupational disease under a workers' compensation law, the disease must meet these requirements:

- Arise out of employment
- Be due to causes or conditions characteristic of, and peculiar to, the particular trade, occupation, process, or employment

The requirement of peculiarity to a particular employment means that workers' compensation coverage does not apply for any ordinary diseases to which the general public is exposed.

It is possible that an employee might contract a disease that arises out of, and in the course of, employment but is not an occupational disease. Consider a heart attack, ulcers, or even alcoholism. These are not deemed occupational diseases, yet employment could have played a part in inducing any of them. Different states treat this type of situation differently; some states may award compensation, and others may not.

If a chemical engineer develops a throat disease caused by working with toxic materials in his employer's laboratory, this would likely qualify as an occupational disease. However, if a school teacher develops bronchitis in the classroom, this probably is not an occupational disease, even if the teacher was exposed to students with bronchitis. Bronchitis is a condition to which the general public is exposed.

All states mandate coverage for most occupational diseases as part of the workers' compensation system. In most states, occupational diseases are eligible for the same compensation that applies to occupational injuries.

23. 12. 4 Types of Disability

Four types of disability are defined under workers' compensation law:

- Permanent total
- Permanent partial
- Temporary total
- Temporary partial

The difference between permanent and temporary is as simple as it appears: it will last forever, or it will not last forever.

The difference between total and partial depends on the disabled person's ability to work. If a worker is disabled to the extent that the worker cannot perform any job, this is considered a total disability.

On the other hand, if a worker is disabled but able to perform some job (even if it is not the same as the previous employment), then this is considered a partial disability. You'll recognize the parallels between these definitions and those of *own occupation* and *any occupation* discussed in the lesson covering income insurance.

Now let's look individually at each of the four types of disability.

A **permanent total disability** usually results in a complete and permanent loss of earning power, with no ability to perform gainful employment. Many state compensation laws specify that certain injuries, such as total loss of sight or loss of both hands or both feet, constitute permanent total regardless of the insured's ability to do some type of work.

Tanika, a research physicist, permanently loses her eyesight when a batch of chemicals in the laboratory explodes in her face. She suffers a permanent total disability.

A **permanent partial disability** usually refers to a permanent physical impairment that leaves the individual incapable of performing the previous regular job, yet results in only partial loss of earning power because other jobs may be performed. In other words, the employee may be able to perform some other type of work.

Simon, a machinist, severs his leg when it is caught in a machine. Simon can no longer perform his former job, but he has had experience as a dispatcher and has been transferred to that position within his company. This is a permanent partial disability.

A **temporary total disability** usually refers to a total disability that lasts for a short period, after which the employee is fully able to return to work. For example, Andre strains his back while lifting heavy boxes at work. He is in traction and off work for five months before he is able to resume his former job.

A **temporary partial disability** usually refers to a temporary disablement that allows the employee to continue the same job, but with a diminished capability. Francesca, who is a photographer and a graphic designer, twists her ankle and is unable to shoot on location. However, she can complete a graphic illustration for her client, so she is only partially disabled and will be temporarily disabled only until her ankle heals.

UNIT TEST

1. Which of the following individuals is least likely to be eligible for Medicare?
   A. Mannie, who is 65 and just registered for his Social Security benefits
   B. Margaret, who is not eligible for Social Security, but is willing to pay a fee for her insurance
   C. Karl, who has been diagnosed with end-stage liver disease
   D. Genevieve, who has been receiving benefits from Social Security for 3 years

2. Under Medicare Part B, individuals pay a deductible each
   A. benefit period
   B. week
   C. month
   D. year

3. After the deductible is satisfied, Part B pays what percentage of all approved charges?
   A. 10%
   B. 20%
   C. 80%
   D. 100%

4. Doctors and suppliers who agree to accept the amount Medicare will pay are said to have agreed to
   A. payment
   B. assignment
   C. assessment
   D. capitation

5. All of the following outpatient services are covered under Part B EXCEPT
   A. artificial limbs
   B. emergency room services
   C. most immunizations
   D. physical therapy

6. Which of the following outpatient services is excluded from Part B coverage?
   A. Casts and splints
   B. Laboratory tests billed by hospitals
   C. Medically necessary ambulance services
   D. Hearing exams

7. The Original Medicare Plan consists of
   A. Medicare Part A
   B. Medicare Part B
   C. Medicare Parts A and B
   D. Medicare Parts C and D

8. Michelle is 65 and starting to receive Social Security benefits. To receive Medicare Part A, she needs to
   A. fill out an enrollment form at her local Social Security office
   B. pay a monthly premium
   C. prove eligibility
   D. do nothing

9. The annual general enrollment period for Medicare Part B begins on
   A. January 1
   B. March 1
   C. March 31
   D. July 1

10. Does Medicare pay all medical costs for its beneficiaries?
    A. Yes
    B. No

11. Some kind of supplement to Medicare is needed by almost everyone covered by Medicare. Which of the following individuals would NOT need Medicare supplement insurance?
    A. George, whose medical conditions are currently under control
    B. Ken, whose income is low enough to qualify him for help from Medicaid
    C. Carl, whose net worth is high enough to cover any medical bills that might incur
    D. Larry, who has high blood pressure that is controlled with medication

12. Medicare SELECT policies offer _______________ coverage, compared with standard Medigap policies.
    A. the same
    B. more extensive
    C. less extensive
    D. unlimited

13. Which type of policy requires use of approved doctors and hospitals to receive benefits?
    A. Medicare SELECT
    B. Standard Medigap policies
    C. Both A and B
    D. Neither A nor B

14. Medicare supplement policies are also known as
    A. Medicare policies
    B. Medigap policies
    C. Medicaid policies
    D. Medichoice policies

15. All of the following statements about Medigap insurance are correct EXCEPT
    A. Medigap policies are available through Medicare
    B. Medigap policies are sold by private insurance companies
    C. Medigap policies were standardized by the NAIC
    D. Medigap Plan A covers basic benefits

16. Which of the following benefits are NOT required in any Medicare supplement policy?
    A. Skilled nursing care benefit that covers the Part A co-payments for the 21st through the 100th day of skilled nursing facility care
    B. Part A co-payments for the 61st through the 90th day of hospitalization
    C. Part B co-payments on Medicare-approved charges for physician's and medical services
    D. All charges for 365 days of hospitalization after all Part A inpatient hospital and lifetime reserve days are used up

17. Which of the following individuals is NOT likely to be eligible for Medicaid?
    A. Pam, a single mom who relies on Aid to Families with Dependent Children to help feed her family
    B. Darrell, who has been unable to work since becoming blind 2 years ago
    C. Carmen, who has not been able to work since losing both legs in an accident
    D. Ginny, who is over 65 and working as a manager of a retail outlet

18. Fully insured and disability insured are defined by
    A. state legislatures
    B. Social Security regulations
    C. individual insurers
    D. state departments of insurance

19. Under Social Security benefits, disabled workers receive a benefit equal to
    A. their earnings at the time of the disability
    B. 66% of their earnings at the time of the disability
    C. their preferred insurance amount
    D. their primary insurance amount

20. Carla is 67 and eligible for Social Security and Medicare. When she comes out of retirement to work at a large corporation that provides health benefits
    A. her private benefits become secondary to Medicare benefits
    B. her Medicare benefits become secondary to her private benefits
    C. the employer is not required to offer her private benefits
    D. she will cease to be eligible for Medicare benefits

21. Medicare is administered by
    A. the Social Security Administration
    B. individual state governments
    C. the Centers for Medicare and Medicaid Services (CMS)
    D. the Health Care Focus Association

22. Medicare Part A covers all of the following EXCEPT
    A. charges for a private room
    B. skilled nursing facility care
    C. home health care
    D. hospice care

23. For each benefit period, Medicare will pay the full cost of up to how many days of hospital care?
    A. 30
    B. 60
    C. 90
    D. 365

24. Medicare will pay the entire cost for skilled nursing facility care for the first
    A. 0 days
    B. 20 days
    C. 80 days
    D. 100 days

25. Individuals who are eligible for Social Security benefits become eligible for Medicare Part A benefits as of
    A. the day they become eligible for Social Security benefits
    B. the first day of the month in which they become eligible for Social Security benefits
    C. the day they turn 65
    D. the first day of the month in which they turn 65

26. Medicare Part A provides coverage for all of the following kinds of care EXCEPT
    A. private-duty nursing
    B. skilled nursing facility care
    C. home health care
    D. hospice care

27. Medicare Part B provides coverage for all of the following kinds of care EXCEPT
    A. skilled nursing facility care not covered by Part A
    B. doctors' services
    C. home health care not covered by Part A
    D. outpatient medical services and supplies

28. Which of the following Medicare supplement plans covers the Part A and Part B deductible?
    A. Plan B
    B. Plan C
    C. Plan D
    D. Plan E

29. Which of the following Medicare supplement plans covers the Part B excess at 80%?
    A. Plan E
    B. Plan F
    C. Plan G
    D. Plan H

30. Which of the following statements about Medicare supplement plans is NOT true?
    A. Benefits must automatically change to coincide with changes in Medicare deductibles and co-payments.
    B. Losses resulting from sickness may not be treated differently than losses resulting from accidents.
    C. The definition of accident may employ an accidental means test.
    D. Policies must be at least guaranteed renewable.

31. To be compensable as interpreted in workers' compensation law, an injury must meet all of the following criteria EXCEPT
    A. it must be accidental
    B. it must arise out of the individual's employment
    C. it must arise in the course of the individual's employment
    D. it must be unforeseeable

32. Juanita is employed in California. She takes a business trip to Colorado to demonstrate some techniques to workers in another facility and is injured in the process. Her workers' compensation benefits will be paid according to the laws of
    A. California
    B. Colorado
    C. whichever state would provide the greater benefit
    D. whichever state would provide the lesser benefit

ANSWERS AND RATIONALES TO UNIT TEST

1. **C.** An individual diagnosed with permanent kidney failure (not end-stage liver disease) would be eligible for Medicare.

2. **D.** Part B deductibles are annual.

3. **C.** After the deductible is satisfied, Part B pays 80% of all approved charges.

4. **B.** Doctors and suppliers who agree to accept the amount Medicare will pay are said to have agreed to assignment.

5. **C.** Part B excludes immunizations.

6. **D.** Hearing exams are excluded from Part B coverage.

7. **C.** Part A and B made up the Original Medicare Plan.

8. **D.** To receive Medicare Part A, she needs to do nothing.

9. **A.** The annual general enrollment period for Medicare Part B begins on January 1.

10. **B.** Medicare has deductibles and coinsurance features.

11. **B.** Low-income people eligible for Medicaid do not need Medicare supplement insurance.

12. **A.** Compared with standard Medigap policies, Medicare SELECT policies offer the same coverage, but the coverage is delivered by hospitals and doctors.

13. **A.** Medicare SELECT policies require the use of approved doctors and hospitals to receive benefits.

14. **B.** A Medicare supplement is also known as Medigap.

15. **A.** Medigap policies are not available through Medicare.

16. **A.** A skilled nursing care benefit covering the Part A co-payments for the 21st through the 100th day of skilled nursing facility care is not required in any Medicare supplement policy.

17. **D.** Medicaid is not age related; it is lack of income related.

18. **B.** Fully insured and disability insured are defined by Social Security regulations.

19. **D.** Under Social Security benefits, a disabled worker receives a benefit equal to the worker's primary insurance amount.

20. **B.** If an individual is eligible for group insurance through a large group and Medicare, Medicare becomes the secondary payor.

21. **C.** Medicare is administered by the CMS, which is part of the Health Care Financing Administration.

22. **A.** Medicare Part A does not cover charges for a private room.

23. **B.** For each benefit period, Medicare will pay the full cost of up to 60 days of hospital care.

24. **B.** Medicare will pay the entire cost for skilled nursing facility care for the first 20 days.

25. **D.** Individuals who are eligible for Social Security benefits become eligible for Medicare Part A benefits as of the first day of the month when they turn 65.

26. **A.** Medicare Part A does not cover private-duty nursing.

27. **A.** Medicare Part B does not cover skilled nursing facility care not covered by Part A.

28. **B.** Medicare supplement plan C covers the Part A and Part B deductible.

29. **C.** Medicare supplement plan G covers the Part B excess at 80%.

30. **C.** The definition of accident may not employ an accidental means test.

31. **D.** The injury need not be unforeseeable.

32. **A.** Her workers' compensation benefits will be paid according to the laws of California.

UNIT 23 EXERCISE ANSWERS

Exercise 23.A

1. **C.**
2. **B.**
3. **E.**
4. **D.**
5. **A.**

Exercise 23.B

1. **T**
2. **F**
3. **T**
4. **F**

Exercise 23.C

1. Totally and permanently
2. Fully insured
3. 12
4. Death
5. 5

Exercise 23.D

1. **C.**
2. **B.**
3. **D.**
4. **A.**

24

Long-Term Care

24. 1 INTRODUCTION

Better medical care means many individuals are living into their 80s, 90s, and beyond. Unfortunately, although life expectancy has increased, many older individuals have serious health problems that keep them from living on their own or completely caring for themselves. Long-term care pays for the kind of care needed by individuals who have chronic illnesses or disabilities. It often covers the cost of nursing home care and provides coverage for home-based care—visiting nurses, chore services, and respite care for daily caregivers who need time away from these difficult duties. Such coverage becomes important when one considers that the annual cost for nursing home confinement can reach $67,000 or more.

Many people believe Medicare or Medicare supplement policies will pay for this care if they need it. Medicare will cover nursing home care if it is part of the treatment for a covered injury or illness, but care needed because of aging is not covered by Medicare or Medicare supplements. Medicare and supplementary insurance pay for skilled nursing care, but the coverage is extremely limited (the care must immediately follow a period of hospital confinement, and no benefits are provided after the 100th day). Medicaid does pay for nursing home care but provides coverage only for needy families. Sadly, many people must pay for their own nursing home care and eventually turn to Medicaid when their life savings are gone.

24. 2 LEARNING OBJECTIVES

After completing this lesson, you will be able to:

- explain the purpose of long-term care (LTC) insurance;
- explain who is eligible for LTC insurance;
- list and describe the different care levels covered under LTC policies;
- explain how benefit amounts are generally defined in an LTC policy;
- define activities of daily living, and explain how they affect LTC policies; and
- describe the standards required of qualified LTC plans.

24. 3 HISTORY OF LTC COVERAGE

The earliest long-term care policies were relatively more restrictive than the current generation of plans, often requiring prior hospitalization and a level of service greater than mere custodial care. Many covered care in a nursing facility only, rather than also providing coverage for services in the home of the individual or in an adult day care center. Most excluded Alzheimer's and dementia—two common illnesses of the elderly and the reason many older persons require such care.

Some long-term care policies were so closely tied to Medicare's restrictions that they paid little that Medicare did not already pay. During the early development period, policies often had so many restrictions that few insureds qualified for payment of benefits.

LTC policies are still evolving. However, with attention to the problem of long-term care firmly focused, legislators and the insurance industry have begun to come to grips with the far-reaching ramifications of health services for an older population. With the federal government responding to consumer interests in long-term care coverages, the National Association of Insurance Commissioners (NAIC) developed a model to help state legislatures in an effort to keep regulation on a state level. More than half of the states currently use the NAIC or a similar model. Key issues include the following:

- A benefit period of at least one year
- Strict restrictions on cancellation, specifically prohibiting cancellation because of the insured's aging; most policies now guarantee renewability
- Standards for covering preexisting conditions
- A free-look period
- Prohibition of exclusions for Alzheimer's disease

Another factor in the evolution and increasing availability of LTC policies is that consumers, too, are more aware that:

- Medicare does not cover long-term care (much to the surprise of most of the population, who at one time believed Medicare did cover most nursing home care);
- one in four people are likely to spend at least some time in a nursing home after age 65, increasing to about one in three if they live to age 85; and
- the average cost for nursing home confinement is currently about $3,300 per month and can be as high as $5,000 per month, depending on location and level of care. These costs are likely to continue growing.

The increased knowledge of insurance buyers has played a part in the development and refinement of LTC policies. In addition, law changes have clarified the tax status of long-term care policies, which now are treated like accident and health policies. Proceeds of qualified long-term care policies are generally received income tax free, and premiums may be deductible as a medical expense, within certain limitations. Federal law now determines what constitutes a qualified long-term care policy eligible for these tax advantages. The law spells out when benefits must be paid and what options must be offered to prospects for long-term care insurance.

Note, however, that insurers are not required to offer and consumers are not required to purchase qualified long-term care policies. Nonqualified policies may offer benefits that are more attractive or easier to obtain than qualified policies and may be more desirable to certain consumers even if the nonqualified policies do not offer the tax advantages of qualified policies.

24. 4 WHO NEEDS LTC INSURANCE?

LTC insurance enables qualified individuals to maintain their independence. With adequate coverage, the individual does not have to rely on friends or family to provide custodial needs or necessary funds to help defray the costs of a nursing home stay.

Protection of personal assets may be the most important reason for purchasing LTC insurance. Possibly, the question isn't, "Can I afford to buy LTC insurance?" but rather, "Can I afford not to purchase LTC insurance?"

When an individual has substantial financial assets (and retirement income), the possibility that LTC expenses could mean a significant reduction in the person's assets and standard of living is a real threat. Thus, the purchase of LTC insurance to protect one's personal financial resources may be a wise financial decision.

24. 5 PROBABILITY OF NEEDING CARE

It is estimated that by the year 2030, there will be more than 64 million Americans age 65 and over.

In addition, life expectancy is increasing in the United States. People reaching 65 today can expect to live 10 or even 20 years in retirement. These retirees will face a greater potential need for long-term medical care simply because of longer life expectancy.

The likelihood of a nursing home confinement increases as age increases. By 2050, it is expected that over 20 million Americans 65 or older will need long-term care.

24. 6 OPTIONS OTHER THAN INSURANCE

What are the available options for the senior citizen facing a stay in a nursing home? Following are some of the alternatives:

- Using personal assets
- Depending on relatives
- Depending on government programs

Depending on friends and relatives for custodial care may not be practical because of changing socioeconomic trends. Today's family is no longer a cohesive unit but a fragmented group; family members live great distances from each other.

The Medicare program is not designed to provide custodial care. It will cover a limited amount of rehabilitative care in a skilled nursing facility approved by Medicare. Because Medicare will pay only for rehabilitative services, it requires prior hospitalization before admission to the skilled nursing facility. Another avenue is Medicaid, which requires the individual to prove financial need. This normally requires that the individual get rid of financial resources and spend down to a poverty level to obtain Medicaid eligibility. The Health Care Financing Administration reports that about one-half of all Medicaid spending goes to people who had financial resources when they entered a nursing home but reached the poverty level while in the nursing home.

24. 7 RATING FACTORS

One way in which LTC policies differ from other health plans concerns how risks are rated. Although people afflicted with heart disease or diabetes, for example, would be rated as substandard risks under most health insurance plans, LTC policies, because of their focus on aging people, use a different means of classification. The key for LTC policies is whether an individual can perform the activities of daily living (ADLs) and, if so, with what degree of proficiency. ADLs include such things as dressing, bathing, eating, walking, and similar activities to care for oneself. Thus, an individual who has a heart disease but is still able to perform ADLs is a standard risk under LTC policies.

Example

Corey, age 60, has had several strokes during the past five years but is completely capable of performing the activities of daily living. Under a major medical policy, it is likely that Corey would be classified as a substandard risk. Under an LTC policy, Corey would be classified as a standard risk.

Exercise 24.A

Mark the following statements as true (T) or false (F).

____ 1. Medicare provides skilled nursing care incident to a period of hospitalization for up to 100 days per benefit period.

____ 2. Medicaid provides LTC benefits for all retired workers over age 65.

____ 3. Consumers are now required to purchase LTC coverage.

____ 4. One-half of all Medicaid spending goes to people who consumed all their resources and became impoverished while in a nursing home.

Answers to the exercises can be found at the end of the Unit 24 answers and rationales.

24. 8 TYPES OF BENEFITS

Three terms regarding the type of long-term care an individual requires are important to understand in order to determine what an LTC policy covers.

- **Skilled nursing care** is nursing and rehabilitative care that is required daily and can be performed only by skilled medical practitioners on a doctor's orders.

- **Intermediate care** is nursing and rehabilitative care that is required occasionally and can be performed only by skilled medical practitioners on a doctor's orders.
- **Custodial or residential care** is help in performing ADLs and can be performed by someone without medical skills or training, but still must be based on a doctor's orders.

Of these, custodial, or residential, care is the type most elderly people will require at some time in their later years, and it is also the type that is not covered by Medicare.

Other important terms are as follows:

- **Home health care** refers to services performed from time to time in the individual's home. It may include skilled nursing, various types of therapy, help with ADLs, and help with housework.
- **Adult day care** provides company, supervision, and social and recreational support during the day for people who live at home and need assistance. This service is especially useful for those who are cared for by relatives who work during the day.

Exercise 24.B

Match the following types of skilled nursing care to the appropriate definition.

_____ 1. Skilled nursing care

_____ 2. Intermediate care

_____ 3. Custodial care

_____ 4. Home health care

_____ 5. Adult day care

A. Provides companionship, supervision, and socialization during the day

B. Assistance with the activities of daily living performed by unskilled helpers

C. Medical or rehabilitative care performed by skilled medical personnel on a continuous basis

D. Medical or rehabilitative care performed on an intermittent basis

E. Both medical and non-medical care, including housework

Answers to the exercises can be found at the end of the Unit 24 answers and rationales.

24.9 COMMON PROVISIONS

Now that you understand some of the terms and concepts involved in long-term care policies, let's look at provisions that are commonly included in these coverages. You might also want to glance back at the NAIC model requirements for comparison purposes.

Currently, most LTC policies include provisions or options to include those described in the following paragraphs.

24.9.1 Eligibility

What are the youngest and oldest ages at which LTC policies may be purchased? Most minimum ages range between 50 and 60 years, but more recent policies may include a much lower minimum age, including some as low as age 18. Upper age limits at which policies may be purchased range from age 69 to 89.

24.9.2 Renewability

Virtually all of the current generation of LTC policies are guaranteed renewable and cannot be canceled except for nonpayment of premium. The insurer cannot cancel the policy but does reserve the right to increase premiums in accordance with the policy provisions. If the premiums are to be increased, they will be changed on the policy anniversary, and the increased premium will be for an entire class of insureds, not just a single individual.

Some LTC policies are noncancelable, which means the insured has the right to continue the coverage by timely payment of premiums, and the insurer has no right to make any change in policy provisions, cannot decline to renew, and cannot change the premium rate at renewal for any reason.

24.9.3 Premiums

Similar to life insurance, premiums are generally based on when an individual purchases this insurance. The younger the individual is at the time of purchase, the lower the premium. In addition, premiums will fluctuate according to the elimination and benefit periods selected—the longer the elimination period, the lower the premium; the longer the benefit period, the higher the premium. Finally, premium variations may result from underwriting considerations. Underwriters consider risk factors, including an applicant's current ability to perform activities of daily living. The premium will be higher if an applicant needs assistance with an ADL at the time of application than it would be if the applicant did not need such assistance.

24.9.4 Waiver of Premium

Nearly all LTC policies include a waiver of premium provision that takes effect after the insured has been confined for a specified period of time. The usual period is 90 days, but it is as long as 180 days in some policies. A few policies have no such provision, which means the insured will be required to continue premium payments no matter how long care continues. When waiver of premium applies, premium payment generally resumes when the care ceases.

24. 9. 5 Prior Hospitalization

Formerly, most nursing home policies required a hospital stay before confinement to a nursing home in order for benefits to be paid. This is no longer the case.

24. 9. 6 Care Level

This refers to whether the policy pays only if skilled nursing, intermediate, or custodial care, as specified in the policy, is required at the time the individual enters the nursing home. This is extremely important, since some policies pay only if intermediate or skilled care is involved, whereas custodial care, which is the most common type required by elders, may not be included. The best policies are those that will pay regardless of the level of care.

24. 9. 7 Hospice Care

Hospice care is often offered as an optional benefit under LTC policies. The primary focus of hospice care is pain control, comfort, and counseling for the terminally ill patient and the patient's family. A hospice is simply a facility whose purpose is to help terminally ill patients die with dignity and with as little suffering as possible. Typically, the expenses incurred in a hospice will be room and board and medication for pain.

24. 9. 8 Respite Care

Respite care is normally associated with hospice care. With this benefit, the patient is admitted to a nursing home for needed care for a short period, or the LTC policy will cover the cost of replacing for a short period (a day or weekend perhaps) the primary care giver, usually a family member, who is looking after an elderly person in the home.

24. 9. 9 Home Health Care

Most LTC policies now cover home health care as an alternative to nursing home care. Home health care is provided in the individual's home and must begin within a prescribed period following a nursing home stay. Usually, the home health care benefit under the policy will be 60% of the regular daily nursing home benefit. Home health care is an extension of intermediate custodial care. The patient is in need of some health care but is able to generally function without the need to be confined to a nursing home. Home health care might include physical therapy and some custodial care, such as meal preparation.

24. 9. 10 Adult Day Care

LTC policies also increasingly make provision for adult day care to allow primary caregivers who work the opportunity to tend to their employment responsibilities. The day care may be provided in the home or in an adult day care facility. Adult day care is basically social and health care services for functionally impaired adults. This benefit provides reimbursement for expenses pertaining to an adult day care center such as a neighborhood recreational center, a community center, and others. Typically, adult day care includes transportation to and from a day care center and a variety of health, social, and related activities. This care usually also includes meals and certain medical services. Specialized care for patients with Alzheimer's is usually included in adult day care benefits.

24. 9. 11 Professional Care Advisor

Coverage may be provided for the services of a care coordinator to help design the most appropriate plan of treatment.

24. 9. 12 Benefit Amount

The prospective insured may be offered a choice of the maximum daily benefit amount for a nursing home stay or covered home health care. Naturally, higher daily benefits mean higher annual premiums.

Most LTC policies provide a daily benefit during confinement. Traditionally, this benefit has been provided as a maximum daily amount (reimbursement for charges up to the stated limit, but not more than the daily limit). Benefit amounts range from $50 per day to $150 or $200 per day. However, some insurers provide coverage on an expense-incurred basis (full reimbursement for the actual charges incurred). The maximum policy benefit may be calculated by multiplying the daily benefit by the number of days in the benefit period.

To illustrate these points, let's use the example of Kim, who has an LTC policy with a 30-day elimination period, a daily benefit of $75 per day, and a two-year benefit period. Her maximum policy benefit is $54,750 ($75 a day times 730 days). If Kim is confined to a nursing home for a total of seven months, her benefit calculation will be as follows:

- First 30 days: no benefit paid (elimination period)
- Next six months: $75 per day (assumes 30-day month)
- $75 × 180 = $13,500

If Kim's actual charges were more than $75 per day, she would have to pay the additional amount.

Most policies specify the dollar amount per day that will be paid for skilled nursing care. Some policies may include sublimits for special types of care or services (e.g., home health care or adult day care). The benefit for home health care or adult day care is usually a fixed percentage of the specified daily benefit, usually 50%. In addition, there may be a deductible amount that must be satisfied before the policy begins to pay.

24. 9. 13 Benefit Periods

LTC policies vary as to the maximum period for which benefits will be paid, usually from three to five years. Some policies offer unlimited benefit periods. Some policies may contain both a benefit period per stay plus a lifetime maximum benefit period. The benefit period may also end when a maximum amount has been paid out.

24. 9. 14 Exclusions

Each policy should be read carefully to determine what is excluded. A major stride in current policies is that most now cover Alzheimer's disease and organic-based mental illness, both of which formerly were often excluded. However, some exclusions remain. Among these are war and acts of war, alcohol or drug dependency, self-inflicted injuries, mental illness and nervous disorders without a demonstrable organic cause, and treatment provided without cost to the insured (such as that received in a veteran's hospital).

24. 9. 15 Preexisting Conditions

Most—but not all—LTC policies do not cover conditions that existed during the six months before the policy effective date. A few policies have no such exclusion.

24. 9. 16 Elimination Period

Similar to a disability income policy, no LTC benefits will be paid until the elimination period is satisfied. Most long-term care policies provide for a period, usually expressed in days or months, at the beginning of a confinement in a long-term care facility, during which no benefits are payable. The elimination period could be defined as a "time deductible." The elimination period could be 30 days or longer. Thus, after the insured is confined to a nursing home for a period of 30 days, LTC benefits begin.

The longer the waiting period, the lower the premium, all other facts being equal. The waiting period can be viewed as the deductible in an LTC policy.

24. 10 BENEFIT TRIGGERS

24. 10. 1 Activities of Daily Living

ADLs are functions or activities that are performed by individuals without assistance, thus allowing personal independence in everyday living. These functions are used as measurement standards to determine the level of personal functioning capacity. Examples of ADLs would include:

- mobility (or transferring)—the ability to walk;

- dressing—being able to adequately clothe one's self;
- personal hygiene—being able to go to and from the toilet and remain continent;
- eating—being able to take in food; and
- bathing.

An individual who cannot accommodate these needs will need some type of care.

Some LTC policies base eligibility for nursing home benefits on the inability to perform some of the activities of daily living in lieu of sickness or injury. These contracts do not require prior hospitalization or that the insured be admitted to a nursing facility as a result of sickness or injury. Federal standards that determine whether an LTC policy is tax qualified also base eligibility on ADLs.

24. 10. 2 Cognitive Impairment

This means a deficiency in the ability to think, perceive, reason, or remember, which results in the inability of individuals to take care of themselves without the assistance or supervision of another person. LTC policies may base eligibility for nursing home benefits on cognitive impairment.

24. 10. 3 Medical Necessity

An LTC policy by definition provides coverage only for medically necessary diagnostic, therapeutic, rehabilitative, maintenance, or personal care services.

24. 11 QUALIFIED PLANS

A qualified long-term care policy must stipulate that the insured be incapable of performing at least two of the ADLs without assistance for at least 90 days to qualify for benefits. The cognitively impaired must require substantial supervision. A physician must certify that the insured is chronically ill and provide a plan of care. A long-term care policy will not be qualified if it does not conform to these standards.

Remember, however, that nonqualified long-term care policies do not have to conform to these federal standards. A nonqualified policy, for example, might require that the insured need assistance with only one ADL with no stipulated time period in order to be eligible for policy benefits. The prospective insured's concern over qualification for benefits must be weighed against tax consequences when considering qualified versus nonqualified long-term care policies.

24. 12 REGULATION

Just as with Medicare supplement insurance, long-term care policies are heavily regulated by the state Insurance Departments. States frequently regulate minimum standards, renewability, the insured's right to return the policy, replacement, marketing standards, and the appropriateness of recommending the purchase of LTC insurance. As with Medicare supplement insurance, frequently the delivery of a buyers guide and outline of coverage is mandatory.

Federal law allows the sale of long-term care coverage that "substantially" duplicates that provided under Medicare or Medicaid (but not multiple policies) to Medicare beneficiaries, provided the company discloses the duplication and the policy pays without regard to other benefits.

24. 13 EMERGING LTC ISSUES

Long-term care insurance is still in an evolutionary state. There are literally hundreds of individual contracts, which have not been standardized like Medicare supplement policies. Some emerging issues in the LTC field include inflation protection and nonforfeiture provisions. New federal standards that determine whether an LTC policy is tax qualified require consumer protections, such as the offer of inflation protection and nonforfeiture provisions, as well as imposing additional disclosure requirements.

24. 13. 1 Inflation Protection

Many states require that insurers offer optional inflation protection at the time of policy purchase. The feature must increase benefit levels annually, cover a specific percentage of actual or reasonable charges, or allow the insured to periodically increase benefit levels without needing to provide evidence of continued insurability.

24. 13. 2 Nonforfeiture Provisions

These protect the policyholder from forfeiting all policy values or benefits when the policyowner stops paying premiums and lapses the policy for any reason. Standard nonforfeiture options may include cash surrender value (a lump sum payable upon policy surrender), reduced paid-up insurance (a reduced daily benefit payable for the policy's benefit period with no further premium payments required), or extended term insurance (a limited extension of coverage for the full amount of policy benefits, without further premium payments required). Nonforfeiture provisions are not commonly included in LTC policies but are beginning to appear in some contracts.

24. 14 MARKETING LTC COVERAGE

In addition to individual LTC policies, a growing number of insurers offer group LTC plans with provisions similar to those mentioned previously. Still, a third marketing device involves attaching an LTC rider to a life insurance policy called an accelerated benefits rider or a living benefits rider.

Accelerated benefits may be available to insureds who are chronically ill and need money for long-term care. Such riders are subject to the same rules as individual long-term care policies, especially with respect to benefit triggers. They also may be designed to cover home health care and nursing home care. Adding an accelerated benefits rider to a life policy costs money in the form of additional premium.

How much may be paid by such a rider varies from policy to policy. Some limit benefits to 50 or 75% of the policy's face value. Others place an absolute ceiling on the amount paid out: for example, $250,000. All, however, take into consideration any outstanding loans against the policy. Payments are ordinarily made to the insured on some kind of periodic basis. Naturally, any accelerated benefits paid out are subtracted from the death benefit paid to the beneficiary when the insured dies.

UNIT TEST

1. Nursing home care is generally covered by
   A. Medicare
   B. Medicare supplements
   C. long-term care policies
   D. all of the above

2. Which of the following would be least likely to be a good candidate for an LTC policy?
   A. George, whose law practice has allowed him to fund a generous retirement fund for himself and his wife
   B. Nina, a single mother whose financial struggles raising her children have left her with few assets and no independent retirement savings
   C. Carla, whose 25 years of civil service have provided a generous retirement, but who worries about the legacy she will leave her children
   D. Darrell, whose inherited estate has provided him with over $6 million in net worth

3. An individual age 65 or older has what chance of being confined to a nursing home?
   A. 25%
   B. 50%
   C. 75%
   D. 90%

4. Early long-term care policies were
   A. more restrictive than current policies
   B. less restrictive than current policies
   C. the same as current policies
   D. prohibited by law

5. Which of the following individuals is most likely to be rated a substandard risk under an LTC policy?
   A. Gerald, who lives alone and has no trouble taking care of himself, but who has been diagnosed with an inoperable brain aneurysm that, if it bursts, would almost certainly kill him immediately
   B. Ken, who is on medication to bring down his blood pressure, but who gets around and takes care of himself easily
   C. Brenda, whose diabetes is under control
   D. Garrison, who has been diagnosed with early-stage Alzheimer's disease

6. Which of the following is the type of care most people will require at some time during their later years?
   A. Inpatient hospital care
   B. Skilled nursing care
   C. Custodial or residential care
   D. Intermediate care

7. Virtually all of the current LTC policies are guaranteed renewable. This means the insurer cannot cancel the policy
   A. but does reserve the right to increase policy premiums on specified classes of policies
   B. but does reserve the right to increase policy premiums on individual policies
   C. or increase policy premiums on specified classes of policies
   D. or increase policy premiums on individual policies

8. When waiver of premium applies
   A. the premium is waived immediately upon disability
   B. the premium payment is suspended permanently once it is invoked
   C. the premium payment generally resumes when care ceases
   D. the premium payment is waived only if disability is considered permanent and total

9. Typically, the expenses incurred in a hospice will be
   A. surgical and room and board
   B. room and board and physical therapy
   C. surgical and physical therapy
   D. room and board and medication for pain

10. The elimination period may be thought of as
   A. a dollar amount deductible
   B. a time deductible
   C. a dollar amount co-payment
   D. a time co-payment

11. Which of the following is NOT considered an activity of daily living?
   A. Transferring
   B. Dressing
   C. Bathing
   D. Working

ANSWERS AND RATIONALES TO UNIT TEST

1. **C.** Nursing home care is generally covered by long-term care policies.

2. **B.** A good candidate for an LTC policy has substantial financial assets to protect.

3. **A.** An individual age 65 or older has a 25% chance of being confined to a nursing home.

4. **A.** Early long term care policies were more restrictive and harder to qualify for.

5. **D.** LTC policies rate risks according to how well the individual can perform ADLs.

6. **C.** Most people will require custodial or residential care at some time during their later years.

7. **A.** Guaranteed renewable means the insurer cannot cancel the policy but does reserve the right to increase policy premiums on specified classes of policies.

8. **C.** When waiver of premium applies, the premium payment generally resumes when care ceases.

9. **D.** Typically, the expenses incurred in a hospice will be room and board and medication for pain.

10. **B.** The elimination period may be thought of as a time deductible.

11. **D.** Working is not an activity of daily living.

UNIT 24 EXERCISE ANSWERS

Exercise 24.A

1. **T**
2. **F**
3. **F**
4. **T**

Exercise 24.B

1. **C.**
2. **D.**
3. **B.**
4. **E.**
5. **A.**

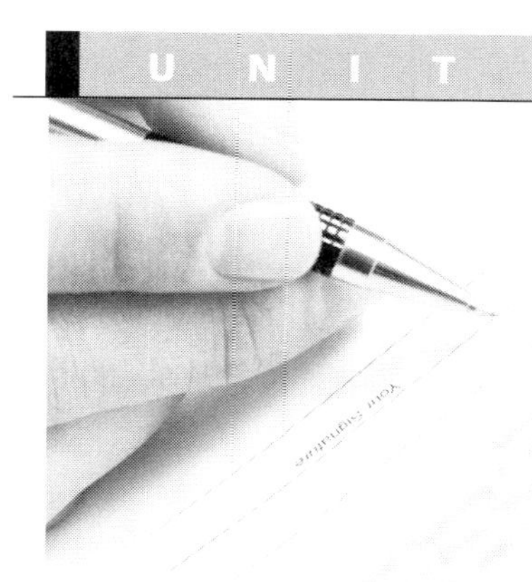

UNIT

25

Health Insurance and Taxation

25. 1 INTRODUCTION

To understand how health insurance is taxed, we need to organize coverage into the following groups:

- Individually owned
- Group
- Sole proprietors and partners
- Business

Then we'll discuss the taxation of disability insurance, Medicare Supplement insurance, and long-term care insurance. We'll conclude by addressing the taxation of government health programs.

25. 2 LEARNING OBJECTIVES

After completing this lesson, you will be able to:

- explain how the various types of health insurance are taxed, when premiums are deductible, and when the benefits are taxed;
- explain when and how disability insurance premiums and benefits are taxed; and
- explain when and how Medicare supplement and long-term care insurance premiums and benefits are taxed.

25. 3 TAXATION OF HEALTH INSURANCE POLICIES

25. 3. 1 Individual Policies

The premiums for individually owned accident, health, disability, or long-term care policies generally are not deductible to the individual taxpayer. However, if the taxpayer's medical expenses exceed 10% of adjusted gross income during a taxable year, any medical expenses, including premiums for accident and health insurance (but not disability insurance), incurred above the 10% threshold can be deducted. For long-term care insurance, there is an annual dollar limit for deductions. This limit is based on the taxpayer's age. Benefits paid by individually owned accident, health, disability, or long-term care policies generally are received income-tax free by the taxpayer, provided the benefits do not exceed actual expenses.

Congress has determined that individual long-term care insurance policies must be treated the same as accident and health policies tax wise, as long as such policies are qualified according to federal law. Individual premiums may be deductible if the 10% of adjusted gross income threshold is exceeded.

All qualified long-term care policy benefits are received income-tax free, so long as they do not exceed actual expenses. As for nonqualified long-term care policy premiums and benefits, it's not clear what their precise status is. Until Congress or the IRS clarifies that status, however, it would be wise to treat nonqualified policies as if they did not have the tax advantages of qualified policies.

25. 3. 2 Group Policies

The premiums paid by a company for group accident, health, and dental coverage for its employees are generally deductible by the company as a business expense. The premiums are not taxed to the employees. The benefits are received by the employees income-tax free to the extent the benefits do not exceed actual expenses.

The premiums paid by a company for group disability insurance for its employees are generally deductible by the company as a business expense. The premiums are not taxed to the employees, but the benefits are taxable. However, if an employee pays all or part of the premiums for group disability coverage, he may not deduct these premiums, but the benefits will be received income-tax free to the extent that the employee paid the premiums. Let's look at an example to see how this works.

Wanda's company pays the entire premium for her group disability coverage. If Wanda became disabled, all of her benefits from this coverage would be subject to tax. However, if Wanda paid 50% of the premiums, then 50% of her benefits would be tax free. And if she paid 100% of the premiums, all of her benefits would be tax free.

Note, however, that disability benefits are subject to Social Security tax (FICA) and federal unemployment tax (FUTA) for the first six calendar months following the last month the employee was on the job.

Group accidental death and dismemberment coverage premiums may be deducted as a business expense by companies. The premiums are not taxable to the employees, and the benefits are received income-tax free.

Qualified group long-term care insurance, like individually owned long-term care, is treated the same as other group health policies. Companies offering this coverage may deduct any premiums paid as a business expense. The employee is not taxed on these premiums, and the benefits are tax exempt.

Companies offering group long-term care coverage can deduct any premiums paid as a business expense. The employee is not taxed on these premiums, and the benefits are tax exempt. However, these tax advantages do not apply to group long-term care coverage provided through a Section 125 cafeteria plan, and expenses for long-term care services cannot be reimbursed under flexible spending arrangements.

25. 3. 3 Sole Proprietors and Partnerships

Self-employed persons are allowed to deduct from their gross incomes 100% of the amount they pay for health insurance (including qualified long-term care insurance). To claim this deduction, however, self-employed persons:

- must show a net profit for the year; and
- cannot claim the deduction for any month in which they were eligible to participate in a health plan subsidized by their employer or by the employer of their spouse.

Payments of premiums by a partnership for a partner's accident and health insurance policy is generally deductible by the partnership. The amount of the premiums is included in the partner's gross income, but it is deductible on the same basis as that for self-employed persons.

25. 3. 4 Business Policies

The premiums paid for business overhead expense insurance are deductible as a business expense whether the business is a sole proprietorship, partnership, or corporation. The proceeds of business overhead expense insurance, however, are taxable.

The premiums paid for a disability policy used to fund a buy-sell agreement are not deductible, nor are the proceeds taxable.

Similarly, the premiums paid for a key employee disability policy are not deductible, nor are the proceeds taxable.

25. 4 DISABILITY INCOME INSURANCE

Premiums paid by the insured for individually owned disability income insurance are not tax deductible. However, benefits paid in this type of situation are tax free to the insured.

In situations in which the business is providing disability income coverage for its employees, the premium paid by the business is tax deductible as a business expense. This is true whether the coverage is provided by a group policy or individual contracts. Naturally, the benefits received by the employees would then be taxable as income.

In situations where the business is providing disability income coverage to protect itself (e.g., key person or disability buy-sell insurance), premiums paid by the business are not tax deductible as a business expense. The basic premise is that either the premium or the benefit will be taxed. If the premium is not deductible to the business, the benefits will be received tax free. If the premium is deductible, then the benefits are taxable as with the BOE policy.

Exercise 25.A

Mark each of the following health insurance products as taxed (T) or not taxed (NT) in regards to their premiums (P) and benefits (B).

P	B		
____	____	1.	Individual MEI, MM, and most other health policies
____	____	2.	Sole Proprietor and Partnership MEI, MM, and most health
____	____	3.	Group health insurance (paid by employer)
____	____	4.	Individual DI or individual share of group DI
____	____	5.	Group DI (paid by employer)
____	____	6.	Business Overhead Expense (BOE)

Answers to the exercises can be found at the end of the Unit 25 answers and rationales.

25. 5 MEDICARE SUPPLEMENT AND LONG-TERM CARE INSURANCE

Individual Medicare supplement insurance premiums are considered deductible medical expenses to the extent that the combination of premiums paid plus other unreimbursed medical expenses exceeds 10% of adjusted gross income. Benefits are considered reimbursements for medical expenses already incurred and are therefore received tax free. Premiums paid by an employer for group Medicare supplement insurance are tax deductible to the employer, and benefits are received tax free.

The Health Insurance Portability and Accountability Act of 1996 provided that premiums paid for individually owned long-term care insurance are tax deductible to the extent that combined premiums and unreimbursed medical expenses exceed 10% of adjusted gross income.

Premiums for group LTC insurance paid by employers are deductible as a business expense, but the coverage cannot be part of a cafeteria plan or flexible spending account. Benefits are received tax free up to specified limits, which are indexed annually for inflation.

LTC policies issued on or after January 1, 1997, must meet federal standards for tax-qualified status. LTC policies issued before that date are grandfathered and are automatically tax qualified.

The federal standards establish new eligibility requirements. The individual must be certified by a licensed health care professional to be chronically ill with a condition that is expected to last at least 90 days and must have a plan of care. **Chronically ill** means that the individual:

- is unable without substantial help from another person to perform at least two of five (or six) activities of daily living for at least 90 days (ADLs include bathing, dressing, toileting, transferring, eating, and continence; state legislatures determine whether to include five or all six of the ADLs); and
- needs substantial supervision because of a cognitive impairment (i.e., Alzheimer's disease).

The individual must be recertified as chronically ill on an annual basis.

The new federal standards also establish consumer protection standards such as guaranteed renewability and the option to add inflation protection and nonforfeiture benefits (but not in the form of cash surrender values) and impose new disclosure requirements.

Exercise 25.B
Fill in the blank to complete the following section.

Generally, premiums for individual health policies are paid using after-tax dollars. However, there is a provision in the internal revenue code wherein individuals may aggregate their premiums and other out-of-pocket medical expenses, and to the extent that these costs exceed ____ of their adjusted gross income, they may be used as an itemized deduction from taxable income.

Answers to the exercises can be found at the end of the Unit 25 answers and rationales.

25. 6 TAXATION OF GOVERNMENT HEALTH PROGRAMS

25. 6. 1 Medicare

As a government social program, Medicare is largely paid for by federal taxes.

Medicare Funding

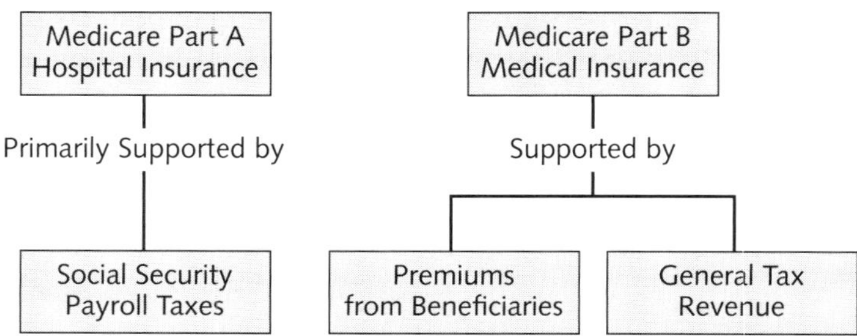

25. 6. 2 Social Security Disability Benefits

Social Security disability benefits are financed through a payroll tax. The tax rate is applied to an employee's gross wages (up to the current wage base), and an appropriate amount is deducted from the employee's wages each pay period. A like amount is contributed by the employer. The self-employed must pay 100% of the combined employee/employer tax rate.

Although employers may take a tax deduction for contributions on behalf of their employees as a routine and necessary cost of doing business, employees are not entitled to a deduction for their share of the Social Security tax. In other words, employee Social Security taxes are paid with after-tax dollars.

25. 6. 2. 1 Taxation of Social Security Benefits

Social Security benefits are generally received free of income tax. However, federal income taxes are imposed on some benefits if the taxpayer has a substantial amount of additional income.

The specifics of the calculations are not important at this stage of your training. However, it is important to understand that Social Security benefits may not be entirely free from federal income taxes.

UNIT TEST

1. Wanda's company pays the entire premium for her group disability coverage. If Wanda became disabled, how much of her benefits from this coverage would be subject to tax?
   A. All
   B. None
   C. Half
   D. It depends on her tax bracket

2. If Wanda paid 50% of premiums, what percentage of her benefits would be tax free?
   A. 0%
   B. 50%
   C. 100%
   D. It depends on her tax bracket

3. If Wanda paid 100% of her premiums, what percentage of her benefits would be tax free?
   A. 0%
   B. 50%
   C. 100%
   D. It depends on her tax bracket

4. The Delectable Doughnut Company may deduct its premiums for business overhead expense insurance
   A. only if it is a corporation
   B. only if it is a partnership or a corporation
   C. if is a corporation, partnership, or sole proprietorship
   D. premiums are not deductible.

5. The premiums are deductible for which of the following?
   A. Disability policy to fund a buy-sell agreement
   B. Key employee disability policy
   C. Both A and B
   D. Neither A nor B

6. Social Security disability income and medical benefits are financed through
   A. voluntary contributions
   B. Mandatory payroll taxes
   C. State government
   D. ERISA

7. The taxes to finance Social Security benefits are paid
   A. solely by employees
   B. solely by employers
   C. equally by employees and employers
   D. the federal governmnet

8. Medicare Part A hospital insurance is primarily funded by
   A. general tax revenue
   B. premiums from beneficiaries
   C. state government taxes
   D. Social Security payroll taxes

9. Social Security taxes are paid by employees with
   A. pretax dollars
   B. tax-deductible dollars
   C. after-tax dollars
   D. tax-deferred dollars

10. Premiums for individually owned health policies may be deductible if the taxpayer's medical expenses exceed
    A. 5% of their adjusted gross income during the taxable year
    B. 5% of their adjusted net income during the taxable year
    C. 10% of their adjusted gross income during the taxable year
    D. 10% of their adjusted net income during the taxable year

11. The premiums paid by a company for group health for its employees are
    A. not tax deductible to either the company or the business
    B. tax deductible by the company and not considered taxable income to the employees
    C. tax deductible by the company and considered taxable income to the employees
    D. tax deductible to the employees and the company

12. Benefits paid by individually owned accident, health, disability, or long-term care policies generally are
    A. received income-tax free by the taxpayer, provided benefits do not exceed actual expenses
    B. received income-tax free by the taxpayer, even if benefits exceed actual expenses
    C. received partially tax free by the taxpayer, provided benefits do not exceed actual expenses
    D. taxed upon receipt by the taxpayer

13. Qualified group long-term care coverage is
    A. deductible by both the company and the employee
    B. not deductible by either the company or the employee
    C. deductible by the company but not the employee
    D. deductible by the employee but not the company

14. Individual disability insurance premiums are
    A. deductible to the insured, and the benefits are received tax free
    B. not deductible to the insured, but the benefits are received tax free
    C. deductible to the insured, but the benefits are taxed
    D. not deductible to the insured, and the benefits are taxed

15. An individual who is considered chronically ill must be recertified as such
    A. every month
    B. every 6 months
    C. annually
    D. every 2 years

ANSWERS AND RATIONALES TO UNIT TEST

1. **A.** Since Wanda's company can deduct the premiums, all of Wanda's benefits are taxable.

2. **B.** 50% of her benefits would be tax free.

3. **C.** 100% of her benefits would be tax free.

4. **C.** Corporations, partnerships, and sole proprietorships can deduct premiums from business overhead expense insurance.

5. **D.** The premiums are not deductible for either a disability policy to fund a buy-sell agreement or a key employee disability policy.

6. **B.** Social security benefits are financed through mandatory payroll taxes.

7. **C.** The taxes to finance Social Security benefits are paid equally by employees and employers.

8. **D.** Medicare Part A hospital insurance is primarily funded by Social Security payroll taxes.

9. **C.** Social Security taxes are paid by employees with after-tax dollars.

10. **C.** Premiums for individually owned health policies may be deductible if the taxpayer's medical expenses exceed 10% of their adjusted gross income during the taxable year.

11. **B.** The premiums paid by a company for group health for its employees are tax deductible by the company and not considered taxable income to the employees.

12. **A.** Benefits paid by individually owned accident, health, disability, or long-term care policies generally are received income-tax free by the taxpayer, provided benefits do not exceed actual expenses.

13. **C.** Qualified group long-term care coverage is deductible by the company but not the employee.

14. **B.** Individual disability insurance premiums are not deductible to the insured, but the benefits are received tax free.

15. **C.** An individual who is considered chronically ill must be recertified as such annually.

UNIT 25 EXERCISE ANSWERS

Exercise 25.A

1. P=T, B=NT
2. P=NT, B=NT
3. P=NT, B=NT
4. P=T, B=NT
5. P=NT, B=T
6. P=NT, B=T

Exercise 25.B

1. 7½%

Glossary

A

absolute assignment Policy assignment under which the assignee (person to whom the policy is assigned) receives full control over the policy and also full rights to its benefits. Generally, when a policy is assigned to secure a debt, the owner retains all rights in the policy in excess of the debt, even though the assignment is absolute in form. (See assignment)

accelerated benefits rider A life insurance rider that allows for the early payment of some portion of the policy's face amount should the insured suffer from a terminal illness or injury.

acceptance (See offer and acceptance)

accident and health insurance Insurance under which benefits are payable in case of disease, accidental injury, or accidental death. Also called health insurance, personal health insurance, and sickness and accident insurance.

accidental bodily injury provision Disability income or accident policy provision that requires that the injury be accidental in order for benefits to be payable.

accidental death and dismemberment (AD&D) Insurance providing payment if the insured's death results from an accident or if the insured accidentally severs a limb above the wrist or ankle joints or totally and irreversibly loses eyesight.

accidental death benefit rider A life insurance policy rider providing for payment of an additional benefit when death occurs by accidental means.

accidental dismemberment Often defined as "the severance of limbs at or above the wrists or ankle joints, or the entire irrevocable loss of sight." Loss of use in itself may or not be considered dismemberment.

accidental means provision Unforeseen, unexpected, unintended cause of an accident. Requirement of an accident-based policy that the cause of the mishap must be accidental for any claim to be payable.

accumulation unit Premiums an annuitant pays into a variable annuity are credited as accumulation units. At the end of the accumulation period, accumulation units are converted to annuity units.

acquired immune deficiency syndrome (AIDS) A life-threatening condition brought on by the human immunodeficiency virus; insurers must adhere to strict underwriting and claims guidelines in regard to AIDS risks and AIDS-related conditions.

acute illness A serious condition, such as pneumonia, from which the body can fully recover with proper medical attention.

adhesion A life insurance policy is a "contract of adhesion" because buyers must "adhere" to the terms of the contract already in existence. They have no opportunity to negotiate terms, rates, values, and so on.

adjustable life insurance Combines features of both term and whole life coverage with the length of coverage and amount of accumulated cash value as the adjustable factors. Premiums may be increased or decreased to fit the specific needs. Such adjustments are not retroactive and apply only to the future.

administrative-services-only (ASO) plan Arrangement under which an insurance company or an independent organization, for a fee, handles the administration of claims, benefits, and other administrative functions for a self-insured group.

admitted insurer An insurance company that has met the legal and financial requirements for operation within a given state.

adult day care Type of care (usually custodial) designed for individuals who require assistance with various activities of daily living, while their primary caregivers are absent. Offered in care centers.

adverse selection Selection "against the company." Tendency of less favorable insurance risks to seek or continue insurance to a greater extent than others. Also, tendency of policyowners to take advantage of favorable options in insurance contracts.

agency Situation wherein one party (an agent) has the power to act for another (the principal) in dealing with third parties.

agent Anyone not a duly licensed broker, who solicits insurance or aids in placing risks, delivering policies, or collecting premiums on behalf of an insurance company.

agent's report The section of an insurance application where the agent reports personal observations about the applicant.

aleatory Feature of insurance contracts in that there is an element of chance for both parties and that the dollar given by the policyholder (premiums) and the insurer (benefits) may not be equal.

alien insurer Company incorporated or organized under the laws of any foreign nation, providence, or territory.

ambulatory surgery Surgery performed on an outpatient basis.

annually renewable term (ART) A form of renewable term insurance that provides coverage for one year and allows the policyowner to renew coverage each year, without evidence of insurability. Also called **yearly renewable term** (YRT).

annuitant One to whom an annuity is payable, or a person upon the continuance of whose life further payment depends.

annuity A contract that provides a stipulated sum payable at certain regular intervals during the lifetime of one or more persons, or payable for a specified period only.

annuity unit The number of annuity units denotes the share of the funds an annuitant will receive from a variable annuity account after the accumulation period ends and benefits begin. A formula is used to convert accumulation units to annuity units.

any occupation A definition of total disability that requires that for disability income benefits to be payable, the insured must be unable to perform any job for which the insured is "reasonably suited by reason of education, training, or experience."

apparent authority The authority an agent appears to have, based on the principal's (the insurer's) actions, words, deeds or because of circumstances the principal (the insurer) created.

application Form supplied by the insurance company, usually filled in by the agent and medical examiner (if applicable) on the basis of information received from the applicant. It is signed by the applicant and is part of the insurance policy if it is issued. It gives information to the home office underwriting department so it may consider whether an insurance policy will be issued and, if so, in what classification and at what premium rate.

appointment The authorization or certification of an agent to act for or represent an insurance company.

approval receipt Rarely used today, a type of conditional receipt that provides that coverage is effective as of the date the application is approved (before the policy is delivered).

assessment insurance Plan by which either the amount of insurance is variable or the number and amount of the assessments are variable. It is offered by assessment associations, either pure or advance.

assignee Person (including corporation, partnership, or other organization) to whom a right or rights under a policy are transferred by means of an assignment.

assignment Signed transfer of benefits of a policy by an insured to another party. The company does not guarantee the validity of an assignment.

assignment provision (health contracts) Commercial health policy provision that allows the policyowner to assign benefit payments from the insurer directly to the health care provider.

assignor Person (including corporation, partnership, or other organization or entity) who transfers a right or rights under an insurance policy to another by means of an assignment.

attained age With reference to an insured, the current insurance age.

authority The actions and deeds an agent is authorized to conduct on behalf of an insurance company, as specified in the agent's contract.

authorized company Company duly authorized by the insurance department to operate in the state.

automatic premium loan provision Authorizes insurer to automatically pay any premium in default at the end of the grace period and charge the amount so paid against the life insurance policy as a policy loan.

average indexed monthly earnings (AIME) The basis used for calculating the primary insurance amount (PIA) for Social Security benefits.

aviation exclusion Either attached by rider or included in standard policy language excepting from coverage certain deaths or disabilities due to aviation, such as "other than a fare-paying passenger."

B

backdating The practice of making a policy effective at an earlier date than the present.

basic medical expense policy Health insurance policy that provides "first dollar" benefits for specified (and limited) health care, such as hospitalization, surgery, or physician services. Characterized by limited benefit periods and relatively low coverage limits.

beneficiary Person to whom the proceeds of a life or accident policy are payable when the insured dies. The various types of beneficiaries are primary beneficiaries (those first entitled to proceeds), secondary beneficiaries (those entitled to proceeds if no primary beneficiary is living when the insured dies), and tertiary beneficiaries (those entitled to proceeds if no primary or secondary beneficiaries are alive when the insured dies).

benefit May be either money or a right to the policyowner upon the happening of the conditions set out in the policy.

benefit period Maximum length of time that insurance benefits will be paid for any one accident, illness, or hospital stay.

binding receipt Given by a company upon an applicant's first premium payment. The policy, if approved, becomes effective from the date of the receipt.

blackout period Period following the death of a family breadwinner during which no Social Security benefits are available to the surviving spouse.

blanket policy Covers a number of individuals who are exposed to the same hazards, such as members of an athletic team, company officials who are passengers in the same company plane, and so on.

broker Licensed insurance representative who does not represent a specific company but places business among various companies. Legally, the broker is usually regarded as a representative of the insured rather than the company.

business continuation plan Arrangements between the business owners that provide that the shares owned by any one of them who dies or becomes disabled shall be sold to and purchased by the other co-owners or by the business.

business overhead expense insurance A form of disability income coverage designed to pay necessary business overhead expenses, such as rent, should the insured business owner become disabled.

buyer's guides Informational consumer guide books that explain insurance policies and insurance concepts; in many states, they are required to be given to applicants when certain types of coverages are being considered.

buy-sell agreement Agreement that a deceased business owner's interest will be sold and purchased at a predetermined price or at a price according to a predetermined formula.

C

cafeteria plan Employee benefit arrangements in which employees can select from a range of benefits.

cancellable contract Health insurance contract that may be terminated by the company or that is renewable at its option.

capital sum Amount provided for accidental dismemberment or loss of eyesight. Indemnities for loss of one member or sight of one eye are percentages of the capital sum.

case management The professional arrangement and coordination of health services through assessment, service plan development, and monitoring.

cash or deferred arrangements A qualified employer retirement plan under which employees can defer amounts of their salaries into a retirement plan. These amounts are not included in the employee's gross income and so are tax deferred. Also called 401(k) plans.

cash refund annuity Provides that, upon the death of an annuitant before payments totaling the purchase price have been made, the excess of the amount paid by the purchaser over the total annuity payments received will be paid in one sum to designated beneficiaries.

cash surrender option A nonforfeiture option that allows whole life insurance policyowners to receive a payout of their policy's cash values.

cash surrender value Amount available to the owner when a life insurance policy is surrendered to the company. During the early policy years, the cash value is the reserve less a "surrender charge"; in later policy years, it usually equals or closely approximates the reserve value at time of surrender.

cash value The equity amount or "savings" accumulation in a whole life policy.

churning The practice by which policy values in an existing life insurance policy or annuity contract are used to purchase another policy or contract with that same insurer for the purpose of earning additional premiums or commissions without an objectively reasonable basis for believing that the new policy will result in an actual and demonstrable benefit.

class designation A beneficiary designation. Rather than specifying one or more beneficiaries by name, the policyowner designates a class or group of beneficiaries. For example, "my children."

classification Occupational category of a risk.

close corporation A corporation owned by a small group of stockholders, each of whom usually has a voice in operating the business.

COBRA "Consolidated Omnibus Budget Reconciliation Act of 1985," extending group health coverage to terminated employees and their families for up to 18 or 36 months.

coinsurance (percentage participation) Principle under which the company insures only part of the potential loss, the policyowners paying the other part. For instance, in a major medical policy, the company may agree to pay 75% of the insured expenses, with the insured to pay the other 25%.

collateral assignment Assignment of a policy to a creditor as security for a debt. The creditor is entitled to be reimbursed out of policy proceeds for the amount owed. The beneficiary is entitled to any excess of policy proceeds over the amount due the creditor in the event of the insured's death.

commercial health insurers Insurance companies that function on the reimbursement approach, which allows policyowners to seek medical treatment then submit the charges to the insurer for reimbursement.

Commissioner Head of a state insurance department; public officer charged with supervising the insurance business in a state and administrating insurance laws. Called "superintendent" in some states, "director" in others.

Commissioner's Standard Ordinary (CSO) Table Table of mortality based on intercompany experience over a period of time, which is legally recognized as the mortality basis for computing maximum reserves on policies issued within past years. The 1980 CSO Table replaced the 1958 CSO Table.

common disaster provision Sometimes added to a policy and designed to provide an alternative beneficiary in the event that the insured as well as the original beneficiary dies as the result of a common accident.

competent parties To be enforceable, a contract must be entered into by competent parties. A competent party is one who is capable of understanding the contract being agreed to.

comprehensive major medical insurance Designed to give the protection offered by both a basic medical expense and major medical policy. It is characterized by a low deductible amount, a coinsurance clause, and high maximum benefits.

concealment Failure of the insured to disclose to the company a fact material to the acceptance of the risk at the time application is made.

conditional contract Characteristic of an insurance contract in that the payment of benefits is dependent on or a condition of the occurrence of the risk insured against.

conditionally renewable contract Health insurance policy providing that the insured may renew the contract from period to period, or continue it to a stated date or an advanced age, subject to the right of the insurer to decline renewal only under conditions defined in the contract.

conditional receipt Given to the policyowners when they pay a premium at time of application. Such receipts bind the insurance company if the risk is approved as applied for, subject to any other conditions stated on the receipt.

consideration Element of a binding contract; acceptance by the company of payment of the premium and statements made by the prospective insured in the application.

consideration clause The part of an insurance contract setting forth the amount of initial and renewal premiums and frequency of future payments.

contestable period Period during which the company may contest a claim on a policy because of misleading or incomplete information in the application.

contingent beneficiary Person(s) named to receive proceeds in case the original beneficiary is not alive. Also referred to as secondary or tertiary beneficiary.

continuing care Type of health or medical care designed to provide a benefit for elderly individuals who live in a retirement community; addresses full-time needs, both social and medical. Also known as residential care.

contract An agreement enforceable by law whereby one party binds itself to certain promises or deeds.

contract of agency A legal document containing the terms of the contract between the agent and company, signed by both parties. Also called agency agreement.

contributory plan Group insurance plan issued to an employer under which both the employer and employees contribute to the cost of the plan. Generally, 75% of the eligible employees must be insured. (*See* **noncontributory plan**)

conversion factor A stated dollar-per-point amount used to determine benefit amounts paid for the cost of a procedure under a health insurance plan. For example, a plan with a $5-per-point conversion factor would pay $1,000 for a 200-point-procedure.

conversion privilege Allows the policyowner, before an original insurance policy expires, to elect to have a new policy issued that will continue the insurance coverage. Conversion may be effected at attained age (premiums based on the age attained at time of conversion) or at original age (premiums based on age at time of original issue).

convertible term Contract that may be converted to a permanent form of insurance without medical examination.

coordination of benefits (COB) provision Designed to prevent duplication of group insurance benefits. Limits benefits from multiple group health insurance policies in a particular case to 100% of the expenses covered and designates the order in which the multiple carriers are to pay benefits.

corridor deductible In superimposed major medical plans, a deductible amount between the benefits paid by the basic plan and the beginning of the major medical benefits.

cost of living (COL) rider A rider available with some policies that provides for an automatic increase in benefits (typically tied to the Consumer Price Index), offsetting the effects of inflation.

credit accident and health insurance If the insured debtor becomes totally disabled due to an accident or sickness, the policy premiums are paid during the period of disability or the loan is paid off. May be individual or group policy.

credit life insurance Usually written as decreasing term on a relatively small decreasing balance installment loan that may reflect direct borrowing or a balance due for merchandise purchased. If borrower dies, benefits pay balance due. May be individual or group policy.

credit report A summary of an insurance applicant's credit history, made by an independent organization that has investigated the applicant's credit standing.

cross-purchase plan An agreement that provides that upon a business owner's death, surviving owners will purchase the deceased's interest, often with funds from life insurance policies owned by each principal on the lives of all other principals.

currently insured Under Social Security, a status of limited eligibility that provides only death benefits.

custodial care Level of health or medical care given to meet daily personal needs, such as dressing, bathing, getting out of bed, and so on. Though it does not require medical training, it must be administered under a physician's order.

D

death rate Proportion of persons in each age group who die within a year; usually expressed as so many deaths per thousand persons. (*See* **expected mortality**)

debit insurer (*See* **home service insurer**)

decreasing term insurance Term life insurance on which the face value slowly decreases in scheduled steps from the date the policy comes into force to the date the policy expires, while the premium remains level. The intervals between decreases are usually monthly or annually.

deductible Amount of expense or loss to be paid by the insured before a health insurance policy starts paying benefits.

deferred annuity Provides for postponement of the commencement of an annuity until after a specified period or until the annuitant attains a specified age. May be purchased either on single-premium or flexible premium basis.

deferred compensation plan The deferral of an employee's compensation to some future age or date. These plans are frequently used to provide fringe benefits, such as retirement income, to selected personnel.

defined benefit plan A pension plan under which benefits are determined by a specific benefit formula.

defined contribution plan A tax-qualified retirement plan in which annual contributions are determined by a formula set forth in the plan. Benefits paid to a participant vary with the amount of contributions made on the participant's behalf and the length of service under the plan.

delayed disability provision A disability income policy provision that allows a certain amount of time after an accident for a disability to result, and the insured remains eligible for benefits.

dental insurance A relatively new form of health insurance coverage typically offered on a group basis, it covers the costs of normal dental maintenance as well as oral surgery and root canal therapy.

dependency period Period following the death of the breadwinner up until the youngest child reaches maturity.

deposit term Has modest endowment feature. Normally is sold for 10-year terms with a higher first-year premium than for subsequent years. If policy lapses, insured forfeits the "deposit" and receives no refund.

disability Physical or mental impairment making a person incapable of performing one or more duties of his occupation.

disability buy-sell agreement An agreement between business co-owners that provides that shares owned by any one of them who becomes disabled shall be sold to and purchased by the other co-owners or by the business using funds from disability income insurance.

disability income insurance A type of health insurance coverage, it provides for the payment of regular, periodic income should the insured become disabled from illness or injury.

disability income rider Typically a rider to a life insurance policy, it provides benefits in the form of income in the event the insured becomes totally disabled.

discrimination In insurance, the act of treating certain groups of people unfairly in the sale and/or pricing of policies; treating any of a given class of risk differently from other like risks. Discrimination is expressly prohibited in most state insurance codes.

dividend Policyowner's share in the divisible surplus of a company issuing insurance on the participating plan.

dividend options The different ways in which the insured under a participating life insurance policy may elect to receive surplus earnings: in cash, as a reduction of premium, as additional paid-up insurance, left on deposit at interest, or as additional term insurance.

domestic insurer Company within the state in which it is chartered and in which its home office is located.

dread disease policy (*See* **limited risk policy**)

E

elimination period Duration of time between the beginning of an insured's disability and the commencement of the period for which benefits are payable.

employee benefit plans Plans through which employers offer employees benefits such as coverage for medical expenses, disability, retirement, and death.

employee stock ownership plan (ESOP) A form of defined contribution profit-sharing plan, an ESOP invests primarily in the securities or stock of the employer.

endowment Contract providing for payment of the face amount at the end of a fixed period, at a specified age of the insured, or at the insured's death before the end of the stated period.

endowment period Period specified in an endowment policy during which, if the insured dies, the beneficiary receives a death benefit. If the insured is still living at the end of the endowment period, the insured receives the endowment as a living benefit.

enrollment period Period during which new employees can sign up for coverage under a group insurance plan.

entire contract provision An insurance policy provision stating that the application and policy contain all provisions and constitute the entire contract.

entity plan An agreement in which a business assumes the obligation of purchasing a deceased owner's interest in the business, thereby proportionately increasing the interests of surviving owners.

equity indexed annuity A fixed deferred annuity that offers the traditional guaranteed minimum interest rate and an excess interest feature that is based on the performance of an external equities market index.

errors and omissions insurance Professional liability insurance that protects an insurance producer against claims arising from service the producer rendered or failed to render.

estate Most commonly, the quantity of wealth or property at an individual's death.

estate tax Federal tax imposed on the value of property transferred by an individual at the individual's death.

estoppel Legal impediment to denying the consequences of one's actions or deeds if they lead to detrimental actions by another.

evidence of insurability Any statement or proof regarding a person's physical condition, occupation, and so forth, affecting acceptance of the applicant for insurance.

examiner Physician authorized by the medical director of an insurance company to make medical examinations. Also, person assigned by a state insurance company to audit the affairs of an insurance company.

excess interest Difference between the rate of interest the company guarantees to pay on proceeds left under settlement options and the interest actually paid on such funds by the company.

exclusion ratio A fraction used to determine the amount of annual annuity income exempt from federal income tax. The exclusion ratio is the total contribution or investment in the annuity divided by the expected ratio.

exclusion rider Health insurance policy rider that waives insurer's liability for all future claims on a preexisting condition.

exclusions Specified hazards listed in a policy for which benefits will not be paid.

exclusive provider organization (EPO) A variation of the PPO concept, an EPO contracts with an extremely limited number of physicians and typically only one hospital to provide services to members; members who elect to get health care from outside the EPO receive no benefits. (*See also* **preferred provider organization**)

expected mortality Number of deaths that theoretically should occur among a group of insured persons during a given period, according to the mortality table in use. Normally, a lower mortality rate is anticipated and generally experienced.

experience rating Review of the previous year's claims experience for a group insurance contract in order to establish premiums for the next period.

express authority The specific authority given in writing to the agent in the contract of agency.

extended term insurance Nonforfeiture option providing for the cash surrender value of a policy to be used as a net single premium at the insured's attained age to purchase term insurance for the face amount of the policy, less indebtedness, for as long a period as possible, but no longer than the term of the original policy.

F

face amount Commonly used to refer to the principal sum involved in the contract. The actual amount payable may be decreased by loans or increased by additional benefits payable under specified conditions or stated in a rider.

facility-of-payment provision Clause permitted under a uniform health insurance policy provision allowing the company to pay up to $1,000 of benefits or proceeds to any relative appearing entitled to it if there is no beneficiary or if the insured or beneficiary is a minor or legally incompetent.

Fair Credit Reporting Act Federal law requiring an individual to be informed if that individual is being investigated by an inspection company.

family plan policy All-family plan of protection, usually with permanent insurance on the primary wage earner's life and with spouse and children automatically covered for lesser amounts of protection, usually term, all included for one premium.

FICA Contributions made by employees and employers to fund Social Security benefits (OASDI).

fiduciary Person in a position of special trust and confidence (e.g., in handling or supervising affairs or funds of another).

fixed-amount settlement option A life insurance settlement option whereby the beneficiary instructs that proceeds be paid in regular installments of a fixed dollar amount. The number of payment periods is determined by the policy's face amount, the amount of each payment, and the interest earned.

fixed annuity A type of annuity that provides a guaranteed fixed benefit amount, payable for the life of the annuitant.

fixed-period settlement option A life insurance settlement option in which the number of payments is fixed by the payee, with the amount of each payment determined by the amount of proceeds.

flat deductible Amount of covered expenses payable by the insured before medical benefits are payable.

foreign insurer Company operating in a state in which it is not chartered and in which its home office is not located.

franchise insurance Life or health insurance plan for covering groups of persons with individual policies uniform in provisions, although perhaps different in benefits. Solicitation usually takes place in an employer's business with the employer's consent. Generally written for groups too small to qualify for regular group coverage. May be called wholesale insurance when the policy is life insurance.

fraternal benefit insurer Nonprofit benevolent organization that provides insurance to its members.

fraud An act of deceit; misrepresentation of a material fact made knowingly, with the intention of having another person rely on that fact and consequently suffer a financial hardship.

free look Provision required in most states whereby policyholders have either 10 or 20 days to examine their new policies at no obligation.

fully insured A status of complete eligibility for the full range of Social Security benefits: death benefits, retirement benefits, disability benefits, and Medicare benefits.

funding In a retirement plan, the setting aside of funds for the payment of benefits.

G

general agent Independent agent with authority, under contract with the company, to appoint soliciting agents within a designated territory and fix their compensation.

government insurer An organization that, as an extension of the federal or state government, provides a program of social insurance.

grace period Period of time after the due date of a premium during which the policy remains in force without penalty.

graded premium whole life Variation of a traditional whole life contract providing for lower than normal premium rates during the first few policy years, with premiums increasing gradually each year. After the preliminary period, premiums level off and remain constant.

gross premium The total premium paid by the policyowner, it generally consists of the net premium plus the expense of operation minus interest.

group credit insurance A form of group insurance issued by insurance companies to creditors to cover the lives of debtors for the amounts of their loans.

group insurance Insurance that provides coverage for a group of persons, usually employees of a company, under one master contract.

guaranteed insurability (guaranteed issue) Arrangement, usually provided by rider, whereby additional insurance may be purchased at various times without evidence of insurability.

guaranteed renewable contract Health insurance contract that the insured has the right to continue in force by payment of premiums for a substantial period of time during which the insurer has no right to make unilaterally any change in any provision, other than a change in premium rate for classes of insureds.

guaranty association Established by each state to support insurers and protect consumers in the case of insurer insolvency, guaranty associations are funded by insurers through assessments.

H

hazard Any factor that gives rise to a peril.

health insurance Insurance against loss through sickness or accidental bodily injury. Also called accident and health, accident and sickness, sickness and accident, or disability insurance.

health maintenance organization (HMO) Health care management stressing preventive health care, early diagnosis, and treatment on an outpatient basis. Persons generally enroll voluntarily by paying a fixed fee periodically.

home health care Skilled or unskilled care provided in an individual's home, usually on a part-time basis.

home service insurer Insurer that offers relatively small policies with premiums payable on a weekly basis, collected by agents at the policyowner's home.

hospital benefits Payable for charges incurred while the insured is confined to or treated in a hospital, as defined in a health insurance policy.

hospital expense insurance Health insurance benefits subject to a specified daily maximum for a specified period of time while the injured is confined to a hospital, plus a limited allowance up to a specified amount for miscellaneous hospital expenses, such as operating room, anesthesia, laboratory fees, and so on. Also called hospitalization insurance. (*See* **medical expense insurance**)

hospital indemnity Form of health insurance providing a stipulated daily, weekly, or monthly indemnity during hospital confinement; payable on an unallocated basis without regard to actual hospital expense.

human life value An individual's economic worth, measured by the sum of the individual's future earnings that is devoted to the individual's family.

I

immediate annuity Provides for payment of annuity benefit at one payment interval from date of purchase. Can only be purchased with a single payment.

implied authority Authority not specifically granted to the agent in the contract of agency, but which common sense dictates the agent has. It enables the agent to carry out routine responsibilities.

incontestable clause Provides that, for certain reasons such as misstatements on the application, the company may void a life insurance policy after it has been in force during the insured's lifetime, usually one or two years after issue.

increasing term insurance Term life insurance in which the death benefit increases periodically over the policy's term. Usually purchased as a cost of living rider to a whole life policy. (*See* **cost of living rider**)

indemnity approach A method of paying health policy benefits to insureds based on a predetermined, fixed rate set for the medical services provided, regardless of the actual expenses incurred.

independent agency system A system for marketing, selling, and distributing insurance in which independent brokers are not affiliated with any one insurer but represent any number of insurers.

indexed whole life A whole life insurance policy with a death benefit that increases according to the rate of inflation. Such policies are usually tied to the Consumer Price Index (CPI).

individual insurance Policies providing protection to the policyowner, as distinct from group and blanket insurance. Also called personal insurance.

individual retirement account (IRA) A personal qualified retirement account through which eligible individuals accumulate tax-deferred income up to a certain amount each year, depending on the person's tax bracket.

industrial insurance Life insurance policy providing modest benefits and a relatively short benefit period. Premiums are collected on a weekly or monthly basis by an agent calling at insured's homes. (*See* **home service insurer**)

inspection receipt A receipt obtained from an insurance applicant when a policy (upon which the first premium has not been paid) is left with the applicant for further inspection. It states that the insurance is not in effect and that the policy has been delivered for inspection only.

inspection report Report of an investigator providing facts required for a proper underwriting decision on applications for new insurance and reinstatements.

installment refund annuity An annuity income option that provides for the funds remaining at the annuitant's death to be paid to the beneficiary in the form of continued annuity payments.

insurability All conditions pertaining to individuals that affect their health, susceptibility to injury, or life expectancy; an individual's risk profile.

insurability receipt A type of conditional receipt that makes coverage effective on the date the application was signed or the date of the medical exam (whichever is later), provided the applicant proves to be insurable.

insurable interest Requirement of insurance contracts that loss must be sustained by the applicant upon the death or disability of another and loss must be sufficient to warrant compensation.

insurance Social device for minimizing risk of uncertainty regarding loss by spreading the risk over a large enough number of similar exposures to predict the individual chance of loss.

insurance code The laws that govern the business of insurance in a given state.

insurer Party that provides insurance coverage, typically through a contract of insurance.

insuring clause Defines and describes the scope of the coverage provided and limits of indemnification.

integrated deductible In superimposed major medical plans, a deductible amount between the benefits paid by the basic plan and those benefits paid by the major medical. All or part of the integrated deductible may be absorbed by the basic plan.

interest adjusted net cost method A method of comparing costs of similar policies by using an index that takes into account the time value of money.

interest-only option (interest option) Mode of settlement under which all or part of the proceeds of a policy are left with the company for a definite period at a guaranteed minimum interest rate. Interest may either be added to the proceeds or paid annually, semiannually, quarterly, or monthly.

interest-sensitive whole life Whole life policy whose premiums vary depending upon the insurer's underlying death, investment, and expense assumptions.

interim term insurance Term insurance for a period of 12 months or less by special agreement of the company; it permits a permanent policy to become effective at a selected future date.

intermediate nursing care Level of health or medical care that is occasional or rehabilitative, ordered by a physician, and performed by skilled medical personnel.

irrevocable beneficiary Beneficiary whose interest cannot be revoked without the beneficiary's written consent, usually because the policyowner has made the beneficiary designation without retaining the right to revoke or change it.

J

joint and last survivor policy A variation of the joint life policy that covers two lives but pays the benefit upon the death of the second insured.

joint and survivor annuity Covers two or more lives and continues in force so long as any one of them survives.

joint life policy Covers two or more lives and provides for the payment of the proceeds at the death of the first among those insured, at which time the policy automatically terminates.

juvenile insurance Written on the lives of children who are within specified age limits and generally under parental control.

K

Keogh plans Designed to fund retirement of self-employed individuals; name derived from the author of the Keogh Act (HR-10), under which contributions to such plans are given favorable tax treatment.

key-person insurance Protection of a business against financial loss caused by the death or disablement of a vital number of the company, usually individuals possessing special managerial or technical skill or expertise.

L

lapse Termination of a policy upon the policyowner's failure to pay the premium within the grace period.

law of large numbers Basic principle of insurance that the larger the number of individual risks combined into a group, the more certainty there is in predicting the degree or amount of loss that will be incurred in any given period.

legal purpose In contract law, the requirement that the object of, or reason for, the contract must be legal.

legal reserve Policy reserves are maintained according to the standard levels established through the insurance laws of the various states.

level premium funding method The insurance plan (used by all regular life insurance companies) under which, instead of an annually increasing premium that reflects the increasing chance of death, an equivalent level premium is paid. Reserves that accumulate from more than adequate premiums paid in the early years supplement inadequate premiums in later years.

level term insurance Term coverage on which the face value remains unchanged from the date the policy comes into force to the date the policy expires.

license Certification issued by a state insurance department that an individual is qualified to solicit insurance applications for the period covered; usually issued for one year, renewable on application without need to repeat the original qualifying requirements.

licensed insurer (*See* **admitted insurer**)

life annuity Payable during the continued life of the annuitant. No provision is made for the guaranteed return of the unused portion of the premium.

life expectancy Average duration of the life remaining to a number of persons of a given age, according to a given mortality table. Not to be confused with "probable lifetime," which refers to the difference between a person's present age and the age at which death is most probable (i.e., the age at which most deaths occur).

life income settlement option A settlement option providing for life insurance or annuity proceeds to be used to buy an annuity payable to the beneficiary for life-often with a specified number of payments certain or a refund if payments don't equal or exceed premiums paid.

life insurance Insurance against loss due to the death of a particular person (the insured) upon whose death the insurance company agrees to pay a stated sum or income to the beneficiary.

life settlement transaction Transfer of an ownership interest in a life insurance policy to a third party for compensation less than the expected death benefit under the policy, or the sale of a life insurance policy for a dollar amount that is less than the policy's face amount.

limited pay life insurance A form of whole life insurance characterized by premium payments only being made for a specified or limited number of years.

limited policies Restrict benefits to specified accidents or diseases, such as travel policies, dread disease policies, ticket policies, and so forth.

limited risk policy Provides coverage for specific kinds of accidents or illnesses, such as injuries received as a result of travel accidents or medical expenses stemming from a specified disease. (*See* **special risk policy**)

Lloyd's of London An association of individuals and companies that underwrite insurance on their own accounts and provide specialized coverages.

loading Amount added to net premiums to cover the company's operating expenses and contingencies; includes the cost of securing new business, collection expenses, and general management expenses; excess of gross premiums over net premiums.

loan value Determinable amount that can be borrowed from the issuing company by the policyowner using the value of the life insurance policy as collateral.

long-term care Refers to the broad range of medical and personal services for individuals (often the elderly) who need assistance with daily activities for an extended period of time.

long-term care policy Health insurance policies that provide daily indemnity benefits for extended care confinement.

loss sharing (*See* **risk pooling**)

lump sum Payment of entire proceeds of an insurance policy in one sum. The method of settlement provided by most policies unless an alternate settlement is elected by the policyowner or beneficiary.

M

major medical expense policy Health insurance policy that provides broad coverage and high benefits for hospitalization, surgery, and physician services. Characterized by deductibles and coinsurance cost-sharing.

managed care A system of delivering health care and health care services, characterized by arrangements with selected providers, programs of ongoing quality control and utilization review, and financial incentives for members to use providers and procedures covered by the plan.

master contract Issued to the employer under a group plan; contains all the insuring clauses defining employee benefits. Individual employees participating in the group plan receive individual certificates that outline highlights of the coverage. Also called master policy.

McCarran-Ferguson Act Also know as Public Law 15, the 1945 act exempting insurance from federal antitrust laws to the extent insurance is regulated by states.

Medicaid Provides medical care for the needy under joint federal-state participation (Kerr-Mills Act).

medical examination Usually conducted by a licensed physician; the medical report is part of the application, becomes part of the policy contract, and is attached to the policy. A "nonmedical" is a short-form medical report filled out by the agent. Various company rules, such as amount of insurance applied for or already in force, or applicant's age, sex, past physical history and data revealed by inspection report, and so on, determine whether the examination will be "medical" or "nonmedical."

medical expense insurance Pays benefits for nonsurgical doctors' fees commonly rendered in a hospital; sometimes pays for home and office calls.

Medical Information Bureau (MIB) A service organization that collects medical data on life and health insurance applicants for member insurance companies.

medical report A document completed by a physician or other approved examiner and submitted to an insurer to supply medical evidence of insurability (or lack of insurability) or in relation to a claim.

Medicare Federally sponsored health insurance and medical program for persons age 65 or older; administered under provisions of the Social Security Act.

Medicare Part A Compulsory hospitalization insurance that provides specified inhospital and related benefits. All workers covered by Social Security finance its operation through a portion of their FICA tax.

Medicare Part B Voluntary program designed to provide supplementary medical insurance to cover physician services, medical services, and supplies not covered under Medicare Part A.

Medicare Part C Medicare Part C is called Medicare Advantage. The program offers a variety of managed care plans, a private fee-for-service plan, and Medicare specialty plans. These specialty plans provide services that focus care on the management of a specific disease or condition.

Medicare Part D A program that offers a prescription drug benefit to help Medicare beneficiaries pay for the drugs they need. The drug benefit is optional and is available to anyone who is entitled to Medicare Part A or enrolled in Part B. This benefit is available through private prescription drug plans (PDPs) or Medicare Advantage (PPO) plans.

Medicare supplement policy Health insurance that provides coverage to fill the gaps in Medicare coverage.

minimum deposit insurance A cash value life insurance policy having a first-year loan value that is available for borrowing immediately upon payment of the first-year premium.

miscellaneous expenses Hospital charges, other than for room and board (e.g., x-rays, drugs, laboratory fees, and so forth) in connection with health insurance.

misrepresentation Act of making, issuing, circulating, or causing to be issued or circulated, an estimate, illustration, circular, or statement of any kind that does not represent the correct policy terms, dividends, or share of the surplus or the name or title for any policy or class of policies that does not in fact reflect its true nature.

misstatement of age or sex provision If the insured's age or sex is misstated in an application for insurance, the benefit payable usually is adjusted to what the premiums paid should have purchased.

modified endowment contract (MEC) A life insurance policy under which the amount a policyowner pays in during the first years exceeds the sum of net level premiums that would have been payable to provide paid-up future benefits in seven years.

modified whole life Whole life insurance with premium payable during the first few years, usually five years, only slightly larger than the rate for term insurance. Afterwards, the premium is higher for the remainder of life than the premium for ordinary life at the original age of issue but lower than the rate at the attained age at the time of charge.

money purchase plan A type of qualified plan under which contributions are fixed amounts or fixed percentages of the employee's salary. An employee's benefits are provided in whatever amount the accumulated or current contributions will produce for the employee.

moral hazard Effect of personal reputation, character, associates, personal living habits, financial responsibility, and environment, as distinguished from physical health, upon an individual's general insurability.

morale hazard Hazard arising from indifference to loss because of the existence of insurance.

morbidity The relative incidence of disability due to sickness or accident within a given group.

morbidity rate Shows the incidence and extent of disability that may be expected from a given large group of persons; used in computing health insurance rates.

mortality The relative incidence of death within a group.

mortality table Listing of the mortality experience of individuals by age; permits an actuary to calculate, on the average, how long a male or female of a given age group may be expected to live.

mortgage insurance A basic use of life insurance, so-called because many family heads leave insurance for specifically paying off any mortgage balance outstanding at their death. The insurance generally is made payable to a family beneficiary instead of to the mortgage holder.

multiple employer trust (MET) Several small groups of individuals that need life and health insurance but do not qualify for true group insurance band together under state trust laws to purchase insurance at a more favorable rate.

multiple employer welfare arrangement (MEWA) Similar to a multiple employer trust (MET) with the exception that in a MEWA, a number of employers pool their risks and self-insure.

multiple protection policy A combination of term and whole life coverage that pays some multiple of the face amount of the basic whole life portion (such as $10 per month per $1,000) throughout the multiple protection period (such as to age 65).

mutual insurer An insurance company characterized by having no capital stock; it is owned by its policyowners and usually issues participating insurance.

N

National Association of Health Underwriters (NAHU) NAHU is an organization of health insurance agents that is dedicated to supporting the health insurance industry and to advancing the quality of service provided by insurance professionals.

National Association of Insurance and Financial Advisors (NAIFA) NAIFA is an organization of life insurance agents that is dedicated to supporting the life insurance industry and to advancing the quality of service provided by insurance professionals.

National Association of Insurance Commissioners (NAIC) Association of state insurance commissioners active in insurance regulatory problems and in forming and recommending model legislation and requirements.

natural group A group formed for a reason other than to obtain insurance.

needs approach A method for determining how much insurance protection a person should have by analyzing a family's or business's needs and objectives should the insured die, become disabled, or retire.

net premium Calculated on the basis of a given mortality table and a given interest rate, without any allowance for loading.

nonadmitted insurer An insurance company that has not been licensed to operate within a given state.

noncancellable and guaranteed renewable contract Health insurance contract that the insured has the right to continue in force by payment of premiums set forth in the contract for a substantial period of time, during which the insurer has no right to make unilaterally any change in any contract provision.

noncontributory plan Employee benefit plan under which the employer bears the full cost of the employees' benefits; must insure 100% of eligible employees.

nondisabling injury Requires medical care, but does not result in loss of time from work.

nonduplication provision Stipulates that insureds shall be ineligible to collect for charges under a group health plan if the charges are reimbursed under their own or their spouse's group plan.

nonforfeiture options Privileges allowed under terms of a life insurance contract after cash values have been created.

nonforfeiture values Those benefits in a life insurance policy that, by law, the policyowner does not forfeit even if the policyowner discontinues premium payments; usually cash value, loan value, paid-up insurance value, and extended term insurance value.

nonmedical insurance Issued on a regular basis without requiring a regular medical examination. In passing on the risk, the company relies on the applicant's answers to questions regarding the applicant's own physical condition and on personal references or inspection reports.

nonparticipating Insurance under which the insured is not entitled to share in the divisible surplus of the company.

nonqualified plan A retirement plan that does not meet federal government requirements and is not eligible for favorable tax treatment.

notice of claims provision Policy provision that describes the policyowner's obligation to provide notification of loss to the insurer within a reasonable period of time.

O

offer and acceptance The offer may be made by the applicant by signing the application, paying the first premium and, if necessary, submitting to a physical examination. Policy issuance, as applied for, constitutes acceptance by the company. Or, the offer may be made by the company when no premium payment is submitted with application. Premium payment on the offered policy then constitutes acceptance by the applicant.

Old-Age, Survivors, Disability and Hospital Insurance (OASDI) Retirement, death, disability income, and hospital insurance benefits provided under the Social Security system.

open-panel HMO A network of physicians who work out of their own offices and participate in the HMO on a part-time basis.

optionally renewable contract Health insurance policy in which the insurer reserves the right to terminate the coverage at any anniversary or, in some cases, at any premium due date, but does not have the right to terminate coverage between such dates.

ordinary insurance Life insurance of commercial companies not issued on the weekly premium basis; amount of protection usually is $1,000 or more.

other insureds rider A term rider, covering a family member other than the insured, that is attached to the base policy covering the insured.

outline of coverage Informational material about a specific plan or policy of insurance that describes the policy's features and benefits; in many states, an outline of coverage is required to be given to consumers when certain types of coverages are being considered.

overhead insurance Type of short-term disability insurance reimbursing the insured for specified, fixed, monthly expenses, normal and customary in operating the insured's business.

overinsurance An excessive amount of insurance; an amount of insurance that would result in payment of more than the actual loss or more than incurred expenses.

own occupation A definition of total disability that requires that in order to receive disability income benefits the insured must be unable to work at his or her own occupation.

P

paid-up additions Additional life insurance purchased by policy dividends on a net single premium basis at the insured's attained insurance age at the time additions are purchased.

paid-up policy No further premiums are to be paid and the company is held liable for the benefits provided by the contract.

parol evidence rule Rule of contract law that brings all verbal statements into the written contract and disallows any changes or modifications to the contract by oral evidence.

partial disability Illness or injury preventing insured from performing at least one or more, but not all, of the insured's occupational duties.

participating Plan of insurance under which the policyowner receives shares (commonly called dividends) of the divisible surplus of the company.

participating physician A doctor or physician who accepts Medicare's allowable or recognized charges and will not charge more than this amount.

participation standards Rules that must be followed for determining employee eligibility for a qualified retirement plan.

partnership A business entity that allows two or more people to strengthen their effectiveness by working together as co-owners.

payor rider Available under certain juvenile life insurance policies, upon payment of an extra premium. Provides for the waiver of future premiums if the person responsible for paying them dies or is disabled before the policy becomes fully paid or matures as a death claim, or as an endowment, or the child reaches a specific age.

per capita rule Death proceeds from an insurance policy are divided equally among the living primary beneficiaries.

peril The immediate specific event causing loss and giving rise to risk.

period certain annuity An annuity income option that guarantees a definite minimum period of payments.

permanent flat extra premium A fixed charge added per $1,000 of insurance for substandard risks.

personal producing general agency system (PPGA) A method of marketing, selling, and distributing insurance in which personal producing general agents (PPGAs) are compensated for business they personally sell and business sold by agents with whom they subcontract. Subcontracted agents are considered employees of the PPGA, not the insurer.

per stirpes rule Death proceeds from an insurance policy are divided equally among the named beneficiaries. If a named beneficiary is deceased, that beneficiary's share then goes to the living descendants of that individual.

policy In insurance, the written instrument in which a contract of insurance is set forth.

policy loan In life insurance, a loan made by the insurance company to the policyowner, with the policy's cash value assigned as security. One of the standard nonforfeiture options.

policy provisions The term or conditions of an insurance policy as contained in the policy clauses.

precertification The insurer's approval of an insured's entering a hospital. Many health policies require precertification as part of an effort to control costs.

preexisting condition An illness or medical condition that existed before a policy's effective date; usually excluded from coverage, through the policy's standard provisions or by waiver.

preferred provider organization (PPO) Association of health care providers, such as doctors and hospitals, that agree to provide health care to members of a particular group at fees negotiated in advance.

preferred risk A risk whose physical condition, occupation, mode of living, and other characteristics indicate a prospect for longevity for unimpaired lives of the same age.

premium The periodic payment required to keep an insurance policy in force.

premium factors The three primary factors considered when computing the basic premium for insurance: mortality, expense, and interest.

prescription drug coverage Usually offered as an optional benefit to group medical expense plans, this coverage covers some or all of the cost of prescription drugs.

presumptive disability benefit A disability income policy benefit that provides that if an insured experiences a specified disability, such as blindness, the insured is presumed to be totally disabled and entitled to the full amount payable under the policy, whether or not the insured is able to work.

primary beneficiary In life insurance, the beneficiary designated by the insured as the first to receive policy benefits.

primary insurance amount (PIA) Amount equal to a covered worker's full Social Security retirement benefit at age 65 or disability benefit.

principal An insurance company that, having appointed someone as its agent, is bound to the contracts the agent completes in its behalf.

principal sum The amount under an AD&D policy that is payable as a death benefit if death is due to an accident.

private insurer An insurer that is not associated with federal or state government.

probationary period Specified number of days after an insurance policy's issue date during which coverage is not afforded for sickness. Standard practice for group coverages.

proceeds Net amount of money payable by the company at the insured's death or at policy maturity.

producer A general term applied to an agent, broker, personal producing general agent, solicitor, or other person who sells insurance.

professional liability insurance (*See* **errors and omissions insurance**)

profit-sharing plan Any plan whereby a portion of a company's profits is set aside for distribution to employees who qualify under the plan.

proof of loss A mandatory health insurance provision stating that the insured must provide a completed claim form to the insurer within 90 days of the date of loss.

pure endowment Contract providing for payment only upon survival of a certain person to a certain date and not in the event of that person's prior death. This type of contract is just the opposite of a term contract, which provides for payment only in the event the injured person dies within the term period specified.

pure risk Type of risk that involves the chance of loss only; there is no opportunity for gain; insurable.

Q

qualified plan A retirement or employee compensation plan established and maintained by an employer that meets specific guidelines spelled out by the IRS and consequently receives favorable tax treatment.

R

rate-up in age System of rating substandard risks that assumes the insured to be older than the insured really is and charging a correspondingly higher premium.

rating The making of insurance also creates the premium classification given an applicant for life or health insurance.

reasonable and customary charge Charge for health care service consistent with the going rate of charge in a given geographical area for identical or similar services.

rebating Returning part of the commission or giving anything else of value to the insured as an inducement to buy the policy. It is illegal and cause for license revocation in most states. In some states, it is an offense by both the agent and the person receiving the rebate.

reciprocal insurer Insurance company characterized by the fact its policyholders insure the risks of other policyholders.

recurrent disability provision A disability income policy provision that specifies the period of time during which the reoccurrence of a disability is considered a continuation of a prior disability.

reduced paid-up insurance A nonforfeiture option contained in most life insurance policies providing for the insured to elect to have the cash surrender value of the policy used to purchase a paid-up policy for a reduced amount of insurance.

re-entry option An option in a renewable term life policy under which the policyowner is guaranteed, at the end of the term, to be able to renew coverage without evidence of insurability, at a premium rate specified in the policy.

refund annuity Provides for the continuance of the annuity during the annuitant's lifetime and, in any event, until total payment equal to the purchase price has been made by the company.

reimbursement approach Payment of health policy benefits to insured based on actual medical expenses incurred.

reinstatement Putting a lapsed policy back in force by producing satisfactory evidence of insurability and paying any past-due premiums required.

reinsurance Acceptance by one or more insurers, called reinsurers, of a portion of the risk underwritten by another insurer who has contracted for the entire coverage.

relative value scale Method for determining benefits payable under a basic surgical expense policy. Points are assigned to each surgical procedure and a dollar per point amount, or conversion factor, is used to determine the benefit.

renewable option An option that allows the policyowner to renew a term policy before its termination date without having to provide evidence of insurability.

renewable term Some term policies prove that they may be renewed on the same plan for one or more years without medical examination, but with rates based on the insured's advanced age.

replacement Act of replacing one life insurance policy with another; may be done legally under certain conditions. (*See* **twisting**)

representation Statements made by applicants on their applications for insurance that they represent as being substantially true to the best of their knowledge and belief, but that are not warranted as exact in every detail. (*See* **warranties**)

reserve Fund held by the company to help fulfill future claims.

reserve basis Refers to mortality table and assumed interest rate used in computing rates.

residual disability benefit A disability income payment based on the proportion of income the insured has actually lost, taking into account the fact that the insured is able to earn some income.

respite care Type of health or medical care designed to provide a short rest period for a caregiver. Characterized by its temporary status.

results provision (*See* **accidental bodily injury provision**)

revocable beneficiary Beneficiary whose rights in a policy are subject to the policyowner's reserved right to revoke or change the beneficiary designation and the right to surrender or make a loan on the policy without the beneficiary's consent.

rider Strictly speaking, a rider adds something to a policy. However, the term is used loosely to refer to any supplemental agreement attached to and made a part of the policy, whether the policy's conditions are expanded and additional coverages added, or a coverage of conditions is waived.

risk Uncertainty regarding loss; the probability of loss occurring for an insured or prospect.

risk pooling A basic principle of insurance whereby a large number contribute to cover the losses of a few. (*See* **loss sharing**)

risk selection The method of a home office underwriter used to choose applicants that the insurance company will accept. The underwriter must determine whether risks are standard, substandard, or preferred and adjust the premium rates accordingly.

rollover IRA An individual retirement account established with funds transferred from another IRA or qualified retirement plan that the owner had terminated.

S

salary continuation plan An arrangement whereby an income, usually related to an employee's salary, is continued upon employee's retirement, death or disability.

salary reduction SEP A qualified retirement plan limited to companies with 25 or fewer employees. It allows employees to defer part of their pretax income to the plan, lowering their taxable income. (*See* **simplified employee pension plan**)

savings incentive match plan for employees (SIMPLE) A qualified employer retirement plan that allows small employers to set up tax-favored retirement savings plans for their employees.

schedule List of specified amounts payable, usually for surgical operations, dismemberment, fractures, and so forth.

secondary beneficiary An alternative beneficiary designated to receive payment, usually in the event the original beneficiary predeceases the insured.

Section 457 plans Deferred compensation plans for employees of state and local governments in which amounts deferred will not be included in gross income until they are actually received or made available.

Self-Employed Individuals Retirement Act Passed by Congress in 1962, this Act enables self-employed persons to establish qualified retirement plans similar to those available to corporations.

self-insurance Program for providing insurance financed entirely through the means of the policyowner, in place of purchasing coverage from commercial carriers.

self-insured plan A health insurance plan characterized by an employer (usually a large one), labor union, fraternal organization, or other group retaining the risk of covering its employees' medical expenses.

service insurers Companies that offer prepayment plans for medical or hospital services, such as health maintenance organizations.

service provider An organization that provides health coverage by contracting with service providers, to provide medical services to subscribers, who pay in advance through premiums. Examples of such coverages are HMOs and PPOs.

settlement options Optional modes of settlement provided by most life insurance policies in lieu of lump-sum payment. Usual options are lump-sum cash, interest-only, fixed-period, fixed-amount, and life income.

simplified employee pension plan (SEP) A type of qualified retirement plan under which the employer contributes to an individual retirement account set up and maintained by the employee.

single dismemberment Loss of one hand or one foot, or the sight of one eye.

single-premium whole life insurance Whole life insurance for which the entire premium is paid in one sum at the beginning of the contract period.

skilled nursing care Daily nursing care ordered by a doctor; often medically necessary. It can only be performed by or under the supervision of skilled medical professionals and is available 24 hours a day.

Social Security Programs first created by Congress in 1935 and now composed of Old-Age, Survivors and Disability Insurance (OASDI), Medicare, Medicaid, and various grants-in-aid, which provide economic security to nearly all employed people.

sole proprietorship The simplest form of business organization whereby one individual owns and controls the entire company.

special class Applicants who cannot qualify for standard insurance but may secure policies with riders waiving payment for losses involving certain existing health impairments.

special risk policy Provides coverage for unusual hazards normally not covered under accident and health insurance, such as a concert pianist insuring his hands for a million dollars. (*See* **limited risk policy**)

specified disease insurance (*See* **limited risk policy**)

speculative risk A type of risk that involves the chance of both loss and gain; not insurable.

spendthrift provision Stipulates that, to the extent permitted by law, policy proceeds shall not be subject to the claims of creditors of the beneficiary or policy-owner.

split-dollar life insurance An arrangement between two parties where life insurance is written on the life of one, who names the beneficiary of the net death benefits (death benefits less cash value), and the other is assigned the cash value, with both sharing premium payments.

spousal IRA An individual retirement account that persons eligible to set up IRAs for themselves may set up jointly with a nonworking spouse.

standard provisions Forerunners of the Uniform Policy Provisions in health insurance policies today.

standard risk Person who, according to a company's underwriting standards, is entitled to insurance protection without extra rating or special restrictions.

stock bonus plan A plan under which bonuses are paid to employees in shares of stock.

stock insurer An insurance company owned and controlled by a group of stockholders whose investment in the company provides the safety margin necessary in issuance of guaranteed, fixed premium, nonparticipating policies.

stock redemption plan An agreement under which a close corporation purchases a deceased stockholder's interest.

stop-loss provision Designed to stop the company's loss at a given point, as an aggregate payable under a policy, a maximum payable for any one disability or the like; also applies to individuals, placing a limit on the maximum out-of-pocket expenses an insured must pay for health care, after which the health policy covers all expenses.

straight life income annuity (straight life annuity, life annuity) An annuity income option that pays a guaranteed income for the annuitant's lifetime, after which time payments stop.

straight whole life insurance (*See* **whole life insurance**)

subscriber Policyowner of a health care plan underwritten by a service insurer.

substandard risk Person who is considered an under-average or impaired insurance risk because of physical condition, family or personal history of disease, occupation, residence in unhealthy climate, or dangerous habits. (*See* **special class**)

successor beneficiary (*See* **secondary beneficiary**)

suicide provision Most life insurance policies provide that if the insured commits suicide within a specified period, usually two years after the issue date, the company's liability will be limited to a return of premiums paid.

supplemental accident coverage Often included as part of a group basic or major medical plan, this type of coverage is designed to cover expenses associated with accidents to the extent they are not provided under other coverages.

supplementary major medical policy A medical expense health plan that covers expenses not included under a basic policy and expenses that exceed the limits of a basic policy.

surgical expense insurance Provides benefits to pay for the cost of surgical operations.

surgical schedule List of cash allowances payable for various types of surgery, with the respective maximum amounts payable based upon severity of the operations; stipulated maximum usually covers all professional fees involved (e.g., surgeon, anesthesiologist).

surrender value (*See* **cash surrender value**)

T

taxable wage base The maximum amount of earnings upon which FICA taxes must be paid.

tax-sheltered annuity An annuity plan reserved for nonprofit organizations and their employees. Funds contributed to the annuity are excluded from current taxable income and are only taxed later, when benefits begin to be paid. Also called tax-deferred annuity and 403(b) plan.

temporary insurance agreement (*See* **binding receipt**)

term insurance Protection during limited number of years; expiring without value if the insured survives the stated period, which may be one or more years, but usually is 5 to 20 years, because such periods generally cover the needs for temporary protection.

term of policy Period for which the policy runs. In life insurance, this is to the end of the term period for term insurance, to the maturity date for endowments and to the insured's death (or age 100) for permanent insurance. In most other kinds of insurance, it is usually the period for which a premium has been paid in advance; however, it may be for a year or more, even though the premium is paid on a semiannual or other basis.

tertiary beneficiary In life insurance, a beneficiary designated as third in line to receive the proceeds or benefits if the primary and secondary beneficiaries do not survive the insured.

third-party administrator (TPA) An organization outside the members of a self-insurance group which, for a fee, processes claims, completes benefits paperwork, and often analyzes claims information.

third-party applicant A policy applicant who is not the prospective insured.

time limit on certain defenses A provision stating that an insurance policy is incontestable after it has been in force a certain period of time. It also limits the period during which an insurer can deny a claim on the basis of a preexisting condition.

total disability Disability preventing insureds from performing any duty of their usual occupations or any occupation for remuneration; actual definition depends on policy wording.

traditional net cost method A method of comparing costs of similar policies that does not take into account the time value of money.

transacting insurance The transaction of any of the following, in addition to other acts included under applicable provisions of the state code: solicitation or inducement, preliminary negotiations, effecting a contract of insurance, transacting matters subsequent to effecting a contract of insurance, and arising out of it.

travel-accident policies Limited to indemnities for accidents while traveling, usually by common carrier.

trust Arrangement in which property is held by a person or corporation (trustee) for the benefit of others (beneficiaries). The grantor (person transferring the property to the trustee) gives legal title to the trustee, subject to terms set forth in a trust agreement. Beneficiaries have equitable title to the trust property.

trustee One holding legal title to property for the benefit of another; may be either an individual or a company, such as a bank and trust company.

twisting Practice of inducing a policyowner with one company to lapse, forfeit, or surrender a life insurance policy for the purpose of taking out a policy in another company. Generally classified as a misdemeanor, subject to fine, revocation of license, and sometimes imprisonment. (*See* **misrepresentation**)

U

unallocated benefit Reimbursement provision, usually for miscellaneous hospital and medical expenses, that does not specify how much will be paid for each type of treatment, examination, dressing, and so forth, but only sets a maximum that will be paid for all such treatments.

underwriter Company receiving premiums and accepting responsibility for fulfilling the policy contract. Company employee who decides whether or not the company should assume a particular risk. The agent who sells the policy.

underwriting Process through which an insurer determines whether, and on what basis, an insurance application will be accepted.

Unfair Trade Practices Act A model act written by the National Association of Insurance Commissioners (NAIC) and adopted by most states empowering state insurance commissioners to investigate and issue cease and desist orders and penalties to insurers for engaging in unfair or deceptive practices, such as misrepresentation or coercion.

Uniform Individual Accident and Sickness Policy Provisions Law NAIC model law that established uniform terms, provisions, and standards for health insurance policies covering loss "resulting from sickness or from bodily injury or death by accident or both."

Uniform Simultaneous Death Act Model law that states when an insured and beneficiary die at the same time, it is presumed that the insured survived the beneficiary.

unilateral Distinguishing characteristic of an insurance contract in that it is only the insurance company that pledges anything.

uninsurable risk One not acceptable for insurance due to excessive risk.

universal life Flexible premium, two-part contract containing renewable term insurance and a cash value account that generally earns interest at a higher rate than a traditional policy. The interest rate varies. Premiums are deposited in the cash value account after the company deducts its fee and a monthly cost for the term coverage.

utilization review A technique used by health care providers to determine after the fact if health care was appropriate and effective.

V

valued contract A contract of insurance that pays a stated amount in the event of a loss.

variable annuity Similar to a traditional, fixed annuity in that retirement payments will be made periodically to the annuitants, usually over the remaining years of their lives. Under the variable annuity, there is no guarantee of the dollar amount of the payments; they fluctuate according to the value of an account invested primarily in common stocks.

variable life insurance Provides a guaranteed minimum death benefit. Actual benefits paid may be more, however, depending on the fluctuating market value of investments behind the contract at the insured's death. The cash surrender value also generally fluctuates with the market value of the investment portfolio.

variable universal life insurance A life insurance policy combining characteristics of universal and variable life policies. A VUL policy contains unscheduled premium payments and death benefits and a cash value that varies according to the underlying funds whose investment portfolio is managed by the policyowner.

vesting Right of employees under a retirement plan to retain part or all of the annuities purchased by the employer's contributions on their behalf or, in some plans, to receive cash payments or equivalent value, on termination of their employment, after certain qualifying conditions have been met.

viatical broker An insurance producer licensed to solicit viatical settlement agreements between providers and policyowners of life insurance contracts.

viatical provider A company that buys a life insurance policy from a policyowner who is suffering from a terminal illness or a severe chronic illness.

viatical settlement contract An agreement under which the owner of a life insurance policy sells the policy to another person in exchange for a bargained-for payment, which is generally less than the expected death benefit under the policy.

viator An individual suffering from a terminal illness or severe chronic illness who sells his life insurance policy to a viatical company. The company becomes the policyowner and assumes responsibility for paying premiums. When the insured dies, the company receives the death benefits.

vision insurance Optional coverage available with group health insurance plans, vision insurance typically pays for charges incurred during eye exams; eyeglasses and contact lenses are usually excluded.

void contract An agreement without legal effect; an invalid contract.

voidable contract A contract that can be made void at the option of one or more parties to the agreement.

voluntary group AD&D A group accidental death and dismemberment policy paid for entirely by employees, rather than an employer.

W

waiting period (*See* **elimination period**)

waiver Agreement waiving the company's liability for a certain type or types of risk ordinarily covered in the policy; a voluntary giving up of a legal, given right.

waiver of premium Rider or provision included in most life insurance policies and some health insurance policies exempting the insured from paying premiums after the insured has been disabled for a specified period of time, usually six months in life policies and 90 days or six months in health policies.

war clause Relieves the insurer of liability, or reduces its liability, for specified loss caused by war.

warranties Statements made on an application for insurance that are warranted to be true; that is, they are exact in every detail as opposed to representations. Statements on applications for insurance are rarely warranties, unless fraud is involved. (*See* **representation**)

whole life insurance Permanent level insurance protection for the "whole of life," from policy issue to the death of the insured. Characterized by level premiums, level benefits, and cash values.

wholesale insurance (*See* **franchise insurance**)

workers' compensation Benefits paid workers for injury, disability, or disease contracted in the course of their employment. Benefits and conditions are set by law, although in most states the insurance to provide the benefits may be purchased from regular insurance companies. A few states have monopolistic state compensation funds.

Y

yearly renewable term insurance (YRT) (*See* **annually renewable term**)

Index

P

Q

R

S

T

U

V

W

Notes

Notes

Notes

Notes

Notes

Notes

Notes

Notes

Notes